CHURCH ROBBERS AND REFORMERS
IN GERMANY, 1525-1547

STUDIES IN MEDIEVAL AND REFORMATION TRADITIONS

History, Culture, Religion, Ideas

FOUNDED BY HEIKO A. OBERMAN †

EDITED BY

ANDREW COLIN GOW, Edmonton, Alberta

IN COOPERATION WITH

THOMAS A. BRADY, Jr., Berkeley, California
JOHANNES FRIED, Frankfurt
BRAD GREGORY, University of Notre Dame, Indiana
BERNDT HAMM, Erlangen
SUSAN C. KARANT-NUNN, Tucson, Arizona
JÜRGEN MIETHKE, Heidelberg
M. E. H. NICOLETTE MOUT, Leiden
GUSTAV HENNINGSEN, Copenhagen

VOLUME CXIV

CHRISTOPHER OCKER

CHURCH ROBBERS AND REFORMERS
IN GERMANY, 1525-1547

CHURCH ROBBERS AND REFORMERS IN GERMANY
1525-1547

CONFISCATION AND RELIGIOUS PURPOSE
IN THE HOLY ROMAN EMPIRE

BY

CHRISTOPHER OCKER

BRILL
LEIDEN · BOSTON
2006

Cover illustration: from the *Klagrede der armen verfolgten Götzen und Tempelbilder über so ungleich urtayl und straffe.* Colored woodcut, circa 1530, 463 x 387 mm, Schlossmuseum Gotha Inv. Nr. G 74,4. Used by permission.

Brill Academic Publishers has done its best to establish rights to use of the materials printed herein. Should any other party feel that its rights have been infringed we would be glad to take up contact with them.

This book is printed on acid-free paper.

Library of Congress Cataloging-in-Publication Data

Ocker, Christopher.
  Church robbers and reformers in Germany, 1525-1547 : confiscation and religious purpose in the Holy Roman Empire / by Christopher Ocker.
    p. cm. — (Studies in medieval and Reformation traditions, ISSN 1573-4188 ; v. 114)
  Includes bibliographical references (p.   ) and index.
  ISBN-13: 978-90-04-15206-9
  ISBN-10: 90-04-15206-7 (hardback : alk. paper)
  1. Holy Roman Empire—Church history—16th century. 2. Reformation. 3. Church property. 4. Luther, Martin, 1483-1546. Schmalkaldischen Artikel. I. Title. II. Series.

BR307.O25 2006
274.3'06—dc22

                                                                                2006043917

ISSN   1573-4188
ISBN-13: 978-90-04-15206-9
ISBN-10: 90-04-15206-7

PRINTED IN THE NETHERLANDS

For Gabriel, Tanya, and Stella

CONTENTS

LIST OF ILLUSTRATIONS

ABBREVIATIONS

CICan	*Corpus Iuris Canonici*
CICiv	*Corpus Iuris Civilis*
CR	*Corpus Reformatorum*
CSEL	*Corpus Scriptorum Ecclesiasticorum Latinorum*
MBW	*Melanchthons Briefwechsel*
PL	*Patrologia Cursus Completus, series Latina*
WA	*D. Martin Luthers Werke, kritische Gesamtausgabe*
WABr	*D. Martin Luthers Werke, kritische Gesamtausgabe, Briefe*
WATisch	*D. Martin Luthers Werke, kritische Gesamtausgabe, Tischreden*

Nemo plus iuris ad alium transferre potest, quam ipse haberet.

No one can transfer to another more of a right than one has.

Ulpian, as cited by Justinian, *Digestum*, 50.17.54

Nemo potest plus iuris transferre in alium, quam sibi competere dignoscatur.

No one can convey more of a right to another than is recognized to belong to oneself.

Pope Boniface VIII, *De regulis iuris*, Rule 79

Sine possessione praescriptio non procedit.

A claim does not proceed without possession.

Pope Boniface VIII, *De regulis iuris*, Rule 3

Nemo dat quod non habet . . . Non est possibile creaturam iuste conferre quidquam, nisi prius naturaliter sit iustum quod habeat . . . A solo Deo potest natura racionalis habere talem potenciam.

No one gives what one doesn't have . . . It's not possible for a creature to confer something justly, unless what one first has naturally were just . . . A human being can have such power from God alone.

John Wyclif, *De civili dominio*, i.5

PREFACE

This is a study of the religious controversy that broke out with Martin Luther and eventually produced a Holy Roman Empire of two churches. The story has been told many times before, but seldom from the vantage of church property. This is surprising, because acceptance of the new church in Germany, where Protestantism began, came only through the acceptance of the property claims of rulers who supported the clergy who embraced Luther's teachings (imperial[1] acceptance of Lutheran churches had nothing to do with tolerance of Luther's faith). This is not a history of confiscation as such, for reasons explained in the Introduction, but a book about the *acceptance* of confiscation within the political community of the Holy Roman Empire and the contribution of theologians to that out-come. Acceptance was essential for the survival of evangelical reforms, the establishment of Protestant churches, and the success of what is sometimes called a crucial if early stage of confessional state-building.

I became interested in church property while studying late medieval controversies over mendicant friars (the Dominicans, Franciscans, Carmelites, and Augustinian Hermits) in Central European towns. This book grew unexpectedly out of that continuing project. I thought there might be a simple progression from late medieval anti-mendi-cant polemic through the widening German anti-clericalism of the 1520's to the confiscations and closures of monasteries in the 1530's and 1540's. It turned out differently. The mendicant orders, always at issue in urban reformations and a persistent trope for church cor-ruption, became less significant by the 1530's, when the League of Schmalkalden shaped the Protestant movement into a political force. Rationales for confiscation had to aim at the far greater possessions of all other kinds of monasteries, which were firmly embedded in the dense webs of aristocratic social relations. This embedment amplified the importance of church property for ruling authority. In the last twenty years, political historians of the Holy Roman Empire

---

[1] By "imperial," I mean the political community of the Holy Roman Empire, not the ruling authority of the emperor per se.

have increasingly viewed the early sixteenth century as a middle
phase within longer trends. Similarly, I see the religious controversy
as occupying a middle position between the localized clerical debates
typical of late medieval towns and the broad discussions of sovereignty
of the late sixteenth and seventeenth centuries. The subject assumes
a complicated position in the history of European monasticism.
Whereas the numbers of new houses belonging to some religious
orders in Central Europe decreased in the fourteenth and fifteenth
centuries, at least one order grew, the Carthusians, only to be confronted, along with the rest, by widescale attrition in the sixteenth
century. Although attrition was most strongly felt in Protestant-con-
trolled territories, it affected the Catholic territories of Central Europe
at the same time, before the renewed and often remarkable growth
of monasteries throughout the continent in the seventeenth and eighteenth centuries. This final period of monastic growth was followed
by the rapid elimination of nearly all monasteries in Europe between
the 1780's and 1830, excepting Sicily, Portugal, parts of Spain, and
parts of Austria.[2] The European Catholic church as we know it today
emerged out of the recovery from those secularizations. One could
therefore say that, with regard to church property, the Reformation
belongs to the pre-history of European secularization. My subject is
limited to the first generation of the new faith, when Europe's most
respected spiritual institution, monasticism, experienced its first great
crisis of legitimacy and when the religious and political terms of the
on-going conflict were established.

Confiscations of church property in Germany were treated in a
comprehensive article by Henry Cohn in the Festschrift for Geoffrey
Elton and in an important ten-page subsection of Thomas A. Brady's
Protestant Politics, but to my knowledge there is no general monograph on this subject in English.[3] In German, the standard monograph, by Kurt Körber, was published in 1913. Hans Lehnert's 1935

[2] Derek Beales, *Prosperity and Plunder: European Catholic Monasteries in the Age of Revolution, 1650–1815* (Cambridge University Press, 2003), pp. 2, 8, 27–83, and for Italy, which experienced no monastic crisis in the sixteenth century, p. 136.
[3] Henry J. Cohn, "Church Property in the German Protestant Principalities," *Politics and Society in Reformation Europe. Essays for Sir Geoffrey Elton on his Sixty-Fifth Birthday*, ed. E.I. Kouri, T. Scott (London: Macmillan, 1987), pp. 158–87, and for Brady and Deetjen see the bibliography.

monograph is restricted to church law.[4] A detailed monograph by
Werner-Ulrich Deetjen on the confiscations of churches in the duchy
of Württemberg appeared over two decades ago. While meticulously
researched, it is a difficult book to navigate.[5] There are a number
of studies of particular territories and cities and Walter Ziegler's
important, recent essay on the closure of monasteries in general.[6]

It is a good time to return to this subject. Access to the sources
is greatly aided by Heinz Scheible's under-utilized *Melanchthons
Briefwechsel*, the new *Akten der deutschen Reichsreligionsgespräche im 16.
Jahrhundert*, and the published letters and memoranda of reformers.[7]
Anton Schindling and Walter Ziegler's seven-volume *Die Territorien
des Reichs im Zeitalter der Reformation und Konfessionalisierung. Land und
Konfession 1500–1650* provides an indispensible survey of territories
and their churches. Gabriele Haug-Moritz's *Der Schmalkaldische Bund
1530–1541/42* is an equally indispensible reconstruction of all aspects
of the first decade of the Protestant League's history, including careful treatment of the question of church property by jurists and in
the League's diets. Jörn Sieglerschmidt's *Territorialstaat und Kirchenregiment*
remains the most important study of benefice law in the Reformation
era. Several studies have put an intense spotlight on theological dialogue and exchange across the confessions, on their political functions
(see, for example, T. Fuchs, Henze, and Kohnle in the bibliography),
and on the development of the "right of reform" (*ius reformandi*) and
the "guardianship of religion" (*cura religionis*; Schneider and Estes in
the bibliography). My debt to these scholars is enormous and constant.

The first three chapters review topics generally familiar to historians. They examine the complex nature of church property as it
existed and as it was thought, the character of evangelical confiscations
throughout the Holy Roman Empire, and the political context of
property gains. I have assumed relatively little prior knowledge of the
church on the part of my readers, especially in the first third of the

---

[4] Hans Lehnert, *Kirchengut und Reformation. Eine kirchengeschichtliche Studie* (Erlangen:
Palm und Enke, 1935).

[5] A helpful summary of it may be found in Martin Brecht, Hermann Ehmer,
Südwestdeutsche Reformationsgeschichte (Stuttgart: Calwer, 1984), pp. 215–22.

[6] See Cahill, Miller, J. Schilling, Schindling (in *Der Passauer Vertrag von 1552.
Politische Entstehung, reichsrechtliche Bedeutung und konfessionsgeschichtliche Bewertung*), Sitzmann,
and Ziegler in the bibliography.

[7] See these and the following works in the bibliography.

book. Chapter One surveys the material church, as it was known in
the late Middle Ages. Chapters Two and Three, drawing on recent
studies, describe the nature and progress of confiscations in illustra-
tive cities and territories, review the development of the League of
Schmalkalden, and examine the League's protection of property
gained.

Chapters Four to Seven focus on the religious rationales that took
shape in the early Reformation and supported the political effort to
consolidate and preserve confiscations. These rationales were created
and debated by clerical advisors, who conducted the religious controversy begun by Luther and who struggled to resolve it. Theological
advice on church property during the rise of German Protestantism
has never been studied as a whole. Scholars have often approached
the most prominent of these intellectuals separately, extracting political thought from their religious writings, and I mean no disrespect
by abandoning this approach. The case of church property allows
us to view theologians within a dynamic and fissiparous political environment. Confiscation has been most often treated as a legal problem. My focus will be on the effect of the clergy as a group contributing
to discussions among the imperial estates over two decades. I do not
examine the individual development of a particular ruler, territory,
thinker, or theory. This is not a study of ruling ideology or political philosophy.[8] A non-ideological approach has at least three advantages. First, it recognizes the specific place of theologians at court
(no one sought a new political philosophy from them in Luther's
generation). Second, it acknowledges the diverging and converging
interests of temporal rulers and clergy (clergy did not merely serve
rulers). And third, it allows arguments to be used in their malleable
ways (there is no need to force the flow of ideas into actions, but
the actions of groups determine the significance of historical ideas).

Evangelical opinions on church property are difficult to characterize
before 1537, as odd as that may seem, given the importance of property to the future of Protestant churches. Until then, the advice of
evangelical theologians was occassional and inchoate (Chapters 4

---

[8] For the political thought of the two most influential German reformers, Luther
and Melanchthon, see now James M. Estes, *Peace, Order and the Glory of God: Secular
Authority and the Church in the Thought of Luther and Melanchthon 1518–1559* (Leiden:
E.J. Brill, 2005).

and 5). In 1537, theologians petitioned the Schmalkald League to form a consistent position on church property, to which end the estates then solicited theological opinions, finally gathering theologians to the League's diet at Schmalkalden in 1540 to declare their agreement, which was adapted in the diet's recess. These developments between 1537 and 1540 allow a more coherent presentation (Chapters 5 and 6). The consensus achieved in 1540 played an important role in the imperial religious colloquies of 1540–1541 and gave shape to the imperial policy legalized by the Truce of Passau (1552) and the Peace of Augsburg (1555; Chapter Seven). Having traced theological discussions to this achievement, I consider, on the basis of the case of church property, the contribution of earliest Protestantism to the development of German states (Chapter Eight and the Conclusion).

I am grateful to the Baden-Württembergisches Staatsarchiv Stuttgart, the Stadtarchiv Braunschweig, the Stadtarchiv Ulm, and the Hessisches Staatsarchiv Marburg, for providing copies of manuscripts or allowing me to use their collections. Research that contributed to this book was made possible by a fellowship from the Alexander von Humboldt Foundation in 1995, which brought me to the Max-Planck-Institut für Geschichte in Göttingen, where I especially enjoyed the guidance of Prof. Dr. Otto-Gerhard Oexle, but also Prof. Dr. Hartmut Lehmann and the Institute's extraordinary company of *Mitarbeiter*. The book took shape during a 2003 research leave supported by the American Philosophical Society. I am far more grateful than I can adequately express to friends and colleagues who have deeply colored and corrected my thinking. My thanks go especially to those who read the manuscript as a whole or in part or who gave advice along the way, above all to Prof. Thomas A. Brady, a mentor and friend since I arrived at the Bay Area fifteen years ago, but also to Prof. Robert Coote, Prof. Elizabeth Gleason, Prof. Geoffrey Koziol, Prof. Thomas Dandelet, Dr. Bruce Elliot, Prof. Philip Wickeri, Dr. Michael Printy, Mr. John Morrow Hackmann, Mr. Larry Jannuzi, Mr. Darin Jensen, Mr. Michael Flanigan, Prof. Hillay Zmora, Prof. Markus Wriedt, Mr. Brad Peterson, Mr. Gabriel Koch Ocker, Ms. Varda Koch Ocker, students of my seminars at the Graduate Theological Union, and two anonymous readers. My special thanks to Prof. Andrew Gow for his encouragement, and to Prof. Dr. Gabrielle Haug-Moritz for permission to adapt her maps for use in this volume. For permissions to reproduce the illustrations and help acquiring copies, I thank Director Bernd Schäfer of the Schlossmuseum xviii

Friedenstein in Gotha, M. Patrick Graham of the Pitts Theological Library at Emory, and Nicole Rivette of the Toledo Museum of Art. Dean Arthur Holder of the Graduate Theological Union helped with the cost of reproductions and the map. The map was drawn by Jessica Rorem. I am grateful to Ms. Shelley Calkins for help assembling the bibliography. Of course, the responsibility for whatever mistakes remain is entirely my own.

A brief note on language. In the following pages there are frequent references to the meetings of the League of Schmalkalden and the Imperial estates. Hoping to make these references less confusing, I use lower case "diet" when referring to the meetings of the League of Schmalkalden and upper case "Diet" when referring to Imperial Diets. When quoting original sources from manuscripts in Chapters Five and Six or early sixteenth-century imprints elsewhere, I follow the variable and often inconsistent spelling of the originals. I translate the original German nouns for briefs written by court theologians for rulers as advice (*Ratschlag*), memorandum (*Bedencken, Bekantnus*), and recommendation (*Gutachten*). The sources use the terms more or less synonymously. I sometimes leave untranslated a common sixteenth-century German term for governing authority, *Obrigkeit*, and when referring to a specific text, I follow the spelling that appears in the source, as in, for example, *oberkeit*. *Obrigkeit* can refer to the personal authority of a prince as well as the constitutional authority of city councils. In the sixteenth century, the term had the advantage and the disadvantage of begging distinctions of ruling authority, which was necessary to achieve a common policy on church property in the League, an alliance of princes and cities. I refer to the governing bodies of cities simply as councils, although the names and structures of governing assemblies in German cities somewhat varied.[9] Such councils usually contained a relatively small body of magistrates in an inner circle, drawn from a narrow slice of the city's wealthy families and chosen by an electoral committee or coopted for a term that ranged from 28 days (e.g. Nürnberg) to life (e.g. Lübeck). Usually, there also existed an additional broader body of representatives either drawn from the guilds or chosen by some other

[9] Eberhard Isenmann, *Die deutsche Stadt im Spätmittelalter* (Stuttgart: Ulmer, 1988), pp. 131–9.

electoral body; sometimes, especially in the north, citizens' assemblies exercised a similar role to the large council. These distinctions, so vital in a local study, are of little significance here, where the emphasis must fall upon the relations between cities and princes within the League of Schmalkalden.

The anonymous broadside, *Complaint of the Poor, Persecuted Idols and Temple Images over So Unfair a Judgement and Penalty* (No place: no publisher, circa 1530). Image by permission of the Stiftung Schloss Friendenstein, Gotha.

INTRODUCTION

How did they imagine church robbers? The anonymous *Complaint of the Poor, Persecuted Idols and Temple Images over So Unfair a Judgement and Penalty*[1] is a single-leaf woodcut depicting church robbers in action at the height of the early Protestant movements. It has been ascribed to Erhard Schön, the Nürnberg student of Albrecht Dürer.[2] The patrician Thomas Blarer may have composed its text in conjunction with the reformation of the city of Constance, but authorship and artist are both uncertain.[3] The locale is equally anonymous. It represents any iconoclastic event, reduced to its physical and moral fundamentals.

The image pictures the interior of a church with an exterior scene. Inside the church, two candles burn on the high altar: a mass has just been interrupted. Laborers and two men of higher social standing, who wear collared cloaks, dismantle the interior of the church. Outside, a man dressed in a costly, fur-collared overcoat and a fancy hat—a patrician or nobleman—stands in the background, his left hand extended (offering payment?), while his pointing right hand directs a worker who carries a pitcher to the project (he will take his payment in drink).[4] This rich man superintends the operation. He stands before a huge wine flagon and a large pot of coins with two women behind him, which has been taken to indicate that he is not only wealthy but a bigamist.[5] He may simply be an adulterer, a crime of which the text complains. A wooden beam protrudes

---

[1] *Klagrede der armen verfolgten Götzen und Tempelpilder über so ungleich urtayl und straffe* (No place: no publisher, circa 1530).

[2] *Glaube und Macht. Sachsen im Europa der Reformationszeit*, edited by Harald Marx, Cecilie Hollberg, and Eckhard Kluth, 2 vols. (Dresden: Michel Sandstein, 2004), 2:120–2, nr. 159 for this, a brief description, and bibliography. For a review of the literature, iconographical analysis, and detailed interpretation, consider also Sonja Neubauer, "Bildanalyse und Interpretation," www.uni-tuebingen.de/dekarat-geschichte/hsrd/index.htm, and the link "Quellen."

[3] *Glaube und Macht*, 2:120–2, nr. 159.

[4] Another depiction of such a man directing an iconoclastic operation may be found in the anonymous account of the Peasants War, *Eyn Warhafftig erschröcklich Histori von der Bewrischen uffrur* (1525). See Norbert Schnitzler, *Ikonoklasmus-Bildersturm. Theologischer Bilderstreit und ikonoklastisches Handeln während des 15. und 16. Jahrhunderts* (Munich: Wilhelm Fink, 1996), p. 308, Abb. 27.

[5] *Glaube und Macht.*, 2:120.

from his eye. It refers to the saying of Jesus, "Why do you see the speck in your neighbor's eye, but do not notice the log in your own eye?" (Matthew 7.3, Luke 6.41).

In the far right foreground, some of the statues are destroyed by a worker, who is about to throw a bearded Apostle Paul (he bears his sword-emblem, Ephesians 6.17) into a bonfire. The fire is already consuming a statue of St. Francis, his tonsure clearly visible, as is his right hand, raised to display an absent stigmatum (his left hand is also raised). St. Francis lies in the flames beside a crowned King David to his right and an unidentifiable saint to his left. The smoke billows below them and towers above the rich man who directs the scene. Outside the church, another laborer is about to carry the statue of an unidentified saint through a portal into a courtyard adjoining the church. We can see within the courtyard the back of one end of an opened altarpiece, turned toward a wall in shadow. We may assume it had earlier adorned the high altar.

Within the church, the dismantling goes on. A laborer is about to strike a statue of St. Peter mounted on a pedestal on the right wall. The saint carries his emblems of key and book, which mark him as the origin of penitential and doctrinal authority. A bishop's mitre has fallen against the wall on the floor below St. Peter. Another laborer, his axe about to be raised, strides across the sanctuary. He passes a martyr abandoned on the tiled floor (the statue holds a raised martyr's palm), advancing toward a burgher who has put his axe down to embrace a statue of the Blessed Virgin, preparing to lift it from its pedestal. The statue is a familiar depiction of the Virgin offering fruit to the Christ Child in her arms. Two side altars have already been cleared. The wall niches above them are empty.

The interior and exterior form two contiguous spaces that are bridged by the third of the three robed men of higher social standing. He carries a crucifix out of the church while eyeing the fire. It is not clear which way he will turn, to the portal or the bonfire. The contiguity of the interior and exterior spaces is divided at the point where the interior and courtyard walls meet, but the two spaces, the tiled floor and the outside ground, merge beneath the feet of the man bearing the crucifix. The image portrays the church building and the outside as distinct spaces, contrasting the apparent safety of the church's courtyard with the open air destruction of statues, but it also obscures the boundary between church and world beneath the feet of a man of rank bearing the cross.

Not all the statues are being destroyed. At least some are being preserved, apparently within the church courtyard (to store, sell, distribute, return to donors?). The picture leaves ambiguous the intentions of the man of higher social standing within the church and the other man of rank leaving the sanctuary. To embrace the Virgin and Child and to shoulder the cross mimick pious actions. But the man directing the scene is grotesquely marked as a hypocrite.

The accompanying text emphasizes the injustice of the destruction of images, while ironically confirming the evangelical view of the powerlessness of "idols" by presenting a lengthy complaint in their voice. The idols argue in verse that they bear no responsibility or guilt for the false worship that has been rendered to them, since statues never have claimed to possess the miraculous powers ascribed to them by others. The very people who now persecute statues bear full responsibility for that false worship. They now ignore their worser crimes of theft, murder, gaming, taverning, drunkenness, dissolute living (*bubenleben*), whoring, etc. The validity of gift-giving to churches is presupposed: "and now some guy wants to devour us, who has himself so forgotten that he in his entire life never gave God the slightest thing, and he wants to play the knight against us."[6] An idolatrous immorality affects young and old alike.[7] The world is such a mess, the iconoclasts confuse faith with theft.[8] Without legal order, the removal of images from churches fails to serve God.[9] In fact, the gospel reference, the beam in the director's eye, reinforces a contrary idea, that the veneration of saints is a far lesser sin than the moral idolatries of iconoclasts who destroy the property of the church. The text concludes with a warning of divine punishment. Iconoclastic idolaters will suffer just as they persecute innocent statues. The bonfire foreshadows the fires of hell.

This broadsheet criticizes the violation of the church's property entirely within a pious framework. It ignores the obvious question, whether any of these people has a right to do what he does. All this

---

[6] "Und yetzund wil uns mancher fressen / Der doch sein selbst so gar vergessen / Des er in allem seinem leben / Kain dinglin nie umb got hat geben / Und wil an uns zu ritter werden."

[7] "Der götzen sind so vil on zal / Schier alle menschen überal / Vil schand laster und büberey / Fressen sauffen und gots lestrung / Jst yetz gemain bey alt und jung / Ebruch ist yetzund so gemain / Schier nymand lebt seins weibs allain."

[8] "Da ist die welt mechtig geschwind / Das sy nit anders waiß vom glauben / Dann es sol sein, den negsten rauben."

[9] "Gesatz und ordnung machen güt."

handling of material objects is neither celebrated as purification nor decried as stealing in the accompanying text, which makes the reformist's point that to recognize the error of worshipping idols is a trivial accomplishment. A hypocrite conducts, some men destroy, one man preserves, and others must choose. The text provokes the viewer to speculate over their moral condition and the broad context of their intentions and choices, which affect the character of the event as a whole. The two places portrayed here, the church interior and the outdoors, are simultaneously distinct and contiguous spaces. The operation threatens to profane both, instead of their desired sanctification. The iconoclastic operation is morally dangerous. The broadsheet promotes a spiritual revolution that has already been betrayed. But not everyone in this picture is necessarily a church robber, and the readers' choices will determine whether things get better or worse—whether these will prove to be the deeds of thieves or of reformers.

The name "church robber," *Kirchenrauber*, was applied to iconoclasts and revolutionaries by their Catholic and Protestant opponents, to Protestants by Catholics, and to Catholics by Protestants. One person's theft was another's reform. The rise of Protestantism created a controversy over church theft in the Holy Roman Empire.

Stealing was elusive by definition. In civil law it was said, "theft is the deceitful handling of a thing for the sake of making a profit, or for the sake of the thing itself, or just for the sake of its use or possession, which natural law prohibited."[10] A thief was a deceitful user or possessor of property. By definition, they were hard to catch. Conrad Lagus (d. 1546), a jurist active at Wittenberg and, for the last six years of his life, a syndic of Danzig, summarized a standard legal doctrine by explaining how there can be no such thing as an accidental thief.[11] A robber tries to escape the consequences of his or her actions; a thief evades detection. A deranged mind, an acquisition by mistake, an inheritance received upon an erroneous presumption of a testator's death, mere counsel or influence to take something without actually abducting the goods from their owner— all these could disqualify the charge of theft. The stolen goods must

---

[10] *Digestum* 47.2.1.3. CICiv 1:814.

[11] Conrad Lagus, *Iuris utriusque traditio methodica* (Frankfurt: Christianus Egenolphus, 1543), ff. 187v–188r. Lagus also limits the definition of theft to movable property.

be handled, and they must be handled with an intent to profit or possess. A fuller or tailor who receives clothes for finishing or mending may meet the handling rule and bear liability for their safe-keeping, but lacks fraudulent purpose. An act of violence performed by a motive other than profit, for example, a lust-crazed man dragging off a prostitute, may be depraved but is not theft.[12] The thief committed an intentional deceit in a transgression of nature's just order. This reflected a Europe-wide standard.

Theft was a transgression of legitimate possession or use. Mere entitlement did not make an owner. One must actually control an object, and others must accept this control. "No one can convey more of a right to another than is recognized to belong to oneself," said the legal maxim.[13] In an interesting concession to the importance of social recognition, Lagus' contemporary, Johannes Oldendorp, perhaps the most famous Protestant jurist of Luther's generation, once defined possession as "the public rite." By that rite, an heir is summoned, a will is read before a magistrate, immoveable property is transferred, and a public record is made.[14] To Oldendorp, such customary performances reflected the adaptations of ancient Rome's civil law to new places, persons, and times. But ancient models of legal order had to be adapted before a living public, where a right was only as good as its recognition.

The recognition of legitimate owners—the social norms that determined legitimacy—made the protection of sacred property difficult,

---

[12] Ibid., "Fullo igitur uel sarcinator, qui polienda uel sarcienda uestimenta accepit, si forte ea induat, furtum e contrectatione rerum fecisse uidetur l. 'fullo' *Digestum* eodem [*Digestum*, 47.2.12, CICiv 1:814]. Non autem fur iudicari potest, qui meretricem libidinis causa rapuit, l. 'uerum' *Digestum* eodem [*Degestum* 47.2.39, CICiv 1:818]." The Digest describes the prostitute as enslaved to someone else, i.e. is someone's property. By dropping this anachronistic reference, Lagus emphasizes the problem of will in the example.

[13] Pope Boniface VIII's rule 79, CICan 2:1124.

[14] Ioannes Oldendorp, *De copia verborum et rerum in iure civili* (Cologne: Ioannes Gymnicus, 1542), p. 124: "Hoc tempore, bonorum possessio appellari potest caeremonia illa, quam ex statutis adhibens succedentes ab intestato, uel ex testamento: dum testamenta post mortem recitantur publice apud magistratum: dum bona immobilia adsignantur haeredi, et describuntur in publicis monumentis. Ad bonorum possessionem item pertinent ordinationes statuariae: scilicet, ne qui haeres admittatur, nisi probatione prius, saltem per duos testes, audita, de gradu cognationis promixo: et si quae sunt similes. . . ." For Oldendorp in general, John Witte, *Law and Protestantism: the Legal Teachings of the Lutheran Reformation* (Cambridge University Press, 2002), pp. 154–7.

and it was hard to detect a church robber. The property posed special problems of ownership, required guardians, and was treated as
its own domain.[15] A guardian could seem, or be, a dissembling thief
while posing as the church's true servant. Like any accusation of
theft, the charge stood or fell on the accused's intentions and on
social agreements over the property's legitimate use, or on perceptions of intentions and uses. The accused must prove the legitimacy
of his actions. Accordingly, controversy over church robbers involved
far more than material things. It involved intentions for property,
agreements over its proper use, shared perceptions about those who
use it, and the arguments that shaped those perceptions. During the
last twenty-five years of Martin Luther's life and for decades after
he died, in some cases centuries, what came to be known as the old
faith and the new faith—each in its own ways—helped demonstrate
legitimate treatments of church property.

   The importance of church property goes far beyond the small
places and intimate choices depicted in the anonymous *Complaint of
the Poor, Persecuted Idols*. The medieval church was the most extensive
trans-regional institution of any kind in Europe.[16] In the sixteenth
century, some of its parts, for example, the papal court and the
larger religious orders, were the only continent-wide multinational
associations in existence. The church at large still provided the most
pervasive structural support for whatever common culture existed.[17]

---

[15] See Chapter 1.

[16] The Roman Catholic Church has since grown to be over a billion strong
today, nearly one-sixth of the world's population of 6 $1/2$ billion, and one of the
three largest organizations in the world, while the Protestant movement's subsequent myriad subdivisions form the largest share of the remaining billion of the
world's Christians. About half of those baptized as Catholics now live in the western hemisphere, although the most rapid growth is taking place in Africa. "Anuario
Shows Slight Rise in Catholic Population," *Catholic World News* 1 February 2005.
The other two organizations of comparable size to the Catholic church now are
the nations of China and India. For Protestants, I combine the designations Protestant
and Independent in David B. Barrett, George T. Kurian, Todd M. Johnson, *The
World Christian Encyclopedia: A Comparative Survey of Churches and Religions in the Modern
World* (Oxford University Press, 2001). For the use of such estimates, consider Philip
Jenkins, "After the Next Christendom," *International Bulletin of Missionary Research*
(January 2004).

[17] This is true in the broad sense of the historical role of monasteries and cathedral schools in establishing and framing the content of learning in medieval Europe,
but also in a narrow sense, as Jörn Sieglerschmidt has suggested. Church benefices
funded late medieval university students and were used by Protestants to provide
scholarships and fund schools. Jörn Sieglerschmidt, *Territorialstaat und Kirchenregiment*

Any change in the nature and exercise of its power must be considered a central problem of Europe's past. Once the power of the traditional church deteriorated in evangelical lordships, the new clergy had the task of preserving what was left of that universal culture. The problem of church property occurred at the foundation of efforts to rebuild Christianity without the papacy and the complex of church courts.

No question of church property can be confined within a narrow chronology of reform. It was an ancient problem. The problem began when the Roman Emperor Constantine applied and expanded benefits enjoyed by pagan holy places to Christian churches. The benefits included endowments of income-producing real estate and the first immunities of church personnel and properties from the jurisdiction of lay courts. Such immunities were routinely violated in the early Germanic kingdoms, where property was often confiscated and used by those whose lineages donated it to begin with or taken as plunder by victors in war. Bishops, abbots, and abbesses periodically recalled Roman-Byzantine norms, condemning church robbers, as is evident, for example, in the writings of the bishop Gregory of Tours (d. 594).[18] The autonomy of the church's control of its own property and personnel was largely ignored by Carolingian collections of canons but recovered in decrees of the late eleventh-century reform papacy and then published in Gratian's *Decretum*, the most important medieval collection of church laws.[19] These laws and the papal reforms that produced many of them did little to resolve competition

(Cologne: Böhlau, 1987), p. 28. Consider also Beales, *Prosperity and Plunder*, pp. 7, 13–14, 46–7.

[18] Consider, for example, his treatment of king Chilperic's robbery of churches. Gregory of Tours, *The History of the Franks*, trans. by Lewis Thorpe (London: Penguin, 1974), p. 380.

[19] P. Landau, "Eigenkirchenwesen," *Theologische Realencyklopedie* 9:399–404 is the best brief survey. See also idem, *Jus patronatus. Studien zur Entwicklung des Patronats im Dekretalenrecht und der Kanonistik des 12. und 13. Jahrhunderts* (Cologne: Böhlau, 1975), passim, and Paolo Cammarosano, "Il ruolo della proprietà ecclesiastica nella vita economica e sociale del medioevo europeo," *Gli spazi economici della chiesa nell' occidente mediterraneo (secoli xii–meta xiv)* (Pistoia: Centro Italiano di studi di storia e d'arte, 1999), pp. 1–17. The second redaction of Gratian was used, which may have been expanded by a student of Gratian's. See Anders Winroth, *The Making of Gratian's Decretum* (Cambridge University Press, 2000), pp. 77–121 for Causa 11 and 122–145, 192 for the problem of authorship and date. For the ninth century, consider also Susan Reynolds, *Fiefs and Vassals: the Medieval Evidence Reinterpreted* (Oxford: Clarendon, 1994), pp. 90–91 and passim.

for the church's things. The church's autonomy remained one of the most contentious political problems of medieval Europe, a matter over which popes and temporal rulers collided again and again. Were confiscations of churches and monasteries in Reformation Germany an end to this conflict, an ultimate defeat of ecclesiastical control? So could it seem as early as the Peace of Westphalia (1648) and still seems to some scholars today.[20] The Peace of Westphalia ended post-Reformation Catholic attempts to win the restoration of church properties confiscated by Protestants, and it halted Protestant attempts to establish evangelical prince-bishoprics, while guaranteeing the legality of those parts of the imperial church that became evangelical since the Peace of Augsburg (1555): the territory of the bishop of Lübeck, part of the territory of the bishop of Osnabrück, some imperial women's monasteries, part of the Teutonic Order, and the Hospitallers of St. John.[21] By contrast, in early Protestant Germany, by which I mean Luther's generation, secularization—an end to the church's official place in political life—was neither the stated ambition nor the assured outcome.

But the controversy over Martin Luther produced an Empire of two churches. In the twenty-one years of organization, consolidation, and negotiation that followed the Peasants' War of 1524/5, the confessional churches of early modern Germany began to take shape.[22]

---

[20] A French delegate to the Peace of Westphalia called the dissolution of the great prince-bishoprics "secularization." Martin Heckel, "Das Problem der 'Säkularisation' in der Reformation," *Zur Säkularisation geistlicher Institutionen im 16. und im 18./19. Jahrhundert*, ed. Irene Crusius (Göttingen: Vandenhoeck und Ruprecht, 1996), p. 33. Robert Scribner described the reforming legislation that followed the Peasants' War of 1524/5 as "the conclusion of a long struggle between church and state . . . and the state clearly emerged as the victor." Robert W. Scribner, C. Scott Dixon, *The German Reformation*, 2nd edition (London: Palgrave, 2003), pp. 37–42, here 37; cf. also p. 80, which considers it "fairly certain" that "Protestant theology could provide important ideological support for the evolving state." And Steven Ozment has characterized the German princes as "spectacular winners" in a 300-year-old controversy with the papacy. Luther joined his new faith to their ancient political struggle at the Diet of Worms in 1521. Steven Ozment, *A Mighty Fortress: A New History of the German People* (New York: Harper Collins, 2004), pp. 66, 78–9. See also Thomas A. Brady, "Fortress Under Siege: A New German History," *Central European History*, 39 (2006): 107–122.
[21] Anton Schindling, "Der Passauer Vertrag und die Kirchengüterfrage," *Der Passauer Vertrag von 1552. Politische Entstehung, reichsrechtliche Bedeutung und konfessionsgeschichtliche Bewertung*, edited by Winfried Becker (Neustadt a.d. Aisch: Degener, 2003), pp. 105–123, here 119.
[22] Peter Blickle has helped shape a widely accepted view that traces the coop-

Hesse, Electoral Saxony, Lüneburg, Brandenburg, Württemberg, among the twenty-one German principalities whose rulers adapted Protestant reform between 1523 and 1546,[23] and many cities large and small, confiscated church properties and redeployed their incomes for religious and not-so-religious purposes.

Several conditions complicated the process. Germany's many law-givers and legal jurisdictions were more resistant to centralizing authority than in any other part of Europe.[24] They formed a crowded landscape with unclear geographical boundaries. In stark contrast to Denmark, the temporal domains of German bishops could be taken only one bishopric at a time, with difficulty and seldom completely, and in stark contrast to England, the confiscation of monasteries often also occurred by increments.[25] The process had only begun when the emperor defeated the Protestant League of Schmalkalden in 1547. The confiscations of monasteries varied so much city by city and territory by territory, they cannot be called a dissolution of the monasteries, as they are commonly known in England.[26]

---

eration between state power and reformers to their response to the Peasants' War of 1524/5. Peter Blickle, *Die Reformation im Reich* (Stuttgart: Ulmer, 1982), p. 141. Bernd Hamm has emphasized how after the Peasants' War among the most influential reformers the "original ideals of a spiritually justified lay Christianity give way to a new theological and practical stress on the divinely legitimated secular office to care for the ordering of the Church and the ecclesiastical office of the minister of the Church, educated at university and legally appointed—i.e. with the support of the civic authorities." Bernd Hamm, *The Reformation of Faith in the Context of Late Medieval Theology and Piety*, edited by Robert J. Bast (Leiden: E.J. Brill, 2004), pp. 218–9. See also Scribner in note 20, above.

[23] These are conveniently listed in a table by Euan Cameron, *The European Reformation* (Oxford: Clarendon, 1991), p. 269.

[24] Thomas A. Brady, "Reformation als Rechtsbruch: Nationalisierung und Territorialisierung der Religionen als Rechtsbruch," *Die Säkularisation im Prozess der Säkularisierung Europas* edited by Peter Blickle, Rudolf Schlögl (Epfendorf: Bibliotheca Academica, 2005), pp. 141–152. The comparison is very strikingly and thoroughly illustrated by Armin Wolf, *Gesetzgebung in Europa, 1100–1500: Zur Entstehung der Territorialstaaten*, 2nd revised and expanded edition (Munich: C.H. Beck, 1996), pp. 96–148 and passim.

[25] For England, Denmark, and Sweden, see Chapter 8, below.

[26] Martin Heckel distinguishes between the *Kirchengutsäkularisation*, the seculariza-tion of church property in the sixteenth century, which first appeared as a techni-cal legal term after the Peace of Westphalia in 1648, and the broader concept of secularization characteristic of a later conflict of the state against the church. The later concept, he noted, is unsuitable for the "inner-religious and inner-ecclesiasti-cal processes" of the reordering of church property in the sixteenth century. Martin Heckel, "Das Problem der 'Säkularisation,'" pp. 33–4, 43. Alois Hahn distinguishes sixteenth-century secularizations from those of modern Europe in two ways. They

Confiscation started with an inventory of monastery holdings ordered by a prince or by city magistrates. Such inventories were not new. They had been made in the fifteenth century in conjunction with reforms of monasteries or simply as an expression of a ruler's church guardianship (*Kirchenvogtei*). In the fifteenth century, rulers sometimes also installed a lay officer to oversee or manage the material business of a monastery. The appointment gave rulers direct knowledge of the monastery's finances, which could be exploited in excises or in other ways, while ostensibly freeing monks or nuns to pursue religious perfection or intercede for the dead without material distractions. In the sixteenth century (this was new), the inventory could be accompanied or followed by the appointment of evangelical preachers, who would declare the vows of monks and nuns to be wrong, unbinding, impermanent, and revocable. Princes might then lay claim to monastic incomes and/or precious objects through confiscation decrees and/or appointed collectors. The inventories and decrees were legally defended as protective acts, the ruler posing as custodian of the church's deposit or as a sequester keeping a disputed property in trust, free of liability, until a settlement should determine a rightful owner.[27]

Little else can be said about the process of confiscation in Reformation Germany without further qualification or reserve.[28] It remained perfectly orthodox and legal, according to both imperial

---

were not "mental" and intellectual, which if they were, would assume for sixteenth-century Europe a distinction between the sacred and the profane that is simply anachronistic, even Hegelian, and in the sixteenth century secular control was often limited and justified on religious grounds. Alois Hahn, "Religion, Säkularisierung und Kultur," *Säkularisierung, Dechristianisierung, Rechristianisierung im neuzeitlichen Europa*, ed. Hartmut Lehmann (Göttingen: Vandenhoeck und Ruprecht, 1997), pp. 17–31. By contrast, Harm Klueting describes the confiscation of church property as an early secularization of "social fields of responsibility" (*gesellschaftliche Aufgabenfelder*). Harm Klueting, "Enteignung oder Umwidmung? Zum Problem der Säkularisation im 16. Jahrhundert," *Zur Säkularisation geistlicher Institutionen*, ed. Crusius, p. 82. See also Enno Bünz, "Das Ende der Klöster in Sachsen. Vom 'Auslaufen' der Mönchen bis zur Säkularisation (1521–1543)," *Glaube und Macht*, 2:81–2.

[27] Lagus, *Iuris utriusque traditio methodica*, ff. 96v–97r for the definition of deposit and sequestration.

[28] Wolfgang Brandis noted differentiations of confiscation in Lüneburg. This may be applied to any number of territories in the Holy Roman Empire, as will become evident in chapter 2. Wolfgang Brandis, "Quellen zur Reformationsgeschichte der Lüneburger Frauenklöster," *Studien und Texte zur literarischen und materiellen Kulture der Frauenklöster im späten Mittelalter*, edited by Falk Eisermann, Eva Scholtheuber, Volker Honemann (Leiden: E.J. Brill, 2004), pp. 357–398, here 361.

and church laws, to inventory and confiscate church holdings, if a ruler followed certain principles and enjoyed ecclesiastical approval (discussed in Chapter 1). Confiscation was not an exclusively Protestant affair, although Protestants posed the greatest challenge to the place of church property in German society. In addition, the progression from inventory to confiscation and closure was often very slow, sometimes never completed, and sometimes reversed (Chapter 2). Many of the monasteries were not dissolved but simply faded away by attrition, at different rates. In these cases the immediate anti-monastic agent was a relatively powerless individual, namely the preacher who inspired a voluntary abandonment of monastic vows. In some cases, abandoned monasteries stood empty for years or were put to temporary uses, but without transfer of title: the confiscating parties let the previously entitled languish until more convenient legal circumstances or the sheer passage of time confirmed the new dominion. Finally, confiscations were interrupted, reversed, or complicated by three wars between 1546 and 1555 and by the settlements agreed in 1552 (Treaty of Passau) and 1555 (Peace of Augsburg).

The study of secularization in Central Europe therefore makes special demands of its students. The twenty-two years of my title hardly render the subject more manageable. A complete history of the confiscations of church property in Reformation Germany would require the systematic examination of surviving records of princes and cities in every region, now scattered in very many archives.[29] This information should be compared, when possible, to surviving indications of the new uses of property, in order to determine the character and success of confiscations in each place and their effect on social networks, territorial government, and ruling power. Aristocratic networks are now widely recognized as the building blocks of the state in late medieval and early modern Europe.[30] In early sixteenth-century Germany, the composition of local and regional aristocracies and their networks were especially diverse. Without a true

---

[29] It is still true, as Sieglerschmidt has noted (*Territorialstaat*, p. 145 n. 44), that we lack studies of the economic impact of the policy of a territorial state on church property, which should also compare Protestant and Catholic territories. Published accounts are incomplete and often marred by confessional biases, which conspire in an unexpected way to exaggerate Protestant successes.

[30] Hillay Zmora, *Monarchy, Aristocracy, and the State in Europe, 1300–1800* (New York: Routledge, 2001), pp. 1–36.

monarchy, the links between artistocracies, princes, cities, and other
regional authorities varied all the more. These links were the very
substance of German political life. The connections of aristocratic
networks to monasteries, cathedral chapters, and collegiate churches
conditioned both resistance to confiscation and success.[31] But the
study of relations between aristocratic networks and church corporations is young.[32] Ultimately, one must try to determine not just
how the church lost property but how the redistribution of property
affected these lateral relationships. For the Empire in the first half
of the sixteenth century, this question cannot yet be answered in any
complete way.[33]

This book may therefore be considered an interim report. I have
tried to take advantage of several regional studies that highlight the
variableness of seizures in the first, formative generation of the
Protestant movement, from which one can also trace the link between
confiscation and an emerging Protestant identity (Chapter 2). Research
into the politics of conversion, the League of Schmalkalden, and the
Imperial Chamber Court (the Empire's highest appelate court) demonstrate the importance of church property discussions among the imperial estates (Chapter 3). My goal throughout is to understand two
things. First, what led to the official acceptance of confiscations—
not the idea of it, nor the mere fact of it, but as a historical precipitate in the Holy Roman Empire? Second, how did this process
affect the rise and character of early Protestantism? Acceptance of
confiscations was the result of no particular plan, least of all a plan
by reformers. The actions of groups, not individuals, created it. It
was a political by-product of negotiations within the League of
Schmalkalden and between the League, the Catholic princes, and
the emperor. I will have nothing to say about individual nuns retrieved
from their convents by evangelical parents, monks exiled from their
towns, the personalities of magistrates and princes, or personal con-

---

[31] Discussed in chapter 1.
[32] Auge, Fouquet, Hoffmann, and Hersche in the bibliography.
[33] So, for example, the fullest survey of churches in territories, and therefore the
best reflection of the state of scholarship on the imperial church as a whole, *Die
Territorien des Reichs im Zeitalter der Reformation und Konfessionalisierung. Land und Konfession
1500–1650*, 7 vols., edited by Anton Schindling, Walter Ziegler, (Münster: Aschendorf,
1991–6), does not consistently record fundamental data, such as the closing dates
(and reopening and/or reclosing dates) of *all* closed monasteries, much less the
movement of their assets. Consider also Cohn, "Church Property," pp. 158–87.

versions.[34] The question of church property hinged on a ruler's traditional obligation to protect religion and on a specific political need to preserve a formal separation of ecclesiastical and secular jurisdictions (Chapter 3), not on personalities.

The League's cities and princes required the active support of their clergy to maintain the devout posture demanded by judicial circumstances. I give special attention to theologians, the technicians of religious legitimacy. They circulated their rationales for the new uses of church property in memoranda. These are among the most overlooked works of sixteenth-century reformers. Here, their advice conveniently reveals the thinking of learned clergy in the wings of courts and diets while they debated the fate of their Christian Revolution. The memoranda merit patient review. They are examined in chronological order in Chapters 4–6. The political effect of the theologians' advice can then be traced out in the imperial religious colloquies of 1540–1541 (Chapter 7).

A historian must handle theology with care. It was an intricate and changing discipline. In addition, theologians viewed society and politics obliquely and in a self-aggrandizing way, as a Franciscan cathedral preacher of Mainz, Johannes Wild, may serve to remind us. Wild was a "mediating" Catholic at the height of the religious controversy, one of a number who strived to moderate clerical distemper by conceding the need for reform; he was the sort of theologian quickly dismissed by his many angry contemporaries, while his moderation usually wins our respect. But in a gesture of partisan self-confidence, he dismissed new churches and political alliances, following the polemical trend to assert rigid confessional lines.[35] Alliances come and go, he said. The true church remains[36]—as

---

[34] Consider Johannes Schilling, *Gewesene Mönche. Lebensgeschichten in der Reformation*, in *Schriften des Historischen Kollegs*, Vorträge 26 (Munich: Stiftung Historisches Kolleg, 1990), and Merry Wiesner-Hanks, editor, Joan Skocir and Merry Wiesner-Hanks, translators, *Convents Confront the Reformation: Catholic and Protestant Nuns in Germany* (Milwaukee: Marquette University Press, 1996), pp. 11–64.

[35] Georg Kuhaupt, *Veröffentlichte Kirchenpolitik. Kirche im publizistischen Streit zur Zeit der Religionsgespräche (1538–1541)*, (Göttingen: Vandenhoeck und Ruprecht, 1998), passim. Political behavior and law suggested dimmer boundaries. See Thomas A. Brady, *Protestant Politics: Jacob Sturm (1489–1553 and the German Reformation* (Atlantic Highlands: Humanities Press, 1995), pp. 142–291; Gabriele Haug-Moritz, *Der Schmalkaldische Bund, 1530–1541/42* (Leinfelden-Echterdingen: DRW-Verlag, 2002); Sieglerschmidt, *Territorialstaat und Kirchenregiment*, pp. 146–154.

[36] "Laß Sturmwind kommen und große Gewässer, dies Haus [the true church]

though to say, let schismatics and their league drift into their obliv-
ion while we remain firmly anchored. He thought himself moored
to God. Protestants alleged the same, especially when they were vanquished.[37] It was an implicit appeal to the metaphysical circumstances
of a resplendent, invisible world of saints. Although Catholics and
the varieties of Protestants, and the pacifiers or aggressors in either
camp, conceived of the communion of saints differently, they framed
their identities around this imagined kinship with an indivisible, happy
company of souls at rest before God's unchanging presence, where
the only remaining betterment was reunion with perfected bodies at
the final resurrection, unmoved and unmoveable in every respect but
that final reunion with glorified flesh. True doctrines presaged a pre-
determined, if unseen, victory. Every partisan in whatever camp
thought he or she belonged to the party of ultimate peace.

Actual circumstances contradicted the comfortable stasis of spiritual kinship. All around the clergy making such claims stood the
plain truth of an unresolved controversy over Martin Luther. Both
religious parties needed encouragement. The schism contradicted
Catholic claims of a singular temporal church, and the tenacity of
Catholic institutions in many locales undermined evangelical hopes
for a total eclipse of papal authority in a given place. Luther had
been condemned and remained under imperial ban. He kept on living, but he might be punished at any time. To both parties, an ultimate Catholic restoration under or alongside a weakened papacy
could seem a near possibility. From 1520 to 1547, the controversy
progressed like a religious movement in the modern sense—charis-
matic, apocalyptic, and susceptible to multiple outcomes. Perhaps
nowhere is this unresolved condition more apparent than when studying theological memoranda to sixteenth-century cities and princes.

The state[38] in sixteenth-century middle Europe requires its own

---

wird unbeschädigt bleiben. Neue Kirchen kann man bauen, neue Rotten und
Verbündnisse kann man anrichten. Daß sie aber allweg bleiben, das vermag Niemand.
Das hat die wahre Kirche oft befunden, daß die Ketzer und ihre Kirchen sind zu
nichts geworden, sie ist geblieben und wird bleiben. Gott hat sie gebaut ewiglich."
Johannes Wild, *Etliche Psalmen Christlich und Catholisch außgelegt* (Mainz 1565), p. 178a,
quoted by Thomas Berger, "Johannes Wild (1495–1554)," *Katholische Theologen der
Reformationszeit*, 6 vols. (Münster: Aschendorff, 1984–1988, 2004), 6:121.
[37] Gabriele Haug-Moritz, "The Holy Roman Empire, the Schmalkald League,
and the Idea of Confessional State-Building," *Identities: Four Dialogues* (Philadelphia:
American Philosophical Society, forthcoming).
[38] I take "state" as the name for all the political means of human interaction,

special considerations. It belongs to a distant, pre-nationalist world.[39] We should not assume that every conjuncture of Lutheran faith with a confiscation of church property represents the state's ideological expansion. Confiscators had immediate objectives, namely gold, silver, buildings, farmlands, rents, and other incomes. "The German Reformation was a struggle for faith; it was also a struggle for property."[40] More often than not, rulers claimed that confiscation was an emergency measure taken on the basis of traditional rights and obligations, while posing the terms, conditions, and ultimate consequences of their actions as traditionally as they could. This was extremely important, given the arguable terms of robbery. In a very real way, the accusation of theft came to hinge on the soul of the man of power directing the clearing of a church. Church law, Roman law, theology, and the actual management of church lands and incomes left sufficient room for debate. Moreover, the state was a work in progress; early Protestantism might variously relate to its future. Protestant ideologies covered a spectrum of views of ruling authority and resistance. They had no intrinsic connection to monarchical or republican standpoints.[41] Communal ideals, which were conceived very differently than princely authority was, dominated the first urban evangelical movements. Princes did not uniformly control geographical territories. And the papacy's power was changing: it no longer formed,

---

to borrow the early sociologist Franz Oppenheimer's comprehensive definition. Franz Oppenheimer, *Der Staat*, 3rd ed. (Berlin: Libertad Verlag, 1990 reprint from 1929), pp. 131–2. Oppenheimer contrasted "state" with "society," the latter indicating all the economic means of human interaction. As witness to the many valences of the term, see *Oxford English Dictionary*, second edition (Oxford University Press, 1989), s.v. "state," (consider especially definition 29a).

[39] Nation-states, as we know them, took shape throughout Europe in reaction to the French Revolution. Jonathan Sperber, *The European Revolutions, 1848–1851* (Cambridge University Press, 1994). Linda Colley, *Britons: Forging the Nation, 1707–1837* (London: Pimlico, 2003). Haug-Moritz, "The Holy Roman Empire, the Schmalkald League, and the Idea of Confessional State-Building."

[40] Brady, *Protestant Politics*, p. 162.

[41] "The political and social impact of a confession was ambivalent and depended on historical circumstances." Heinz Schilling, *Civic Calvinism in Northwestern Germany and the Netherlands, Sixteenth to Nineteenth Centuries* (Kirksville, Missouri: Sixteenth Century Journal Publishers, 1991), pp. 5–6, 69–104. The association of Luther with the development of authoritarian rule, Calvin with democracy, is equally problematic. James Tracy, "Luther and the Modern State: Introduction to a Neuralgic Theme," *Luther and the Modern State in Germany*, ed. James D. Tracy (Kirksville, Missouri: Sixteenth Century Publishers, 1986), pp. 19, esp. 17.

if it ever really did, a kind of super-state in competition with other European powers, as Leopold von Ranke once alleged.[42] The confessional division and continued political fragmentation of Germany are evidence of the limitations of state-formation, making it difficult to assume that the confiscations of monasteries and other church lands *necessarily* corresponded to the growth of state power. The confiscations of church property in Reformation Germany may deserve less fanfare than they have sometimes received. But something did happen. The Reformation established an Empire of two churches.

---

[42] Thomas A. Brady, "Ranke, Rom und die Reformation: Leopold von Rankes Entdeckung des Katholizismus," *Jahrbuch des Historischen Kollegs 1999* (Munich: Oldenbourg, 2000), pp. 43–60, here 54–55. Haug-Moritz, "The Holy Roman Empire, the Schmalkald League, and the Idea of Confessional State-Building." Thomas A. Brady, *Turning Swiss: Cities and Empire, 1450–1550* (Cambridge University Press, 1985). Ernst Schubert, "Vom Gebot zur Landesordnung. Der Wandel fürstlicher Herrschaft vom 15. zum 16. Jahrhundert," *Die deutsche Reformation zwischen Spätmittelalter und Früher Neuzeit*, edited by Thomas A. Brady (Munich: Oldenbourg, 2001), pp. 19–61. Thomas Dandelet, *Spanish Rome: 1500–1700* (New Haven: Yale University Press, 2001). Tom Scott, *Society and Economy in Germany, 1300–1600* (Houndmills: Palgrave, 2002), pp. 153–248.

CHAPTER ONE

CHURCH PROPERTY

Canon law broadly defined any confiscation of church lands, precious objects, and incomes by non-clergy as theft.[1] A principle behind this definition is the inalienability of church property. Once dedicated to a religious purpose, it would so have to remain. When the sale or "alienation" of church property was allowed, it must first serve a religious purpose, then public welfare, from the surplus remaining after the needs of divine worship and ministry have been met, as Thomas Aquinas said in an unremarkable opinion.[2] The principle was also entrenched in Roman law.[3] When Protestant princes and

---

[1] *Decretum* C. 12 q. ii.70 CICan 1:710, quoting a famous passage of Ambrose, *De officiis* ii.140–141. Ambrose, *De officiis*, edited and translated by Ivor J. Davidson, 2 vols. (Oxford University Press, 2001), 1:347. See also *Decretales Gregorii IX* III.xiii.1–III.xix.9, CICan 2:512–25, *Liber Sextus* III.ix.1–2, CICan 2:1042–3, *Liber Clementinarum* III.iv.1–2, CICan 2:1160, *Extravagantes Johannis XXII* III.iv.1, CICan 2:1269.

[2] *Summa Theologiae* 2a2ae q. 185 a. 7, commenting on Ambrose and the *Decretum* and Augustine's Ep. 185.9. PL 33:809. See also *Decretales Gregorii IX* III.xlix.2, 4, 7; Alan Gewirth, *Marsilius of Padua: The Defender of Peace*, 2 vols. (New York: Columbia University Press, 1956), 2:266–7; and P. Fourneret, "Biens ecclésiastiques," *Dictionnaire de theologie catholique*, 2/1:843–78, here 857, 874. A maxim of Pope Boniface VIII summarized the non-revocability of a gift to the church: *semel deo dicatum non est ad usos humanos ulterius transferendum. Liber Sextus, De regulis iuris*, li. Sieglerschmidt, *Territorialstaat*, p. 113.

[3] The study of Roman law in medieval and early modern Europe was based on the *Corpus Iuris Civilis*, containing the *Digest, Codex, Institutes*, and *Novellae* compiled by order of the Byzantine emperor Justinian. Accordingly, it represents early Byzantine regulations concerning the church. The first prohibition of confiscation of church property was a constitution of the Emperor Leo I from 470 prohibiting the sale of any real estate or annuities of the church of Constantinople. It apparently served as the basis of the Ostrogothic king Odoacer's prohibition of the sale of the property of the church of Rome, issued a decade later, and it was extended to the entire Byzantine church by the emperor Anastasis shortly after. The two previous imperial constitutions were taken up in Justinian's *Codex* (1.2.14, CICiv 2:13–14), to which he added his own detailed prohibitions (*Codex* 1.2.21, CICiv 2:16; *Novellae* 7, CICiv 3:48–63), but he also authorized the alienation of houses of the church of Jerusalem (*Novellae* 40, CICiv 3:258–61), permitted the sale of church property under certain conditions to relieve debt (*Novellae* 46, CICiv 3:280–83), allowed the exchange of goods between churches (*Novellae* 54, CICiv 3:306–10), permitted the church of Constantinople to exchange property with his own fisc (*Novellae* 55, CICiv 3:308–10),

cities violated the administrative authority of the courts of popes, archbishops, and bishops by independently appointing pastors, assuming the management of church properties, and/or redistributing them, they also needed to describe their actions as the preservation of church rights. Church robbers thus became reformers.

What was the church's property? The answer to this question is complex, for two reasons. First, the nature of the church's ownership of property was peculiar. Second, the late medieval church's material holdings were very diverse, as one may see by reviewing the main types of properties and institutions the Protestants exploited, or liberated, as one may have it. I will consider each of these matters in turn.

Ownership and Churches

In medieval Europe, ownership was conceptualized between two extremes. At one extreme stood the ideal case of paradise, with an earth shared among equals. No private possession was possible, necessary, or useful there. At the other extreme stood the absolute, individual control of material things. The majority of medieval intellectuals believed that in the pristine state of nature before the sin of Adam and Eve all things were shared in common and nothing was individually owned.[4] Individual ownership was generally held to be a divinely sanctioned accommodation to original sin, accomplished through the institutions of temporal rulers or as a change of or addition to natural law serving the common good in imperfect human society.[5] Franciscan theologians insisted that the unpropertied con-

---

and permitted the sale of ritual objects to redeem captives or pay off debts to avoid the sale of church real estate (*Novellae* 120.9–10, CICiv 3:601–3). Fourneret, "Biens ecclésiastiques," 2/1:863. Although Constantine had exempted the clergy from public obligations, both the Theodosian Code and Justinian's *Novellae* allowed special taxes of the clergy in special circumstances. See ibid., 2/1:868–70.

[4] Diana Wood, *Medieval Economic Thought* (Cambridge University Press, 2002), pp. 17–41 provides an excellent introduction to medieval intellectual approaches to ownership. For examples of the view that nothing was owned in paradise, see Odd Langholm, *Economics in the Medieval Schools* (Leiden: E.J. Brill, 1992), pp. 74 (William of Auxerre), 90 (Roland of Cremona), 151–2, 154 (Bonaventure), 213 (Thomas Aquinas), 252 (Henry of Ghent), 351 (Peter John Olivi), 382 (Giles of Rome), 406 (John Duns Scotus).

[5] Langholm, *Economics*, p. 570. An exception to this prevailing view was that of

dition was revived in the apostolic church, and many agreed that
poverty, in one form or another, ideally characterized the communal life of those most committed to religious perfection.[6] Absent was
the Enlightenment's conviction that ownership is a free and unlim-
ited right conveyed by nature to human beings, which governing
powers should recognize and preserve.[7] Absent, too, was the supervening right of a sovereign authority—be it king, parliament, or the
state—to the property of a place, as in the exercise of eminent
domain. Rather, ownership required the personal exercise of power,
in Latin *dominium*, over an object. Ideally, it required an unrestricted
exercise of power. Dominion over an owned thing was supposed to
be unencumbered by other obligations. Or as presupposed by the
Mirror of Saxony, the first written code of Germanic law, a true possession (*egen*) is not held in fief, that is, from a superior upon obligations to perform service, but is given to heirs free of obligations to
pay tribute.[8] Simple enough, where the forms of ownership were
limited to a small number of people whose social debts were clearly
defined, or where ownership and use coincided, which was increasingly rare in late medieval Europe, if it had ever been very clear.[9]

---

the French publicist, John of Paris, who believed that individual property was the
natural consequence of labor, subject to the laborer alone and to no other lordship. Wood, *Medieval Economic Thought*, pp. 24–5.

[6] Langholm, *Economics*, pp. 72 (William of Auxerre), 91 (Roland of Cremona),
147 (Bonaventure), 210 (Thomas Aquinas, poverty by counsel not precept), 351
(Peter John Olivi), 383 (Giles of Rome, poverty a duty rather than a necessity), 498
(Guido Terreni, communal property ideal for contemplatives). Wood, *Medieval Economic
Thought*, pp. 27–30 and the literature noted there. For the laity and poverty, con-
sider Michael Bailey, "Religious Poverty, Mendicancy, and Reform in the Late
Middle Ages," *Church History* 72(2003):457–83.

[7] Gerhard Köbler, *Lexikon der europäischen Rechtsgeschichte* (Munich: C.H. Beck, 1997),
pp. 118–19, s.v. Eigentum. Helmut Coing, *Europäisches Privatrecht* 2 vols. (München:
Beck, 1985, 1989), 1:222.

[8] The *Sachsenspiegel* thus distinguished between encumbered property in an inheritance, whose obligations are transferred to an heir, and property transferred unencumbered upon the testimony of seven witnesses. *Sachsenspiegel Landrecht*, I.viii.1, ed.
Karl August Eckhardt (Göttingen: Musterschmidt, 1955), p. 78. Consider also the
gloss by Johann von Buch (c. 1330), *Glossen zum Sachsenspiegel-Landrecht. Buch'sche Glosse*,
ed. Frank-Michael Kaufmann, 3 vols. (Hannover: Hahnsche Buchhandlung, 2002),
1:184–7, and see Charles du Fresne Du Cange, *Glossarium mediae et infimae latinitis*,
10 vols. (Graz: Akademische Verlagsanstalt, 1954), 6:535, s.v. proprietates, quoting
Melchior Goldast on the *Sachsenspiegel*.

[9] A conviction of absolute disposition of property may also be considered a lay
adaptation of the church's claims to immunity, and an extension of the heritability
of property. Consider Reynolds, *Fiefs and Vassals*, pp. 60–61, 63, 72, 124, 141, and
passim.

By the end of the fourteenth-century, transactions could involve such diverse things as easements, debts of service, usufruct, shares of freight vessels, communal bond-issues, and other forms of credit, all of which tended to divide rights of use from ownership.[10]

The relative quality of ownership is also expressed in the terms that denoted ownership and control. *Proprietas* and *dominium*, "ownership" and "dominion," both referred to property, with *dominium* as the broader concept indicating both lordship in the widest sense and a legal person with constricted rights over a thing, as in cases of usufruct, easements, or ecclesiastical patronage rights (more on patronage, below), all of which comprise a partial dominion.[11] In the case of partial dominion, one's freedom to consume or destroy was limited, the right to consume or destroy being a litmus test of absolute disposition; but limited, too, was the risk taken in the event of property loss or damage.[12] Scholars of Roman law believed that *proprietas* refers to the total disposition of property, and they emphasized how free that disposition must be. Yet here too, as Helmut Coing has remarked, the definition of "ownership" simply "did not correspond to legal reality" in many places in Europe. The definition appears rather to have been intended to correct the limitations on the disposition of property known to exist in economic life.[13] Seldom did ownership involve an unencumbered power over things. Accordingly, scholastic economic thought can be seen "as a set of corollaries to a theory of limited property rights."[14]

The actual power to control things corresponded to one's status (it was not attributed to a natural right). The growing complexity of property transactions in late medieval Europe—involving rents, annuities, easements, usufruct, and so forth—was matched by the increasing complexity of distinctions of status. In Central Europe, status did

---

[10] Wood, *Medieval Economic Thought*, pp. 18, 36. Odd Langholm, *The Legacy of Scholasticism in Economic Thought* (Cambridge University Press, 1998), pp. 66–76. Edwin S. Hunt, James M. Murray, *A History of Business in Medieval Europe, 1200–1550* (Cambridge University Press, 1999), pp. 49, 61–2, 204–55.

[11] Coing, *Europäisches Privatrecht*, 1:291–92. For the distinction between direct and indirect dominion see also Köbler, *Lexikon*, p. 119, and *Lexikon Latinitatis Nederlandicae Medii Aevi*, 7 vols.+ (Leiden: E.J. Brill, 1970+), 3:1580–82. Consider also Sieglerschmidt, *Territorialstaat*, pp. 60–7 for the Roman concept of dominion.

[12] Consider John T. Noonan, *The Scholastic Analysis of Usury* (Cambridge: Harvard University Press, 1957), pp. 28–29, 40, 137–70.

[13] Coing, *Europäisches Privatrecht*, 1:291–92.

[14] Langholm, *Economics in the Medieval Schools*, p. 21.

not strictly correspond to titles, such as count, duke, or prince, nor did it depend exclusively on property or military might; in late medieval cities, money-wealth helped differentiate ranks within the broad spectrum of middling classes, but moneyed status did not supplant distinctions of honor, or fancy titles, especially among the cities' ruling classes.[15] In the broad, ruling sense, *dominium* implied a relative degree of power over things or people, be it a free peasant's control of family and a plot of land; a tradesman's control of tools, resources, and productivity; or a prince's control of regional lineages and peasants. Since the thirteenth century, all manner of property was increasingly subject to written rules, taxation, and professional administration.[16] This reflected the growth of economic complexity, while the expansion of the European economy also multiplied the possibilities of partial ownership.

Finally, there was no truly impersonal concept of property outside of the church. A concept of public property did not exist. An *allmende*, a field or wood for common use by a village, for example, was by definition not ownable. There was no idea of the state as an abstract and impersonal entity with absolute claims. The power to own was obtained by inheritance, gift, purchase, or might, or conveyed and acquired by groups acting with the legal force of individuals—partnerships or corporations like cities or village communes.[17]

But the church presented a special case. Ecclesiastical persons, in particular bishops, abbots, and abbesses, were lords alongside others, and they, together with religious corporations, such as monastic convents and other fraternal bodies, controlled property. Bishoprics and monasteries exercised, at best, a quasi-personal dominion over lands and laborers. Power to control their properties, at least in law, and by the late Middle Ages in fact, was attached to an office or a corporation, not to the person. It could not be inherited, at least not openly. The church's governance was since the twelfth century

---

[15] Karl-Heinz Spieß, *Familie und Hochadel im deutschen Hochadel des Spätmittelalters* (Stuttgart: Steiner, 1993), passim. Isenmann, *Die deutsche Stadt im Spätmittelalter*, pp. 250–54 and the literature noted there.

[16] Reynolds, *Fiefs and Vassals*, pp. 476–8, for this and the rise of institutions of feudal vassalage.

[17] The authority of village communes was gradually supplanted by the integration of peasants into territorial states as something approaching citizens after the period studied in this book. Scott, *Society and Economy*, pp. 48–55.

distinguished from lay rule by church law, yet ecclesiastical lords
transacted the same business as lay rulers, and little, if anything, distinguished the routine business of one from the other. This was especially the case in Germany, where since the tenth-century Saxon
dynasty most bishops enjoyed the temporal status of imperial princes,[17a]
and many of the oldest monasteries also enjoyed substantial temporal domains. The rule of bishoprics and monasteries was embellished
by spiritual, pastoral lordship, inherent in the office of bishop but
also possessed by monasteries, which also established churches on
their lands and provided religious services to noble families.

If the rule of cathedrals and monasteries overlapped that of princes,
the rule of princes, nobility, urban aristocrats, communes, and other
corporations touched the spiritual governance of the church, in part
because the church could not form an organization free of lay involve-
ment, in spite of the principles of church law, for example, the general rule on the inalienability of church property. Neither the seven
(before 1344, six) church provinces of the Holy Roman Empire nor
the bishops within them ever formed an independent political block,
and there was no national synod of bishops.[18] Rather, the archbishops competed with each other for preeminence in imperial affairs,
and the bishops' ties to princes were more important than their relations within the church as such.[19] Because kings once dominated the
appointment of bishops, these appointments were extremely political,
giving shape to what has usually been called the "imperial church
system." The name refers first and foremost to the pronounced role
played by bishops in imperial politics, as that role took shape during
the Saxon and Franconian (known also as Ottonian and Salian)
dynasties of the Holy Roman Empire, which ruled from 919 to 1125,
a central European variant on the role played by bishops at the courts
of other European rulers, for example the kings of France and
England.[20] Since the thirteenth century, imperial influence in epis-

[17a] Thomas A. Brady, "The Holy Roman Empire's Bishops on the Eve of the
Reformation," *Continuity and Change: The Harvest of Late Medieval and Reformation History*,
edited by R.J. Bast, A. Gow (Leiden: E.J. Brill, 2000), pp. 20–47.
[18] Michael Borgolte, *Die mittelalterliche Kirche*, (Munich: Oldenbourg, 1992), p. 72.
[19] Borgolte, *Die mittelalterliche Kirche*, p. 80.
[20] Borgolte, *Die mittelalterliche Kirche*, pp. 73–5. T. Reuter, "The Imperial Church
System' of the Ottonian and Salian Rulers: a Reconsideration," *Journal of Ecclesiastical
History* 33(1982):347–74. Kings and emperors could also conceive of their office in
religious terms, as Marc Bloch and Ernst Kantorowicz once emphasized; Ernst
Schubert has pointed out the survival of religious notions of kingship in late medieval
Germany. Ernst Schubert, *König und Reich. Studien zur spätmittelalterlichen deutschen*

copal appointments declined for a time, leaving governing authority in the late medieval church of the Holy Roman Empire all the more dispersed among the bishops, and the avenues of temporal influence dispersed among various kinds of ruling authority.[21]

The influence of the laity may have been most broadly felt in the complex rules governing the lay foundation of churches and chapels and the rights retained by donors and their ancestors as patrons—their patronage right.[22] The right was connected to gifts large and small, including those that supported routine clerical offices, or minor benefices, which is to say this system affected every level of society.[23] Patrons retained a right to present candidates for office (a right of presentation), called a patron's "honor" by the jurists, to which there corresponded the obligation to defend the church and a kind of insurance policy, that if the patron fell into want, the church would provide for the patron.[24] In the course of the fifteenth century the right of presentation was used increasingly by all kinds of lay donors, from princes and wealthy townsmen to village and urban bodies (e.g. communes, guilds, fraternities), to influence the church's governance.[25]

Verfassungsgeschichte (Göttingen: Vandenhoeck und Ruprecht, 1979), p. 35. Borgolte, *Die mittelalterliche Kirche*, p. 81.

[21] Charles IV, the mid fourteenth-century king of Bohemia and Holy Roman Emperor, was an important exception to the general decline of imperial influence in church appointments. See Ferdinand Seibt, *Karl IV. Ein Kaiser in Europa, 1346–1378*, 2nd ed., (Munich: Süddeutscher Verlag, 1978), p. 304; Gerhard Losher, *Königtum und Kirche zur Zeit Karls IV*, (Munich: R. Oldenbourg Verlag, 1985), pp. 182–95; and Borgolte, *Die mittelalterliche Kirche*, pp. 27, 86.

[22] Sieglerschmidt, *Territorialstaat und Kirchenregiment*, passim. Borgolte, *Die mittelalterliche Kirche*, pp. 36, 55, 114. R.N. Swanson, *Religion and Devotion in Europe, c. 1215–1515* (Cambridge University Press, 1995), pp. 214–15, 230, 245–6.

[23] A benefice is a right granted by a bishop to an income usually attached to a parish, in particular the right to collect its tithes. Although the parish represented the lowest point in the church's elaborate hierarchical structure, it was considered extremely important, was deeply embedded in village society, and involved a certain reciprocity between the community and the clergy (the village was not the mere passive recipient of pastoral care). "The relationship of pastor and community was marked by a close entanglement of church and world," concluded Enno Bünz. Enno Bünz, "'Die Kirche im Dorf lassen...' Formen der Kommunikation im spätmittelalterlichen Niederkirchenwesen," *Kommunikation in der ländlichen Gesellschaft vom Mittelalter bis zur Moderne*, edited by Werner Rösener (Göttingen: Vandenhoeck und Ruprecht, 2000), pp. 77–167, esp. 142–162, 165 (for the quote). For tithes, p. 32, below.

[24] Sieglerschmidt, *Territorialstaat*, p. 92 n. 117, for this doctrine in the Ordinary Gloss to the *Decretum*, Gottofredo da Trani, Sinibaldo dei Fieschi (Pope Innocent IV), Hostiensis, Johannes Andreae, Johannes de Anania, and Antonius de Butrio.

[25] The dukes of Braunschweig-Lüneburg and Württemberg, among many others,

Benefices could be used to secure incomes for friends, family, and other favored individuals and groups, including people who represented one's religious ideals.[26]

Legal rights associated with patronage thus corresponded to a growing sense of shared clergy-laity responsibility for religious renewal and spiritual welfare, and this sensibility was attached to property. Gifts established enduring relationships. In addition, lay and ecclesiastical princes and city councils promoted spiritual renewal in religious houses by initiating or supporting the subjection of the house to a new, usually trans-regional, "observant" structure, an extension of the lay rulers' protection of the church.[27] Clerical administrators and lay owners participated in the same economy, which fact was variously accommodated by canon law, the norms of which were readily adapted to real life. For example, canon law insisted that the asset given had been lost to the world and became the church's, but if taken absolutely, this would greatly hamper a churchman's ability to conduct business and decrease the benefit of the gift. Jurists therefore qualified this formal inalienability with provisos such as this, by the prominent sixteenth-century scholar Diego de Covarrubias y Leyva: a prelate *could* rent out church properties for strictly limited periods, never on a lifetime contract.[28] Likewise, the property could be pawned for a specific religious or charitable purpose, such as the redemption of prisoners of war or emergency poor relief.[29] These were useful conditions. War emergencies were many and varied, and "poor" was a relative term. Moreover, a property may have entered the church encumbered in the first place. For example, when

---

used a patronage right to introduce reform. Sieglerschmidt, *Territorialstaat*, pp. 228–9 n. 19.

[26] The early sixteenth-century Catholic jurist, Caesar Lambertinus, said a gift could even stipulate that a benefice be restricted to the donor's kin. Sieglerschmidt, *Territorialstaat*, p. 98.

[27] Sieglerschmidt, *Territorialstaat*, pp. 280–86, who shows that the rights of patrons were gradually superceded by the prerogatives claimed by territorial lords over the course of the sixteenth and early seventeenth centuries. Rosi Fuhrmann, *Kirche und Dorf: religiöse Bedürfnisse und kirchliche Stiftung auf dem Lande vor der Reformation* (Stuttgart: G. Fischer, 1995), passim. Manfred Schulze, *Fürsten und Reformation* (Tübingen: J.C.B. Mohr, 1991), pp. 139–42. Christopher Ocker, "Religious Reform and Social Cohesion," *The Work of Heiko A. Oberman*, ed. Thomas A. Brady, Katherine G. Brady, Susan Karant-Nunn, James D. Tracy (Leiden: Brill, 2003), 69–91 and the literature noted there.

[28] Diego de Covarrubias y Leyva, *Variarum Resolutionum*, II.xi.1–9, *Opera omnia*, 2 vols. (Coloniae Allobrogum: Samuelis de Tournes, 1679), 2:248–258.

[29] Ibid., II.xi.8–9.

pawned property was given to a monastery, the monastery would ordinarily receive whatever benefits might accrue from it (value of agricultural products or rent, for example) until the property was redeemed. At redemption, the monastery would receive the price of redemption. But the gift might come with conditions attached to the original security pledge, for example, that the donor's family or heirs might exclusively redeem the property, thus limiting the monastery's disposition of this asset. In the event that a donor's clan had died out, the clan's overlord could often make claims on the property.[30] That same right could be claimed by city councils, in cases where the lineages of urban patrons had died out.[31]

The religious imaginary complemented the actual entanglement of clerical and lay business. Gifts of property to churches or monasteries were personal acts of devotion. They implied exchanges of service and protection between heaven and earth and were transacted with the utmost seriousness. When various social groups, from princely courts to cities or villages, gave gifts and influenced appointments to church offices, they presupposed these bonds and reciprocities between heaven and earth.

In summary, church governance involved spiritual and temporal rule. Church authority was distinguished from lay power but overlay it, and likewise, the laity exercised considerable influence over the church. What finally differentiated church governance from the laity was a peculiar *concept* of power. This difference is crucial. The

---

[30] A statute of Archduke Ferdinand of Austria 14 October 1524, addressed to the people of all social ranks in Württemberg, attempted to regulate this (Stuttgart, Baden-Württembergisches Staatsarchiv, A 64 Nr. 1 Teil 1, a bundle of documents that include the inventories of ornments, chalices, monstrances, and liturgical garments from 36 places in 1535). Ferdinand granted churches and monasteries the right to sell such encumbered properties outside the family when redemption by heirs or relatives proved impossible. But in the event that a donor's clan had died out, the archduke claimed a right to redeem the gift. In a distant example of such a prerogative, Count Enno II of East Frisia, in 1528, declared himself heir of empty cloisters and claimed the right to confiscate their precious goods for defense of the land. Ziegler, "Reformation und Klosterauflösung," p. 596. Such conditions may have prevented the conferral of a patronage right, at least in theory, since Catholic jurists, for example Paulus de Citadinis and Caesar Lambertinus, insisted that the right could only be conferred when the church received direct dominion over the gift, but it was possible to distinguish patronage, at least formally, from mixed transactions. Sieglerschmidt, *Territorialstaat*, pp. 65 with n. 36, 85–6, 119 (the patron may retain a right of use, while the church holds direct dominion).

[31] Wolfgang Schlenck, *Die Reichsstadt Memmingen und die Reformation* (Memmingen: Memminger Geschichtsblätter, 1968), p. 27.

church had, in the centuries before Martin Luther, defined its own
dominium as impersonal and absolute, whereas lay rulers generally did
not. The definition of power in impersonal and absolute terms appears
most clearly in two distinct series of well known conflicts. One series
involved the property rights of religious communities. The other
involved the power of popes over kings. Both obscure the dynamic
quality of the church's property relationships with a few religious
ideas that were, in the late Middle Ages, extremely compelling.

The first conflict began as an internal debate within a religious
order, the order that "problematized" ownership more than any
other in the Middle Ages.[32] It displays well the late medieval difficulties
with reconciling property to an idealized, spiritual good, but also the
impossibility of the church avoiding property. Although St. Francis
intended his followers to live strictly as hermits, shunning money and
property both individually and as a collective, his order began to
accumulate real estate within a decade of his death, enjoyed an
established urban ministry that competed with the pastoral care
offered in parishes, and appeared, to themselves and others, to compromise St. Francis' ideal. Bonaventure, the prominent Parisian master elected minister general of the order in 1257, who was responsible
for codifying the order's statutes and publishing the official biogra-
phy of its founder, allowed that property might support the life and
work of the community, so long as the order had no title to it. His
intention was to preserve Francis' ideal in changing circumstances.
His doctrine of poverty was challenged by Dominican theologians.
It was considered a dangerous compromise by two "spiritual" factions
that emerged within the Franciscan Order soon after Bonaventure's
death. And it was officially approved by Pope Nicholas III in 1279,
on three conditions: the Franciscans must not themselves handle
money, must refuse unconditional bequests, and must live in want,
as did the poor.[33] The mere use of property nevertheless seemed

---

[32] A summary of the Franciscan debate may be found in *Nicolaus Minorita: Chronica*,
ed. Gedeon Gál, David Flood (St. Bonaventure, N.Y.: Franciscan Institute, 1996),
pp. 1–53. See also Malcolm Lambert, *Franciscan Poverty* (St. Bonaventure, N.Y.:
Franciscan Institite, 1998), and for the late stages of the conflict, David Burr, *The
Spiritual Franciscans* (University Park: Pennsylvania State University Press, 2001).
[33] For the emergence of two "spiritual" factions, Burr, *Spiritual Franciscans*, pp.
43–65 and passim for the problem of the name "spiritual Franciscans." Nicholas
III's 1279 bull, *Exiit qui seminat* approved the Bonaventuran distinction between *usus
domini* and *usus facti* or *usus simplex*—the use associated with dominion and a mere

dangerously close to the actual possession of communal things. To prevent this arrangement from becoming an excuse for luxury, Franciscan theologians, in particular the intellectual leader of the more moderate "spiritual" faction, Peter John Olivi, insisted that Franciscans live in some impoverished way, which was known as the "poor use" of property, *usus pauper*. This condition, advocated as a necessary interpretation of the Franciscan rule, rested upon the formal propertylessness of the order. To protect that claim and to promote "poor use," Pope Clement V, in 1312, declared that the papacy held formal title to all property used by the Franciscans.[34] This papal-Franciscan cooperation was soon broken. At the end of the thirteenth century, the doctrine of poor use came increasingly to be associated with radicals within the order, whose apocalyptic views undermined papal authority. Pope John XXII imposed ownership on the Franciscan Order by denying that the use of property and dominion were separable and by formally renouncing Clement V's provision, which left Franciscan users the owners of their convents, books, robes, and other effects.[35] The papacy was soon further antagonized when the principal supporters of the moderate, Bonaventuran view, the Franciscan minister general Michael of Cesena, and the friars Bonagratio of Bergamo and William Ockham, supported Ludwig of Bavaria in his conflict with the pope over his imperial election. The pope responded to the moderates by attempting to extinguish all possible rebellion among the Franciscans.

Conflicts over religious dominion continued. To many clergy the connection between property and dominion undermined the claim of anyone who was said to practice religious poverty but was not personally and obviously impoverished, such as, for example, very many Franciscans, Dominicans, Augustinian Hermits, or Carmelites of the fourteenth and fifteenth centuries. This, by the way, would include members of Observant houses in the fifteenth century. They

---

use with no claim to dominion. *Exiit qui seminat*, articles 7, 9, 11, 12 and passim. http://www.franciscan-archive.org/bullarium/exiit-e.html.

[34] *Exivi de paradiso*, http://www.franciscan-archive.org/bullarium/exivi-e.html.

[35] *Quia nonnunquam* (1322), *Ad conditorem* (1322), and *Quum inter nonnullos* (1323). *Extravagantes Johannis XXII, De verborum significatorum*, ii–v. CICan 2:1224–29. http://www.franciscan-archive.org/index2.html. On the composition of *Quum inter nonnullos*, see Patrick Nold, *Bertrand de la Tour and the Apostolic Poverty Controversy under Pope John XXII* (Oxford: Clarendon, 2004), chapters 7, 8.

may have lived simpler than their "conventual" confreres, but they could scarcely have been considered to be actually impoverished.[36] At Paris in the 1250's a master named Guillaume de St. Amour had developed an argument against the mendicant orders that focused on their hypocrisy, hypocrisy defined as a spurious claim to be poor.[37] The argument was expanded to make a case for the dissolution of the four mendicant orders, which was forcefully promoted at the papal court (and in England) by an archbishop of Armagh, Richard FitzRalph. When the members of a religious order fraudulently claimed to be poor, FitzRalph said, they committed a mortal sin, and the mortal sin disproved their claim to pursue religious perfection. FitzRalph adapted a view for dominion first developed by papal publicists earlier in the fourteenth century, known as "dominion by grace," according to which all dominion must be traced to a spiritual source. Papal publicists named that source as the priesthood, with the papacy as the foremost priest of Christendom. In FitzRalph's version of this doctrine, mortal sin cancels a right to own and use the gifts of the faithful or the properties of the church. The charge helped widen opposition to the friars in the fourteenth century.[38] The argument was expanded yet again by the Oxford master John Wyclif in the 1370's as an argument for the royal expropriation of the church altogether. Wyclif adapted this to an argument against the papacy and for the nationalization of the English church.

That is, the concept of Christ's rule could be used both to estab-

---

[36] Bernhard Neidiger, "Armutsbegriff und Wirtschaftsverhalten der Franziskaner im 15. Jahrhundert", *Erwerbspolitik und Wirtschaftsweise mittelalterlicher Orden und Klöster*, edited by Kaspar Elm (Berlin: Duncker und Humboldt, 1992), pp. 213–14. Ocker, "Religious Reform and Social Cohesion," p. 85.

[37] For Guillaume de Saint Amour, M.M. Dufeil, *Guillaume de Saint-Amour et la polémique universitaire parisienne, 1250–1259* (Paris: A. et J. Picard, 1972), and Penn R. Szittya, *The Antifraternal Tradition in Medieval Literature* (Princeton University Press, 1986). For FitzRalph and Wyclif, Katherine Walsh, *Richard FitzRalph in Oxford, Avignon, and Armagh: a Fourteenth-Century Scholar and Primate* (Oxford: Clarendon, 1981), pp. 377–79 and passim; Christopher Ocker, *Johannes Klenkok: A Friar's Life, c. 1310–1374* (Philadelphia: American Philosophical Society, 1993), pp. 32–40.

[38] Christopher Ocker, "Die Armut und die menschliche Natur: Konrad Waldhauser, Jan Milíč von Kroměříž und die Bettelmönche," *Die neue Frömmigkeit: eine europäische Kultur am Ende des Mittelalters*, edited by Martial Staub and Marek Derwich (Göttingen: Vandenoeck und Ruprecht, 2005), and idem, "'*Lacrima ecclesie.*' Konrad von Megenberg, the Friars, and Beguines," *Konrad von Megenberg (1309–1374), das Wissen der Zeit*, edited by Gisela Drossbach, Martin Kintzinger, Claudia Märtl, forthcoming as a *Beiheft* of the *Zeitschrift für Bayerische Landesgeschichte*.

lish and to undermine church dominion. Its use to undermine church dominion was roundly condemned among the errors of John Wyclif at the Council of Constance in May, 1415,[39] and so would it be remembered in theology faculties up to the dawn of the Protestant movements, whenever teachers and readers fell upon discussions of these famous debates in their books. The importance of this migration of the poverty debate is this. It underscored the validity of church dominion and linked the rejection of church property to heresy.

In the second conflict over dominion, between popes and kings, the papacy came to define its own power as both indirectly acquired and absolute, through the series of quarrels that began with Pope Gregory VII in the eleventh century and culminated in the controversy between Pope Boniface VIII and the king of France at the turn of the fourteenth century. According to the conception developed by Pope Boniface VIII and subsequent papal publicists, papal power is absolute insofar as it is nothing but the earthly exercise of the power of Christ, who possesses heavenly rule over the visible and invisible universe. [40] It is indirect, insofar as the papal office exercises it as a kind of special subdelegate, the only plenipotentiary subdelegate of Christ on earth, a point which was made against another of Ludwig of Bavaria's publicists, Marsiglio of Padua, who insisted on the imperial derivation of the church's temporal possessions.[41] The papacy saw its ruling authority as both derivative and absolute. It is often said that this controversy marked an important stage in the development of European political thought, in that it quickened the debate over absolute rule among kings and churchmen alike, inspiring alternative views of the derivation of governmental authority: theological, individual, or corporate. The debate

---

[39] *Enchiridion Symbolorum*, nr. 1127–7, 1137, 1160, 1166, 1168, and Martin V in his condemnation of the heresy of Jan Hus in February 1418, ibid., nr. 1274–6.

[40] Michael J. Wilks, *The Problem of Sovereignty in the Later Middle Ages* (Cambridge University Press, 1963).

[41] *Enchiridion Symbolorum Definitionum et Declarationum de Rebus fidei et Morum*, ed. Heinrich Denzinger, Adolf Schönmetzer, 36th ed. (Freiburg im Briesgau: Herder, 1965), nr. 941. John of Paris, the early fourteenth-century theologian and royal publicist, similarly argued that all church property belongs to the entire community of the church, but is dispensed by the papal office. Should the pope fail to employ it for the common good, he may be deposed. Michael Wilks, *The Problem of Soveriengty*, pp. 480–81 n. 4.

showed that power, *dominium* could be derived in various ways—from
the people, from God, or from a body of representatives of the
people.

Ultimately, the owners of church property were believed to be
supernatural figures, for example, Christ, as the Bolognese jurist
Johannes Andreae said, or patron saints.[42] But an irony of late
medieval debates over church property, when compared to prevailing secular views of dominion in medieval Europe, is that of all the
social configurations that existed, including urban communes, the
church's view was closest to a concept of public property, despite—
perhaps because of—its supernaturalism (we will return to this in
the Conclusion). Not that the church conceived of its power as publicly derived. Marsiglio of Padua's famous arguments were usually
rejected by theologians, and conciliar theories, when the conciliar
movement faded soon after Pope Eugenius IV left the Council of
Basel in 1439, had only, in the end, justified emergency action by
the Christian faithful in the face of the papal schism. The church's
power was supernaturally derived: its dominion was impersonal, a
power of office, and no human being could claim to own it, which
papal critics like Marsiglio of Padua also believed. One could only
manage it. Bishops often viewed their spiritual jurisdiction as absolute
within their dioceses, but a diocese in Germany was not a geographically delimited region, a territory; it was a space of episcopal
legal authority, and monasteries in particular were accustomed to
dispute its absolute character.[43] Religious power also implied some
set of doctrinal and moral assumptions, for example, that those who
exercise dominion represent themselves honestly (as in FitzRalph's
arguments against the friars), or that those who administer church
property do not use it for private gain. It is perhaps not surprising
that the most widespread revolution known to pre-modern Europe,

---

[42] For Andreae, Wood, *Medieval Economic Thought*, p. 31. Sieglerschmidt pointed
out that while the degree of a Catholic jurist's papalism can be measured by the
degree of proprietary-like powers a jurist ascribes to the pope, Catholic jurists well
into the seventeenth century ascribed dominion of church property to Christ, with
the clergy as its administrators. Sieglerschmidt, *Territorialstaat*, pp. 121–3 with n. 213,
p. 216.
[43] Consider Ilona Riedel-Spangenberger, "Konrad von Megenberg und die Paro-
chialstruktur," *Konrad von Megenberg (1309–1374). Das Wissen der Zeit*, ed. Drossbach,
Kintzinger, Märtl (forthcoming).

the Peasants' Revolt of 1524/5, justified its actions by appealing to a divine source, the "godly law," a normative atom bomb.[44]

In short, at the dawn of the Protestant movement, the church possessed a view of dominion that was very abstract, absolute in its dimensions, and more impersonal than secular views of power and ownership.[45] The church's *sense* of dominion (it was more than a doctrine) reinforced the conviction of its autonomy, as a complete society governed by its own laws, while the *exercise* of dominion was entangled with lay society. The sacramental power of the priesthood allowed the clergy to view this practical entanglement in metaphysical and paternalistic terms. The church facilitated salvation. There was nothing more important in human life. Ecclesiastical rulers—as priests differentiated from other human beings by their indelible sacramental power—could simply ignore the distinction between their temporal and spiritual jurisdictions and regard interference in their temporal affairs as aggression against the church. It was easy to blur the line between the temporal and the spiritual church.

What the Church Owned in Late Medieval Germany and How Much It Was Disrupted

The church in society was a propertied entity governed by prelates and administrators closely tied to regional aristocracies. Its properties were many and diverse.

The material church consisted of buildings for worship and shelters for monks, nuns, some priests, the poor, and the infirm. In addition to churches, chapels, cloisters, parsonages and other houses, a piece of farmland attached to the parsonage, hospitals, and the like, the property of the church also included the precious objects used

---

[44] Brady, *Protestant Politics*, p. 163. Peter Blickle, *The Revolution of 1525*, trans. Thomas A. Brady and H.C. Erik Midelfort (Baltimore: Johns Hopkins, 1981), pp. 87–100. Peter Bierbrauer, "Das Göttliche Recht und die naturrechtliche Tradition," *Bauer, Reich und Reformation. Festschrift für Günther Franz zum 80. Geburtstag am 23. Mai 1982*, edited by Peter Blicke (Stuttgart: Eugen Ulmer, 1982), pp. 210–234.

[45] Its abstract quality is perhaps also a reflection of the role of law in the church's self-understanding. Consider Peter Landau, "Der Einfluß des kanonischen Rechts auf die europäische Rechtskultur," *Europäische Rechts- und Verfassungsgeschichte: Ergebnisse und Perspecktive der Forschung*, ed. Reiner Schulze (Berlin: Duncker und Humboldt, 1991), pp. 39–57, here 44, 49–52.

to perform and enhance religious rites and devotions, from reliquaries and liturgical gear to books, paintings, and statues.[46] Although sometimes destroyed or confiscated, to great psychological effect,[47] these movable things comprised a small portion of the material church. Income-producing real properties were the most significant part of the church's wealth, mostly farmlands but also houses, often managed by monastic communities or canons (more on canons in a moment) but also leased-out for rental incomes. To these incomes were added tithes, owed by people of a parish to support its rector. The tithe was a portion of product of arable land ostensibly owed for the maintainence of the church. Since the thirteenth century, it was often assessed as a money payment attached to a parcel.[48] It was often given in fief by bishops to lay nobles. Earlier efforts, in the twelfth century, of reforming bishops to restrict lay possession of tithes were long past. Tithes were eminently tradable. Since the thirteenth century, land was increasingly exchanged in money transactions, and soon rights to tithes were also exchanged, pawned, and sold outright. Clergy, laity, and corporations all traded tithes, only a portion of which went to support priests (how much was dictated by local custom).

The rector of a parish was a priest appointed to the office who enjoyed whatever ecclesiastical income, or benefice, was attached to it. He was in turn obliged to provide for pastoral services, usually by appointing a "vicar" to the task. Incomes were attached to other offices, as well: cathedral dignities and canonries. Appointments to

---

[46] For the development of church properties, see Sieglerschmidt, *Territorialstaat*, pp. 12–15 and the literature noted there.

[47] See Lee Palmer Wandel, *Voracious Idols and Violent Hands* (Cambridge University Press, 1995); Schnitzler, *Ikonoklasmus-Bildersturm*, pp. 144–73; Olivier Christin, *Une révolution symbolique* (Paris: Éditions de Minuit, 1991) for France. Schnitzler has pointed out that, in spite of Luther's denial that iconoclasm could be the last resort of a reform program, it continued to be taken as the proof of the «load-capacity» (*Tragfähigkeit*) of the new church or the prerequisite for the successful establishment of the new church. Idem, "Wittenberg 1522—Reformation am Scheideweg?," *Bildersturm. Wahnsinn oder Gottes Wille?* ed. Cécile Dupeux, Peter Jezler, Jean Wirth (Munich: Wilhelm Fink, 2000), pp. 68–74, here 72–3.

[48] Catherine E. Boyd, *Tithes and Parishes in Medieval Italy* (Ithaca: Cornell, 1952), pp. 26–177, although treating Italy, remains a useful introduction. For Germany, see Rudolf Harrer, *Der kirchliche Zehnt im Gebiet des Hochstifts Würzburg im späten Mittelalter. Systematische Analyse einer kirchlichen Einrichtung im Rahmen der Herrschaftsstrukturen einer Zeit* (Würzburg: Echter, 1992), pp. 89–118.

offices fell under the power of bishops and, according to terms and conditions that expanded greatly in the fourteenth and fifteenth centuries, under the power of the papal court. Although Catholic lay patrons retained a right of presentation—the right to present candidates to a post—the bishop held the formal right of appointment, which according to canon law could only be trumped by the papal court under specific conditions. When Protestants confiscated church buildings and incomes, they hoped to achieve total control over the management of church personnel. They inevitably encroached on the religious government of cathedrals and the papacy alike, not by merely staking a claim on church incomes, but by assuming control entirely apart from existing church courts.

The most valuable properties confiscated from the church in Reformation Germany were almost exclusively monastic. A monastery was an institution in which clergy or laity, men or women, lived a commonly structured religious life prescribed by a *regula* or rule (priests who belong to such a community may also be called regular clergy, while priests who have not taken monastic vows may be called secular clergy). That is about the only thing all monasteries had in common, due to a long and variegated history of monastic foundation and organization. Many monasteries owed their foundation to noble dynasties, with which they would continue to have close relations, enjoying the patronage of one or a few families, receiving children of the lineages and friends as novices, and sometimes being ruled by significant lineage members. They may be called noble foundations (*Adelsstifte*). Other monasteries owed their establishment to emperors or came to enjoy imperial privileges: legal rights, promises, and exemptions meant to protect the monastery from other powers, generally regional noble dynasties, who might make claims upon their lands. In Germany, these are usually called imperial foundations (*Reichsstifte*).

The same monasteries can also be named after the rule, the *regula*, the written regulations that stipulated life within the community, which in turn usually pointed to regional and trans-regional relationships with other monasteries of the same rule. The oldest foundations in Germany, reflecting the preferences of the Carolingians long ago, adhered to the Benedictine rule. Many others were organized by the various reform movements of the eleventh and twelfth centuries, the most important in Central Europe being the Premonstratensians, the Cistercians, and the Carthusians (one of the most successful monastic movements of late medieval Germany).[49] Still others were organized locally around the Augustinian Rule, so called because it derives from a letter of Augustine.[50] Some took the form of collegiate foundations (*Kollegiatstifte*) or collegiate churches, named after their corporate structure, although many collegiate churches were not "regular" (as in *regula*, a monastic rule). The colleges consisted of canons or canonesses, and in the latter case, their houses are sometimes called canoness foundations (*Kanonissenstifte*). The male collegiate foundations often played an important role in diocesan administration, having close relations with the cathedral and the college of men, the cathedral canons, who comprised a body known as the cathedral chapter, a diocesan managerial elite.

Over the centuries monasteries sometimes accumulated vast properties. In addition to lands, their wealth was stockpiled and impressively displayed in liturgical objects and reliquaries made of precious metals and gemstones. Rulers of monasteries (abbots, abbesses, priors, or prioresses) had temporal responsibilities, lordship. Temporal power was matched by quasi-episcopal ones. Monasteries had often established churches on their lands, held rights to tithes, and enjoyed rights and responsibilities as patrons, namely the right to nominate priests to serve parishes and altars (priests were technically appointed by the bishop, but monasteries were famously independent) and the responsibility to provide for those pastoral incomes. Having these claims, monasteries traded them, just as other ecclesiastical and lay people did, in the process acquiring control of new churches, which were "incorporated" to the monastery. A monastery might have rights to present candidates to serve altars or churches on their farmlands, but also in churches in villages and towns under other lordships.

Church corporations—in particular, cathedral chapters, collegiate churches, and monasteries—were enmeshed in social networks, which

---

[49] For Carthusian expansion, see Manfred Oldenburg, *Die Trierer Kartause St. Alban von der Gründung (1330/31) bis zur Mitte des 15. Jahrhunderts* (Salzburg: Institut für Anglistik und Amerikanistik, 1995), pp. 2–38; Heinrich Rüthing, "Die Ausbreitung der Kartäuser bis 1500," *Atlas zur Kirchengeschichte*, edited by Hubert Jedin, Kenneth Scott Latourette, and J. Martin, 2nd edition (Freiburg: Herder, 1986), pp. 38, 51.

[50] For its compostion and history, George Lawless, *Augustine of Hippo and His Monastic Rule* (New York: Oxford University Press, 1987).

in turn conditioned the vulnerability or resistance to reform of each. These networks varied in membership, arrangement, and relationship to one another. Gerhard Fouquet has demonstrated the entanglement of church corporation and aristocracy in a thorough study of the personnel of the cathedral chapter of Speyer, where bonds of kinship, regional origin, friendship, and patronage all shaped the chapter's social connectivity.[51] Olivier Auge demonstrated the same on the example of Württemberg's collegiate churches.[52] Although the relations of church corporations to social networks have only begun to be studied, it is obvious that they existed and affected every clerical corporation. The networks were formed around distinct kinds of people. Patron-client relationships, for example, might include foreign ecclesiastical powers, like the pope, or a regional power who might fill canonries with children from families close to his court, as dukes of Württemberg did with the collegiate Church of the Holy Spirit in Stuttgart.[53] Bonds of friendship might exist between families within one stratum of the nobility, or between the lower nobility and urban aristocracies, or between ecclesiastical persons and corporations, as was the case between cathedral chapters in the German northwest.[54] Given the current state of scholarship, few generalizations can be made about these relationships and their role in church and society. One permissible conclusion is this. There was, apparently, a chronologically broad trend in the changing social backgrounds of chapters. Over the course of the sixteenth and seventeenth centuries, membership in many cathedral chapters became exclusively noble, increasing the distance between the chapters and the ruling families of the cities in which they lived, for example at Speyer, Münster, Paderborn, Osnabrück, and Magdeburg—a small but geographically dispersed number.[55] This trend, however, was of

---

[51] Gerhard Fouquet, *Das Speyerer Domkapitel im späten Mittelalter (ca. 1350–1540). Adlige Freundschaft, fürstliche Patronage und päpstliche Klientel*, 2 vols. (Mainz: Gesellschaft für Mittelrheinische Kirchengeschichte, 1987), pp. 203–302.

[52] Olivier Auge, *Stiftsbiographien. Die Kleriker des Stuttgarter Heilig-Kreuz-Stifts (1250–1552)* (Leinfelder-Echterdingen: Weinbrenner, 2002), pp. 128–141.

[53] Auge, *Stiftsbiographien*, p. 136.

[54] Christian Hoffmann, *Ritterschaftlicher Adel im geistlichen Fürstentum. Die Familie von Bar und das Hochstift Osnabrück: Landständewesen, Kirche und Fürstenhof als Komponenten der adeligen Lebenswelt im Zeitalter der Reformation und Konfessionalisierung 1500–1651* (Osnabrück: Verein für Geschichte und Landeskunde von Osnabrück, 1996), pp. 100–5.

[55] Peter Hersche, "Adel gegen Bürgertum? Zur Frage der Refeudalisierung der Reichskirche," *Weihbischöfe und Stifte. Beiträge zu reichskirchlichen Funktionsträgern der Frühe*

no particular significance to the early evangelical movements. Before 1547, most cathedral chapters, it seems, continued to receive a full third or half of their membership from burghers.[56] Collegiate churches and monasteries appear to have continued to draw members more variably, although in at least some cases, presumably many, nobles vied for control of high offices.[57] Some collegiate churches were predominantly noble, some included people of lower nobility and knights, others included people born to the ruling families of cities, and others drew from peasants and knights.[58] In other words, in the early sixteenth century, the social networks tied to foundations involved more diverse social strata than later in the century. In some instances, the specific bonds of a convent to a social rank left a monastery virtually unassailable. The best known examples are the women's monasteries that chose to resist evangelical reforms, which were overwhelmingly aristocratic. But in other instances, the specific bonds of a convent to social rank left a monastery vulnerable. Such appears to have been the case for monasteries of Franconia, which lacked noble protectors, and lacking protection, they suffered heavy property losses in the Peasants' War.[59] The church was an autonomous society only in the ideal world of canon law. In the early sixteenth century, its social entanglements were in fact spread across the panoply of social classes.

At one time, cathedral chapters in Europe found themselves in frequent conflict with bishops, especially during an episcopal succession. Bishops were dropped down on these regional, aristocratic communities from the stratosphere of high imperial, royal, and papal

---

Neuzeit, ed. Friedhelm Jürgensmeier (Frankfurt: J. Knecht, 1995), pp. 195–208, here 200–8. R. Po-Chia Hsia, *Society and Religion in Münster, 1535–1618* (New Haven: Yale, 1984), pp. 32–42. Gottfried Wentz, Berent Schwineköper, *Domstift St. Moritz zu Magdeburg* (Berlin: Walter De Gruyter, 1972), p. 116.

[56] Hersche, "Adel gegen Bürgertum," pp. 200–8.

[57] For example in Osnabrück and Württemberg. Hoffmann, *Ritterschaftlicher Adel*, p. 94. Auge, *Stiftsbiographien*, pp. 132–3.

[58] Auge, *Stiftsbiographien*, pp. 132–141. Hoffmann, *Ritterschaftlicher Adel*, pp. 93–9. Hermann Ehmer, "Ende und Verwandlung: Südwestdeutsche Stiftskirchen in der Reformation," *Die Stiftskirche in Südwestdeutschland*, ed. Sönke Lorenz, Olivier Auge (Leinfelden-Echterdingen: Weinbrenner, 2003), pp. 224–6, pp. 211–237. Henze, "Orden und ihre Klöster," p. 96, and *Die Territorien des Reichs*, 4:191–2. Hsia, *Society and Religion*, pp. 32–44. Brady, *Ruling Class, Regime and Reformation*, pp. 222–3.

[59] Henze, "Orden und ihre Klöster," p. 97 with n. 41 and its references for further examples for women's houses, p. 96 for Franconia. Ziegler, "Reformation und Klosterauflössung," pp. 608–9.

politics.[60] In the thirteenth, fourteenth, and fifteenth centuries, the papacy increased its ability to make appointments to church offices throughout Europe—all kinds of offices, from the benefices of parish rectors to archbishop-imperial electors.[61] At the same time, kings and magnates became very good at manipulating appointments to high church office to their own advantages, especially in countries that were more effectively developing centralized kingship in the late Middle Ages, in particular, Spain, France, and England. But in Germany there was no true king, which left the most ambitious and powerful noble dynasties to vie for these valuable offices among themselves. As a result of the absence of monarchy, the bishops of Germany were the most independent of Europe, and as a result of that, the leading noble dynasties in Germany competed hard for their control.

One type of monastery was intended to be distinct from the monastic and clerical communities so far considered, to what extent was a matter of debate in late medieval Europe (the poverty debate was largely a debate over the uniqueness of their charism). Cloisters of the mendicant or begging orders (principally four, the Franciscans, the Dominicans, the Augustinian Hermits, and the Carmelites) were relatively poor, compared to all other monasteries, but hardly without possessions. They, too, had enjoyed powerful benefactors—including kings and magnates, as well as lesser nobility—alongside a wide economic range of donors in the cities in which their cloisters were concentrated. Their accumulation of houses in cities, their enjoyment of tax exemptions, and their competition with parish clergy had irritated urban communes and many clergy ruled by bishops since soon

---

[60] Lawrence G. Duggan, *Bishop and Chapter. The Governance of the Bishopric of Speyer to 1552* (New Brunswick: Rutgers, 1978); Gottfried Wentz and Bernkt Schwineköper, *Das Erzbistum Magdeburg*, (Berlin: Walter de Gruyter, 1972), 1:90–92. Wilhelm Kohn, *Das Domstift St. Paulus zu Münster*, (Berlin: Walter de Gruyter, 1987), 1:148. Sieglerschmidt, *Territorialstaat*, p. 18 n. 26, for the older literature on cathedral chapters.

[61] Many of these were awards of expectative benefices, that is the assignment of a benefice to an individual when it should become vacant, a contestable and ineffective method of appointment that nevertheless kept the papal court involved in many church transactions in northern Europe. See Brigide Schwarz. "Klerikerkarrieren und Pfründenmarkt im Spätmittelalter," *Quellen und Forschungen aus italienischen Archiven und Bibliotheken* 71(1991):243–65; Andreas Meyer, "Der deutsche Pfründenmarkt im Spätmittelalter," *Quellen und Forschungen aus italienischen Archiven und Bibliotheken* 71(1991):266–79.

after the friars arrived in Germany in the early thirteenth century.
That irritation was still amply reflected in the pamphlets of the early
sixteenth century, when the evangelical movement came to towns.
The pamphlets mock friars for lewd behavior, a phony practice of
poverty, divisiveness, heresy, and more.[62] When city councils decided
to support evangelical preachers, they soon found themselves taking
over mendicant cloisters, often because their membership had been
depleted by evangelical preaching and loss of incomes (the friars'
welfare was uniquely dependent on charitable gifts). Their churches
were unencumbered by patronage rights. Once the princes put their
sights on the properties of the church, the significance of this bogey-
man, as evidence of monastic corruption, had to decrease. An inventory could quickly show that mendicant incomes hardly exceeded
the cloister's expenses, while old foundations, like those of Benedictines
and Cistercians, enjoyed broad, seductive profits, as Duke Heinrich
of Saxony discovered in the twenty-nine cloisters of his realm soon
after coming to power in 1539.[63] His realm offers a vivid example.
The Cistercians of Altzella, among the richest monasteries of his
land, possessed 12 farmsteads, monetary rents from villages and individuals in 109 locales worth a little over 50,100 fl., leases in 6 locales
worth 4,170.5 fl., and payment in kind of grain, hay, wine, eggs,
and cattle from all the aforementioned places. The monastery also
held patronage rights in 23 parishes. By contrast, the Franciscans of
Dresden held a single satellite house in the town of Dippoldiswalde
and received rents worth between 2500 and 3000 fl. The Dominicans
of Freiberg were better off, but hardly rich. They held one or two
pastures, field(s) producing 18 bushels of grain, a number of mining
shares, 22 cows, monetary rents from 5 cities and 4 private individuals and other properties worth a little over 325 fl., and payments in kind of butter and herring.

Walter Ziegler has estimated the number of monasteries about the
year 1500 within the territory that is today Germany: 160 Benedictine
houses, 120 Premonstratensian, 80 Cistercian; 125 Franciscan con-

---

[62] Consider Ocker, "'Rechte Arme' und 'Bettler Orden,'" and Geoffrey Dipple,
Antifraternalism and Anticlericalism in the German Reformation (Aldershot: Scolar Press,
1996).
[63] Helga-Maria Kühn, *Die Einziehung des geistlichen Gutes im Albertinischen Sachsen,
1539–1553* (Cologne: Böhlau, 1966), pp. 114–115, 119–20, 123.

vents, 70 Domincan, 50 Carmelite, 60 Augustinian; 30 Carthusian (56 in the Empire as a whole), and 85 commends of the Teutonic Knights and the Hospitallers of St. John.[64] In addition, in the broader region of the entire Holy Roman Empire, there were some 500 collegiate churches in the year 1520.[65] There is no reliable estimate of the entire portion of Central European property in ecclesiastical hands before the religious controversy began, much less when the controversy formally ended at the Peace of Augsburg (1555). The sheer variableness of German territories and confiscations within them prevents a useful preliminary estimate. Our knowledge of the closures of monasteries, even disregarding the more complicated fate of their properties, is also limited. But a few religious orders and collegiate churches allow an overview of closures, and they suggest the extent of ecclesiastical disruption during the religious controversy. Let us consider some examples.

The easiest assessment may be made of Martin Luther's own Order of Augustinian Hermits. It yields a picture of severe crisis, but not devastation. Ninety-six of the 160 cloisters of the German provinces (which included regions east, south, and west of Germany today) were closed during the religious controversy.[66] The province that covered Luther's area of immediate influence, Saxony and Thuringia, together with the Reformed Congregation led by Luther's close friends Johannes Stauptiz and Wenzeslaus Linck, were the most strongly affected (both entities ceased to exist in the Reformation, their surviving convents incorporated into other provinces). They lost thirty-five cloisters from 1523 to 1538, largely as a result of the controversy,[67] then another nine after the conversion of Albertine Saxony

---

[64] Ziegler, "Reformation und Klosterauflösung," p. 587.

[65] I have counted these in the register by Alfred Wendehorst, Stefan Benz, *Verzeichnis der Säkularkanonikerstifte der Reichskirche* (Neudstadt an der Aisch: Degener, 1997), which lists foundations by locale in alphabetical order. The register does not include Augustinian canons, which to my knowledge have never been counted.

[66] Adalbero Kunzelmann, *Geschichte der deutschen Augustinereremiten*, 7 vols, (Würzburg: Augustinus-Institut, 1969–1979), 5:516–8. See also ibid., 6:1–8 and 7:113–162.

[67] 8 from 1523 to 1524 (in no particular order): Gewitsch, Zürich, Antwerp, Eisleben, Sternberg, Rössel, Quedlinburg, Patollen. 11 in 1525 alone: Wittenberg, Erfurt (but restored within months, only to die out in 1560), Königsberg i/Fr., Himmelpforten, Windesheim, Magdeburg, Neustadt a/O, Herzberg, Gotha, Zerbst, Nürnberg. 15 from 1526 to 1538, the period from the end of the Peasants' War to the second expansion of the League of Schmalkalden: Helmstedt, Alsfeld, Eschwege, Gartz a/O, Anklam, Kulmbach, Grimma, Constance, Tübingen, Neustettin, Stargard, Königsberg i/N (2), Wilster, Friedeberg.

and Brandenburg.[68] The Bavarian province lost eighteen cloisters, six before 1538 and another six up to 1548.[69] The vast majority of Augustinian Hermit houses closed when incomes had fallen below sustainable levels or their membership dwindled as a result of the impact of evangelical doctrine, which even affected cloisters that managed to keep their doors open. Luther's Order surely reflects an extreme example: his influence on monks was most strongly felt there. But the same occurred on a smaller scale among the Carmelites.[70]

The religious controversy reversed the fortunes of the Carthusian Order. The Order experienced its greatest growth in Central Europe during the two hundred years before Luther. Of the fifty-six Carthusian monasteries established in the Holy Roman Empire before 1500, thirty-two were founded or incorporated in the fourteenth century and eighteen in the fifteenth. Fifteen of these cloisters closed as a result of sequestration or similar actions by evangelical authorities between the beginning of the religious controversy and 1555.[71] One to five years of inventory, confiscation of documents, reassignment

---

[68] From the second expansion of the League of Schmalkalden after 1537 through its defeat in 1547 and to the Leipzig Interim in 1548: Einbeck, Sangerhausen, Waldheim, Langensalza, Dresden, Schmalkalden, Herford, Osnabrück, Lippstadt, Appingedam.

[69] Nürnberg 1525, Windsheim 1525, Mindelheim 1526, Klosterneuburg 1529, Memmingen 1531/8, Marchegg 1537, Radkersburg 1542, Kornenburg 1545, Baden bei Wien 1545, Judenburg 1545, Bruck an der Leithe 1546, Kulmbach 1547, Ramsau 1549, Hohenmauthen 1549, Völkermarkt 1550, Laibach 1555, Schönthal 1559, Rattenberg 1560, not including the cloisters of Silesia, which were all lost as a result of Prussian secularization. Ibid., 3:51–63.

[70] Of the 24 cloisters of the Carmelite province of Upper Germany, which extended from southwest Hungary through Austria, Bavaria, and Franconia into Swabia, 8 were closed as a result of the evangelical movement (Nürnberg 1525, Neustadt/Kulm 1527, Esslingen 1531–6, Augsburg 1534, Heilbronn 1535, Sparneck 1537, Rothenburg am Neckar 1538, Nördlingen 1538). An additional cloister died of attrition with no apparent connection to evangelical preaching (Gösing, 1548), another was relocated to Vienna due to the Turkish occupation of parts of Hungary (Fünfkirchen), and another was destroyed in the Turkish occupation (Priwitz). Adalbert Deckert, Matthäus Hösler, *Acta des Karmelitenprovinzials Andreas Stoss (1534–1538)* (Rome: Edizioni Carmelitane, 1995), pp. 46–112.

[71] The following information is compiled from *Monasticon Cartusiense*, vol. 2, edited by Gerhard Schlegel, James Hogg (Salzburg: Institut für Anglistik und Amerikanistik, 2004), passim. Nürnberg 1525, Mariefred 1526 (by the King of Sweden), Eppenberg 1527, Bern 1528, Eisenach 1529, Konradsburg 1530, Crimmitschau 1531, Güterstein 1535, Frankfurt/Oder 1540, Letanovce 1543, Legnica 1548, Darłowo 1548, Szczecin (Stettin) 1551, Lövöld 1552, Świdwin (Schivelbein) 1552.

of properties, and/or pensioning of monks preceded most closures.[72] Six additional Carthusian monasteries closed between 1556 and 1600.[73] One closed in the seventeenth century.[74] But thirty-six Carthusian monasteries were secularized between 1772 and 1848, the majority in 1802–1803.[75] One had been destroyed by the Hussites in the fifteenth century.[76]

Collegiate foundations depict similar losses. Of the 500 collegiate foundations of the Holy Roman Empire, seventy-nine were closed or converted to Protestantism by 1548; an additional two were closed by Catholic authorities (their personnel and/or property combined to another foundation or incorporated to a religious order).[77] At least six foundations were obliged to divide canonries between both confessions or to share the church.[78] Only fourteen collegiate foundations converted or were closed between 1549 and 1565, just before the inconoclastic "wonder-year" in the Habsburg Netherlands. Between 1565 and 1600, another fifty-six converted or were closed, many in connection with the Dutch Revolt. By contrast, of those 500 foundations of 1520, 253 would meet their end in the French Revolution or the Napoleonic invasion (counting the years 1789–1811). But only five had fallen to the Hussites a century before Luther's rebellion

---

[72] See *Monasticon Cartusiense* v. 2, s.v. Nürnberg, Eppenberg, Eisenach, Konradsburg, Crimmitschau, Güterstein, Frankfurt/Oder (but it took 8 years at Legnica and 13 years at Szczecin and Świdwin).

[73] Rostock 1557, Basel 1564, Ahrensbök 1564, Wesel 1590, Strasbourg 1591, Pleterje 1595.

[74] Christgarten (Nördlingen) 1648.

[75] Kartuzy (Danzig) 1772, Hildesheim 1777, Jurklošter (Gairach) 1780, Mainz 1781, Žiče (Seitz) 1782, Bistra (Freudenthal) 1782, Lechnic (Lechnitz) 1782, Mauerbach 1782, Gaming 1782, Brno 1782, Aggsbach 1782, Olomouc (Olmütz)-Dolany 1782, Schnals 1782, Freiburg/Briesgau 1782, Valdice 1782, Roermond 1783, Molsheim 1791, Rettel 1792, Koblenz 1802, Trier 1802, Köln 1802, Vogelsang 1802, Xanten 1802, Grünau 1803, Würzburg 1803, Tückelhausen 1803, Erfurt 1803, Buxheim 1803, Astheim 1803, Ilmbach 1803, Prüll (Regensburg) 1803, Weddern 1804, Gidle 1819, Bereza 1831, Ittingen 1848.

[76] Prague in 1419. But another four Carthusian monasteries were plundered in the Hussite wars: Frankfurt/Oder 1432, Letanovce 1433, Brno 1428, Olomouc 1425 and 1437. In other wars, Kartuzy (Danzig) was plundered during the conflict between the Teutonic Order and the *Pommerellenstädtebund* in 1455, in 1458 by Polish troops, and in 1466 by the Teutonic Order. Mauerbach 1462 was plundered by the Austrian duke and in the 1480s by the Hungarians, then in 1529 by the Turks, in 1619 by the Bohemians, and in 1683 by the Turks again.

[77] Wendehorst, Benz, *Verzeichnis*, passim.

[78] Wendehorst, Benz, *Verzeichnis*, s.v. Bielefeld, Herford, Minden, Möckmühl, Soest, Wetzlar.

against the pope.[79] In short, taken as a whole, the closures of collegiate churches in the sixteenth century were considerable, but not
quite cataclysmic. The Augustinian Hermits and Carthusians give
the same impression.

This, however, could hardly diminish a pervasive sense of monastic and ecclesiastical crisis. Consider the despair of the Saxon
Franciscan, Fortunatus Huber, over his order's fate in Germany:[80]

> Here hot tears should flow from the pen. O how miserably the most
> beautiful cloisters and divine houses have been put down! . . . Oh, their
> fickle monks, how quickly have they learned perjury from Peter [the
> apostle who betrayed Christ three times] and have committed it. There,
> my angelic father Francis, look around, how is it for your order in
> Germany, where your preciously built cloisters have perished? How
> scornfully and miserably your unarmed friars are hunted down, starved
> out, imprisoned, tortured, or killed!

Antonius Bomhouwer, Franciscan lector in remotest Riga, noted in
the mid-1520's that the heresy began with an apostate monk and
was spread by apostate monks to devastating effect, "in fact, in
Saxony many monasteries stand empty" (*atque in Saxonia plura monas-
teria sunt vacua*).[81] The Chronicler of the Doesburg house of the
Brethren of the Common Life complained that the spread of Luther's
teachings led to the destruction of many religious communities in
the 1520's.[82] Such claims were diffuse and could exaggerate the role

---

[79] Ibid., s.v. Grossenhain/Ozzek, Karlstein/Karlštein, Lipnitz/Lipnice, Melnik/
Mělník, Moldauthein/Týn nad Vltavou.

[80] Quoted in Franz Wilhelm Woker, *Geschichte der Norddeutschen Franziskaner-Missionen
der sächsischen Ordens-Provinz vom heiligen Kreuz. Ein Beitrag zur Kirchengeschichte Norddeutschlands
nach der Reformation* (Freiburg im Breisgau: Herder, 1880), p. 28: "Hie sollte die
Feder von haissen Thränen flüessen. O wie armselig liegen zu Boden die schön-
sten Klöster und Gotteshäuser! . . . O ihr wankelmüthige Ordensleut, wie bald habt
ihr von Petro die Meineidigkeit gelernt und geübt. Da, mein Seraphischer Vatter
Franziskus, siehe umb, wie es steht umb deinen Orden in Teutschland, wo deine
so theuer erhebte Klöster seynd hingekommen? Wie verrächtlich und armselig deine
unbewaffnete Ordensbrüder seynd verjagt, ausgehungert, verkerkeret, verpeiniget
oder ermordet worden!"

[81] *Informacio, quo pacto commodius resistendum Lutheranae heresij*, edited in *Urkundenbuch
der alten sächsischen Franziskanerprovinzen*, 2 vols., edited by Leonhard Lemmens (Düsseldorf:
L. Schwann, 1913), 1:64–6 nr. 287.

[82] Ulrich Hinz, *Die Brüder vom Gemeinsamen Leben im Jahrhundert der Reformation. Das
Münstersche Kolloquium* (Tübingen: J.C.B. Mohr, 1997), pp. 42–4, and 45–69 for the
actual extent of the spread of Lutheran ideas among the Brethren of the Münster
Colloquy. Hinz has pointed out that estimates of the Brethren's conversion to the
new faith, like their alleged contribution to the spread of the evangelical movement,

of evangelical preaching in monastic decline, as the Brethren's troubles
in the next decades suggest. The Münster Colloquy of the Brethren
comprised ten houses in the north of Germany. The houses at
Marburg and Kassel were closed with the vast majority of Hessian
monasteries in 1527. But it took ten to twenty years of external evangelical pressure to close the houses at Magdeburg and Merseburg.[83]
The Brethren's houses at Hildesheim, Herford, and Wesel survived
to the end of the century, Wesel as an evangelical community and
a continuing member of the Münster Colloquy.[84] Likewise, houses
in Catholic territories, such as Münster after the fall of the Anabaptist
regime, Cologne, and Hildesheim, suffered attrition, loss of gifts, and
a sharp decline in the number of brothers.[85] Only one house enjoyed
economic growth after the failure of evangelical reform—Cologne,
in the third quarter of the century. Herford stagnated. The danger
to the Brethren proved to be a pervasive malaise that followed the
religious controversy. It was the malaise of a broader monastic crisis. The fact of the religious controversy seems to have undermined
the attraction of monasteries as objects of devotion, their ability to
recruit, and the public's sense of monastic legitimacy.

In addition to monasteries and collegiate foundations, there were
the temporal domains of bishops—in Germany, prince-bishops. They
experienced no disruption of their office comparable to monastic tur-
moil. Prince-bishops had lands, vassals, the ability to raise and deploy
an army, impose taxes, judge conflicts, and so forth, while they also
claimed spiritual authority as the foremost pastors of dioceses. They
held their temporal possessions as imperial fiefs. Although temporal
power was technically distinct from pastoral authority (pastoral functions were carried out by auxiliary bishops, who managed the diocese with archdeacons, cathedral chapters, other canons, and various

---

have been exaggerated. Consider ibid., pp. 49, 78–80. He describes their position,
as a semi-religious community, as standing between Lutherans and Catholics and
vulnerable to both, ibid. pp. 286–7. Although the Brethren of the Common Life
originated as a lay movement, they had become increasingly monastic over the previous century. Theo Klausmann, *Consuetudo Consuetudine Vincitur. Die Hausordnungen der
Brüder vom gemeinsamen Leben im Bildungs- und Sozialisationsprogramm der Devotio moderna.*
(Bern: Peter Lang Publishing, 2003), passim.

[83] Hinz, *Die Brüder vom Gemeinsamen Leben*, pp. 70–4. Magdeburg closed 1541,
Merseburg 1537.

[84] Hinz, *Die Brüder vom Gemeinsamen Leben*, pp. 40–80, 247–255.

[85] For this and the following, Hinz, *Die Brüder vom Gemeinsamen Leben*, pp. 188–201,
220–236, 243–4, and passim.

officers), the highest ruler of the cathedral could be disentangled neither from his sacramental power nor from his temporal concerns.[86]
Their grip on the urban communes that grew around their cathedrals had weakened long before the Reformation, but they remained
powerful members of the imperial community. The most successful
prince-bishop of the early sixteenth-century was probably Albrecht
of Brandenburg.[87] His brother, Elector Joachim of Brandenburg, engineered his election as archbishop of Magdeburg in 1513. Their intent
was to extend the Brandenburg dynasty's influence, following a policy begun by their father, Elector Johann Cicero. Albrecht was
appointed administrator of the prince-bishopric of Halberstadt that
same year, and one year later he was elected archbishop of Mainz,
through intricate negotiations with the papacy. Already one of the
most powerful princes of Germany and the foremost ecclesiastical
prince, he was made a cardinal in 1518. Albrecht was a master of
political affairs and adapted quickly to their changing demands. He
played a crucial role in the election of Charles V as Holy Roman
Emperor in 1519, yet he indulged the princes and cities that refused
to implement the imperial edict against Luther until the late 1530's,
when the Habsburgs became newly inclined toward reconciliation
with Protestants.

To confiscate the properties of prince-bishops was alluring and
unrealistic. It would ultimately have meant the overthrow of the
dominion of a significant piece of the Holy Roman Empire's ecclesiastical estates (the Empire's ecclesiastical estates consisted of the
electoral archbishops of Mainz, Cologne, and Trier, other archbishops and bishops, abbots, other prelates, and the Grand Masters of
the Teutonic Knights and the Hospitallers of St. John). That was a
far greater ambition than early Protestants had, at least at first, and
apart from the special case of Prussia, the first efforts aimed at monastic properties.[88] Scattered were the claims of bishops to spiritual and

---

[86] Leo Santifaller, *Zur Geschichte des ottonisch-salischen Reichskirchensystems* (Vienna:
Hermann Böhlaus Nachfolger, 1964), pp. 46–7.

[87] *Die Bischöfe des Heiligen Römischen Reiches, 1448 bis 1648. Ein biographisches Lexikon*,
ed. Erwin Gatz (Berlin: Duncker und Humboldt, 1996), pp. 13–16. Georg May,
Die deutschen Bischöfe angesichts der Glaubensspaltung des 16. Jahrhunderts (Vienna: Vediatrix,
1983), pp. 232–9.

[88] For Prussia, pp. 69f. For Protestant designs on the sees of Naumburg, Merseburg,
and Münster in the 1540's, pp. 70–1. Such designs increased in the second half of
the sixteenth century, but largely by the gradual replacement of episcopal consti-

temporal holdings, churches and altars on the one hand and farms and peasants on the other (episcopal treasuries, including reliquary collections, were often under direct control of cathedral chapters), a dispersion of interests like that of all German rulers of every kind and status. Bishops claimed to possess comprehensive authority in the administration of the churches of their dioceses, often regionally concentrated, but not exclusively so. That authority was most direct in the case of parish churches, but in every other case, for example the churches incorporated by monasteries or those established by the patronage of a city or village council, the bishop claimed a right to approve appointments and an exclusive authority to control the sacraments, the priests of his diocese acting as his sacramental surrogates. Much could be said about a bishop's ability to exercise such power, or the lack thereof. For my purpose, it is important to realize that prince-bishops, even if their temporal domains were not immediately threatened, could take any change in any church of the diocese as an infringement on their spiritual dominion. It may therefore seem remarkable that bishops were relatively complacent toward the religious controversy in the first decades of the Protestant movement.[89]

---

tution with a consistorial one, for example in Samland and Pomesanien, or when the bishops in evangelical territories died out, their properties were added to princely domains, for example the bishoprics of Brandenburg, Havelberg, and Lebus (to Brandenburg); Merseburg, Naumburg, and Meißen (Saxony); Camin (Pomerania); and Schwerin (Mecklenburg). From 1571 in Brandenburg and 1598 in Havelberg and Lebus, the administration of the bishopric was claimed by the territorial lord. Haug-Moritz, *Der Schmalkaldische Bund*, pp. 520–21. Wolgast, *Hochstift*, passim. Heckel, "Das Problem der 'Säkularisation,'", p. 33. *Realencyklopädie für protestantische Theologie und Kirche*, 24 volumes (Leipzig, J.C. Hinrichs, 1896–1913), s.v. Säkularisation, 21:838–858, here 844. See also Thomas A. Brady, "Luther und die Beseitigung der Reichskirche—ein versäumter Weg?," *Luther zwischen den Kulturen*, edited by Hans Medick, Peer Schmidt (Göttingen: Vandenhoeck und Ruprecht, 2004), pp. 89–101, and Karlheinz Blaschke, "The Reformation and the Rise of the Territorial State," *Luther and the Modern State in Germany*, p. 63.

[89] Wolgast, *Hochstift und Reformation*, pp. 190–94. Albrecht Pius Luttenberger, *Glaubenseinheit und Reichsfriede. Konzeptionen und Wege konfessionsneutraler Reichspolitik 1530–1552 (Kurpfalz, Jülich, Kurbrandenburg)* (Göttingen: Vandenhoeck und Ruprecht, 1982), p. 140, for the large number of ecclesiastical estates who avoided the religious controversy, other bishops who both avoided confessional confrontation and promoted reconciliation (Moritz of Eichstätt, Johann of Weeze bishop of Constance, Wolfgang of Passau, and Archbishop Johann III of Trier), and still other prelates who promoted Catholic reform (Abbot Philip of Fulda, Bishop Erasmus of Strasbourg, the Archbishop Herman of Wied, Bishop Johann of Meißen, Bishop Franz of Münster, Minden, and Osnabrück).

Their complacency reflects, perhaps, their preoccupation with temporal domains.

Their political autonomy was locally challenged by urban communes, who, once the bishop's court was safely settled outside rebellious towns, came in frequent conflict with the cathedral canons who were left behind.[90] The competition was most keenly felt in towns where prince-bishops claimed lordship over the city, a lordship that many cities had tried to ignore or deny (for example, Würzburg, Erfurt, Worms, and Magdeburg). Protestantism did not merely provide many cities with a rationale for independence. It also invited a bishop's litigation or intervention by force of arms, both of which reactions had often undermined urban independence in the past. An urban rebellion threatened the hegemony of the local ruling class from within and a loss of ruling independence from without.

So, to cite one example that involved Archbishop Albrecht of Brandenburg, at Magdeburg, mid-August 1524, after a year of growing tension inspired by increasingly radical evangelical preaching, a mob ransacked several churches of the old city (Magdeburg, like many German cities, was divided into two communes ruled by separate councils).[91] The burgomaster had brought in Luther two months before to preach against the radicals, led by a certain Wolfgang Cyclops. By July, evangelicals were preaching from pulpits in all of the old city's churches, alongside Catholic clergy, thanks to the old city council's adherence to the tamer Lutheran reforms. To little effect. The riots came, and after the riots, the council promised to protect the Catholic clergy and their properties, looked for defensive alliances against the archbishop with other princes and cities, and tried to negotiate with the archbishop. Nothing worked. The

---

[90] For Constance and Augsburg, consider J. Jeffery Tyler, *Lord of the Sacred City: The Episcopus Exclusus in Late Medieval and Early Modern Germany* (Leiden: E.J. Brill, 1999), pp. 170–201 and passim.

[91] *Die Chroniken der niedersächsischen Städte: Magdeburg*, v. 2 (= *Die Chroniken der deutschen Städte vom 14. bis ins 16. Jahrhundert*, v. 27) (Göttingen: Vandenhoeck und Ruprecht, 1899, reprinted 1962), pp. 200–203. Helmut Asmus, et al. *Geschichte der Stadt Magdeburg*, 2nd ed. (Berlin: Akademie-Verlag, 1977), pp. 71–81. Friedrich Hülße, "Die Einführung der Reformation in der Stadt Magdeburg," *Geschichtsblätter für Stadt und Land Magdeburg* 18(1883):209–369. For the Magdeburg *Bildersturm* and the criminalization of iconoclasm in northern cities, Schnitzler, *Ikonoklasmus-Bildersturm*, pp. 194–211, 306. For longterm consequences, Manfred Sitzmann, *Mönchtum und Reformation. Zur Geschichte monastischer Institutionen in protestantischen Territorien (Brandenburg-Ansbach/Kulmbach, Magdeburg)*, (Neustadt a.d. Aisch: Degener, 1999), and Gottfried Wentz, Schwineköper, *Das Erzbistum Magdeburg*, 1/1:96–99, 749, 753–6.

city must have expected Archibishop Albrecht of Brandenburg's suit against them before the Imperial Chamber Court, in September of that year (it was the first time the court heard a case related to the new church controversy).[92] The citizenry responded by demanding that clergy of the old faith be thrown out of town, at the urban assembly when the court's decision was announced. The council, however, payed the 10,000 fl. fine.

Many urban aristocracies were reluctant to endorse Lutheran preaching in their towns (examples appear in chapters 2 and 4, below). It helped that Luther seemed much less fanatical than some, like Andreas Bodenstein von Karlstadt, who helped inspire and justify iconoclasm at Wittenberg in 1521–2, and Wolfgang Cyclops, who inspired the 1524 riots in Magdeburg, and Thomas Müntzer, who in 1525 led revolting peasants in Thuringia and was executed after the brutal suppression of the Thuringian revolt at Frankenhausen. Yet like all ruling authorites, city councils seized opportunities to expand their control over their sphere, including religious life, with a close eye to increasing government incomes. Cities therefore had to negotiate a difficult course between two poles, avoiding confrontation with prince-bishops and increasing their social control. Magdeburg's council managed to maintain peace with its archbishop for another two decades. In Würzburg, Bamberg, Mainz, Salzburg, Trier, Freising, and Passau, bishops ended evangelical movements.[93] In Hildesheim, the city council halted the spread of evanglicalism, while at the same time commandeering properties of the Brethren of the Common Life to improve city battlements and a water conduit.[94] (The Brethren's money problems had begun earlier, when after the feud between the city's bishop with Duke Heinrich the Younger of Braunschweig-Wolfenbüttel, 1519–1523, they found themselves subject to the duke's onerous taxes, while the bishop lost part of his domain.)[95] When a church fell into a council's hands, for example, after a riot, it could be difficult to give it back. The city

---

[92] Martin Heckel, "Die Reformationsprozesse im Spannungsfeld des Reichskirchensystems," *Die politische Funktion des Reichskammergerichts* (Cologne: Böhlau, 1993), pp. 9–40, here 11.

[93] Hans-Christoph Rublack, *Gescheiterte Reformation* (Stuttgart: Klett-Cotta, 1978), p. 126 and passim.

[94] Hinz, *Die Brüder vom Gemeinsamen Leben*, p. 50.

[95] Hinz, *Die Brüder vom Gemeinsamen Leben*, pp. 210–1, 223.

could then expect demands for restitution and the imposition of fines. Whether a city could avoid restitution and payments would vary from place to place (chapter 2), and it would depend on the ability of Protestant rulers to interefere with law suits effectively or exercise a military threat. Such a coalition was the League of Schmalkalden (chapter 3).

Any ruler who was at least conventionally religious—and that would be every ruler of sixteenth-century Europe—was also accustomed to business with the church, both temporal (management of lands, trade, taxation, war) and spiritual (endowments of altars and gifts to cloisters, religious renewal, the exercise of charity, the memorial of the dead). Given these entanglements, it is not surprising that clergy and laity would manipulate the terms under which business was conducted, and lay rulers of all kinds, from village elders and urban magistrates to magnates, became good at it. The conventional means of increasing control over the church was to impose excises, to place kin in significant ecclesiastical offices, or in the case of monasteries to endorse a reform group that would replace existing leadership. These could and often had been perfectly orthodox things to do. The Protestant confiscation of ecclesiastical properties involved the endorsement of a reform group, namely evangelical preachers, but it exceeded earlier precedents by replacing *parish* priests, not just monks and/or cloister leaders, by sometimes reorganizing parishes, and by diverting monastic incomes to other public institutions or uses (schools, hospitals, and poor chests). If Protestant governments contributed to the welfare of Christian society, their expenses met a religious necessity and were payable from church properties. But only insofar as a ruler's actions could be conceived as the promotion of religion and protection of the church.

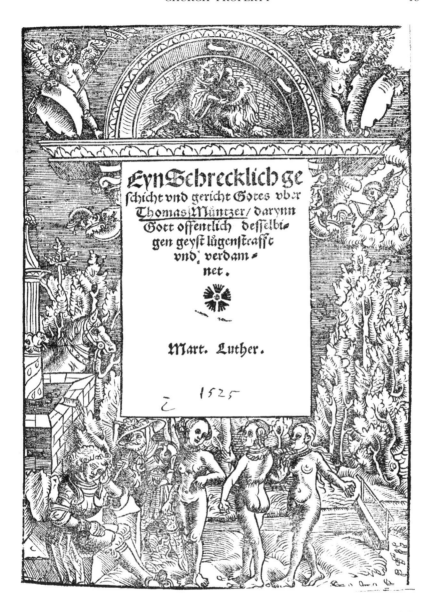

The title page of Martin Luther's *A Terrible History and the Judgement of God on Thomas Müntzer, in which God Clearly Punishes and Condemns the Same* (Wittenberg: Joseph Klug, 1525), depicting the Judgement of Paris in the lower register and Samson rending the Lion in the upper. For a detailed description, see Appendix 2. Image courtesy of the Richard C. Kessler Reformation Collection, Pitts Theology Library, Candler School of Theology, Emory University.

CHAPTER TWO

CHURCH ROBBERS

The evangelical movement began by accident, then coalesced as a bold experiment. Church property made the movement a matter of ruling authority, in the aftermath of the Peasants War of 1524/5. The war provoked experimental thinking, and it created property dilemmas that contributed to the formation of Protestantism. These dilemmas may have affected confessional identity as much as Luther's resistance to papal and imperial condemnation, the popular spread of his ideas, and sympathy and support among urban elites and territorial rulers.

Let us begin at the beginning of the religious controversy. It rapidly progressed from academic obscurity, as a debate among theologians, to public notariety. Luther's ninety-five theses for an academic disputation on indulgences was a professorial reaction to objectionable preaching, which reaction was published in autumn 1517. The theses treated part of a much discussed tangle of theological questions surrounding the sacrament of penance, including the numerical (even monetary) assessment of moral value and compensation, both of which Luther rejected out of hand.[1] Luther's response to the indulgence preached by the Dominican Johannes Tetzel is fabled, in a story first reported after Luther's death, that on the eve of All Saints' Day he hammered his list of ninety-five onto the door of the Wittenberg church. He never did post theses on the door, or if he did, it was not until mid-November, two weeks after the Feast of All Saints, nor does it really matter, as Luther's best biographer has said.[2] The

---

[1] See now Bernhard Felmberg, *Die Ablaßtheologie Kardinal Cajetans 1469–1534* (Leiden: E.J. Brill, 1998), pp. 17–27, and for the subsequent debate, consider pp. 187–345. Determining a penance involved not only assessing moral compensation for sin, but also assessing the moral value of business transactions. For the latter, Odd Langholm, *The Merchant in the Confessional: Trade and Price in the Pre-Reformation Penitential Handbooks* (Leiden: E.J. Brill, 2003), passim. Nikolaus Paulus, *Geschichte des Ablaßes am Ausgange des Mittelalters* (Paderborn: Ferdinand Schöningh, 1923) remains a useful survey.

[2] Martin Brecht, *Martin Luther*, 3 vols. (Minneapolis: Fortress, 1985–93), 1:190–202, esp. 200. The circumstances of the indulgence are described ibid., pp. 178–83.

preaching of this particular indulgence was arranged by Albrecht of Brandenburg—archbishop of Mainz, imperial chancellor, and one of three ecclesiastical electoral princes (alongside the archbishops of Cologne and Trier)—in part to raise funds to help satisfy debts incurred when he was chosen as archbishop four years earlier. Luther's response was academic. A process against him began in the summer of 1518. It culminated in January 1521 with Luther's excommunication.[3] Soon after, the affair erupted into the most enduring schism of western Christendom.

The church was enormously powerful, in economic and judicial, as well as symbolic ways. Its structures of governance and its sources of revenue were the most pervasive in Europe. The papal court probably touched the lives of priests everywhere in the Empire, insofar as the papacy may have become an important factor in all the clergy's competion for incomes in almost every imperial diocese, and priests were known in every European town and nearly all villages.[4] The church's power was famously displayed in the first decade of the century by Pope Julius II (1503–1513), who began the campaign of opulent renovation that promised to reestablish Rome as the capital of Christendom. Tetzel's audience must have been reminded of that distant spiritual lord, for the indulgence he preached was Pope Leo X's (1513–1521) plenary indulgence of 1515, which was intended to raise funds to complete the building program begun by Julius (Tetzel's audience could not have known that only part of the proceeds were destined for Rome; another part went to pay Albrecht's loan from the Fuggers, the famous Augsburg bankers).

Luther won the predictable response. Confronted with a summons to appear at the papal court to answer charges of heresy, he chose within a year of October 1517 to expand his criticisms to an indictment of the papal office altogether. He began to reject papal authority in 1518, when he questioned the papacy's competence to decide his case, and he appealed to a general council.[5] In 1519 his uncertainty

[3] Remigius Bäumer, "Der Lutherprozess," *Lutherprozess und Lutherbann. Vorgeschichte, Ergebnis, Nachwirkung*, edited by Remigius Bäumer (Münster: Aschendorff, 1972), pp. 20–48.
[4] See note 61 in chapter 1, above.
[5] Brecht, *Martin Luther*, 1:239–73, 306–7 for this and the following, and Hans-Jürgen Becker, *Die Appellation vom Papst an ein allgemeines Konzil* (Cologne: Böhlau, 1988), pp. 244–60.

blossomed into a complete rejection of the papacy as such, and he began to call Pope Leo X's *office* the beast of the Apocalypse, the Antichrist who heralded the coming of the final judgement and the end of history. This must have seemed especially bold to Luther's contemporaries, given the accusation's heretical pedigree, until it became clear that even so resounding a threat as Leo X's threat of excommunication (15 June 1520) might be impossible to execute. 17 November 1520, Luther repeated the appeal to a general church council. 10 December he publicly burned Pope Leo X's bull threatening excommunication. The excommunication was confirmed and published by another bull of January 1521, then extended by the imperial ban, approved 25 May 1521: the emperor acted against Luther's heresy, according to his own report, as protector of religion.[6] It made Luther an imperial outlaw for the remaining twenty-five years of his life. He was ready for the challenge. A few weeks after burning the papal threat of excommunication, he reported the deed to his mentor Johannes Staupitz, noting that it made him happier than he had been at any other time in his life.[7]

By summer 1521, a tide of German discontent carried Luther along. That discontent was, at best, vaguely evangelical. The tide rose among the imperial estates, too, who hoped it might overwhelm foreign taxation. So, for example, at the Imperial Diet of 1522, they refused to deliver Luther to the papal court. To the refusal, they added a list of 100 grievances, with a demand: papal annates, fees collected when higher church offices like bishoprics and abbacies were filled, should be applied to the common good of the Empire. After the Diet, a pamphlet conveniently published the grievances and the demand. The pamphlet surveyed the accounts delivered to the papal nuncio Francesco Chieregati region by region and calculated the sum to leave Germany for the papal treasury at 15,634 fl., 10 schilling, 8 heller.[8] The pamphlet ended with the New Testament

---

[6] Brecht, *Martin Luther*, 1:473–4.

[7] WABr 2:245, and Bäumer, "Der Lutherprozeß," p. 47.

[8] Anonymous, *Was Bebstliche heyligkeyt auß Teütscher nation järlicher Annata, und eyn yeder Bistum und Ebbtey, besondern taxirt* (no place: no publisher, 1523), Flugschriften des frühen 16. Jahrhunderts, Fiche 6 nr. 16. For payment of annates directly to the apostolic treasury and not to collectors, Christiane Schuchard, *Die päpstlichen Kollektoren im späten Mittelalter* (Tübingen: Max Niemeyer, 2000), p. 322. For expansion of Lutheran support after the Diet, Jean Delumeau, Thierry Wanegffelen, *Naissance et affirmation de la Réforme* (Paris: Presses universitaires de France, 1997), pp. 76–78.

verse (Romans 13.11), "brother, it is time to wake up" (*Brůder es ist zeyt vom schlaff uffzůsteen*). As it turns out, the amount calculated was hardly exceptional, nor was the estates' request to apply it to the Empire's common good unprecedented. Annates and other fees cost Albrecht of Brandenburg 29,000 fl. alone when he was elected to the archbishopric of Mainz in 1514.[9] But the ever Catholic Duke Georg of Saxony at the Diet of Worms in 1521—the Diet famous for its imperial condemnation of Luther—had complained that annates diverted too much money out of Germany. There was nothing unusual in his complaint. Annates had been criticized as simoniacal, a money crime against the church, at least since the days of Guillaume Durand, the early fourteenth-century bishop of Mende and critic of the decline of a bishop's pastoral office.[10] Many must have shared the suspicions of Ulrich of Hutten, who complained that Pope Leo X was a tyrannt draining Germany to irrigate a luxuriating curia.[11]

Normally, a roundly condemned heretic like Luther was quickly dispatched or isolated. But a German sense of alienation from the papacy rendered Luther more resilient. The 1522 Diet marks the beginning of a long succession of compromises with and condemnations of Luther and his followers. The Empire's religious controversy unfolded in its complex and uncertain way because the new heretical movement in part flowed with established moral antipathies, in no way uniquely evangelical, against what seemed a remote court.

The most widespread uprisings known in Europe up to that time, the so-called Peasants' Revolt of 1524/5, then helped raise the evangelical party as a transregional, organized movement. Only after did evangelicals develop the church rites and organizational structures on a wide scale that replaced those of Catholic bishops and the pope in Protestant lands. The rites and structures were designed by theologians and implemented by evangelical clergy under the coercive authority of urban magistrates or princes, when those urban magistrates and princes chose to reform the church in their realms. The churches were therefore designed by and within city-states and territories, and they are known as territorial churches.

---

[9] Anton Störmann, *Die städtischen Gravamina gegen den Klerus am Ausgange des Mittelalters und in der Reformationszeit* (Münster im Westfallen: Achendorf, 1916), pp. 32 n. 2; 36 n. 6; 37; 39 for this and the following. Brecht, *Martin Luther*, 1:178–9.
[10] Störmann in the previous note.
[11] Ulrich von Hutten, *Opera*, ed. E. Böcking, 7 vols. (Leipzig: B.G. Teubner, 1859–99), Epp. 188 and 189, 1:371–99.

The reform of a church in a city or territory involved: assigning favored preachers to pulpits, using or trying to use church incomes to support them, establishing disciplinary courts to oversee public morality, publishing and prescribing an evangelical liturgy and management structure(s), and prohibiting religious rites and practices that were considered inconsistent with evangelical doctrine, in particular, the performance of the mass and intercessory prayers for the dead, to saints or before images. To reform a church in the Protestant manner in the sixteenth century was to do several or all of these things. In Germany, it could not occur without the support of princes or city magistrates, unless a territorial church would be run by voluntary labor, which never happened. To support territorial churches and to increase the opportunities for selective welfare by building hostels for the sick and indigent (there was no general social welfare in sixteenth-century Europe), cities and princes took control of church properties—church buildings, tithes, incomes from rents and annuities, and farmlands. Monasteries held the largest share of the income-producing real estate of the church. Protestants had their doubts about the legitimacy of monasticism, anyway. They were convinced that many monastic practices were inconsistent with the gospel, in particular monastic prayers for the souls of the dead, which service happened to produce the most gifts to monasteries and—directly or indirectly—incomes. Many also held monasticism suspect for sheltering dishonorable men and women, preventing them from living productive and morally justifiable lives.[12]

No one is surprised that monasteries were often closed down. But few consider how the closure of cloisters took place in heterogeneous ways. In many Protestant places monasteries survived for decades. Lutheran ideology did not help as much as it might have. Luther and Melanchthon, in their most principled moments, argued that monasteries had to be reformed, not confiscated.[13] That is, evangelical preachers must be installed and the monks or nuns given the opportunity to convert. They must be hindered from corrupting society through false teaching and superstitious practices, such as prayer to the saints, yet if they remained Catholic but kept to themselves or if they became evangelical yet did not wish to leave the monastery, Lutheran doctrine had little else to throw at cloisters. The confes-

---

[12] Ocker, "'Rechte Arme' und 'Bettler Orden,'" pp. 129–57.
[13] This will be reviewed in chapter 4, below.

sional politics that emerged in the 1530's and characterized German history to the Peace of Westphalia (1648) left the geography of conversion a kaleidoscope. The religious landscape remained divided, its parts shifting, superimposing, and segregating, only eventually to produce a largely Protestant north, a largely Catholic south, and principalities of either confession in the west, with some monasteries, cities, small lordships, and tolerated confessional minorities, Catholic or Protestant, scattered throughout.[14]

Heterogeneous but overlapping social and cultural settings are familiar to scholars of late medieval Germany. It is the environment in which the new faith took shape. More surprising is the fact that Protestantism permanently established itself at all. The question is how. To answer this question we must begin with the Peasants' War, which helped shape the public posture of evangelical preachers and rulers and rapidly accelerated lay designs on church property, under the cover of traditional religious obligations.

An Effect of the Peasants' War

On a Friday morning in early spring, 24 March 1525, two bands of peasants gathered at Brettheim, a village belonging to the city-state of Rothenburg on the Tauber, to ransack the Tauber Valley. 800 strong, they marched into Insingen, circled through Diebach, Ostheim, and Wettringen, then came back to Insingen at the end of the day, fortified by the priests' wine at Betwar and Ostheim and the stores of the mayor's house in Wettringen, which they plundered and distributed among themselves.[15] So began the revolt in Franconia, the third wave of unrest since the late spring of 1524.

The revolt, which had begun in the southern Black Forest ten months earlier, spread quickly around militias formed in bands of various sizes around a headman, rotating recruits, and plundering for their provisions.[16] A strong party of sympathetic burghers in the

---

[14] Marc Venard, et al. *Le temps des Confessions (1530–1620/30)*, v. 8 of *Histoire du Christianisme des origines à nos jours* (Paris: Desclée, 1992), pp. 368–70.

[15] The *Schulthaiß* of Wettringen was in Rothenburg at the time. *Quellen zur Geschichte des Bauernkriegs aus Rotenburg an der Tauber*, edited by Franz Ludwig Baumann, (Stuttgart: Literarischer Verein, 1878), pp. 59–61. A brief account may be found in Martin Brecht, Hermann Ehmer, *Südwestdeutsche Reformationsgeschichte* (Stuttgart: Calwer, 1984), p. 107.

[16] Patterns of organization are summarized by Blickle, *The Revolution of 1525*, pp. xx–xxii.

city of Rothenburg, including guildsmen, reinforced the Franconian
rebels when they came, as in other towns. They were disgruntled
by burdensome taxation and inspired by evangelical preaching. The
reformer Andreas Bodenstein von Karlstadt, who denied instigating
violence, was exiled from Electoral Saxony in 1524, for instigating
violence, and he was exiled from Rothenburg for the same reason
before the revolt reached the city. But he remained there in hiding
for several months.[17] The peasants of Upper Swabia had set precedents for the Franconian rebels, including church raids and the occasional sale of church lands to provision the armies.[18]

  As the revolt swept from southwest Germany west through Alsace,
north into central Germany, and east into Austria, it was inevitable
that the contingents should damage and destroy church property.
Many of the rebels were bound to farmlands belonging to monasteries, particularly in the southwest, where unrest had broken out
periodically over the previous century, a reflection of creeping social
decline among the peasantry.[19] Although most peasants were technically free, the rights of many had been steadily eroding, leaving
some in a position practically identical with that of unfree serfs.[20]
Now, those belonging to ecclesiastical lords violated their lord's prerogatives simply by leaving farms. There were, too, grain, wine, pow-
der, tools, and precious objects to plunder from ecclesiastical and
noble storehouses alike and use for the campaign. Some towns and
villages owed duties in kind to prince-bishops and monasteries.
Villagers often had priests living with them and a church and a parsonage among their houses. Church properties were diverse and
widely distributed. It was easy to transgress the prerogatives of the
church. It was easy, in the revolt, to become a church robber.

  There was also the venal manner of peasant militias. So, for example, when Thomas Müntzer's army of the elect threatened the Thurin-

---

[17] Günther Franz, *Der deutsche Bauernkrieg*, eighth edition (Bad Homurg: Hermann
Gentner, 1969), pp. 176–87. Sigrid Looß, "Andreas Bodensteins von Karlstadt Haltung zum Aufruhr," *Querdenker der Reformation—Andreas Bodenstein von Karlstadt und seine
frühe Wirkung*, ed. Ulrich Bubenheimer, Stefan Oehmig (Würzburg: Religion und
Kultur, 2001), pp. 265–76.
[18] *Quellen zur Geschichte des Bauernkriegs in Oberschwaben*, ed. Franz Ludwig Baumann
(Stuttgart: Literarischer Verein, 1876), pp. 64, 363, 421, 490, 756. Some examples
of violations of church property and persons in the years just before the Revolt
may be found in ibid., pp. 52, 56, 57.
[19] Franz, *Der deutsche Bauernkrieg*, p. 15.
[20] Blickle, *Revolution of 1525*, p. 70.

gian cloister of Naundorf, the Cistercian nuns were tipped off on a Sunday, 30 April 1525, that a *Klostersturm*, an invasion of the cloister, was planned for that evening.[21] The nuns ran to the sheriff of Alstedt (the abbess happened to be away at Eisleben). He refused to offer protection. And the abbess hurried home. She arrived at midnight to find the cloister occupied by peasants (they said, the sheriff let them in). Two barrels of beer, a tun of cheese, and other assorted foodstuff had already been consumed. They let the fowl and livestock run free. They threatened and ridiculed the stunned abbess with unrepeatable words—revelry typical of the revolt. Although the monastery seems to have survived the war, the nuns' situation was precarious.[22] The not-too-distant Cistercian nunnery of Annerode, the Benedictine monastary of Gerode, and the Cistercian monastery of Reifenstein were destroyed by fire about the same time. It took fifteen years to reopen them.[23] Rebels sometimes ostentatiously threatened priests, monks, or nuns, as in the case of the abbess. In Franconia, the priests of Betwar and Ostheim were robbed of their wine.[24] To the southeast, the Dominican cloister of Schwäbisch-Gmünd was plundered.[25] The Carmelites of Heilbronn were forced to run a gauntlet, not of rebels but of citizens, a few days before the city fell to the peasants.[26] In some places, for example, the Kreichgau, other parts of Württemberg, Bamberg, and Elsaß, the leaders of peasant bands planned the destruction of cloisters and/or castles, while in other places it happened spontaneously.[27] The violence against property and persons seemed infectious, for iconoclastic riots broke out

---

[21] For the event, *Akten zur Geschichte des Bauernkriegs in Mitteldeutschland*, ed. Otto Merx, Günther Franz, 2 vols. (Aalen: Scientia Verlag, 1964), 2:186 nr. 1298. For additional examples of violence, Tom Scott, Bob Scribner, editors, *The German Peasants' War: A History in Documents* (New Jersey: Humanities Press, 1991), pp. 108–9 nr. 20, p. 146 nr. 45, pp. 311–12 nr. 149.

[22] R. Hermann, "Verzeichniß der in den Sachsen-Ernestinischen, Schwarzburgischen und Reußischen Landen, sowie den K. Preuß. Kreisen Schleufingen und Schmalkalden bis zur Reformation vorhanden gewesenen Stifter, Klöster und Ordenshäuser," *Zeitschrift für thüringische Geschichte und Alterthumskunde* 8 (1871): 1–176, here 42 nr. 72, which notes that Naundorf is mentioned in 1527 as still existing.

[23] Herman, "Verzeichniß," pp. 85 nr. 3, 105–6 nr. 42, 144–5 nr. 116.

[24] *Quellen zur Geschichte des Bauernkriegs aus Rotenburg*, pp. 59–60.

[25] Brecht, Ehmer, *Südwestdeutsche Reformationsgeschichte*, p. 79.

[26] Blickle, *Revolution of 1525*, pp. 113–14.

[27] Brecht, Ehmer, *Südwestdeutsche Reformationsgeschichte*, pp. 105, 110. Rudolf Endres, *Adelige Lebensformen in Franken zur Zeit des Bauernkrieges* (Würzburg: Ferdinand Schöningh, 1974), p. 10.

in some cities during the season of revolt, sometimes related to it, as for example at Waldshut near the beginning of the war in October 1524 or Heilsbronn and Halberstadt in 1525, and sometimes not, as at Magdeburg and Memmingen in 1524, Strasbourg in 1524 and February 1525, Stralsund in April 1525, or Ribnitz in late September of that year.[28]

The violence included the destruction of church art and holy objects, as the war brought a new movement of iconoclasm to a rapid climax, which lingered on through the 1530's in southwest and central Germany and Switzerland, only fading in the 1540's.[29]

Table: The Number of Cities Affected by Iconoclasm, 1520–1548

	The North[30]	Central Germany	Southwest Germany	Switzerland	Total	Average incidents/ year
1520–1523	2	5	0	3	10	2.5
1524–1525	12	7	19	4	42	21
1526–1529	2	3	3	25	33	3.2
1530–1537	1	9	13	17[31]	40	5
1538–1548	0	0	3	0	3	.28

---

[28] Brecht, Ehmer, *Südwestdeutsche Reformationsgeschichte*, p. 99. Wandel, *Voracious Idols*, pp. 118–19. For the Magdeburg riot of the Feast of the Assumption of the Blessed Virgin, 15 August 1524, *Die Chroniken der niedersächsischen Städte: Magdeburg*, v. 2 (= *Die Chroniken der deutschen Städte vom 14. bis ins 16. Jahrhundert*, v. 27) (Göttingen: Vandenhoeck und Ruprecht, 1899, reprinted 1962), pp. 200–203. Magdeburg did not feel itself threatened by the revolt until spring, 1525. The Memmingen riot of Christmas 1524 occurred months before the city's occupation by the Swabian League and the subsequent siege by the rebels. Schlenck, *Die Reichsstadt Memmingen*, pp. 41–2. For Halberstadt, Silke Logemann, "Grundzüge der Geschichte der Stadt Halberstadt vom 13. Bis 16. Jahrhundert," *Bürger, Bettelmönche und Bischöfe in Halberstadt. Studien zur Geschichte der Stadt, der Mendikanten und des Bistums vom Mittelalter bis zur Frühen Neuzeit*, edited by Dieter Berg (Werl: Dietrich-Coelde-Verlag, 1997), pp. 81–138, here 128–138. For Stralsund, Norbert Schnitzler, "'Kirchenbruch' und 'lose Rotten.' Gewalt, Recht und Reformation (Stralsund 1525)," *Kulturelle Reformation. Sinnformationen im Umbruch, 1400–1600*, pp. 285–316, and Ingo Ulpts, *Die Bettelorden in Mecklenburg. Ein Beitrag zur Geschichte der Franziskaner, Klarissen, Dominikaner und Augustiner-Eremiten im Mittelalter* (Werl: Dietrich-Coelde-Verlag, 1995), pp. 347–8. For Ribnitz, ibid., pp. 375–6.

[29] The table is derived from the summary and maps by Sergiusz Michalski, "Die Ausbreitung der reformatorischen Bildersturms, 1521–1537," *Bildersturm. Wahnsinn oder Gottes Wille?* edited by Cécile Dupeux, Peter Jezler, Jean Wirth (Munich: Wilhelm Fink, 2000), pp. 46–56. I have excluded regional seasons of iconoclasm, noting only cities.

[30] This includes scattered incidents in Denmark, Sweden, Prussia, Livonia, and Estonia.

[31] Almost all of these incidents occurred in French-speaking regions.

After the war, magistrates, whether sympathetic to evangelical doctrine or not, uniformly opposed the disordered iconoclasm of riotous townsfolk (when iconoclasm was officially advocated, it was the orderly removal of images by mandate).[32] But earlier examples—Wittenberg 1521/2, Zürich 1523, Strasbourg 1524, and Magdeburg 1524—suggested to many observers a trajectory from evangelical preaching toward the general deterioration of social order during the war.

The extent of peasant destruction enlarged this vivid impression. In the territory of Bamberg, an area severely affected, nearly 200 castles were damaged or destroyed within a mere eleven days, 15–26 May 1525; only six castles subject to the prince-bishop survived the war unharmed.[33] Frankish castles were especially at risk. Many noble castellans had relocated to Bamberg, some castles were managed by subjects from villages, or the nobles were away fighting with the Swabian League against the rebels in the southwest.[34] In the territories of Bamberg and Würzburg, it has been said, monasteries were rendered especially vulnerable by trends of monastic recuitment. Recruitment had turned from the families of imperial knights to peasants and burghers over the previous decades, placing monasteries within less provident social networks.[35] After the war, damages were assessed and peasants fined. Although the nobility's claims most accurately reflect what lords wanted, and they therefore must amplify injuries, some inventories were published, and they shaped the public impression of the extent of damage, which may have mattered more for the shape of emergent Protestant identity than actual material losses.[36] One pamphlet listed places destroyed in the lands of the

---

[32] In the south, councils controlled riots by removing images. In the north, councils responded with prohibitions of iconoclasm. Schnitzler, *Ikonoklasmus-Bildersturm*, pp. 237–303, 315. For the reliance of iconoclastic actions on late medieval concepts of the image and practices of devotion (in contrast with the view that iconoclasm was a mere *Entmachtung* of images), ibid., p. 320 and passim. See also Cameron, *The European Reformation*, pp. 249–51; Carlos Eire, *War Against the Idols* (Cambridge University Press, 1986), pp. 105–21; Carl C. Christensen, *Art and the Reformation in Germany* (Athens: Ohio University Press, 1979), pp. 66–109; Robert W. Scribner, "Ritual and Reformation," *The German People and the Reformation*, ed. R. Po-Chia Hsia (Ithaca: Cornell, 1988), pp. 122–44.

[33] Endres, *Adelige Lebensformen*, p. 10.

[34] Ibid., p. 10.

[35] Henze, "Orden und ihre Klöster," p. 96, and *Die Territorien des Reichs*, 4:191–2.

[36] Endres, *Adelige Lebensformen*, pp. 11–6. For problems with the lists and the difficulty of assessing the revolt's actual damages, Helmut Gabel and Winfried Schulze, "Folgen und Wirkungen," *Der deutsche Bauernkrieg*, edited by Horst Buszello, Peter Blickle, Rudolf Endres (Paderborn: Ferdinand Schöningh, 1984), pp. 322–349,

prince-bishops of Würzburg and Bamberg and in the Brandenburg-
ruled mark of Ansbach-Kulmbach: 50 destroyed castles in Würzburg,
72 places in Bamberg, 27 in Ansbach-Kulmbach, and 12 cloisters,
all identified by name.[37] Another pamphlet names 179 destroyed
strongholds alone.[38] Although the destruction of cloisters was far less
extensive than castles, sacrilege was attributed to the entire rebellion. This affected the progress of the religious controversy in the
1520's and beyond. Sacrilege seemed to have an obvious source.[39]

> And counter to oath and obligation,
> Your government's mortification,
> All obedience cast away,
> In cities, markets, townships.
> Herded like a horde of pigs,
> Countless buildings torn to shreds.
> Cloisters, churches, and God's houses,
> Monks, pastors, nuns, and Carthusians
> Hunted down, then robbed, and plundered,
> Worship and divine honor ended.
> Holy images chopped to bits,

here 329–30, and for the payment of reparations, ibid., pp. 330–5 and Thomas F.
Sea, "The Economic Impact of the German Peasants' War: the Question of Reparations," *Sixteenth Century Journal* 8 (1977): 75–97.

[37] Anonymous, *Verbrannte unnd abgebrochne Schlosser unnd Cloester, so durch die Bawerschafft
yhn Wuertzburger und Bamberger Stifften beschehen* (n.pl.: n. publ, 1525). Flugschriften des
frühen 16. Jahrhunderts, Fiche 287, nr. 828.

[38] Anonymous, *Die Summa unnd namen der schloß, auch wem eyn iedes zugehort hatt, so
durch versamlung der Bawern, inn Stifftenn, Bamberg, Würtzburg und Brandenburisch Marggraffschafft,
Im iar Dausent Fünffhundert und Fünff und zwentzigsten jämerlich verbrant und verhört sindt*
(Würzburg: n.publ., 1525?). I am grateful to Hillay Zmora for kindly providing me
with a list of these.

[39] *Der bock dryt frey auff disen plan/ Hatt wider Ehren nye gethan/ Wie sehr sie yn gescholten
han/ Was aber Luther für ein man/ Und wilch ein spyl ere gfangen an/ Und nun den man-
tel wenden kan/ Nach dem der wind thüt einher gan/ Findstu in disem Büchlin stan* (No place:
no publisher, 1525), ff. 1v–2r, 3v. Flugschriften des frühen 16. Jahrhunderts, nr.
3375. "Und wider ewer eyd und pflicht / Ewer Oberkeit gar vernicht, / Allen
gehorsam abgeworffen / In stetten, merckten, und in dorffen. / Zusammen flossen
wie die schweyn, / Manchschn gebewd geryssen eyn. / Closter, kirchen, und gottes
hewßer, / Münch, pfaffen, nonnen und Carthewßer / Veriagt, berawbet und geplin-
dert, / Und gottes dienst und ehr verhindert. / Der heylgen bild zu stuck gehawen, /
Die mutter gots und zart junckfrawen. / Gotslesterlich und unbescheyden, / Vergleycht
den alten badmeyden. / Die Fürsten die euch widerstannen, / Gescholten und
genennt Tyrannen. / Dem Adel jre schloß belegert, / Ire zyns, rennt, und dienst
gewegert. / Und euch wider sie auffgebürstet, / Al die nach unglück hat gedürstet. /
Manch burg verwust in teutschen landen, / Die vor dem Türcken wol wer bstanden. /
Das ist das Euangelion, / Das jr von Luthern glernet hon."

Mother-of-Gods and sweet Virgins.
Blasphemous, presumptuous,
Comparing her to bathhouse wenches.
The princes that stood against you,
You scolded and called tyrants.
The castles of noblemen besieged,
Repudiated rents, service, fees.
You ruffled yourselves up against them,
Until everyone yearned for misery.
Many castles in German lands,
Laid waist that should still stand
Against Turks. That is the Gospel,
That Martin Luther taught you.

Such were the tableaux of misfortune. Luther, this anonymous pamphlet later says, was the source of Karlstadt and Thomas Müntzer. The Dominican theologian Johannes Eck declared the revolt the "fruit of Luther's seed" (*fructus germinis Lutheri*).[40] Duke Ferdinand of Austria dismissed the peasants as Lutherans, *paisans Luteriens*. Monastic writers associated both urban and rural unrest with Luther.[41] Anyone not committed to Luther's teaching could easily think that a true reformation would end abuses of the church, such as these that Luther seemed to have spawned.

Luther's sensitivity to these accusations is well known. He answered by insisting on the prince's responsibility to suppress revolt and support reform, while he polemically sacrificed his own heretics.[42] These had been identified before the war broke out. They were also being named by the defenders of the old faith. Müntzer was obvious, having led an army in the rebellion. Karlstadt, who like Müntzer challenged Luther's understanding of the sacraments, did not openly promote the revolt, although he did believe a Christian city should

---

[40] Armin Kohnle, *Reichstag und Reformation* (Gütersloh: Gütersloher Verlagshaus, 2001), p. 248 for this and the following.

[41] Hinz, *Die Brüder vom Gemeinsamen Leben*, p. 53 for the case of Münster, with notes 74–6 for the literature on the social origins of the revolt.

[42] Two works of 1525 were especially meant to prove his distance from Karlstadt and Müntzer: *Wider die himmlischen Propheten* (Against the Heavenly Prophets, completed in January and February 1525), WA 18:62–214, LW 40:79–223; and *Eyn Schreyklich Geschicht und Gericht Gottes über Thomas Müntzer* (A Terrible History and Judgement of God on Thomas Müntzer, completed in May 1525), WA 18:362–74. The title-page of the latter is the frontispiece to this chapter, for an explanation of which see Appendix 2. Blickle, *Revolution of 1525*, pp. 155–61, for the relation of the unrest to Lutheran doctrine.

end the mass; remove all images from churches; expel all priests, monks, and nuns; and expel adulterers and drunkards—demands that Luther had not quite made. When Thomas Müntzer asked Karlstadt to join his movement in July 1524, Karlstadt refused. Expelled from Saxony to Rothenburg, Karlstadt brought the controversy over his symbolic, sacramentarian concept of the eucharist to Franconia. His contribution to the war was at best indirect; the contribution of sacramentarian doctrine to rebellion non-existent.[43] Yet Luther blamed him for the civil war at its outbreak. The allegation stuck among Luther's followers, in spite of Karlstadt's 1525 *Apology against the False Accusation of Revolt*, which he offered at the end of the war, and in spite of Luther's qualified admission of Karlstadt's innocence.[44]

Luther's followers used the association of sacramental doctrine with rebellion—an alleged susceptibility of sacramental heretics to revolution—to resist the accusation of revolution levelled against themselves. They assigned a religious cause to a social problem, a maneuver consistent with Augustinian and Lutheran views of the predominance of sin in human society, and maybe consistent with most preaching in religions whose scriptures originated with (a) prophet(s). Many evangelicals who lobbied princes or magistrates performed this maneuver, alleging either a wrong view and practice of the eucharist, Anabaptism, or both. Their number included religious houses that embraced the new faith, for example, the Brethren of the Common

---

[43] Looß, "Bodensteins Haltung zum 'Aufruhr,'" pp. 265–76. Stefan Oehmig, "'Christlicher Bürger'—'christliche Stadt?' Zu Andreas Bodensteins von Karlstadt Vorstellungen von einem christlichen Geimeinwesen und den Tugenden seiner Bürger," *Querdenker der Reformation*, pp. 151–86, here 164–71. Siegfried Bräuer, "Der Briefwechsel zwischen Andreas Bodenstein von Karlstadt und Thomas Müntzer," ibid., pp. 187–209.

[44] Near the end of the war Karlstadt had been forced from his refuge at Rothenburg. He sought admission to Saxony for himself and his wife in June, just after Thomas Müntzer's execution in Thuringia. To that end, he asked Luther to publish the *Apology* in Wittenberg, in order to clear his name. And Luther did, with a preface exonerating him. But, Luther said, he did so only because Christ bade his followers to love their enemies; he remained completely opposed to Karlstadt's doctrine. Looß, "Bodensteins Haltung," p. 271. *Karlstadts Schriften aus den Jahren 1523–1525*, ed. Erich Hertzsch, 2 vols. (Halle: Neimeyer, 1956–1957), 2:106–18. Martin Luther, *Entschuldigung D. Andreas Karlstadts*, WA 18:436–38. Karlstadt's text was delivered to Luther by Karlstadt's wife 27 June. Karlstadt arrived in Wittenberg soon after and was given secret accommodations in Luther's own home in the Augustinian Friary. WA 18:433–34.

Life at Herford.[45] The maneuver had to seem ludicrous to Luther's opponents, even those relatively close to evangelical movements, such as Erasmus. Erasmus denounced Luther as seditious in 1527, and he challenged the reforming authenticity of Luther's followers in his 1529 "Letter against the Fake Evangelicals."[46] It inspired an immediate, 170-page rebuttal by Martin Bucer.[47] Bucer answered the accusation of evangelical rebellion by appointing the Christian magistrate of Strasbourg to the police force of reform.[48] He is somewhat famous for continuing to defend this magisterial role through the next decade, as he advocated the suppression of Anabaptist dissent in his city. The same necessity confronted other cities, for example Nürnberg in 1530, another well known example of confessional discipline under magistrates in Reformation Germany.[49]

By the Diet of Speyer in 1529, where the evangelical princes made the protests from which the name Protestant derives, the Lutheran refrain about rebels had become sacramentarians and Anabaptists.[50]

---

[45] Hinz, *Die Brüder vom Gemeinsamen Leben*, pp. 69, 92.

[46] *Epistula contra Pseudevangelicos* (Freiburg 1529). For the 1527 *Hyperaspistes*, Timothy Wengert, *Human Freedom, Christian Righteousness: Philip Melanchthon's Exegetical Dispute with Erasmus of Rotterdam* (New York: Oxford University Press, 1998), p. 124, and Estes, *Peace, Order and the Glory of God*, p. 73.

[47] *Martini Buceri Opera Latina* (Leiden: E.J. Brill, 1982), 1:59–225. Gottfried Hammann, *Martin Bucer, 1491–1551: Zwischen Volkskirche und Bekenntnisgemeinschaft*, trans. Gerhard P. Wolf (Stuttgart: Franz Steiner, 1989), p. 49.

[48] Gottfried Hammann explains Bucer's view of the Christian magistrate as standing between Luther's sharp distinction between secular government and church discipline and Zwingli's rejection of any limitation on the sovereignty of secular government over church discipline. Hammann, *Martin Bucer*, pp. 251–2. Luther developed his initial position in the years after the imperial ban was pronounced against him. See Brecht, *Martin Luther*, 2:115–19 and now Estes, *Peace, Order and the Glory of God*, pp. 17–41.

[49] In Nürnberg, an anonymous associate of the city secretary, Lazarus Spengler, advocated open tolerance of religious dissenters, provoking the debate over magisterial authority. James M. Estes, *Whether Secular Government Has the Right to Wield the Sword in Matters of Faith: A Controversy in Nürnberg, 1530* (Toronto: Centre for Renaissance and Reformation Studies, 1994), and idem, *Peace, Order and the Glory of God*, pp. 98–119.

[50] Estes, *Peace, Order and the Glory of God*, pp. 98–119, 184–7. The first protest of 19 April 1529 was against a decision to suspend the article on religion of the recess of the 1526 Diet of Speyer. A second, broader protest was presented to Archduke Ferdinand of Austria on 20 April by a delegation of counselors of five Protestant princes. The Lutheran princes also declared themselves in agreement with a prohibition of Anabaptism and of all defamatory literature. See Kohnle, *Reichstag und Reformation*, pp. 369, 374. Estes has explained how Melanchthon, Johannes Brenz, and probably Wenceslas Linck and Andreas Osiander expanded the role of temporal

Sacramentarians endangered much of the south German and Swiss reformations, as far as Luther was concerned. But many Protestants in the German south belied the first half of Luther's refrain, for they simply did not take sacramentarian doctrine as the mark of a revolutionary, although no manner of objecting ever assuaged Luther's suspicion.

The pressure to define the evangelical movement as an anti-papal orthodoxy continued for years, for evidence of evangelical chaos continued. Münster 1534/5 posed the most extreme evidence. Swollen with apocalyptically expectant Anabaptists who had fled persecution in the Netherlands, its famous social experiment progressed from adult baptism to obligatory polygamy during the long seige of what all rulers outside the city's short-lived Anabaptist kingdom could only regard as a just war.[51] The docile "spiritualism" of Sebastian Franck and Caspar von Schwenckfeld, which hoped to replace external religion with a purely inward faith, dribbled menacingly over Germany throughout the decade, and was lumped together with the earlier Anabaptist disorders. It added to Catholic pressure against all evangelicals. Georg Witzel, a reform advocate at the court of Georg, the Catholic Duke of Saxony, worried over imperial toleration of Protestants because of their propinquity to exactly these sorts of heretics and many more. In his 1538 answer to Luther's Schmalkald Articles, he included in one company Zwingli, Balthasar Hubmaier (the Swiss Anabaptist), Johannes Campanus (he was an Anabaptist antitrinitarian active in Braunschweig and Jülich), Bernhard Rothmann of Münster fame, Melchior Hoffmann (the Anabaptist languishing in the hangman's tower of Strasbourg),[52] and Jacob Schenk (an antin-

---

authority as *cura religionis* in response to the threat of radical preaching in the early 1530's. Estes, *Peace, Order and the Glory of God,* pp. 93–133.

[51] Fühner, *Die Kirchen- und die antireformatorische Religionspolitik,* pp. 262–287, esp. 272–3 for the migration from the Netherlands. Anabaptists also planned a takeover of Amsterdam in March 1534; 300 Anabaptists briefly occuppied the Cistercian abbey of Bloemkamp in Friesland in March 1535; forty Anabaptists managed to storm the Amsterdam Rathaus in May of that year, killing all its guards, a burghomaster, and some others; and finally in early summer a group of radical Anabaptists assembled around the nobleman Jan van Batenburg and plundered houses, cloisters, churches, and forcefully rebaptized people in Groningen and Frisia. Although Jan was executed in 1538, his band of robbers survived to the late 1570's. Ibid., pp. 273, 280–2, and the literature noted there.

[52] He was arrested in 1533 and had been imprisoned since, but left followers in the Netherlands and elsewhere, who flocked to Strasbourg, where they were sup-

omian active in Freiberg). To Luther he asked, "Weren't these all first hidden in your belly?"[53] Luther thought the condemnations of Anabaptists and sacramentarians answered the accusation. The League of Schmalkalden added condemnations of Franck and Schwenckfeld in 1540.[54] In the bi-polar landscape of religious debate, with its doctrines and counter-doctrines, radical evangelicals seemed to prove more than anything else where the Protestant rebellion against the pope would lead. They also presented an opportunity. These most famous evangelical Reformation debates—the sacraments, Anabaptism, other doctrinal and moral experiments—helped the new theologians position themselves as the defenders of religious tradition.

One may also observe a conservative impulse in less pompous settings than religious polemic and high theology, beginning in the Peasants' War. Where political authority remained largely intact and unsympathetic to the revolt (this was perhaps least true in the political patchwork of Müntzer's Thuringia), the rebel extravagances posed many problems. For village elders, like princes, must have wanted to appear, at least, to have tried to protect church property, as one can see in this defensive letter from the council of the Franconian village of Wettringen to their prince, the Bishop of Würzburg, three days after Easter, 18 April 1525:

pressed, and to Münster, where they were destroyed, while expecting the New Jerusalem. Brady, *Turning Swiss*, pp. 109–114. George Huntston Williams, *The Radical Reformation*, 3rd edition (Kirksville, Missouri: Sixteenth Century Publishers, 1992), pp. 539–547. Fühner, *Die Kirchen- und die antireformatorische Religionspolitik Kaiser Karls V.*, pp. 263–9.

[53] Hans Volz, *Drei Schriften gegen Luthers Schmalkaldische Artikel von Cochläus, Witzel und Hoffmeister (1538 und 1539)* (Münster: Aschendorf, 1932), pp. 95–96: "Zele hie Carlstat, Müntzer, Zwingel, Baltzer, Campan, Rotman, Hoffman, Agricol, Jacob etc. Sind dise nicht alle dir, Luter, erstlich im bauch gesteckt?" Witzel's own proposals were vilified by both Cathlics and Protestants. Thomas Fuchs, *Konfession und Gespräch. Typologie und Funktion der Religionsgespräche in der Reformationszeit* (Cologne: Böhlau, 1995), pp. 399–400. For Witzel's unique position as a humanist and Catholic reformer, and the evolution of his efforts to end the German schism, see Barbara Henze, *Aus Liebe zur Kirche Reform: Die Bemühungen Georg Witzels (1501–1573) um die Kircheneinheit* (Münster: Aschendorff, 1995), passim. But during the first religious colloquy, at Hagenau in 1540, Johannes Eck wrote a list of agreements between the parties, which recognized their shared conviction that government should attack Anabaptists. *Akten der deutschen Reichsreligionsgespräche im 16. Jahrhundert*, 2 vols.+, edited by Klaus Ganzer and Karl-Heinz zur Mühlen (Göttingen: Vandenhoeck und Ruprecht, 2000+), 1/2:1141 nr. 399.

[54] CR 3:983–86 nr. 1945, MBW 3:41 nr. 2396. *Martin Bucers Deutsche Schriften*, 9/1:80.

> We would like to inform your princely grace that we with the entire community have confiscated the church and parsonage (*kirchhoff und pfarhoff*) here at Wettringen (they stand next to each other), in case other people come along. We did it under instruction from the steward of the Rotenstein district and with the concurrence of the pastor, Mr. Michael Fen, appointed by Sir Conrad von Bibra. Now the pastor has disappeared, and so, too, a considerable amount of grain, wheat, and rye, about forty bushels, and the men have seized a good two cartloads of wine, from which they drank.[55]

Conrad von Bibra must have held the right of presentation. It seems that Pastor Fen was either swept aside or swept up by the revolt, and the village elders were eager to distinguish their actions from any revolutionary cooperation. They took the two church plots into protective custody. Now they were anxious to avoid the accusation of church robbery. Their dilemma probably confronted the leaders of any modestly wealthy village facing the revolt. But so, too, when the revolt was suppressed in that bloody year, the Swabian League and the German estates in general acted, like the village elders of Wettringen, as protectors of their own interests *and* as emergency protectors of the church.

Protectors of the Church

It may seem ironic that a conservative impulse soon characterized the Protestant rebellion against the papacy. It was an expression of the traditional responsibility to protect religious things. But it should seem familiar to historians of late medieval Germany, insofar as rulers at all levels of society who witnessed or resisted the revolt acted according to well-established habits and convictions, rather than from a new ideological position. Accordingly, in the sequestering seasons that followed the Peasants' War, the seizure of churches happened in ways as various as medieval conditions were, according to different chronologies and with diverse outcomes. To each of these matters, protection and seizure, we now turn.

To begin with a truism of recent scholarship on German religion in the late Middle Ages, church protection reflects growing lay

---

[55] *Akten zur Geschichte des Bauernkriegs in Mitteldeutschland*, 1/1:97–8 nr. 134.

influence. Lay influence had generally grown in the fifteenth century, over churches and monasteries alike, from kings and emperors to urban and village councils—lay authorities trans-regional, regional, and local. Their influence grew both as a function of patronage rights and through increasingly effective taxation of clergy and monasteries. They claimed a right to intervene in the name of reform, sometimes in the event of emergency, such as war.[56] Pious interventions were in certain ways routine. The most conventional interventions included the appointment of lay guardians, urban and territorial taxation, and imposition of obligations of citizenship on priests and members of religious orders.[57] Opportunities to intervene multiplied as princes assumed the custodianship of monasteries as protectors or conducted territorial visitations to promote reform.[58] The pope colluded in princely interventions, for example by granting a papal privilege to nominate bishops and appoint administrators of cloister property, as happened, for example, in electoral Brandenburg, a small instance of the kind of right that helped great kings in other parts of Europe extend their sovereignty over churches.[59]

This stood in tension with what by now were seen as ancient prerogatives, namely those asserted by the ecclesiastical reforms of the eleventh century and of medieval papalism, which tried to postion the church as a distinct society governed by its own hierarchy according to its own laws, in its own courts, and supported by its inalienable property.[60] In any matter of clerical immunity, even if the case appeared before a temporal court, papal law superceded secular law, an expression of the honor and reverence owed to holy matters, the oversight of which fell to popes and church prelates.[61] Church autonomy existed in doctrine, but not quite in fact. Yet it was this conceptual

---

[56] Isenmann, *Die deutsche Stadt*, pp. 214–15. Cohn, "Church Property," pp. 159–62.

[57] Paul Mikat, "Bemerkungen zum Verhältnis von Kirchengut und Staatsgewalt am Vorabend der Reformation," ZRG, KA 67 (1981): 264–309, esp. 290, 297, 301, 305–7. Bernd Moeller, "Kleriker als Bürger," *Festschrift für Hermann Heimpel*, 2 vols. (Gottingen: Vandenhoeck und Ruprecht, 1972), 2:195–224.

[58] Ziegler, "Reformation und Klosterauflösung," p. 594.

[59] Barbara Henze, "Orden und ihre Klöster in der Umbruchszeit der Konfessionalisierung," *Territorien des Reichs*, 7:91.

[60] *Liber Sextus* III.vii.9, CICan 2:1042–3.

[61] So said Diego de Covarrubias y Leyva, the prominent sixteenth-century jurist, *Variarum resolutionum* II.xx.3, *Opera omnia*, 2 vols. (Colonia Allobrogum: Samuelis de Tournes, 1679), 2:270.

independence that protectors of the church were meant to safeguard.

Lay interventions may serve as an index of ruling power. Barbara Henze has recently pointed out that a successful reform is evidence of the extent of a prince's regional authority, his control of estates and power over neighbors.[62] Reform required self-assertion. The ruler had to best others, although a strong lord was no *guarantee* of successful reform.[63] It could happen against reform. In 1534, the ducal counsels of Cammin prevented the bishop from confiscating monastic property to educate noble children, on the advice of his theologians.[64] It could happen for reform. The Elector of Saxony conducted visitations against the will of the lords of Gera, which demonstrated his supremacy to cloisters and to the Teutonic Order. The lack of powerful overlords meant that the monasteries related to Catholic seigneurs in the Lausitz survived attempts to convert them to the evangelical faith, just as churches with powerful and insistent Catholic patrons in Protestant areas could also resist change. Yet a ruler was no guarantee of the *safety* of his confession. In spite of the prince-bishop of Würzburg's opposition to the new doctrine and in spite of the fact that he was named protector of noble monasteries by the emperor in 1534, monasteries in his domain experienced high attrition, to the point that some dissolved themselves.

At the summit of aristocratic networks were a few great princely dynasties in competition. Among them, the needs of the moment easily overwhelmed established church norms. Among the most brazen and illustrious of fifteenth-century violators of church immunities in Germany stands the amazing Margrave Albrecht Achilles of Brandenburg. During his time as elector (1470–1486), he found himself twice under papal interdict for marriage alliances that ignored the canonical rules of affinity, at war with the bishops of Bamberg and Würzburg, whose landholdings he challenged, at war with the archbishop of Mainz, and in conflict with the bishop of Eichstätt and the abbot of Castell.[65] When he received news of imperial taxes to fund the

---

[62] Henze, "Orden und ihre Klöster," pp. 91–2.

[63] Ibid., p. 93 and *Die Territorien des Reichs im Zeitalter der Reformation und Konfessionalisierung*, 4:108–9.

[64] For this and the following, Henze, "Orden und ihre Klöster, p. 92 and *Die Territorien des Reichs im Zeitalter der Reformation und Konfessionalisierung*, in order of mention: 2:195–6, 4:31–2, 6:100–1, 2:30.

[65] *Das kaiserliche Buch des Markgrafen Albrecht Achilles*, ed. Julius von Minutoli (Berlin: F. Schneider, 1850), pp. 331–87.

imperial campaign against the Turks, he passed the burden to the clergy of his realm as an excise, then taxed clergy to fund his own campaign against Burgundy, then finally instituted a general clergy tax, winning concessions from the bishops of Bamberg, Eichstätt, Augsburg, and Regensburg, and an interdict from Würzburg.[66] His justification was the common good. Albrecht Achilles' taxes on clergy were a wonderful thing: even without *Praemunire* or the *Pragmatic Sanction of Bourges*, he whittled away at ecclesiastical immunities.[67] To take church incomes, rents, tithes, and lands was the next step after clerical taxation. Rulers innovated. They moved cases over tithes, benefices, and other properties to their own courts in Bavaria, Württemberg, and the Palatinate; they imposed territorial taxes on monasteries in Bavaria, Pomerania, and Saxony; and they audited monastic incomes in Bavaria (a lay court's adjudication of a conflict over a right to a tithe had precedents before the evangelical rebellion against ecclesiastical courts).[68] Just as their treatments were ad hoc, their accomplishments at building territorial states were fragmentary and partial, as Henry Cohn has pointed out. Such was the fifteenth century.

The most fundamental way to reorganize church business would have been to carve off the church's temporal dominion, then restrict church government to religious affairs and personnel, or in other words, secularize ecclesiastical principalities. This was accomplished in Germany for the first time during the religious controversy in the lands of the Teutonic Order, in 1525, as an aftershock of a 1521 truce between the Order and the Polish crown. The Grand Master, Albrecht of Brandenburg (he was the cousin of the archbishop of Mainz with the same name), realized that Polish absorption of the Order's territory meant the secularization of the Order's domain. In

---

[66] Ibid., pp. 356–69.

[67] In 1438, while the Council of Florence was still in session, a royally assembled French synod issued the Pragmatic Sanction of Bourges to limit papal appointments to benefices and appeals to the papal court, to the advantage of the French crown. In the Empire a year later, a similar resolution was issued, the Acceptation of Mainz, but to no effect. Borgolte, *Die Mittelalterliche Kirche*, p. 75. In the Empire, restrictions on papal interference would not occur Empire-wide, but territory by territory. *Praemunire* is the name given to a series of English statutes that, beginning in 1353, restricted appeals beyond royal courts to the papacy and limited papal controls in episcopal appointments.

[68] Cohn, "Church Property," pp. 158–63. For a case of an urban court deciding a tithe dispute, consider Brady, *Ruling Class*, p. 225.

April of 1525, in order to preserve his own rule and upon Martin
Luther's advice, Albrecht converted the Order's territory into the
duchy of Prussia, took personal possession of its properties, and
became himself a vassal of the Polish crown.[69] In May of that same
year the bishop of Samland, a close associate of the Grand Master-
turned-duke, who had been vexed by the neglect of infant baptism
in his diocese and who had preached against pilgrimages, indulgences, salvation by merit, and the mendicant orders since 1523,
transferred his temporal domain to the duke. In December the same
bishop implemented, with the bishop of Pomesanien, a church order
prescribing eucharistic communion by the laity in both kinds, bread
and cup, and elimiting the feastdays of saints.[70] This was a dramatic
instance of the convergence of secularization and Lutheran Reformation, to be sure, but uniquely so among the first Protestants.

Other early instances of explicitly evangelical attempts to control
bishoprics are relatively few, with mixed results. Elector Joachim II
of Brandenburg tried to move his son, also called Joachim, into the
bishoprics of Brandenburg and Havelberg, and in preparation saw
that the son passed through the lower grades of ordination.[71] The
elector finally forced him upon the Brandenburg cathedral chapter
in 1545, then tried to win papal confirmation. The son returned the
bishop's office to the cathedral chapter in 1560. The elector's grand-
son, the Margrave Joachim Friedrich, was appointed to the see of
Havelberg when he was a seven-year old child. The young appointee's
father, Johann Georg, then assumed the administration of the cathedral's temporal domain. When Johann Georg became elector, he
combined the cathedral's territory with his own. To the south of
Brandenburg, in the early 1540's, the Elector of Saxony tried and
ultimately failed to control the succession of the bishopric of Naumburg,

[69] Hartmut Boockmann, *Ostpreußen und Westpreußen*, v. 1 of *Deutsche Geschichte im Osten Europas* (Berlin: Siedler Verlag, 1992), pp. 231–46.
[70] Ibid. and *Urkundenbuch zur Reformationsgeschichte des Herzogthums Preußen*, ed. Paul Tschackert, 3 vols. (Osnabrück: Otto Zeller, 1965 reprint of the edition of 1890), 1:112, 2:120 nr. 356, for the bishopric of Samland's secularization. For the bishop of Samland's worry over declining baptisms, *Die Reformation im Ordensland Preussen 1523/24*, ed. Robert Stupperich (Ulm: Verlag Unser Weg, 1966), pp. 108–10. Biblical feastdays associated with the conception and birth of Christ (Mary's Puri-fication, Mary's Annunciation) and Pentecost were retained. Ibid., pp. 118–29.
[71] Gustav Abb, Gottfried Wentz, *Das Bistum Brandenburg* (Berlin: Walter De Gruyter, 1929), pp. 19–20; Gottfried Wentz, *Das Bistum Havelberg* (Berlin: Walter De Gruyter, 1933), pp. 27–8.

after a decade's conflict between the city and the bishop.[72] Such evangelical efforts to extend dynastic power into prince-bishoprics, which preoccupied imperial debates in the latter sixteenth century, were few and inconsequential in the first Protestant generation, when they also lacked uniform support from reformers. Luther and Melanchthon disapproved of Johann Friedrich's designs on Naumburg.[73]

To gain a bishopric, one traditionally installed relatives and/or otherwise strengthened the hold of a dynasty's network on the see. When Duke Moritz of Saxony moved on the bishopric of Merseburg in 1544 (this time Melancthon and Luther approved), it was through a canonical election by the cathedral chapter of his brother as administrator of the bishopric's territory, who then appointed Prince Georg III of Anhalt as spiritual "coadjutor."[74] Georg had entered the priesthood as a canon of Merseburg's cathedral in 1524, and quickly enjoyed a relatively succesful ecclesiastical career. He became the provost of the cathedral of Magdeburg that same year and occupied that office during the chapter's early resistance to the Old City Council's promotion of the new faith. He served as legal counsel to Archbishop Albrecht of Magdeburg in 1529. He became coregent of Anhalt-Dessau with his two brothers upon his mother's death in 1530. Soon after becoming prince, he embraced the new faith.[75] He was, in 1544, a prince with both strong regional ecclesiastical credentials and evangelical convictions. Duke Moritz had adapted the traditional tactic of moving a see's property interests closer to a dynasty's control while assigning spiritual roles to an auxiliary, who in this case also belonged to a regionally significant lineage himself.

---

[72] For the bishop and the city, which in 1532 installed evangelical preachers, changed the liturgy, removed altars and chalices, sold off prebends, and destroyed a church to build a cemetery with its masonry, see Sprenger, *Viglius von Aytta*, pp. 87–8, and for the subsequent complaint brought by the bishop of Freising, administrator of Naumburg, to the Imperial Chamber Court in 1537, see Sieglerschmidt, *Territorialstaat*, pp. 147–150. For the rest, Haug-Moritz, *Der Schmalkaldische Bund*, pp. 520–21; Wolgast, *Hochstift*, passim; Martin Heckel, "Das Problem der 'Säkularisation' in der Reformation," *Zur Säkularisation geistlicher Institutionen im 16. und im 18./19. Jahrhundert*, ed. Irene Crusius (Göttingen: Vandenhoeck und Ruprecht, 1996), p. 33.

[73] Estes, *Peace, Order and the Glory of God*, pp. 169–70.

[74] Estes, *Peace, Order and the Glory of God*, p. 170. May, *Die deutsche Bischöfe*, pp. 216–7.

[75] Friedrich Bautz, "Georg III der Gottselige," *Biographisch-Bibliographisches Kirchenlexikon*, 2:210–11.

These efforts foreshadowed future princely ambitions, but they show the early Protestants closer to a late medieval and Catholic world. Grand intrusions of state on the church were usually incremental and may or may not require a religious justification. Examples trickled down from the top of the political stratosphere. Emperor Charles V provided an extraodrinary model of encroachment by degrees, which he demonstrated through the course of his long rule in the Netherlands in many ways. In 1515, he won from the papacy the right to approve all abbatial appointments and another for nominees to benefices. In 1527, the right of nomination was extended to all Netherlandish cloisters, then again in 1530 to the appointment of coadjutors with a right of succession.[76] It proved difficult to limit the jurisdiction of ecclesiastical courts and influence appointments to canonries—though he tried.[77] To greater effect, the emperor revived a policy inaugurated by his great grandfather Charles the Bold requiring the amortization of church properties accumulated in Brabant since 1475; he quickly extended this requirement to at least six more of his Netherlands' provinces.[78] The papacy granted the emperor's brother, the archduke of Austria, a third of clergy incomes in 1523, which Ferdinand then saw partially extended to the Netherlands in 1524, while Charles sought a quarter of benefice incomes in all his domains for support of Ferdinand against the Turks. This failed, but Charles soon proposed, in 1529, that church properties be sold to finance the defense of Austria.[79] Margarete, the emperor's aunt and regent of the Netherlands, objected. But that same year the papacy granted Ferdinand the right to sell church properties to help pay for the cost of defense against the Turks, although Ferdinand did not avail himself of the privilege.[80] During Charles' reign in the Netherlands,

---

[76] This and the following is a brief and partial summary of the emperor's policies, as examined in detail by Jochen A. Fühner, *Die Kirchen- und die antireformatorische Religionspolitik Kaiser Karls V. In den siebzehn Provinzen der Niederlande, 1515–1555* (Leiden: E.J. Brill, 2004), pp. 89–165.

[77] Fühner, *Die Kirchen- und die antireformatorische Religionspolitik*, pp. 89–100, 144–5.

[78] Ibid., pp. 131–3.

[79] Ibid., pp. 135–6.

[80] *Legation Lorenzo Campeggios 1530–1531 und Nuntiatur Girolamo Aleandros 1531* part 1, supplementary volume 1 of *Nuntiaturberichte aus Deutschland, 1533–1559, nebst ergänzenden Aktenstücken,* (Tübingen: Max Neimeyer, 1963), p. 157 nr. 40 with n. 13–15. Campeggio, anxious to persuade Charles V to undertake a war against Luther's supporters, suggested to Rome in June 1531 that the campaign could be made more attractive by permitting him to fund the campaign with church property. Ibid., p. 253 nr. 71.

the papacy repeatedly granted the emperor a portion of benefice incomes (stipulated at 1/2 of the annual income of larger benefices in 1532 and after), while the emperor tried also to restrict the church's own property gains.[81] These privileges were resisted by the estates of Flanders, the church prelates of Brabant, and Premonstratensian abbots.[82] The goal was to increase control of revenues and nominations of ecclesiastical prelates. Conflicts over the right of nomination in Seeland, Luxemburg, Utrecht, and Artois were decided to imperial advantage, and throughout the Netherlands between 1519 and 1540 Charles' rights of nomination and appointment came to be generally acknowledged, as his coadjutors were gradually accepted.[83] Charles and his sister Maria of Hungary, who succeeded Margarete as regent of the Netherlands, also tried to influence the appointment of coadjutors to the archdioceses of Cologne (1534) and Trier (1546), part of which fell within Habsburg territory.[84] More drastically, Charles temporarily confiscated the property of the ten largest Flemish monastaries in a conflict over the succession of the abbot of St. Gertrude's in Louvain.[85] And when his candidate failed to win the see of Utrecht in 1524, the emperor soon forced the winning bishop to surrender the bishopric's temporal holdings and resign (the pretense was compensation for military support required for the Peasants' War), which the bishop did in 1528, upon the promise of an annual payment of 2,000 fl.[86] In 1529, Pope Clement VII ratified the arrangement, which fused the bishop of Utrecht's territory to that of Charles as Duke of Brabant and Count of Holland. Charles then nominated Willem van Enckenvoirt to the bishop's office, who for a decade had advocated Habsburg interests at Rome (the emperor had already helped him become the bishop of Tortosa and a cardinal in 1523).

---

[81] Fühner, *Die Kirchen- und die antireformatorische Religionspolitik*, pp. 134–151. The papal grant of benefice incomes in 1532 stipulated 1/2 the value of annual incomes of all Netherlandish benefices over 24 fl., 1/5 the value of benefices with 12–24 fl. incomes, and none of the income of benefices with less than 12 fl. annual income. Ibid., p. 138. Fühner notes that the necessary estimates of benefice incomes were not made until 1535. The same census was used in 1542/3 for another excise to help fund the emperor's Algerian campaign, and another at the occasion of the Schmalkald War.
[82] Fühner, *Die Kirchen- und die antireformatorische Religionspolitik*, pp. 152–8.
[83] Ibid., p. 108.
[84] Ibid., p. 127.
[85] Ibid., pp. 109–111.
[86] Ibid., pp. 118–120.

As to Utrecht's retired incumbent, the 2,000 were apparently never paid.[87] But the incremental control of nominations had strong effect. When the emperor resigned in 1556, he effectively controlled the bishoprics of Utrecht, Lüttich, Arras, Tournai, and Cambrai, and he was about to establish a new diocese under better Habsburg control out of part of the less maleable diocese of the bishop of Thérouanne.[88] That was a ruler who managed his churches.

Confiscations

As the Prussian duchy was being formed in the northeast corner of Europe, the Peasants' War approached its climax in central Germany. While the war distracted anyone who might have resisted the creation of the duchy,[89] it had another effect in the Empire at large. It accelerated lay designs on church dominion, not always by intention. The revolutionaries were not the perpetrators of this acceleration. For all that they destroyed or damaged, they entertained inconsistent ideas about church government, its prerogatives, and its established dominions. Most often they simply demanded the replacement of prince-bishops or cathedral canons, seldom the secularization of ecclesiastical lordships.[90] Their actions against church property were opportunistic, as in the Tauber Valley and at Wettringen, but opportunities seemed to multiply with the revolt. The most conspicuous of these were created by urban uprisings in several imperial cities. Among other things, the urban rebels imposed citizenship and its burdens on the monks and priests of their towns, as city councils had been trying to do for decades.[91] Yet no revolutionary posed an enduring threat to the properties and jurisdictions of the church. The spoils were temporary; the better part seem to have been moveable goods, not the long-term incomes that come from farmlands, rents, or tithes.

---

[87] The fact was published in *Warhafftige neuewe zeitung. Von den Krieg zwischen keyserlicher Maiestat, dem hauss von Burgundi, Stifft Utricht, und hertzog Karol von Gellern etc. Wie das ergangen und gehandelt worden bis auff natiuitatis Marie, des achten tags September An. etc. xxviii* (Constance: Johan Haselbergk, 1528).

[88] Fühner, *Die Kirchen- und die antireformatorische Religionspolitik*, p. 127.

[89] Boockmann, *Ostpreußen und Westpreußen*, p. 244.

[90] For this and the following, Wolgast, *Hochstift und Reformation*, pp. 61–68.

[91] Blickle, *Revolution of 1525*, pp. 113–14.

It was the *protectors* who posed the enduring threat to the material basis of the church, first because the mere possibility of violence invited cities and princes to take monastic lands into custody, not to secularize, but to preserve as custodians as an act of piety by *Obrigkeit*. What ruler would deny the obligation to hinder abuse of the church and support true religion? A ruler's threat to church property merely reflected the practical entanglement of laity and clergy in the church. Evangelical intrusions into religious affairs were variants on a recognized theme, and the mere fact of encroachment did not really distinguish the new church. As the fenceposts of Lutheran identity went up, the landscape of conversion must have looked like an undulating, bewildering landscape.

Let us consider a southern urban example of confiscation, a city that has been well studied but generally ignored in favor of more famous towns of the German southwest. The city of Breisach took over the properties of Marienau, a Cistercian women's cloister, during the Peasants' War.[92] As in many cities (for example, Nürnberg, Memmingen, Ulm, Esslingen, Wismar, Halberstadt, Magdeburg, and Bremen), by the time the revolt began, evangelical preachers had already aroused tensions between sympathetic citizens and the city council. Monks in city cloisters began to abandon their vocations (by 1526 only two monks and one novice were left in the monastery of Augustinian Hermits at Breisach), and nuns at Marienau began to do the same. This had been happening all over Germany. The convention of imperial cities at Ulm in 1524, in answer to a request from Memmingen, advocated the inventory of monastery properties in such cases.[93] Now the Habsburg government of Anterior Austria in Ensisheim (it administered the western Habsburg domains in the Franche Comté, Alsace, and the southwest corner of Germany) allowed the city of Breisach to inventory and administer the property of the Augustinians until the monastery could be reestablished. Then the war intervened.

In the spring of 1525, facing an army of rebels, the council made a pact with the revolutionaries to prevent passage of an opposing army. Soon after the contract had been made, an opposing army appeared, from the city of Freiburg, with whom Breisach had a prior

---

[92] Berent Schwineköper, "Klosteraufhebungen als Folge von Reformation und Bauernkrieg im habsburgischen Vorderösterreich," *Zeitschrift des Breisgau-Geschichtsvereins* 97 (1978): 61–78.

[93] Schlenck, *Die Reichsstadt Memmingen und die Reformation*, p. 39.

treaty guaranteeing mutual aid. Breisach blocked passage across the
Rhine, which hindered the Freiburg troops from confronting the
rebels. As it happened, Freiburg had earlier taken the same approach
with the rebels, making a similar pact with them after a six-day
seige.[94] When the threat had passed, Freiburg abandoned the rebel
agreement and supported the archduke of Austria. It is easy to imagine how Breisach got caught in the rapidly shifting fortunes of the
war. We might call it today a failure of intelligence. Freiburg later
claimed that Breisach had turned Lutheran, which the Breisach council adamantly denied. How could they not make a treaty of opportunity? The Austrian government in Ensisheim could offer Breisach
no defensive aid. It seemed necessary for a time to risk offending
the Habsburgs.

During the revolt, the Breisach city council had Marienau destroyed
and the convent dissolved—it claimed for purposes of defense—without the permission of the archduke Ferdinand, the Habsburg high
bailiff, or the regime at Ensisheim (other cities, for example Worms
and Strasbourg, did the same during the revolt).[95] After the war,
neighboring cities brokered an agreement between Freiburg and
Breisach, but then complaints against Breisach arrived, first in 1527
from monastery donors who claimed that Archduke Ferdinand, not
Breisach, held lordship over Marienau, and Breisach's actions were
therefore illegal. In the meanwhile, the city took over administration
of Marienau's properties, used monastery incomes to pay fines imposed
for its breach of treaty, and gave stipends from cloister property to
the cloister's nuns. The Habsburg regime's response to these actions
was equivocal: in 1529, it froze the monastery's property, which
Breisach conveniently took as permission to use it for limited ends.

Conversion was not supposed to be like this, tentative about doctrine, built upon an excuse. It was supposed to occur by evangelical teaching, carried by the breeze of the Holy Spirit, converting
monks and priests into gospel preachers, then through their ministry
liberating people from the fear of God's judgment and the burdens

---

[94] Scott and Scribner, *German Peasants' War*, pp. 187–89 nr. 73–74.
[95] So, too, had Cologne in 1474, Breslau in 1529, and Hannover in 1534, all
without the permission of ecclesiastical authorities. Störmann, *Die städtische Gravamina*,
pp. 106–7. Störmann noted a few scattered examples of destruction of church property with permission, ibid., pp. 105–6.

of superstition. According to the reformers' plan, monasteries would either become evangelical base camps or simply fade away. Martin Luther and his Wittenberg associates believed in this, and it seemed to work. By the time the Elector of Saxony sequestered the monastic properties of his lands, in 1531, cloisters had been depleted of their personnel by years of such Lutheran preaching. Electoral Saxony experienced a tame confiscation, one that came after sermons had the intended effect of monastic attrition. A prince or city could thus claim simply to protect empty monasteries, giving assurances that the property will continue to serve a religious purpose of some kind.

Not Breisach. The revolt of 1525 forced it to reconsider the management of monastic property with no sure conversion in the usual, preacherly sense. Not just cities did this, and again, sympathy for Luther was irrelevant. Dynasties large and small alike tried to use the events of 1525 to infringe on holdings of prince-bishops. Count Wilhelm IV of Henneberg moved against Würzburg, just as Philip of Hesse moved against Hersfeld and Fulda; Archduke Ferdinand and the Tyrolean estates took over the prince-bishop of Brixen's territory in a kind of provisional secularization; and Archduke Ferdinand and the dukes of Bavaria moved against Salzburg.[96] Most acquisitions were returned after the war, but not all, and was this required? Of course, evangelical doctrine could help justify the retention of assets, but its role was optional and sometimes inconclusive. The house of the Brethren of the Common Life at Münster was saved from destruction by the protective custody of the city council in the Peasants' War.[97] But after the fall of the Anabaptist regime and the restoration of Catholicism in 1535, the house failed to recover a large part of its properties.[98] The new faith did not enter into it. Nürnberg, which accomplished a near total evangelical conversion of the urban church in 1525, was dragged into litigation over properties taken into protective custody during the uprising.[99] Hesse, whose young and ambitious Landgrave Philip aspired, at the very least, to be a very influential prince among the imperial estates, embraced

---

[96] Wolgast, *Hochstift und Reformation*, pp. 66–67. For Hersfeld and Fulda, Breul-Kunkel, *Herrschaftskrise und Reformation*, pp. 248–304.

[97] Hinz, *Die Brüder vom Gemeinsamen Leben*, p. 55.

[98] Ibid., pp. 225–7.

[99] Gunter Zimmermann, *Prediger der Freiheit. Andreas Osiander und der Nürnberger Rat 1522–1548* (Mannheim: Palatium, 1999), p. 179 n. 100 for two cases.

evangelical teaching the year before the revolt, acted like a good Catholic guardian during the war, and began a systematic program of confiscation and ecclesiastical reorganization within two years after. These were his actions during the war: he conducted an inventory of monasteries in his realm, following the advice of the Swabian League, and he prevented the cities of Fulda and Schmalkalden from forming treaties of opportunity with rebels. His prophylactic moves at Fulda and Schmalkalden encouraged other cities to resist the peasants when they came, as the city of Eisenach did soon after.[100] Once Eisenach was secured, the Landgrave joined forces with Duke Georg of Saxony to make of Mühlhausen another example for the cities of Thuringia. We may be sure that he was evangelical a year earlier, but these deeds as such did not identify him as one. His interventions hardly differ from actions by Catholic estates.

The war was followed by a brief season of liberal, if not promiscuous speculation among the church's just-exercised guardians, some of it by evangelicals, some of it not. Such a climate had not been known since the Council of Basel, nearly a century before. We cannot fully understand the implications of these ideas until the revolt's consequences for property are more fully known. But the speculation reveals how climactic the war seemed in its aftermath, as an event that demanded the reconsideration of church property. When the Imperial Diet met at Speyer in 1526, the Large Committee, formed by the emperor to treat peasant grievances, blamed Rome for the recent Peasants' Revolt and recommended the confiscation of benefices reserved to the pope.[101] The Diet did not agree to confiscate papal reservations. Again, the emperor called on the estates, in the name of the protection of religion, to execute the ban pronounced against Martin Luther at the Diet of Worms in 1521. Most of the princes agreed that there should be no innovations in reli-

---

[100] Richard Andrew Cahill, *Philipp of Hesse and the Reformation* (Mainz: Philipp von Zabern, 2001), pp. 91, 99–108, 117, 169. Other princes who did the same included Duke Ernst of Lüneburg and Casimir the margrave of Ansbach. Duke Ernst had earlier, in 1523 and following the example of Brandenburg, taxed his prelates, and would tax cloisters again in 1526. Casimir inventoried monastic properties and revoked clerical tax and juridical exemptions. Dieter Brosius, "Die lüneburgischen Klöster in der Reformation," *Reformation vor 450 Jahren. Eine Lüneburgische Gedenkschrift*, ed. G. Körner (Lüneburg: Museumsverein für das Fürstentum Lüneburg, 1980), pp. 95–111, here 98. C. Scott Dixon, *The Reformation in Rural Society. The Parishes of Brandenburg-Ansbach-Kulmbach* (Cambridge University Press, 1996), pp. 21, 23.

[101] Blickle, *Revolution of 1525*, pp. 165–66.

gion but an end to religious malpractice, after which, they said, the problem with the Edict of Worms would resolve itself.[102]

There circulated proposals for a reorganization of church dominions. One was composed by Johann von Schwarzenberg, a Franconian knight in the service of the bishop of Bamberg. A renowned legal advisor, he had written a criminal code for Charles V in 1521, which went into effect in 1532 and remained in effect for nearly 300 years, until the end of the Holy Roman Empire in 1803. Schwarzenberg's evangelical sympathies were displayed in November 1524, when he withdrew his daughter from a Bamberg nunnery. Andreas Osiander, the firebrand preacher of Nürnberg's church of St. Lorenz, published Schwarzenberg's letter to the bishop defending his action.[103] In 1525, as *Landhofmeister* at the court of Margrave Casimir in the city of Ansbach, and with the support of the Ansbach chancellor, Georg Vogler, he prepared a recommendation for the Diet called to meet at Augsburg that year (its business was postponed to the Imperial Diet at Speyer in 1526). The recommendation was never presented nor discussed at the Diet.[104] If not representative of that tribunal's deliberations, it nevertheless shows us how in 1525 a significant, intelligent participant in events did think.

Three years later, after Casimir's brother Georg assumed the Brandenburg rule of Ansbach-Kulmbach, Schwarzenberg would coordinate, with the city of Nürnberg's own visitation, the visitation of the territories' cloisters that initiated evangelical conversion there, and in 1529, Johannes Brenz wrote a new cloister-ordinance for the margrave.[105] But in 1525, Margrave Casimir's confiscation of monastic property during the Peasants' Revolt likely inspired Schwarzenberg. Schwarzenberg formulated his advice (*Rathschlag*) as a scheme to

---

[102] Kohnle, *Reichstag und Reformation*, pp. 260–71.

[103] Jürgen Lorz, *Das reformatorische Wirken Dr. Wenzeslaus Lincks in Altenburg und Nürnberg (1523–1547)* (Nürnberg: Stadtarchiv Nürnberg, 1975), p. 152.

[104] *Rathschlag, was man mit geistlichen Gütern zu Gemeinen und des Reichs Nutz fürnemen und handeln solle*, in *Nützliche Sammlung verschiedener meistens ungedruckter Schrifften, Berichte, Urkunden, Briefe, Bedencken*, ed. Christian Gottlieb Buder (Frankfurt and Leipzig: Christian Heinrich Cuno, 1735), pp. 31–37. See also Wolgast, *Hochstift und Reformation*, pp. 69–71.

[105] Osiander, *Gesamtausgabe*, 3:123–5, 230–1 n. 35. The extent of the city council's right to confiscate cloisters was debated at Nürnberg in 1524 and 1525, with the council members favoring the more moderate view (install preachers, wait for attrition, take empty monasteries). Ibid., 1:350–51, 2:148–60. For Brenz, Brecht, Ehmer, *Südwestdeutsche Reformationsgeschichte*, p. 154.

restore security and order in the Empire. He proposed a drastic reduction of clergy, to the mere number of those who performed pastoral ministry (no other clergy should be granted entrance to cities), and he called for the emergency confiscation of most monasteries and their properties, on the grounds that gifts to the church should serve the purpose of their donors, to honor God. Only two or three cloisters should be left in each of the proposed six regions of the Empire to care for daughters of the nobility, who would remain free to leave at will.

Schwarzenberg was not alone. Cities at the June 1526 diet of estates of the duchy of Württemberg proposed the confiscation of church properties to relieve debts incurred during the war.[106] Michael Ott von Echterdingen, imperial Master of Ordnance, in the introduction to his *Kriegsbuch* (*The Book of War*) proposed a church entirely run by a fraternity of veteran noblemen. Most church incomes would be diverted to support reorganized imperial armies, and church livings would be restricted to a reduced number of clergy who provide pastoral care.[107] The reduction of clergy is exactly what later happened when Protestant rulers suppressed Catholicism.[108] Hundreds of kilometers from the nearest rebellion in the Peasants' War (the urban rebellion at Görlitz, which itself was a revolt of opportunity and more than a hundred kilometers from the easternmost peasant armies in Saxony) another proposal was made. Johann Lohmüller, secretary to the free city of Riga in the state of the Teutonic Order, published a plan to carve a new state out of the holdings of the Teutonic Order, the archbishopric of Riga, and the bishoprics of Dorpat, Ösel-Wiek, and Kurland.[109] In Habsburg-ruled Württemberg, after the suppression of the Peasants' Revolt by the Swabian League in May 1525, the nobility of the principality's diet proposed the dissolution of most cloisters, the reduction of clerical benefices, and the future adminstration of the freed properties and benefices by the territorial nobility.[110] The Archduke Ferdinand, who received Württemberg

---

[106] Brecht, Ehmer, *Südwestdeutsche Reformationsgeschichte*, pp. 110–111.

[107] Wolgast, *Hochstift und Reformation*, pp. 71–72.

[108] For example, in the collegiate Church of the Holy Spirit in Stuttgart, the leading church of the territory of Württemberg, 40 canons, vicars, altarists, and chaplains were reduced to two preachers and two deacons. Auge, *Stiftsbiographien*, p. 97.

[109] Wolgast, *Hochstift und Reformation*, pp. 68–69.

[110] Werner-Ulrich Deetjen, *Studien zur Württembergischen Kirchenordnung Herzog Ulrichs 1534–1550* (Stuttgart: Calwer Verlag, 1981), p. 18.

with Austria in 1521, when his brother Emperor Charles V appointed him archduke, rejected the proposal, but he did impose an immunity-busting clergy-tax. The revolt inspired, in some cases required, reexamination of the church's rights. Or rather, the exercise of protective custody during the war suggested the reorganization of church property.

The first large-scale Protestant confiscation of church properties drifted along this postwar stream. Philip of Hesse was the vanguard of aggressive confiscators.[111] He acted as a prince opposed to religious malpractice, as it was defined by evangelical preachers and publicized at the so-called Synod of Homberg in the autumn of 1526. The synod was an assembly of two or three representatives from each cloister and the rectors and priests serving urban parishes in his lands.[112] There he staged a debate between a former friar, François Lambert, and the guardian of the Observant Franciscan cloister at Marburg, Nikolaus Ferber. Lambert had been an Observant Franciscan himself at Avignon. He had earlier risen to the office of apostolic preacher in France but converted to Protestantism in Switzerland. He came to the Landgrave's court just after the Diet of Speyer, at the recommendation of the Strasbourg magistrate, Jacob Sturm.[113] When the proceedings at Homberg opened, the Landgrave's chancellor, Johann Feige, noted Philip's obligation to reform the church. The synod was called by a layman, not a bishop, but Feige claimed it was tacitly approved by the recently concluded recess of the Diet of Speyer.[114] Lambert attacked the usual suspects—the Latin

---

[111] David Bruce Miller, "The Dissolution of the Religious Houses of Hesse During the Reformation," Ph.D. Dissertation, Yale University, 1971, pp. 116–38. See also Cahill, *Philipp of Hesse*.

[112] Cahill, *Philipp of Hesse*, pp. 152–167. The synod was called for 20 October. The summons to the Augustinians of Eschwege is dated 5 October. Schilling, *Klöster und Mönche*, p. 186.

[113] For this and the following, Schilling, *Klöster und Mönche*, pp. 188–99, 201–2. For Lambert, Oskar Hütteroth and Hilmar Milbradt, *Die althessischen Pfarrer der Reformationszeit*, (Marburg N.G. Elwert, 1966), pp. 196–7.

[114] Cahill, *Philipp of Hesse*, p. 159. The recess of the Diet allowed the estates to implement or not implement the Worms Edict condemning Luther and his supporters at the discretion of their own consciences before God and emperor: "jeder Stand möge sich so verhalten, wie er es gegen Gott und kaiserliche Majestät hoffe und wisse zu verantworten." Johannes Schilling, *Klöster und Mönche in der hessischen Reformation* (Gütersloh: Gütersloher Verlags-Haus, 1997), pp. 183–84. Rainer Wohlfeil, Hans-Jürgen Goertz, *Gewissensfreiheit als Bedingung der Neuzeit: Fragen an die Speyerer Protestation von 1529* (Göttingen: Vandenhoeck & Ruprecht, 1980). Cahill, *Philipp of Hesse*, p. 149. Philip and his publicists would later appeal to this decision time and

mass, votive masses, prayer to the saints, and also monasticism.[115] His attack had the effect of announcing the Landgrave's designs on the church of the territory. Another disputation was held in January 1527 at Marburg, and it marked the beginning of confiscations.[116] A month later, the appointment of monastery stewards began: they gave the Landgrave control of all cloister business. In October 1527, Philip published a new law on monastic-property. It stipulated that 1) those who wanted to stay in monasteries might do so, 2) two cloisters were to be converted into schools for noble children, and a common chest was to be established to support needy nobility, while thirty noblemen would receive incomes of fruit and grain so that they may retain arms and serve the state, 3) cloister property was to be used to fund the new university at Marburg (it had opened earlier that year, on 30 May), and 4) the remaining property was to fund a common chest kept by two princely council members, two noblemen, and two urban representatives.[117] Those who left monasteries were asked to sign a document admitting that their vows contradict the gospel, they accept an annual stipend from the Landgrave, and they renounce claims to whatever property they had brought

---

again, most significantly when, in July of 1528, he won from the electors of Mainz, Trier, and the Palatinate and the representatives of Archduke Ferdinand the concession to control ecclesiastical matters in his territories until a general church council should occur or a settlement be reached. Cahill, *Philipp of Hesse*, p. 152.

[115] Schilling, *Klöster und Mönche*, p. 206. Cf. Cahill, p. 160. Ferber was reluctant to concede anything to Lambert, insisting on the traditional prerogatives of monasticism, poverty, the right to beg and not work (clergy in general, says Ferber in paragraphs 273–4, are not required to perform manual labor). When Lambert notes that "the hording of those who possess is the thing most prohibited by the Word of God" (*Possidentium thesaurizatio est ea quae maxime dei verbo est interdicta*, paragraphs 279–83), Ferber grants that he, too, is against hording, for the gospels teach that the kingdom of God has priority, and riches should be dispensed to the poor. He does not excuse the avarice of those who horde pensions, prebends, priorships, deanships, or other like things. But monasteries choose leaders (*primares*) to dispense their property. Princes and magistrates cannot confiscate monasteries and their incomes. Nikolaus Ferber, *Assertiones trecentae ac vigintisex fratris*, (Cologne 1526), Flugschriften des frühen 16. Jahrhunderts, Fiche 37, nr. 103.

[116] Schilling, *Klöster und Mönche*, p. 206.

[117] Schilling, *Klöster und Mönche*, pp. 208–9, 223. The historical basis for the use of monasteries as schools was first asserted in Wittenberg at the end of 1521, in the recommendation written by Andreas Bodenstein von Karlstadt and signed by university theologians, including Justus Jonas, Melanchthon, and Nicolaus Amsdorf, to the Elector near the beginning of the unrest over monasteries and the mass in the city. CR 1:493–510. Hermann Barge, *Andreas Bodenstein von Karlstadt* 2 vols. (Leipzig: Friedrich Brandstetter, 1905), 1:344–5.

into the cloister.[118] The thorough organization of Philip's monastic reforms seemed aggressive enough, but Philip was taken, with the more patient Elector of Saxony, as an example of monastic reform by attrition caused by evangelical preaching and conversion.[119]

Erratic Conversion

In many places, the Peasants' War launched, directly or indirectly, an erratic process of conversion. A good example is the Cistercian monastery of Heilsbronn in the south-Franconian territory of Ansbach-Kulmbach, whose conversion has recently been analyzed by Manfred Sitzmann. Heilsbronn was a noble foundation set-up by counts of Abenberg centuries earlier.[120] It later received imperial privileges, which allowed the monastery to claim the freedoms of an imperial monastery. The counts of Abenberg were succeeded by the Hohenzollern. The Hohenzollern controlled the surrounding territory of Ansbach and the nearby territory to the north, Kulmbach. Over the course of the fourteenth and fifteenth centuries, the city of Nürnberg distended itself squarely between these two Hohenzollern territories.[121] By the beginning of the sixteenth century, it was a city-state some thirty kilometers in diameter. When the emperor Sigismund enfiefed the Hohenzollern Friedrich II (he was the brother of Albrecht Achilles) with the Mark Brandenburg and its electorate in 1415, Ansbach and Kulmbach, flanking Nürnberg on the south and north, were united to that distant northeastern land. The monastery won guarantees of its imperial freedoms from Emperor Sigismund. Its privileges were to continue to enjoy protection by imperial burgraves. But the Hohenzollern margraves simply ignored the renewed privileges. Albrecht Achilles separated Ansbach and Kulmbach from Brandenburg after he was made elector in 1473. At his death in 1486, the three territories were divided among three sons, but at the beginning of the

---

[118] Schilling, *Klöster und Mönche*, pp. 220–21.

[119] For example, in Ansbach. See Osiander, *Gesamtausgabe*, 3:230–31. See also Cohn, "Church Property," p. 165.

[120] Sitzmann, *Mönchtum und Reformation*, pp. 80–170.

[121] For urban territorial expansion in general, see Tom Scott, "Town and Country in Germany, 1350–1600," *Town and Country in Europe, 1300–1800*, edited by S.R. Epstein (Cambridge University Press, 2001), pp. 203–228.

evangelical movement, the eldest son, Casimir, ruled both Ansbach and Kulmbach, until his death in 1527, when his brother Georg, called the Pious, succeeded him.[122] The margrave of Ansbach-Kulmbach continued to treat Heilsbronn as a noble foundation. The reformation of the cloister in the 1530's culminated the erosion of the monastery's independence at the hands of the Hohenzollern for over two hundred years. That process of eroding independence was completed in 1539, when Margrave Georg of Ansbach-Kulmbach published a promise of protection that enshrined the Hohenzollern claim in territorial law.[123] Yet the transformation of the monastery remained incomplete. How did the Protestant faith fit into the process?

In Ansbach-Kulmbach, the reformation began in 1524 with the sermons of Heilsbronn's prior, Johannes Schopper, who taught the doctrine of Luther's 1521 treatise *On Monastic Vows*. Schopper preached that all Christians stand under the one eternal vow made in baptism, and that vow alone is irrevocable.[124] The monastic vows of chastity, poverty, and obedience cannot, he argued, be perpetually binding. Schopper would soon prove himself an ambiguous reformer. But after he published this view, fourteen monks slipped away under the cover of night. The Peasants' Revolt then provided a catalyst for a wave of margravial intrusions. In April 1525, the territorial diet attempted to install evangelical preachers in the monastery. Schopper's abbot sought protection from Margrave Casimir. There followed a margravial inventory, the creation of a margravial office to oversee the monastery's affairs, and the confiscation of some liturgical and precious objects (Casimir did the same in other cloisters and foundations).[125] Casimir first used the proceeds to allay the expense of the war. The number of monks dwindled by mid-summer to a mere three, one of whom was prior Schopper. An August 1525 invitation welcomed runaways to return, with a quasi-evangelical proviso that they were no longer bound to wear the Cistercian habit. The abbot was made the margrave's temporary bailiff for the Waizendorf dis-

---

[122] Bruno Gebhardt, *Handbuch der deutschen Geschichte*, 4 vols, 8th rev. ed., 2nd improved impression, edited by Herbert Grundmann (Stuttgart: Union Verlag, 1958), 2:502. A Protestant state would only be definitively and thoroughly created in Ansbach-Kulmbach after that time, during the reign of Georg Friedrich. Dixon, *Reformation and Rural Society*, pp. 1–5, 51–54.

[123] Sitzmann, *Mönchtum und Reformation*, pp. 80–86.

[124] For this and the following, ibid., pp. 96–99.

[125] For the other cloisters, ibid., p. 32. For later inventories, pp. 51, 55.

trict and a member of the margravial council.[126] But the process of religious change had hardly begun.

In September 1525, Margrave Casimir codified the new arrangement in an ordinance for the cloisters of his realm. He claimed the authority to regulate the return of monks and limit monastery personnel. He tried to limit monastic participation in trade, and he ordered monks to wear the costume of secular clergy. These measures made no appeal to Protestant doctrine. Casimir acted as a Catholic, and in 1529 the order was approved by Pope Clement VII.[127]

He had special plans for Heilsbronn. He wanted to convert it into a collegiate church, which would reduce the monks to benefices under his patronage while he took possession of the monastery's lands. The monks worried. Prior Schopper wondered whether the oppressive terms of the anonymous fifteenth-century reform treatise, the *Reformation of the Emperor Sigismund*, would be imposed on them. He might leave, he noted, if Rome would allow it, if he had any promise of financial security in secular life and if he had no responsibilities for the convent.[128] The monks were divided. One group advocated the cloister's restructuring, another endorsed the margrave's takeover of incomes, another wanted to wait for papal or imperial direction, and yet another wanted to wait for instructions from the next Imperial Diet. But Schopper rallied them around the margrave's plan by the end of the year.[129] Before winter set in, the monastery sent Casimir a delegation to negotiate the details of the restructure. Posing as protector of the monks, the margrave insisted again that the seizure was for their benefit. He guaranteed the cloister's rights to nominate to their benefices, yet asked for a list of nominees. And he wanted to limit the number of canons to twenty-four. He wanted papal approval and imperial confirmation of the reorganized foundation. The monks agreed to it all and formed a commission of seven to negotiate benefice incomes, but they worried that the margrave would impose his own nominees. Casimir ignored this. He answered that he would protect them from the nobility, and he would petition the imperial governor, the Archduke Ferdinand of Austria, to approve the restructure.

---

[126] Ibid., pp. 102–106.
[127] Ibid., pp. 105–6.
[128] Ibid., pp. 106–11 on the conversion to a collegiate foundation, and for Schopper's protocol, which records the following, p. 108.
[129] Ibid., p. 109 for this and the following.

Pope Clement VII approved the reform in 1529, together with Casimir's church order (note 127, above). But in the monastery, little had changed. When Georg the Pious succeeded his brother Casimir in 1527 (a third brother, Albrecht, was the first duke of Prussia we encountered before),[130] he found the monks still in control of many of their properties. And in spite of its reorganization, the monastery continued to regard itself as Cistercian, for when Abbot Wenk chose to step down, in early 1529, the election of his successor took place in the traditional Cistercian manner, under the supervision of the abbot of Erbach and free of margravial interference. Prior Schopper, sympathetic to Luther's doctrine in at least some respects, as we have seen, was elected to replace Wenk.[131] Schopper may have helped the new margrave, Georg, to inventory and confiscate church assets in 1529–1530. But when in 1530 Heilsbronn was included in a special margravial tax, Schopper acted as an abbot traditionally would. He tried to postpone the tax and complained about their poverty, driven into debt by the cost of hospitality, building maintenance, vineyards, and draw-horses, with exactions for the imperial Turkish campaign on the way (that same year the margrave confiscated gems and precious metal from churches and chapels of his realm raising some 24,000 fl. from silver alone).[132] The margrave's response was likewise traditional. He guaranteed the cloister's freedoms, said it was a temporary exaction, and in the following year imposed a tax yet again.[133] The tax was repeated in 1532, 1534, and 1539. In 1534, Schopper passed the tax on to the cloister's small holders as an indirect excise on wine and beer.

Change did not *require* Lutheran teaching. Lutheran teaching did not change everything. A monastic prelate, whatever his or her sympathies, would naturally resist interference, and this left Heilsbronn's conversion a somewhat ambiguous affair, even as it seemed to take firmer shape. On 1 March 1533, a new church order for Ansbach-Kulmbach was published in concert with the city of Nürnberg, which had been trying to promote Protestantism among its neighbors.[134] It

---

[130] In the previous section of this chapter.
[131] Sitzmann, *Mönchtum und Reformation*, pp. 111–12 for this and the following.
[132] Erich Freiherr von Guttenberg, *Das Bistum Bamberg* (Berlin: Walter De Gruyter, 1937), p. 90.
[133] Sitzmann, *Mönchtum und Reformation*, pp. 119, 121, 123.
[134] Ibid., pp. 113–14.

is known as the Brandenburg-Nürnberg Church Order. The order imposed modest reforms on the entire margraviate, all the parishes, foundations, and cloisters included, but the centerpiece of monastic spirituality remained—the daily prayer liturgy of the divine office. In October, Johann Rurer and Andreas Althamer wrote a more thorough reform, at the request of the monastery of St. Gumbert in Ansbach and with Heilsbronn's support. Priors and prioresses of the realm did not know what to do with it. Abbot Schopper, responding to inquiries from Langenzenn and the Cistercian nuns of Frauental and Birkenbelf, tepidly suggested that most churches used it, and he would not advise them against the prince. But at Heilsbronn, they were still using the Cistercian liturgy.

A margravial visitation of 1536 intended to force the implementation of the new order. Heilsbronn responded by complaining: about the loss of incomes from properties in the territories of the bishops of Bamberg and Würzburg, outside Hohenzollern jurisdiction, and about the requirement of margravial approval of new cloister members. The margrave insisted on his good intentions and assumed for the first time an obviously evangelical tone. He imposed a changed liturgy, ended private masses, truncated the divine office, and turned it into public prayer that included laity. There was a Lutheran eucharistic liturgy, eliminating the offertory and canon in public masses, the liturgical portions that made the mass a priestly sacrifice. Intercessory prayers stopped. A strict discipline was imposed on the monks. No new members could be admitted to the monastery.[135] Eleven years after the first reforms, the eventual death of the monastery was planned.

But the monastery survived for another three decades in this Lutheran form. There was some tension between the old and the new. When the abbot took a wife in 1543, the monks worried over what the new heiress would claim at the abbot's death, and they insisted she live outside the cloister on a monastery farm. Margrave Georg, who still did not control all the monastery's properties, took another inventory, planned for the abbot to move out with his wife, ordered margravial counselors and the monks to negotiate an annual provision for the abbot, demanded that the abbot return cloister property that he had removed to Nürnberg, determined that he

---

[135] Ibid., pp. 116–19.

remain in the margrave's service, and appointed the prior and a judge as administrators of cloister property. These moves only raised new fears. The convent worried, to the margrave, that without an abbot (unheard of in the Cistercian order, they said) they would not be able to maintain their properties and incomes, especially in foreign places (Würzburg, Eichstätt, the county of Oettingen, the imperial cities of Nürnberg, Nördlingen, Windsheim, etc.). They wanted therefore to elect a successor within eight or ten days who could be confirmed by the papal legate currently at Nürnberg. Eventually they did elect a successor, a year and a half later, with the support of the officer and counselors of margrave Albrecht Alcibiades, the son of Casimir, who inherited the lands of Kulmbach in 1541.

Albrecht was a Catholic who in 1543 entered the military service of emperor Charles V (he served as a cavalry commander in France and would soon participate in the Schmalkald War on the emperor's side). He was now enlisted to mediate an understanding on the new abbatial election with the counselors of margrave Georg.[136] An understanding was reached, and Georg Greulich was made abbot, to serve for four years, ending a twenty-month vacancy.[137]

By now, Heilsbronn comprised some kind of liminal monasticism, such as a collegiate church might accommodate. After the defeat of the League of Schmalkalden in 1547, it must have been relatively easy to return the cloister to some of the Catholic practices that had slipped away. The tonsure returned in February 1549, for the first time since the Peasants' Revolt, along with the Cistercian habit; the restriction on new recruits was removed; and new monks came from Ebrach, Langheim, and Bildhausen. Private masses and prayer to the saints resumed, as did regular contact with other Cistercian monasteries. After the Peace of Augsburg in 1555, Margrave Georg Friedrich subjected the cloister to an evangelical church order again. The membership quickly dwindled from four monks to one, until the last member of the cloister, Prior Melchior Wunder, died in 1578. His death finally allowed the margrave to take complete control of the cloister's holdings, and the building was made into a school.[138]

---

[136] Albrecht would later prove a "scourge of the Lutheran moralists." Dixon, *Reformation and Rural Society*, pp. 50–51.

[137] Sitzmann, *Mönchthum und Reformation*, 124–28.

[138] Ibid., pp. 128–41. Dixon, *Reformation and Rural Society*, pp. 51–52 for Protestant church order in general.

It had endured fifty years of reform. Through both Catholic restructuring and Protestant conversion to an evangelical monastery, which
happened simultaneously, the cloister never ceased to be known as
an old Cistercian foundation.

Confiscations of monasteries of the old, richer orders left cities at
a clear disadvantage. Like Heilsbronn, the city of Breisach and the
case of Marienau show us how this handicap might be overcome,
by a stubborness that exceeded the competition. Breisach destroyed
the cloister and confiscated its properties during the Peasants' War.
After the revolt of 1525, the city was sued before a variety of courts
with actual or potential jurisdiction.[139] There was a suit before the
Habsburg government in Innsbruck, and the bishop of Constance
received another complaint from the bailiff. There was a suit in 1532
from the abbot of the Cistercian cloister at Lützel, who tried to claim
the Marienau property, which claim the Cistercian order approved
in 1536. It came before the subdelegate papal judge in Altkirch, but
in Altkirch the Habsburg government contested Lützel's claim and
demanded that Breisach account for Marienau property and its use
(1537). The city responded with a petition to use Marienau incomes
to renovate the city's hospital and public works. Maximilian I had,
decades before, promised in his will to fund such a renovation, but
the will's provision was never executed. Either way, the city refused
to surrender account books to any authority less than King Ferdinand.
In 1539, the Austrian court council finally conceded Breisach's use
of cloister incomes until a resolution of the religious controversy in
a church council or otherwise. In 1544, Lützel tried again. The
Austrian government in Ensisheim ordered the rebuilding of the
monastery instead, to no effect. The Edict of Restitution of 1629
was also of no consequence. The monastery was never restored.

In other words, Breisach managed to control the property without Habsburg or any other approval. The sheer intricacy of Marienau
property claims may have aided the city's resistance. So, for example,
after the Marienau abbess left the cloister on the strength of a papal
privilege, married, was widowed, and remarried—all before the
Kirchenräuberkrieg, the "church robber war" of 1525 and Breisach's
confiscation—the city handled claims related to her for over a decade
after Marienau was dissolved. In 1538, her widower from the last

---

[139] Schwineköper, "Klosteraufhebungen," pp. 61–78 and passim for this and the
following.

marriage sought the dowry she long ago brought to the cloister when she took her vows. In 1540, the abbot of Lützel tried to win it, too. By then the widower, Diepold Walter, had, after the former abbess's death, also remarried. Diepold himself died, and in 1543, his widow by that subsequent marriage received from Breisach a settlement from the former abbess's estate. The property of a gone cloister could enter a kind of limbo. No general, Protestant dis-qualification of monasticism, much less anything resembling a proto-nationalization of the church, nullified the legal force of the abbess's dowry, her action, or the subsequent claims built upon it. Nor did Protestantism bring Breisach the cloister's incomes. The city simply took them over and got away with it.

Near-Total Conversion

Opportunity and persistence were the main ingredients of secular-ization in Heilsbronn and Breisach. They were equally present in the most dramatic example of Protestant confiscation, which occurred in the duchy of Württemberg. Ulrich, its exiled duke, had witnessed the reformation of Hesse at the Landgrave's court. Within two years of his restoration in 1534, he carried out a spectacular confiscation of nearly all the monasteries in his lands. He imposed taxes, seized documents, and diverted incomes to his treasury, monastery by monastery.[140] He lacked the pretext of emergency created by the Peasants' Revolt. His program was not designed around a concept of evangelical freedom, which required a two-stage approach: the installment of preachers, then at least some time to let the gospel deplete the ranks of monks or nuns. He simply took inventories, established accounts, appointed officers, and took over the manage-ment of monastic property. Although a portion of benefices went to secure incomes for evangelical pastors, most of the money simply disappeared into the ducal treasury and from there into the hands of his creditors, which included the Catholic archduke of Austria. Let us consider his process.

It is well known that Ulrich had a troubled reputation. The Swabian League, with Habsburg support, had removed him from Württemberg

---

[140] Martin Brecht, Hermann Ehmer, *Südwestdeutsche Reformationsgeschichte*, p. 215. Deetjen, *Studien zur Württembergischen Kirchenordnung*, passim.

in 1519, after an extravagant and vicious infidelity (he murdered his lover's husband, his own equerry).[141] He returned in 1534, in a restoration engineered by Philip of Hesse with the help of Jacob Sturm, the Strasbourg magistrate who worked closely with Philip to build Protestant coalitions. He arrived loudly displaying the faith he studied at the Hessian court, sporting the armband designed by the Landgrave for Lutheran sympathisers at the Diet of Speyer in 1526. V.D.M.I.E. it said, for *verbum domini manet in eternum* (Isaiah 40.8 in the Vulgate, "the grass is whithered, the flower faded, but the word of God stands forever").[142] The day after entering Stuttgart on 15 May 1534, to which he marched after his victory at the battle of Lauffen, he entered the collegiate Church of the Holy Spirit, burial place of his ancestors and the principal territorial church, to pray according to an evangelical liturgy.[143] Ulrich, Philip, and Sturm all took advantage of the reprieve granted by the Truce of Nürnberg in 1532. The Landgrave exploited Wittelsbach-Habsburg rivalry and won Bavarian support to drive the Habsburg administrators from Ulrich's realm, their temporary stronghold in south-central Germany.[144] Despite a substantial gift of French foreign aid, Ulrich returned to power deeply indebted to Philip, on top of which two treaties, of Kaaden and Vienna, added the burden of payments to Austria, and there were the costs of redeeming bonded properties, purchasing rights, and construction projects for the ducal court, including eventually the renovation of that sturdy castle in Stuttgart.[145] Ulrich immediately ordered his nobility to produce 60,000 fl., and he ordered all clergy, from prelates of rich monasteries to individual priests, to hand over half of their annual income.[146]

---

[141] He did this just as the pregnancy of his own wife, a Bavarian princess with whom he had a brief, tempestuous, and politically advantageous marriage, came to full term. His son Christoph was born a few days after the murder, grew up at the Bavarian court, and eventually succeeded his father. Brecht and Ehmer, *Südwestdeutsche Reformationsgeschichte*, p. 196.

[142] Deetjen, *Studien*, pp. xxxi, 16–17, 19–24.

[143] Auge, *Stiftsbiographien*, p. 97.

[144] Brady, *Protestant Politics*, p. 83.

[145] Deetjen, *Studien*, p. 60. These treaties also mark the beginning of the end of Ambrosius Blarer's influence at court. Blarer, a sacramentarian with strong ties to the South German Reformation, was displaced by adherents of the Augsburg Confession. Ibid., pp. 35–36.

[146] Brecht, Ehmer, *Südwestdeutsche Reformationsgeschichte*, p. 215. Deetjen, *Studien*, pp. 187–93.

That was only the beginning. There were some 160 cloisters in the territory of Württemberg, which together held a third of the farmland, the vast majority of it held by a mere fourteen or fifteen male monasteries.[147] Ulrich's ancestors and the Habsburgs after Ulrich's expulsion had been accustomed to see themselves as protectors of these cloisters.[148] That was Ulrich's pretext. When Ulrich returned in 1534, most prelates asked for the confirmation of their historical privileges in cheerful letters of welcome, and Ulrich openly granted it.[149] Then in the next two years he conducted a blitzkrieg against the monasteries.

The duke moved with a relentless stream of decrees. On 12 June 1534 he issued a letter to his officers ordering the surrender of tithes, followed four days later by an order to inventory all benefices.[150] In November he sent his commissioners to get full disclosures of properties from abbots and other officers of monasteries, to be taken under oath, and he prohibited the receipt of new members.[151] Over the next year, beginning in January, he installed evangelical preachers in the large monasteries (by 1536, all but two had them), and although the preachers enjoyed mixed success, they published the duke's intention to convert and reform.[152] Women's cloisters were ordered to dismiss the monks that had provided them pastoral care and to admit evangelical preachers (February 1535).[153] The mass was ended in mendicant cloisters and some monasteries (February/ March).[154] On 8 March 1535 the duke ordered again the inventory of benefices but now included church ornaments.[155] He then led the ducal council in Stuttgart to confiscate convent benefices and con-

---

[147] Brecht, Ehmer, *Südwestdeutsche Reformationsgeschichte*, pp. 215–22. Deetjen, *Studien*, pp. 27–33, 45–6, 60.
[148] Deetjen, *Studien*, pp. 163–64. The Habsburgs improved the territory's administration between 1521 and 1534 through a series of mandates for managing lands, forests, the poor, and planning a university, judicial reform, trade, monasteries, etc. Ibid., p. 15. Ulrich's secularizations built upon Habsburg administrative reforms.
[149] Deetjen, *Studien*, pp. 169–70.
[150] Ibid., pp. 109, 166.
[151] Ibid., pp. 173–75.
[152] Ibid., pp. 194, 200, 203.
[153] Ibid., pp. 194, 199.
[154] Ibid., pp. 93, 205.
[155] Ibid., pp. 37, 111, 169. The benefices included the ducal ones given by the Habsburg government, reflecting his belief that the Habsburgs accepted his restoration. It would only be confirmed by Ferdinand in August of that year.

trol the administration of urban clergy (June 1535). Austrian canons were removed, and monks were retired with annual stipends, some invited to enter ducal service, most likely to help administer the confiscated properties; or they could leave to settle in an approved place.[156] Finally in July Ulrich published a church order to give these accomplishments a religious form. It prohibited the divine office, the mass, penance, fasts, and vows of silence (but gossip was also prohibited). It asserted freedom of dress and denied that vows of obedience were perpetual. It required women's cloisters to hold prayers in German and the women to remain cloistered, and it forbade new recruits, dismissed novices, and offered the return of dowries to those who would leave or an annual stipend of 40 fl. upon renunciation of all future claims. Lay brothers would get a mere 25 fl., beguines to be treated similarly; mendicant friars were to be consolidated in a single cloister, with the elderly and weak receiving special care; those who left voluntarily got a pension.[157]

Ulrich left little to the imagination, and his persistance paid off. On 3 Feburary 1536 he noted that some inventoried church ornaments had not yet reached the treasury, especially small objects of silver and gold. That had to change. He ordered wool and linens not yet sent to be divided among the poor of a locality. He ordered books and liturgical vestments to be sold to the highest bidders. Other valuable objects were to be inventoried and stored. By spring 1536, Ulrich could claim most church property as his own, and he ordered his treasury to collect incomes and conduct business accordingly. Some benefices were left to pay pastors and some to fund poor relief.[158] On 1 June 1536, he published a comprehensive ordinance that established the Protestant basis of public life.[159] It marks the completion of the Reformation of Württemberg.

The repetition of inventories and confiscations in this brief period, 12 June 1534 to 1 June 1536, points to the number and diversity of cloisters in Ulrich's realm, the variety of church jurisdictions upon which such actions infringed (there were five bishops with interests in Württemberg), and the strength of the resistance he met. At least

[156] Ibid., pp. 112–13.
[157] Ibid., pp. 194, 215–18.
[158] Ibid., pp. 118–25, 127. The process of confiscation 1535/36–1547 is reconstructed in ibid., pp. 221–42.
[159] Ibid., p. 93.

one encumbered monastery was out of reach, the collegiate church
of Möckmühl, pawned to the cathedral chapter of Würzburg between
1521 and 1542. After it had been redeemed, most of the seven
canons, with the prior, accepted ducal pensions and took wives.[160]
Then Ulrich confiscated the cloister and its properties, one of his
later acquisitions. More leftovers were seized in 1545. Even in the
ecclesiastical blitzkrieg of 1535/6, confiscation proceeded one monastery
at a time. Prelates hindered the duke's commissioners with excuses,
demurring that their tax appraisals were inaccurate, then they simply ran away, preventing cooperation. Some hid movable goods.
These were landed monasteries, the cloisters least scorned in the
early Protestant movement. Virtually nothing is know of the fate of
the lay branches of the mendicant orders in Württemberg (there
were more than forty-five male and female houses of these), in this
otherwise well documented secularization, because they had little
property to target.[161] As usual in Germany, women's cloisters offered
the stiffest resistance, so much so that little is known of how and
when the duke gained control of the properties of most of them.
Only two were closed outright. An additional two were directly
administered by ducal authorities.[162] Some survived for centuries, for
example the noble women's cloister of Oberstenfeld, which was only
closed in 1920! But the vast majority of monastic lands fell in the
first year of confiscations.[163] For confiscating rulers of the Holy Roman
Empire, it simply did not get any better than this in the sixteenth
century.

The Limits of Confiscation

By 1536, it was clear that success in confiscation came incrementally.
In most evangelical places, incremental gains arrived slower than in
Württemberg, a point easy to overlook if one takes Württemberg or
the most comprehensive conversions of cities as the norm, for example
Basel, Nürnberg, Ulm, or Esslingen, where once city councils decided

---

[160] Ehmer, "Ende und Verwandlung," p. 223.
[161] Deetjen, *Studien*, pp. 162–3, 184–5.
[162] Deetjen, *Studien*, pp. 185–6.
[163] Deetjen, *Studien*, p. 218. The evidence is presented in Deetjen, *Studien*, pp. 29,
178–87. Some cloisters were restored in 1547.

to endorse evangelical preacher-programs, they achieved complete control over parishes and the majority of the local holdings of the few monasteries of their towns. But the rest of the cities, like most of the territories, tell a less triumphal story, a point easily illustrated by the mixed results of several early confiscation campaigns.

For example, the city of Frankfurt assumed the financial administration of foundations and cloisters and the supervision of church tribunals with the approval of the archbishop of Mainz and the pope before the evangelical movement arose.[164] There, Dominicans and Carmelites remained the most resistant to their encroaching city council. After the city endorsed evangelical reforms, the Dominicans and Carmelites survived, through to the War of Schmalkalden. The Franciscans, on the other hand, whose finances the council was supposed to supervise since reforms a half-century earlier and whose pulpit was a center of evangelical teaching, transferred their cloister to the city in 1529. The monastery became a school, while its assets helped fund a common chest. The ties between council and monastery were even closer in the case of the nunnery of St. Catherine, which held the rule of the Teutonic Order, where membership had been reserved for the daughters of citizens since its founding in the fourteenth century. When the nuns converted in 1526, they gave the cloister to the city (the city maintained it as a women's home until 1877, when it was combined with another foundation, the "White Nuns' Cloister," which had been taken over by the city in 1542; the combined entity exists as a public foundation to this day). In other towns, the Holy Clares formed a center of Catholic resistance, on the basis of the same kinds of bonds to urban society, for example at Nürnberg and Memmingen.[165]

[164] For this and the following, Henze, "Orden und ihre Klöster," p. 94, *Die Territorien des Reichs*, 4:43–6, and Roman Fischer, "Das Barfüßerkloster im Mittelalter," *Von Barfüßerkirche zur Paulskirche. Beiträgre zur Frankfurter Stadt- und Kirchengeschichte*, ed. Roman Fischer (Frankfurt: Waldemar Karmer, 2000), 9–109, here 88–95. For the reform of Frankfurt's Franciscans in the fifteenth century, Ocker, "Religious Reform and Social Cohesion," pp. 69–78.
[165] The Nürnberg case is well known by the effective resistance of its abbess Caritas Pirkheimer to the evangelical preaching imposed on the convent by the city council. *Die Denkwürdigkeiten der Äbtissin Caritas Pirkheimer*, edited by Frumentius Renner (St. Ottilien: Erzabtei St. Ottilien, 1982), passim. At Memmingen, the city council commissioned two councilmen, two guild-masters, and a petulant Ambrosius Blarer to move the nuns to embrace the gospel and return to the world. Schlenck, *Die Reichsstadt Memmingen und die Reformation*, p. 65.

The presence of aristocratic women in a monastery greatly slowed, sometimes prevented confiscation. In some cases the monasteries still exist.[166] Similarly in the case of men, the noble privileges of the Teutonic Knights and the Hospitalers of St. John preserved these institutions as evangelical orders long after their priests died out. The ruling families that dominated city councils had the most consistent claims to altars and the dowries of family members who had left cloisters.[167] Few towns held the patronage of their most important churches (Ulm and Nürnberg are significant examples of towns that did).[168] Bishops of Würzburg, Bamberg, Mainz, Salzburg, Trier, Freising, and Passau suppressed the evangelical movement in their cities.[169] About half the towns in the League of Schmalkalden confronted the obstacle of an ecclesiastical lord.[170] In some northern towns, bishops restrained confiscations by town councils, for example at Magdeburg, Halberstadt, and Hamburg, leaving cathedral chapters a part of the town's political and religious landscape at least through Luther's generation, and other collegiate churches and monasteries remained Catholic and also survived for the first decades of the Protestant movement, sometimes much longer.[171] In Augsburg, the city council used a flank manoeuver against the cathedral. Its parish churches were all controlled by the cathedral chapter, collegiate churches, or monasteries. But there was a discretionary fund, under the control of a lay *Zechmeister*, which for two centuries had been used to support preaching, catechism, an altar, a sexton, and purchases of wax and liturgical objects.[172] In the 1530's, the regime

---

[166] Henze, "Orden und ihre Klöster," p. 97 with n. 41 and its references for examples.

[167] Brady, *Ruling Class, Regime and Reformation*, pp. 222–3, 226. Martial Staub, *Une société à l'œuvre: Vie paroissiale et solidarité à Nuremberg, du xiiie siècle à la Réforme* (Paris: École des Hautes Études en Sciences Sociales, 2003) for patronage and its uses by ruling families.

[168] Haug-Moritz, *Der Schmalkaldische Bund*, p. 513 and the literature noted at n. 17.

[169] Rublack, *Gescheiterte Reformation*, p. 126 and passim.

[170] Haug-Moritz, *Der Schmalkaldische Bund*, p. 513 with n. 18.

[171] Franz Schrader, *Reformation und katholische Klöster: Beiträge zur Reformation und zur Geschichte der klösterlichen Restbestände in den ehemaligen Bistümern Magdeburg und Halberstadt* (Leipzig: St. Benno-Verlag, 1973), pp. 85–138, 164–222. Rainer Postel, *Die Reformation in Hamburg 1517–1528* (Gütersloh: Gerd Mohn, 1986), pp. 89–122, 251–317. Ziegler, "Klosteraufhebung und Reformation," pp. 605–6.

[172] Herbert Immenkötter, "Die katholische Kirche in Augsburg in der ersten Hälfte des 16. Jahrhundert," *Die Augsburger Kirchenordnung von 1537 und ihr Umfeld*, ed. Reinhard Schwarz (Gütersloh: Gerd Mohn, 1988), pp. 9–32, here 16–18.

used the fund to support evangelical preachers, sometimes planted alongside Catholic priests (in most if not all cities affected by evangelical preaching, the new faith was promoted by benefice holders who converted to the new doctrine or preachers appointed by towns in competition with benefice holders of the old faith). When cities reassigned church incomes to evangelicals, they could transgress both ecclesiastical immunities and the prerogatives of other lords, making enemies among several social networks, and like Breisach their cases could become mired in the courts of several jurisdictions.

It could take decades to gain control of monasteries even in cities and territories where Protestants were strong. In the far south, Basel, with its dramatically uniform conversion in 1529, had to contend with its estranged cathedral chapter until 1693, when the city council finally decided to stop answering the exiled chapter's complaints against the city's takeover of chapter properties and incomes.[173] Nürnberg, like Basel, experienced one of the more decisive conversions of the early Protestant movement. The city gained several cloisters (the Augustinian Hermits, the Carthusians, the Benedictines) after a few last monks, whose numbers had been depleted by evangelical preaching and the pressures of the religious controversy, handed the cloisters over, soon after the city ended the public celebration of the mass in 1525.[174] The Cistercian nuns of Himmelthron in nearby Großgründlach handed over their property and endowments for masses to the city in 1526. The properties were converted into a rural relief fund. But the Dominican friars, the Augustinian nuns of Pillenreuth, the Observant Franciscans, the Dominican nuns of Engelthal, the Franciscan nuns of Nürnberg, and the Dominican nuns of the city all resisted such pressures. They listened to compulsory evangelical sermons unmoved. They closed forever only much later (in the order I just listed them): 1543, 1552, 1562, 1565, 1590, and 1596. The last nun of the Franciscan Holy Clares died in 1590, the last Dominican nun in 1596.[175] The chapel of St. Elisabeth of the Teutonic Order remained untouched and untouchable.[176] Ulm

---

[173] Paul Roth, *Durchbruch und Festsetzung der Reformation in Basel* (Basel: Helbing und Lichtenhah, 1942), pp. 71–9.
[174] *Die Territorien des Reichs*, 1:37 for this and the following. Also Zimmermann, *Prediger der Freiheit*, pp. 146–7.
[175] Henze, "Orden und ihre Klöster," p. 93. *Die Territorien des Reichs*, 1:37.
[176] *Die Territorien des Reichs*, 1:40. Henze, "Orden und ihre Klöster," p. 94.

never gained control of the local commend of the Teutonic Knights
or the Benedictines of Wiblingen, nor could the city council bring
about the evangelical conversion of the Holy Clares of Söflingen,
even though the council was, by an imperial right confirmed in
1534—after the city joined the League of Schmalkalden—lay guardian
over the cloister, and it remained guardian until 1773.[177] Strasbourg,
the leading urban center of Protestantism in the southwest from 1534
to the Schmalkald War, could not eliminate the celebration of the
mass by the cathedral chapter, the chapters of the collegiate churches
of Old and New St. Peter, the Teutonic Knights, the Knights of St.
John, the Carthusians, the Dominican nuns of St. Margaret and St.
Nicholas, the Penitents of Mary Magdalen, and one beguinage.[178]
The council could only control public access to traditional rites at
these places by issuing prohibitions and fines. Much less could they
gain all their holdings.

Some monastic properties destroyed in the Peasants' War could
be taken by lords within just a few years.[179] Other confiscators had
to wait long for evangelical attrition to run its course. The provost
of the Cistercian nunnery of Frauenberg, Conrad Jonis, who became
an important evangelical preacher in his region, married the Cistercian
abbess in 1521. Prioress and surviving nuns only handed over the
cloister and its properties to the city of Nordhausen in 1557, and
then on the condition that it be used to open a girls' school.[180] The
canons of the Premonstratensian monastery of Veßra, in Thuringia,
embraced evangelical teachings. But Count Georg Ernst of Henneberg
did not confiscate the monastery's properties until the last abbot died
in 1573.[181] The mass was ended in the Augustinian Cloister of St.

---

[177] *Deutsches Städtebuch. Handbuch städtischer Geschichte*, edited by Erich Keyser, 5+
volumes and numerous parts and subdivisions (Stuttgart: W. Kohlhammer, 1939—
present), 4/2/2:275–7.

[178] Lorna Jane Abray, *The People's Reformation: Magistrates, Clergy, and Commons in
Strasbourg, 1500–1598* (Ithaca: Cornell University Press, 1985), p. 42.

[179] E.g. by the Elector of Saxony (Cistercian monasteries of Georgenthal, Mönch-
pfiffel; the Benedictine monastery of Reinhardsbrunn), the Count of Henneberg-
Schleusingen (Cistercian monastery of Georgenzell), the Count of Gleichen (Cistercian
nunnery of Heyda), the city of Jena (the Carmelite monastery of Jena), and the
Count of Mansfeld (Benedictine monastery of St. Peterskloster). Hermann, "Verzeichniß," p. 25 nr. 35, p. 26 nr. 36, pp. 31–3 nr. 46, p. 41 nr. 70, p. 47 nr. 84,
p. 50 nr. 89.

[180] Ibid., pp. 138–9 nr. 104.

[181] Ibid., p. 58 nr. 109.

Moritz, near Naumburg, in 1532. When the last prior died in 1543, the Elector of Saxony dissolved the monastery and sold the buildings and property to the city council of Naumburg, excepting only the church and the prior's house.[182] The Augustinian canons of Jechaburg began to leave the monastery in 1543. Count Gunther of Schwarzburg installed a Lutheran deacon in 1552. The canons' properties were only secularized in 1572.[183] After its destruction in the Peasants War, the Thuringian Benedictine nunnery of Walbeck struggled to reestablish itself. In 1546 the Count of Mansfeld confiscated it over the Abbess of Quedlinburg's objections.[184]

It took decades to control monasteries in the domains of Magdeburg and Halberstadt in the second half of the sixteenth century.[185] Farther north, the six women's monasteries of the duchy of Lüneburg lost some part of their incomes in 1529 and 1530, when Duke Ernst replaced their provosts with his own unilaterally appointed procurators, confiscated whatever account documents his men could lay their hands on, tried to take over incomes, liquidated property without the monasteries' consent, and placed the nuns on state welfare. He did it all as protector, guaranteeing their traditional rights and prerogatives, as the nuns at Wienhausen, Isenhagen, and Lüne carefully noted in several accounts that still commanded their attention in the seventeenth century.[186] At the Cistercian monastery of Wienhausen in 1529, the monastery's provost claimed to confiscate documents on the duke's behalf for their protection, in case the monastery is destroyed in a peasants' war.[187] The nuns at Lüne and Wienhausen resisted the harangues of the duke's preachers and the personal admonitions of the duke, but unwilling to leave the monastery, deprived of the Catholic sacraments, and subjected to a Lutheran, divine office

---

[182] Ibid., p. 136 nr. 100.

[183] Ibid., p. 33, nr. 48.

[184] Ibid., p. 155 nr. 138.

[185] Schrader, *Reformation und katholische Klöster*, pp. 85–138, 164–222.

[186] Brandis, "Quellen zur Reformationsgeschichte der Lüneburger Frauenklöster," pp. 357–398, with excerpts from the Wienhausen and Lüne chronicles.

[187] Brandis, "Quellen zur Reformationsgeschichte der Lüneburger Frauenklöster," p. 367. The same provost had a history of liquidating monastery properties without the convent's approval over the previous five years. The properties were significant: a stud farm, four horses and three oxen with tackle, twelve young steer, thirty-two cows, a large numbers of pigs (160 in 1525; 120 in 1528), etc. Brandis, "Quellen," pp. 393–4.

in German, the community eventually converted by default. At Lüne, their resistance weakened after 1535.[188] But at Wienhausen, the last Catholic abbess came to office as late as 1565.[189] All six Lüneburg women's monasteries exist to the present day as Protestant convents. Their properties were never completely liquidated. In the seventeenth century, although long evangelical, they preserved accounts of their earlier crises that were framed by the perspective of their Catholic predecessors—an indication of their sense of continuity with a Catholic past.[190] The disruption of conversion was neither total nor absolute. In sum, successful confiscations were, to varying degrees, piecemeal. Both cities and territories could only control properties convent by convent.

The progress of confiscation was sometimes hindered by dynastic sharing arrangements in the sixteenth century. Heinrich V, one of two reigning dukes of Mecklenburg, supported evangelical preaching since 1523, but his younger brother, co-regent, and competitor Albrecht II remained Catholic. Heinrich did not join the protest at the Diet of Speyer in 1529 nor subscribe to the Augsburg Confession in 1530 nor ever join the League of Schmalkalden.[191] When he conducted church visitations in 1534 and 1540, he did little to eliminate Catholic worship and monasticism from his territory, something only accomplished after the Augsburg Interim (1548). Similarly, cities in his lands took decades to gain control of monasteries. For example, Wismar's city council supported evangelical preaching since 1524, and in earnest since 1527.[192] But Catholic priests and evangelical clergy worked side by side in city churches until well into the 1540's. The Franciscan cloister was only dissolved and converted into a school in 1541, although attrition had already reached crisis proportions in 1535. Wismar's Dominican cloister remained in tact until 1553, although its public activities were restricted since 1532, and it survived in a truncated form until 1562. A prince could make all the difference to monastic conversion.[193] Duke Heinrich of Mecklenburg

---

[188] Brandis, "Quellen," p. 371.
[189] Ibid., p. 364.
[190] Ibid., p. 391.
[191] For this and the following, Ulpts, *Die Bettelorden in Mecklenburg*, pp. 340–5.
[192] Ulpts, *Die Bettelorden in Mecklenburg*, pp. 345–366 for this and the following.
[193] The same was true in the city of Osnabrück. Heide Stratenwirth, *Die Reformation in der Stadt Osnabrück* (Wiesbaden: Franz Steiner, 1971), pp. 97–100, 126–9.

supported evangelical preaching in the city of Rostock since 1523, and the city council began to support evangelicals in 1526.[194] When attrition from the Franciscan and Dominican cloisters finally mounted in the early 1530's, the council seized their assets and ignored the pleas of lesser noble patrons. But a rump convent of Dominicans nevertheless survived through the 1550's, and in the single person of the prior, Hermann Otto, until the poor man's death in 1575.

Such were the limitations on confiscating ambitions imposed by political circumstances: the diversity of powers and the tenacity of monastic privileges. It is clear that the chronology of confiscations stretched over the century. Hesse or Württemberg might remind us of Denmark or England, but they were exceptions, not the rule.[195] The financial benefits of confiscation were also limited. Where confiscation did occur, it had limited economic impact on a government's finances. Monasteries seem to have made a relatively small contribution to the fisc of confiscating principalities, and their incomes were quickly eaten up by rulers' debts. Monastic incomes amounted to fourteen percent of gross revenues in the districts of Hesse in 1532. The value of confiscated properties had already proved insufficient to pension the 800 monks and nuns of Hesse's 20 male and 17 female monasteries.[196] A centralized administration of church property was hindered by the insufficiency of funds, although the Landgrave did establish hospitals at Haina, Merxhausen, Gronau, and Hofheim, and he converted two noble nunneries, at Wetter and Kaufungen, to hostels for noble daughters. In 1530, the Landgrave pledged monastic properties to raise about half of the credit obtained by his government, and the practice continued through the rest of his long reign. Johann Friedrich of Saxony's sequestrators brought in 100,000 fl. between 1533 and 1543, but more than four times that amount (430,000 fl.) was raised in that same period of time by excises on beer and wine alone.[197] The Elector of Saxony payed debts, promising a repayment to monasteries that never came.[198] So too, in neighboring

---

[194] Ulpts, *Die Bettelorden in Mecklenburg*, pp. 367–374.

[195] Confiscations in England, Denmark, and Sweden are summarized in chapter 8.

[196] For this and the following, Schindling, "Der Passauer Vertrag," pp. 112 n. 21 and 113, and *Die Territorien des Reichs im Zeitalter der Reformation und Konfessionalisierung*, 4:263–4.

[197] Cohn, "Church Property," p. 169.

[198] For this and the following, Gottfried Seebaß, "Martin Bucers Beitrag zu den

Albertine Saxony, when Duke Heinrich introduced the evangelical reform in 1539, he sold most confiscated lands to nobility and officers below value.[199] Duke Ulrich of Württemberg paid for his restoration, but put the property under direct ducal administration. Pomerania's dukes wanted to leave property only to urban cloisters, in order to support the ministry, and confiscate the rest. Confiscations were opportunistic. It was the promotion of evangelical doctrine that elevated confiscations to religious deeds. This may have seemed like a frontal assault on ecclesiastical immunities, but insofar as the property was concerned, the church was never as independent as it claimed to be. Good Catholic rulers were hardly handicapped by church immunities, as the eloquent example of Charles V in the Netherlands shows. Immunities had the advantage of preserving the church as a future revenue source.

In the first and most formative generation of the Protestant religion, it could not have been clear to even the most prescient that reform should lead to a Protestant state, and a Catholic presence remained in most Protestant places. The implications of this for early evangelical preachers (and for confessionalisation) are too seldom considered. The preachers' intolerance of Catholicism pressured towns and encouraged princes to seek total control of churches, but how did the limitations color the emergent culture of Protestantism? How did evangelicals adapt? One may think of the preachers' intensity, pitch, and volume in inverse proportion to the grounds for Protestant confidence in any worldly meaningful sense. There was no direct line-of-fire from evangelical preaching to confessional state-building in early confessional Germany.

Diskussionen über die Verwendung der Kirchengüter," *Martin Bucer und das Recht. Beiträge zum internationalem Symposium vom 1. bis 3. März 2001 in der Johannes a Lasco Bibliothek Emden*, ed. Christoph Strohm (Geneva: Librairie Droz, 2002), pp. 167–83, here p. 172.

[199] Cohn, "Church Property," p. 169.

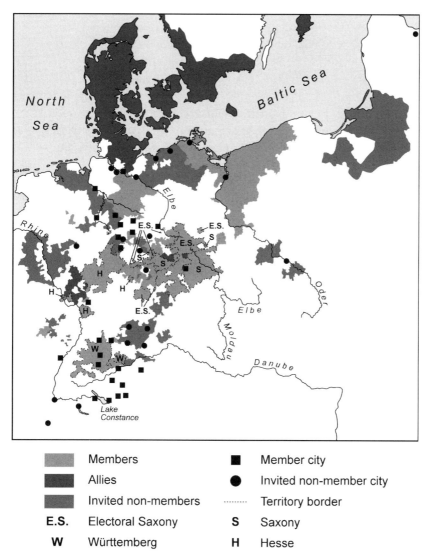

	Members		Member city
	Allies		Invited non-member city
	Invited non-members	⋯⋯	Territory border
E.S.	Electoral Saxony	**S**	Saxony
W	Württemberg	**H**	Hesse

The League of Schmalkalden in 1546. The map shows the extent of the
League's influence and the territories of four of its most important princely
members. "Invited non-members" were those estates sympathetic to the
evangelical cause for whom the membership process had been initiated but,
by reason of choice or circumstance, was not completed.

CHAPTER THREE

THE LEAGUE OF SCHMALKALDEN AND THE IMPERIAL CHAMBER COURT

The League of Schmalkalden, created at the end of December 1530, was formed as a defensive alliance against the Holy Roman Emperor and the majority of Catholic princes in the Imperial Diet. But scholars have come to emphasize its broader political role, born as a coalition just after the breakdown of negotiations over a religious settlement. Its history as a coalition to defend its members' religious confession and as a political body is complex. The religious controversy never entirely conformed to plain, confessional oppositions, nor to purely political ambitions, which were many, varied, and changable. Rather, the League became a second great theater, beside the imperial Diet, in which the members of the German political community handled one another.

Nevertheless, the League took shape in conjunction with several milestones in the development of confessional identity. One was the document composed in response to the 1530 imperial Diet at Augsburg, where Charles V, recently crowned emperor at Bologna, hoped to resolve the religious controversy and unite the German estates under the banner of mutual defense against the armies of Suleiman the Magnificent (the Ottoman Sultan's traumatic siege of Vienna occurred only the year before). Most of the estates at the Imperial Diet who still resisted the condemnations of Martin Luther subscribed to a confession, composed by Philip Melanchthon, known as the Augsburg Confession, which summarized evangelical teachings. When the League was formed, its members also subscribed to the Augsburg Confession. At the Diet, four Protestant cities unwilling to accept Luther's doctrine of the eucharist subscribed to another document, the so-called Tetrapolitan or Four-Cities Confession (Strasbourg, Constance, Lindau, and Memmingen). Of these, the city playing the most important role in the politics of the Holy Roman Empire, Strasbourg, would soon accept the Augsburg Confession, too. Strasbourg then worked to draw other south-German cities into the League, in part by negotiating a theological compromise on the disputed doctrine. The compromise is known as the Wittenberg Concord of 1536. It was composed by Strasbourg's most influential churchman and theologian at the time, Martin Bucer, with Wittenberg's Melanchthon.[1] We will return to the Wittenberg Concord at the beginning of Chapter 5.

The Augsburg Confession expressed an evangelical orthodoxy. The existence of a common orthodoxy was also presupposed by the League's appeal to a general church council. At the 1530 Diet, the adherents of the Augsburg Confession, partly in response to the demand that they restore church properties, insisted on a general council to decide the religious controversy, and the newly formed League did the same. This culminated a long series of such appeals. A general council had emerged in the late Middle Ages as, potentially, an ecclesiastical court of last instance (an alternative to the papacy). In 1518 Martin Luther appealed to such a council when he was summoned to Rome by the pope for trial.[2] The Imperial Diet of Nürnberg in 1524, bowing to anxiety among the estates over potential unrest, made the uncommonly hesitant order that the estates fulfill the Edict of Worms, as far as possible. It was the first time the Diet had said the estates may consider the interests of territorial peace when implementing an edict.[3] It reflects the widespread conviction that any preconciliar solution to the prevailing religious questions was penultimate, at best. The conciliar option enjoyed imperial support. In 1524, Charles V at Rome first insisted on a general council and proposed that it be held at the city of Trent, an imperial free city on the southern side of the Alps.[4] Several members of Charles V's inner circle advocated the political advantages of a council at least since 1526.[5] At Speyer in 1526, the Electoral

---

[1] Bucer's role as an urban religious leader was confirmed by the 1532 Strasbourg synod that established an evangelical church order in the city. François Wendel, *L'Eglise de Strasbourg: sa constitution et son organisation, 1532–1535* (Paris: Presses universitaires de France, 1942), pp. 95–96. Hammann, *Martin Bucer*, pp. 50–1.

[2] Becker, *Die Appellation vom Papst an ein allgemeines Konzil*, pp. 244–60 and passim.

[3] According to Bernd Christian Schneider, *Ius Reformandi. Die Entwicklung eines Staatskirchenrechts von seinen Anfängen bis zum Ende des Alten Reiches* (Tübingen: J.C.B. Mohr, 2001), p. 91.

[4] Charles-Joseph Hefele, J. Hergenroether, H. Leclercq, *Histoire des conciles*, 11 vols. (Paris: Letouzey et Ané, 1907–1952), 8:1145.

[5] Wolfgang Reinhard, "Die Kirchenpolitischen Vorstellungen Kaiser Karls V., ihre Grundlagen und ihr Wandel," *Confessio Augustana und Confutatio. Der Augsburger Reichstag 1530 und die Einheit der Kirche*, ed. Erwin Iserloh (Münster: Achendorf, 1980), pp. 62–100, here 70–86. For the Emperor's religiosity, see also Fühner, *Die Kirchen- und die antireformatorische Religionspolitik*, pp. 167–172, and Heinz Schilling, "Charles

College deadlocked on the question of the extent to which to consider matters of faith, and conceded that a general council should
decide the religious question.[6] The protesting estates at the Diet of
Speyer in 1529 appealed to a general council. The conciliar option
remained in play for a decade following the Augsburg Diet of 1530.

The 1530 Diet contributed to the hardening of confessional lines.
There, theological negotiations broke down. As a result, the Diet's
recess demanded three things: the restoration of traditional church
practices until a council would decide the religious controversy, the
fulfilment of the edict of Worms against Luther, and the threat of
an imperial ban and the loss of property against Luther's supporters.[7]
It was not an effective threat. It had already been mostly neutralized, in the 1520's, but this was a little more than bluster. It was
the emperor's default attitude: Luther was a heretic and his supporters *should* be treated as criminals, even if necessity required greater
circumspection.[8] The emperor demanded that the subscribers of the
Augsburg Confession comply on those points still disagreed at the
Diet (these ranged from original sin to clerical marriage and monastic vows) by 15 April 1531, while he left the door open for himself:
he would consider further measures and arrange for a general council with the pope.[9] Pope Clement VII's conditions for a council were
stringent (the Protestants had to submit to its decisions before it even

---

V and Religion. The Struggle for the Integrity and Unity of Christendom," *Charles
V, 1500–1558, and His Time*, edited by Hugo Soly, Wim Blockmans (Antwerp:
Mercatorfonds, 1999), pp. 285–363, esp. 296–328. The most prominent advocate
of negotiation was Mercurio di Gattinara, imperial chancellor, who in June 1526
proposed a general pardon of Protestants as part of a Habsburg strategy to drive
the French from Italy, if the supporters of Luther agreed to submit to the decision
of a future council and provide the emperor troops. Ferdinand advocated negotiation because of his own need for German troops: he was confronted with a mutiny
after the Turkish siege of Vienna was lifted (15 October 1529), saw the failure of
a strict course against Luther supporters at the Diet of Speyer that year (it brought
about the protestations from which the name Protestant derives), and feared a
Hessian campaign to end his control of Württenberg.

[6] Kohnle, *Reichstag und Reformation*, pp. 266–9.
[7] Klaus Mencke, *Die Visitationen am Reichskammergericht im 16. Jahrhundert* (Cologne:
Böhlau, 1984), pp. 27–8. *Deutsche Reichstagsakten, jungere Reihe*, ed. Historische Kommission
bei der Königlichen Akademie der Wissenschaften, vols. 1–4, *Deutsche Reichstagesakten
unter Kaiser Karl V* (Gotha: Perthes, 1893–1905), 2:640–659 nr. 92. For a review of
property aspects of the recess, Sieglerschmidt, *Territorialstaat*, pp. 133–6.
[8] Reinhard in note 5, above.
[9] Fuchs, *Konfession und Gespräch*, pp. 363–88.

convened), and the French were ambivalent at best, the English opposed (the king, in his "Great Matter" of bringing a legitimate heir into the world, had been forbidden by the pope to remarry in March 1530), while Clement was unwilling to call a council without French and English participation; nor was his curia going to push him.[10] No council was summoned. Yet in spite of the Diet's treatment of the religious controversy as a breach of peace,[11] no one was ready to resolve the religious controversy by force of arms, least of all Charles and Ferdinand, who needed German troops in their Turkish, Italian, and French campaigns: they needed *least* a civil war. The recess of the Diet of Augsburg left in place the condemnation of Luther of 1521, the validity of episcopal courts and jurisdictions, and the illegality of Protestant control of benefices and monastic property. The adherents of the Augsburg Confession refused to accept the recess, leaving them, if not immediately confronted by a threat of force, in a delicate political and legal position. The League of Schmalkalden was formed to strengthen the position of the Protestants. But a total war between the League and the emperor did not occur until 1546.[12]

As for a council, the idea was only truly embraced by the papacy in 1534, at the beginning of Pope Paul III's long, fifteen-year reign.[13] By then it had become obvious, if it had not always been, that at such an event the Protestants could only expect the condemnation of their views and reform measures. The council finally convened in December 1545 at the city of Trent. But its first period (1545–1547) had no immediate significance for Germany. Neither Protestants nor German bishops participated. The council began as a small and predominantly southern European affair.

---

[10] Hefele, Hergenroether, Leclercq, *Histoire des conciles*, 8:1132–39, 1145–52. *Legation Lorenzo Campeggios*, pp. 226–32 nr. 62, pp. 241–2 nr. 68. In 1533, King Henry VIII would appeal his "great matter" to a general council against the papacy. Diarmaid McCullough, *Thomas Cranmer* (New Haven: Yale, 1996), pp. 49, 63, 105–6.

[11] Sieglerschmidt, *Territorialstaat*, p. 135.

[12] Seebaß, "Verwendung der Kirchengüter," p. 178. Kurt Körber, *Kirchengüterfrage und schmalkaldischer Bund* (Leipzig: Verein für Reformationsgeschichte, 1913), pp. 85–86, 91. Brady, *Protestant Politics*, 75–80.

[13] *Le temps des confessions (1530–1620/30)*, pp. 235–39, and Hefele, Hergenroether, Leclercq, *Histoire des conciles*, 9:45–53, 203–22.

The Imperial Chamber Court

The most pressing threat against the subscribers to the Augsburg Confession in 1530 was legal action, not theological opposition or war. The two leading Protestant princes (the Landgrave and the Elector of Saxony) withdrew from the 1530 Diet after the breakdown of religious negotiations and before the publication of the Diet's recess, which, when it came, demanded the restitution of church properties.[14] The Protestants refused to allow any restoration of private masses or the return of exiled monks to what the papal legate, Lorenzo Campeggio, called "occupied monasteries."[15] They had also come to regard themselves as possessing a subjective right to resist imperial decisions on the religious question, not merely on religious grounds but on a constitutional one: they treated the Empire as a confederation of estates with diverse rights and obligations.[16] After the withdrawl of the Elector of Saxony and the Landgrave from the Diet of Augsburg, the assembled estates reinforced the Imperial Chamber Court by appointing more Catholics to it.[17] The Imperial Chamber Court quickly became the frontline of reaction to Protestant reform.

The court was only forty years old. The imperial estates had demanded its creation and used it to resolve conflicts free of the emperor's direct control. To the Emperor Maximillian and his successor Charles V, the court represented German mistrust of their dynastic ambitions.[18] Still, the estates were reluctant to bankroll the

---

[14] Philip of Hesse departed in early August and Duke Johann Elector of Saxony in late September. Their departure was reported to Rome by Campeggio, together with his surprise at Protestant intransigence but pleasure over imperial inflexibility on heresy. *Legation Lorenzo Campeggios 1530–1531 und Nuntiatur Girolamo Aleandros 1531*, pp. 106, 138, 141, nr. 27, 34, 36.

[15] Ibid., p. 129 nr. 32.

[16] Schneider, *Ius Reformandi*, p. 100.

[17] Mencke, *Visitationen*, pp. 41–4.

[18] Reinhard Seyboth, "Kaiser, König, Stände und Städte im Ringen um das Kammergericht, 1486–1495," *Das Reichskammergericht in der deutschen Geschichte. Stand der Forschung, Forschungsperspektiven*, ed. Bernhard Diestelkamp (Cologne: Böhlau Verlag, 1990), p. 12. Heinz Duchhardt, "Das Reichskammergericht," *Oberste Gerichtsbarkeit und zentrale Gewalt*, ed. Bernhard Diestelkamp, (Cologne: Böhlau, 1996), pp. 1–13. A current bibliography of repertories of documents produced by the court, along with a brief review of recent studies, may be found in Ralf-Peter Fuchs, "The Supreme Court of the Holy Roman Empire: the State of Research and Outlook," *The Sixteenth Century Journal* 34(2003):9–27. See also Jörn Sieglerschmidt's review of sources, *Territorialstaat*, pp. 50–1, with appendix 1, ibid., pp. 291–312.

court.[19] Throughout the first half-century of its history, the court's power seldom matched its prestige, even though its prestige was great. On average, the court began 180 new proceedings per year in the first half of the sixteenth century, this in spite of the fact that its processes seldom ended conflicts. Plaintiffs rarely expected the court to end a case.[20] The court rather had a pacifying role; its procedures at best provided the basis for steps toward resolution back home.[21] More commonly it seems to have led to interminable negotiations. So for example, when in July 1533 the court declared the illegality of the city of Hamburg's 1528 reforms, it demanded the restoration of all confiscated church properties. The city entered negotiations with the cathedral chapter about the restoration of Catholic worship in the cathedral, while it also negotiated admission to the League of Schmalkalden.[22] But the town repeatedly postponed the discussion of religious matters, until the religious controversy were settled by a general church council, while conceding the restitution of the chapter's temporal properties, not those meant to support divine worship.[23] Negotiations only ended in 1561, when the city conceded the chapter's right to rule itself and control its benefices; the chapter confirmed the city council's oversight of parishes, and both agreed that the Catholic mass would not return to the cathedral.

The Imperial Chamber Court's business was vast. Its assessors, who usually deliberated in groups of eight, more or less, could receive all manner of suits from any imperial subject, complaints of breach of peace, and as the highest appellate court of the Empire, appeals of decisions by courts of any of the Empire's lordships (appeals dominated the court's business in its first decades).[24] It served as a court

---

[19] Mencke, *Visitationen*, p. 1.

[20] Filippo Ranieri, *Recht und Gesellschaft im Zeitalter der Rezeption*, 2 vols. (Cologne: Böhlau, 1985), 1:139, 198–9. Bernhard Diestelkamp, *Recht und Gericht im Heiligen Römischen Reich* (Frankfurt am Main: Vittorio Klostermann, 1999), p. 257.

[21] Diestelkamp, *Recht und Gericht*, p. 258.

[22] For this and the following, Otto Scheib, *Die Reformationsdiskussionen in der Hansestadt Hamburg, 1522–1528* (Münster: Aschendorff, 1975), pp. 180–8.

[23] Sieglerschmidt, *Territorialstaat*, p. 146 with n. 45, quoting Hamburg's procurator to the Imperial Chamber Court and similar concessions from Minden's procurator.

[24] Ranieri, *Recht und Gesellschaft*, 1:200–211. Ranieri showed that through the course of the sixteenth century, the court moved from its original function as a control of territorial courts to the court to which imperial estates and nobles took recourse. Ibid., pp. 204–5. For the ratio of appeals to new suits, see Sprenger, *Viglius von Aytta*, p. 49. For the three groups of assessors (eight were prescribed but there were often fewer or more), ibid., pp. 54–5.

of first instance in cases of breach of peace and property disputes alike.[25] In the 1520's and 1530's, the court claimed competence to handle Protestant violence against Catholic interests, which was interpreted broadly to include any change or challenge to prebends and church property,[26] including tithes, rents, and other clerical rights, such as the Protestants were diverting to support the evangelical ministry. By treating Protestant confiscations as church robbery, the court avoided handling them as problems of benefice or patronage law.[27] Such cases represented only a fraction of the court's business.[28] But they were the most politically vexatious over the long term.

The 1530 Diet of Augsburg established the centrality of the court in religious disputes, although its competence was hotly debated. In the 1520's the court had become one of many tribunals before which complaints against evangelicals were pursued, and there were very many tribunals. For example, from the diocese of Constance between 1522 and 1531, complaints were brought on behalf of various male and female monasteries and clergy of the diocese before the bishop, the papacy, the Swiss Confederacy, the territorial tribunal (*Landgericht*) of Thurgau, the territorial tribunal of Swabia, the Austrian high bailiff at Altdorf, the city of Constance, the imperial tribunal (*Hofgericht*) at Rottweil, and the Imperial Chamber Court at Speyer.[29] When

---

[25] Gero Dolezalek, "Die juristische Argumentation der Assessoren am Reichskammergericht zu den Reformationsprozessen 1532–1538," *Das Reichskammergericht in der deutschen Geschichte*, p. 29. Ranieri, *Recht und Gesellschaft*, 1:200. Betinna Dick, *Die Entwicklung des Kameralprozesses nach den Ordnungen von 1495 bis 1555* (Cologne: Böhlau, 1981), p. 93.

[26] A prebend in English usage is the income received by a member of a cathedral chapter or collegiate church, which comprised the bulk of desirable church incomes. In Germany, the term may apply to any ecclesiastical benefice, which is how I use it here.

[27] Sieglerschmidt, *Territorialstaat*, p. 170. He notes typical cases related to the end of Catholic worship involving the cities of Hamburg, Minden, Naumburg, and Augsburg; the property of churches and cloisters involving the cities of Haina, Maulbronn, Frankfurt, Ulm, Strasbourg, Hirschfelden, and the duke of Saxony; and the complaints of individual clergy from Strasbourg, Lindau, Ansbach-Kulmbach, and Esslingen. Ibid., n. 101.

[28] How significant a fraction is suggested by the percentage of cases brought by church institutions, 19.8% of all cases between 1520 and 1539, and some 2/3 of them brought by monasteries that had lost property. Ranieri, *Recht und Gesellschaft*, 1:225 n. 24, 1:228.

[29] Hermann Buck, *Die Anfänge der Konstanzer Reformationsprozesse, Österreich, Eidgenossenschaft und Schmalkaldischer Bund 1510/22–1531* (Tübingen: Osiandersche Buchhandlung, 1964), pp. 249–444.

the Diet of 1530 reasserted the court's authority, it underscored the court's central place in disputes over church property and jurisdiction. Its centrality was enhanced by the Protestant refusal to acknowledge papal and episcopal tribunals. By receiving suits and appeals, the court advocated the dismantling of evangelical changes just as they had been and were being achieved, church by church and monastery by monastery.

Anticipating suits before the Imperial Chamber Court, the League of Schmalkalden decided (4 April 1531) to station two procurators at Speyer bearing the "appeal in a matter of faith" (*appellacion in causa fidei*) made at Augsburg and a copy of the recently conceived *exception incompetencie und recusacionis*, an allegation of the court's incompetence in matters of faith.[30] The idea was to keep the religious controversy assigned to ecclesiastical jurisdiction, a convenient tactic, since technically, certainly from their point of view, the Protestants had trumped all church courts by an appeal to a general council. Embedded in the League's strategy from the start was the recognition of the formal distinction between spiritual and temporal jurisdictions, a presupposition shared by Catholics and Lutherans alike. The two procurators would soon receive broad power of attorney from the members of the League. Thus the League had as its stated, dual purpose from the start both military and legal defense, but the latter was for most of the League's history the more pressing and consistent need. Between 1526 and 1544, when the Imperial Diet agreed to suspend the court, suits involving the Reformation, most if not all involving church property and personnel, were brought against seven territorial princes and at least twenty cities.[31] The League supported members in numerous ways. Legal advice was offered by jurists at the universities of Marburg and Wittenberg and at the courts of the Landgrave and the Saxon Elector (such advice

---

[30] *Die Schmalkaldischen Bundesabschiede, 1530–1532*, ed. Ekkehart Fabian, (Tübingen: Osiandersche Buchhandlung, 1958), pp. 18–23. For their power of attorney (9 June 1531), *Urkunden und Akten der Reformationsprozesse*, ed. Ekkehart Fabian, part 1: *Allgemeines 1530–1534* (Tübingen: Osiandersche Buchhandlung, 1961), pp. 31–4 nr. 4. For the League's use of the court in defense against legal attack, Haug-Moritz, *Der Schmalkaldische Bund*, pp. 277–87. For the work of procurators, Sprenger, *Viglius von Aytta*, pp. 58–60.

[31] Gero Dolezalek, "Die juristische Argumentation der Assessoren am Reichskammergericht zu den Reformationsprozessen, 1532–1538," *Reichskammergericht in der deutschen Geschichte*, p. 25.

was given to Pomerania, Hamburg, Riga, Lüneburg, and Constance in 1532 and 1533). The League sent letters and made oral requests on behalf of members to Emperor Charles V and King Ferdinand in the name of the League. The League's two leading princes, the Landgrave of Hesse and the Elector of Saxony, sent emissaries on behalf of members to the Imperial Chamber Court.[32]

Defense of Reform

The League of Schmalkalden quickly became the center stage of the Protestant movement. Through the eight years since its founding, its membership expanded from an original six princes and two cities (Elector of Saxony, Landgrave of Hesse, Duke of Lüneburg, Prince of Anhalt, the two Counts of Mansfeld, the city of Magdeburg, and the city of Bremen) to include one of the largest principalities of southern Germany (Duke Ulrich of Württemberg joined in 1536), the most important imperial cities of the south, and most of the north (the Duke of Pomerania entered in 1536, the Elector of Brandenburg in 1538, and the Duke of Saxony in 1539). The emperor and German bishops indirectly contributed to its early success. German bishops were relatively apathetic toward the evangelical movement, but some worked to prevent a civil war. At the Diet of Nürnberg in 1532, the electoral archbishop of Mainz and the Elector Palatine negotiated a temporary settlement, which Charles V contracted with the League on 22 June 1532 (the Truce of Nürnberg).[33] The truce was fixed until such a time as a general church council could decide the religious disputes. This brought the emperor soldiers from the Protestant estates for the defense of Vienna, but the Catholic princes never ratified the truce. After the Truce of Nürnberg, the threat of hostilities first mounted, then stagnated, then in 1537 mounted again, as both Catholic and Protestant sides confronted the tenacity of their

---

[32] Haug-Moritz, *Der Schmalkaldische Bund*, pp. 278–79. Ferdinand, Archduke of Austria, was elected king of the Romans, making him the presumptive successor to the emperor, in 1531 (long before the actual succession in 1556, a decade after Ferdinand had been pressured to forfeit his claim to Charles V's son Philip).

[33] Luttenberger, *Glaubenseinheit und Reichsfriede*, pp. 139–41, Brady, *Politics*, p. 238 notes 14–15. Also Schneider, *Ius Reformandi*, pp. 108–114 for negotiations at the Diet.

religious differences.[34] The absence of war allowed the Protestant movement to establish its position within the Empire, as we shall see.

The truce of 1532 was supposed to end suits before the Imperial Chamber Court. Instead, there followed prolonged disputes over the court's jurisdiction, while Protestantism and the League spread to new German cities and territories. Strasbourg and its influential churchman, Martin Bucer, tried to create unity among the Protestants, in spite of theological reservations in south German cities over the Augsburg Confession's doctrine of the eucharist. The Wittenberg Concord of 1536, which included a consensus formula on the disputed doctrine, answered these reservations and strengthened the position of the League in the south, although the Concord was rejected by the Swiss Protestant cities. But since Swiss political and military significance for Germany had ended in 1531, when Zürich was defeated by the five Catholic cantons of the Christian Union of Waldshut, this was of no consequence to the League.

After the Diet of Nürnberg in 1532, the German estates negotiated the meaning of the peace edict itself. The Protestants insisted hopefully that it implied the reversal of unfavorable decisions previously issued by the court, while they argued among themselves over the most effective way to handicap their legal opponents. Philip of Hesse preferred to recuse the entire judicial bench. Others wanted to recuse individual judges on grounds of religious bias.[35] Time and again members of the League would accuse the court of bias, sometimes extravagantly.[36] The accusation was not entirely fair. The court was obliged to determine the relevant points of law. So for example, when Strasbourg's bishop, in 1532, brought a complaint against the city for appointing a lay custodian to the women's cloister of St. Stephan's, the court initially confirmed the illegality of this move.[37]

---

[34] Haug-Moritz, *Der Schmalkaldische Bund*, pp. 46–8, 54–69.

[35] Dolezalek, "Juristische Argumentation," pp. 42–43. Brady, *Protestant Politics*, pp. 166–68 emphasizes Strasbourg's leadership among the cities in developing the recusation against the court.

[36] Thomas A. Brady, Katherine G. Brady, "A 'Swabian Conspiracy' at the Imperial Chamber Court (*Reichskammergericht*) in 1540," *Landesgeschichte als Herausforderung und Programm. Karlheinz Blaschke zum 70. Geburtstag*, ed. J. Matzerath, U. John (Leipzig: Sächsische Akademie der Wissenschaften, 1997), pp. 317–27, and Haug-Moritz, *Der Schmalkaldische Bund*, pp. 277–87.

[37] Sprenger, *Viglius von Aytta*, pp. 65–70 for this and the following, and Brady, *Protestant Politics*, p. 168.

But when in 1536 the city answered that they were exempt from
the court's jurisdiction on the strength of a 1435 imperial privilege,
the court, rather than dismiss the evasive maneuver, considered the
privilege at length and had difficulty deciding its validity (the suit
was eventually suspended by Charles V at the Diet of Regensburg
in 1541). Again, when in 1536 the prominent Strasbourg clergyman,
Jakob Abel, presented the assessors with a decision of the papal court
against the reformer Wolfgang Capito, who had assumed Abel's post
as prior of the collegiate church of St. Thomas, the court, rather
than simply confirm the papal decision, debated at length its authenticity, whether they were obliged to accept it, and the merits of
Abel's claim. The League's strategy of recusal was presumptuous to
the point of baffling. The accusation of bias simply ignored the illegality of Lutheran teachings that were used to justify the actions of
Protestant rulers in churches. But it eventually worked. The success
of the League's persistent self-assertion against restitution suits points
us to the importance of conviction, or one could even say faith. The
members of the League had to believe they were simply right, acting as true Christians. Accordingly, through the rest of the League's
history, its members were most consistently agreed about only two
things: the faith of the Augsburg Confession and the validity of
confiscations already made.

Suits against Protestants before the Imperial Chamber Court
mounted over the two years following the failure of the recusation
of 1534.[38] Between 1534 and 1536, six territories and twenty cities
were the subject of complaints involving the reformation of church
rites and properties.[39] In April 1538, Jacob Sturm, the Strasbourg
magistrate, proposed that the League recuse the court in all matters, which the League discussed, only to discover the diversity of
opinions among themselves about the legality, use, and form of recusation, alternatives to it, and the definition of "all matters."[40] The
League eventually formulated a general recusation in 1542 (we will
return to this).[41]

---

[38] Haug-Moritz, *Der Schmalkaldische Bund*, pp. 277–87. Mencke, *Visitationen*, pp.
58–63.
[39] Gerd Dommasch, *Die Religionsprozesse der rekusierenden und die Erneuerung des
Schmalkaldischen Bundes, 1534–1536* (Tübingen: Osiandersche Buchhandlung, 1961),
pp. 88–94. Haug-Moritz, *Der Schmalkaldische Bund*, p. 279.
[40] Haug-Moritz, *Der Schmalkaldische Bund*, p. 285.
[41] Haug-Moritz, *Der Schmalkaldische Bund*, pp. 284–7.

A Question of Mandate

Since 1537, pressure also mounted to extend the League's mandate to secular affairs, or to define religious matters in a way that included secular conflicts, as though any act of aggression against a Protestant ruler could be construed as a problem of religion.[42] The threat of military aggression seemed to mount, too, when in October 1538 the Imperial Chamber Court for the first time placed a member under ban for its religious reforms, the city of Minden in Lower Saxony. The event spurred an intense debate within the League over the obligation to mutual defense and the merits of preventive and defensive war.[43]

That same month, the imperial chancellor, Matthias Held, completed the formation of a Catholic counter-alliance, the Nürnberg League, which was contracted between the king of the Romans, the two dukes of Bavaria, the archbishop of Mainz, the duke of Albertine Saxony, the duke of Braunschweig-Wolfenbüttel, and the duke of Braunschweig-Calenberg. It alarmed the Protestants. But every party still had far more to gain from peace than war. Negotiations between the League and the French crown and the on-going threat of the Turks encouraged the emperor to compromise with the League of Schmalkalden.[44] Matthias Held, imperial chancellor, had not long before (February 1537) communicated to the Protestants the emperor's readiness to tolerate confiscations of church property, and there were those associated with the Schmalkald League, like Jacob Sturm, who doubted the League's readiness for armed conflict and emphasized the wisdom of diplomacy.[45] In 1538, it was more obvious to seek

---

[42] In 1537 the city of Bremen first brought its feud with Balthasar of Esens to the League, which had to do with the free passage of Bremen's ships. The League considered the matter repeatedly over the next four years, together with more famous conflicts of Braunschweig city with the duke of Braunschweig-Wolfenbüttel; Minden with the administrator of its cathedral, the bishop of Münster and Osnabrück; and Goslar with the duke of Braunschweig-Wolfenbüttel. Haug-Moritz, *Der Schmalkaldische Bund*, pp. 82–92, 190. The city of Strasbourg hoped the League would define the Imperial Chamber Court's judgement against it that same year, in a conflict over a disputed case of citizenship with the count of Hanau-Lichtenberg, as a religious matter. Brady, *Protestant Politics*, pp. 166–7.

[43] Brady, *Protestant Politics*, pp. 168, 206.

[44] Schneider makes the point that there was, on this account, no true threat of war. *Ius reformandi*, p. 116.

[45] Haug-Moritz, *Der Schmalkaldische Bund*, pp. 292–95, and 510, where she notes

accommodation in the Empire. Yet in the opening months of the following year, the League prepared for armed confrontation.[46]

The League also looked for new allies among Catholic princes in the party of mediation.[47] The electors of Trier, Cologne, and the Palatinate had proposed a meeting of electoral princes in spring 1538, and Johann Friedrich corresponded with the archbishop of Cologne about a solution in the imperial electoral college.[48] The Elector of Brandenburg, committed to neither the Protestant nor the Catholic (Nürnberg) League and desirous of a reform "neither Roman nor Saxon," worked for an imperial peace apart from Protestant-Catholic reconciliation.[49] His proposal included an end to religious cases at the Imperial Chamber Court, and it excluded sacramentarians, Anabaptists, and all other "unchristian" sects.[50] Since a reconciliation of Protestants with the Catholic church was not forthcoming, his plan was to separate imperial peace from religious agreement. Both Johann Friedrich and Philip of Hesse found this a practical course.[51] In 1539 the archbishop of Trier and the League considered an alliance. They hoped to include the ecclesiastical principalities of electoral Mainz, electoral Cologne, Würzburg, Bamberg, Osnabrück, Münster, and Minden, and the League was even prepared to guarantee the continued existence of ecclesiastical territories.[52] Philip of Hesse, who worried that Charles V intended to consolidate his authority in Germany as efficiently as he had done in Spain (and he was doing just that in the Netherlands), approached the Habsburg's rival in south Germany, the Catholic Duke Wilhelm of Bavaria, to arrange a princes' colloquy (it never happened). The Landgrave insisted that the League had no design on ecclesiastical

---

that church property only became an open topic of discussion at the meetings of the League after the imperial chancellor informed them that progress on church property should not, from the emperor's standpoint, hinder peace negotiations.

[46] Haug-Moritz, *Der Schmalkaldische Bund*, pp. 465–84.

[47] Haug-Moritz, *Der Schmalkaldische Bund*, p. 295.

[48] Luttenberger, *Glaubenseinheit und Reichsfriede*, p. 185. Haug-Moritz, *Der Schmalkaldische Bund*, pp. 288, 348.

[49] Bodo Nischan, *Prince, People, and Confession. The Second Reformation in Brandenburg* (Philadelphia: University of Pennsylvania, 1994), pp. 5–24, here 24.

[50] Luttenberger, *Glaubenseinheit und Reichsfriede*, pp. 187–8. Kuhaupt, *Veröffentlichte Kirchenpolitik*, p. 28.

[51] Luttenberger, *Glaubenseinheit und Reichsfriede*, p. 190 with n. 335.

[52] Wolgast, *Hochstift und Reformation*, p. 72.

principalities: they would accept the dual temporal and ecclesiastical roles of bishops, he said, while hoping to reform religious abuses.[53]

As these arrangements were explored, the League found itself moving simultaneously along two very different but not necessarily incompatible paths, one that could lead ultimately to rebellion against the emperor and another leading to accommodation within the Imperial Diet. In addition to eight new members in 1537–1538, six of whom were princes, including Heinrich of Saxony, the League had concluded its treaty with its northern neighbor, a recently converted Denmark, in April 1538 (Denmark had been the fiercest competitor of north Germany's Hanseatic cities for well over a century; as duke of Schleswig and Holstein the king was a member of the imperial diet).[54] When the Duke of Saxony and the Elector of Brandenburg decided to enter the League, the alliance claimed most of the north.[55] A new wave of Protestant reform then passed over the territories of electoral Brandenburg, Pfalz-Neuburg, Albertine Saxony, Pomerania, Mecklenburg, Braunschweig-Calenberg, the imperial city of Regensburg, and the cathedral cities of Hildesheim and Osnabrück; in all but Regensburg, it involved the confiscation of cloisters and the reassignment of church incomes and properties.[56] At this time (1537–9) in neighboring Bohemia, noble resistance to Ferdinand's royal power, which had grown over the estates since he received the crown in 1526, intensified around the Utraquist confession that had originated with Jan Hus.[57] Ferdinand's ambitions there matched Habsburg ambitions in the Netherlands, Austria, and Spain. Johann Friedrich and the Landgrave both hoped to create an international anti-Habsburg coalition.[58] Northern dominance by the League could only seem worthwhile to Johann Friedrich.

---

[53] M. Lenz, *Briefwechsel Landgraf Philipp's des Grossmüthigen von Hessen mit Bucer*, 3 vols. (Leipzig: S. Hirzel, 1880–91), 1:443–49, esp. 447.

[54] Haug-Moritz, *Der Schmalkaldische Bund*, p. 124 for this and the following.

[55] Haug-Moritz, *Der Schmalkaldische Bund*, p. 273.

[56] Schindling, "Der Passauer Vertrag," pp. 110–111.

[57] Resistance was brief. The third Habsburg territorial ordinance for Bohemia, of 1549, "legalized the shift of power from the Estates to the Monarch." Winfried Eberhard, *Monarchie und Widerstand. Zur ständischen Oppositionsbildung im Herrschaftssystem Ferdinands I. in Böhmen* (Munich: Oldenbourg, 1985), 265–334, esp. 311–5. Jaroslav Pánik, "Land Codes of the Bohemian Kingdom in Relation to Constitutional Changes in Central Europe on the Threshold of the Early Modern Age," *Historica* n.s. 9(2002):7–39, here 8–14, 30–32 (the quotation is from p. 13).

[58] Brady, *Protestant Politics*, p. 221.

In 1539, the emperor embraced princely efforts to accommodate the League.[59] Charles V offered the Protestants a temporary peace in April 1539 (the Truce of Frankfurt), and a two-month moratorium on Protestant cases before the Imperial Chamber Court, then began to negotiate the terms of dialogue.[60] These efforts led to the formulation of an agreed position on church property in the League, and they culminated in imperially sponsored religious colloques at Hagenau, Worms, and Regensburg in 1540 and 1541. At these colloquies, the League tried to keep church property off the table, and they succeeded (Chapter 7, below). The colloquies were supposed to achieve a religious peace. They are still celebrated as ecumenical milestones.[61] In their aftermath, the League won accommodation of its religion by the Empire.

But a sequence of scandal, success, and failure compromised the efforts of 1540 and 1541, even while the Protestant movement seemed to gain unprecedented power. Philip of Hesse, who with Johann Friedrich was leader of the League, provided the scandal. Although married to the daughter of Duke Georg of Saxony (they had had seven children together), the Landgrave secretly wedded a seventeen-year old noblewoman at court in March 1540, just as the League was preparing for the imperial religious colloquies.[62] The matter, when it became public that year, was scandalous to members of the League and opponents alike, but stranger still, the Landgrave was so committed to his new young wife, he threatened to reach an independent peace agreement with the emperor should his colleagues in the League oppose him, and he undertook secret negotiations to that end.[63]

In the meanwhile, the question of whether to extend the League's mandate to temporal conflicts was becoming increasingly acute.

---

[59] Brady, *Protestant Politics*, pp. 207–8.

[60] A majority of the court's assessors decided to uphold the moratorium in August 1539. Sieglerschmidt, *Territorialstaat*, pp. 152–3 with n. 56.

[61] Volkmar Ortmann, *Reformation und Einheit der Kirche: Martin Bucers Einigungsbemühungen bei den Religionsgesprächen in Leipzig, Hagenau, Worms und Regensburg 1539–1540* (Mainz: von Zabern, 2001).

[62] Brady, *Protestant Politics*, pp. 219–23 and the literature noted there. Brecht, *Martin Luther*, 3:205–9.

[63] Brady, *Protestant Politics*, p. 220. As early as 1531, the papal nuntio Girolamo Aleandro believed Philip might return to the old faith if church properties were left to him. *Legation Lorenzo Campeggios 1530–1531 und Nuntiatur Girolamo Aleandros 1531*, p. 427 nr. 120.

Strasbourg, in reaction to the Imperial Chamber Court's fine in 1539 and threat of ban in 1540, advocated a military response to onerous or excessive judgements, on the grounds that the court's sentences expressed bias against the Augsburg Confession (the cases could thus be taken as religious matters).[64] The League had warned of such action before.[65] At the same time, the Elector of Saxony won the League's support for a war in defense of the duke of Jülich, Cleves, and Berg. Since coming to power in 1539, the duke of Jülich, Cleves, and Berg wished to claim the neighboring duchy of Geldern, in violation of Habsburg claims. He, with the League in tow, now formed a third force in French-Habsburg rivalry in the Netherlands.[66]

Charles V was attentive to potential divisions within the League. In 1541, he demanded the support of Philip of Hesse against the duke of Cleves, Jülich, and Berg. Although in the next few years Philip supported Johann Friedrich's campaign for the League's dominance in the north, in this conflict, still pliant from the bigamy scandal, he was neutralized by the emperor.

That same year, the Landgrave and the Elector of Saxony overcame the resistance of the south German cities and persuaded the League to regard the long-standing, entirely non-religious conflicts of a new northern member, the city of Goslar in Lower Saxony, with the duke of Braunschweig-Wolfenbüttel as a religious matter.[67] Johann Friedrich, with the League's support, invaded and conquered Braunschweig in July 1542. The Imperial Chamber Court had an obvious obligation to try such a blatant breach of the peace as the invasion of Braunschweig. When the case came, the League returned to the suggestion made four years earlier by Jacob Sturm: that they should recuse the court in all matters, not just religious ones.

In 1542, the recusation worked. The Protestants first won a temporary, five-year suspension of the Imperial Chamber Court, then at its diet at Schweinfurt in November 1542, the League declared

---

[64] See Brady, *Protestant Politics*, pp. 168–9, 179–80 for this and the following.

[65] During Held's visit to the League's diet in February 1537 the Landgrave and the Elector had threatened to act with force against the court and denounce it publicly, according to Held's subsequent report to the Imperial Chamber Court. Sprenger, *Viglius von Aytta*, p. 83.

[66] The League had pursued a similar course in 1535. Haug-Moritz, *Der Schmalkaldische Bund*, pp. 273–5. Brady, *Protestant Politics*, pp. 151, 159, 254–7.

[67] Brady, *Protestant Politics*, pp. 260–3.

the court incompetent in any matter whatsoever.[68] The Imperial Diet
at Nürnberg in 1543 suspended all cases involving evangelicals. In
1544, the Imperial Diet of Speyer confirmed the suspension. At
Speyer, the emperor again recognized the League's reformation of
church property until a final settlement. The result was, as Thomas
Brady has pointed out, de facto recognition of Protestants within the
Empire.[69] If the recognition fell short of the legalization of Protestant
confiscations of church property, it removed what had become the
principal means of prosecuting confiscations as crimes, and that was
the crucial thing. The constant stream of restitution suits seldom if
ever restored properties, since judgements were mostly ignored, but
they kept confiscations illegal; they hindered legitimation by default,
by the sheer passage of time. They maintained the normative definition
of church robbery. They left the long-term survival of evangelical
churches an open question. The League's successful recusal demon-
strates how imposing a force the League had become. The suspension of the court accommodated, at least temporarily, churches of
the Augsburg Confession within the Empire.

That was one side of it. The other shows the League in a less
resolute light. Although an appetite for domination in the north had
been thoroughly whetted, the League's military policy still wavered.
When the emperor invaded the territory of the duke of Cleves, Jülich,
and Berg in 1543, the League took no action, and the duke was
roundly defeated after a brief campaign, which concluded with the
return of Geldern and Zutphen to the emperor, an end of his brief
alliance with France, and a marriage alliance that put the duke
squarely within the imperial party.[70] Martin Bucer played an important role in the Landgrave of Hesse's effort to move Herman von
Wied, the elector and archbishop of Cologne, from the ranks of
Catholic reconcilers to that of the adherents of the Augsburg

---

[68] Brady, *Protestant Politics*, p. 169. But see Schneider, *Ius reformandi*, pp. 118–9 for
the progressive suspensions of the court.

[69] Brady, *Protestant Politics*, pp. 169–174. Körber and Sieglerschmidt have also
pointed out how the Diet of 1544 anticipated the permanent settlement of 1555.
Sieglerschmidt, *Territorialstaat*, p. 155. Körber, *Kirchengüterfrage*, p. 148.

[70] Hans-Joachim Behr, *Franz von Waldeck, Fürstbischof von Münster und Osnabrück,
Administrator zu Minden (1491–1553). Sein Leben in seiner Zeit*, 2 parts, (Münster:
Aschendorf, 1996, 1998), 1:293.

Confession.[71] When in 1545 Charles obtained a papal sentence that removed Herman von Wied from office, the League determined to provide the archbishop's defense, but this intention was soon overcome by preparations for the Schmalkald War.[72] The archbishop was removed in 1546. In addition to the difficulty of mobilizing the League, divisions within it became more complex. The southern free cities, essential to the League's finances, had little to gain from the aspirations of the princes.[73] In the north itself, the two Saxonies vied for the protective lordship of the bishopric of Naumburg, rekindling the competition that the succession of Duke Heinrich in 1539 and his entry into the League was supposed to overcome (his successor in 1541, Duke Moritz, also Protestant, was far less pliable than his immediate predecessor).[74] Both had intentions for the bishop's temporal domains. The elector appointed and installed, to the objection of Naumburg's cathedral chapter, a Lutheran theologian, Nikolaus Amsdorf, as bishop. Amsdorf, a veteran of urban reform at Magdeburg and Goslar, had been helping Duke Heinrich reform the city of Meissen before Duke Moritz's succession. He had done battle with cathedral chapters several times before. Moritz soon allied himself with the emperor against his neighbor and distant kinsman, causing the most damaging rift in the League. He hoped eventually to see the electorship transferred from Johann Friedrich to himself and the Albertine succession. After the Schmalkald War, it was.

The Defeat of the League

One effect of the League's expansionist adventures, whether put under a broad definition of the defense of religion or not, was to increase competition among its members. Another was to force the emperor and the king of the Romans to recognize, not only the League's threat to peace, but a growing impediment to their own

---

[71] Wolgast, *Hochstift und Reformation*, pp. 91–9, 189. Brady, *Protestant Politics*, pp. 257–60.

[72] Wolgast, *Hochstift und Reformation*, pp. 91–9, 189.

[73] Brady, *Protestant Politics*, pp. 272–81.

[74] Gebhardt, *Handbuch*, 2:95.

ambitions. There were those Protestant military campaigns in Jülich-
Cleves-Berg and Braunschweig, and the reformation of one of the
Empire's ecclesiastical electors, the archbishop of Cologne. The two
Saxonies had designs on the bishopric of Naumburg. There was,
too, Franz von Waldeck, the prince-bishop of Münster and Osnabrück
and the administrator of Minden. Von Waldeck is famous for his
suppression of the Anabaptist kingdom at Münster in 1535 and the
restoration of Catholic order in the diocese.[75] Five years later, he
planned to introduce a Lutheran liturgy in the territories of Münster
and Osnabrück and the diocese of Minden.[76] To support that plan,
he, only a lay subdeacon, chose finally to complete his episcopal
appointment by getting ordained, which required passing through
the prior grades of deacon and priest.[77] Deaconry and priesthood
came on 28 December 1540, episcopacy on 1 January 1541. It was
said, he received the sacrament "with great piety and introspection."[78]
Not to mention convenience. In October, encouraged by that year's
Protestant-Catholic negotiations, he called on the estates of his territories to introduce reform. Conversion would have allowed him to
marry his lover and convert the prince-bishop's lands into a dynastic inheritance. Although several cities of his territories were already
introducing reforms, the estates of Münster and Osnabruck would
not comply. While the Landgrave of Hesse, an ally since 1532, tried
and ultimately failed to win the prince-bishop's admission to the
League of Schmalkalden, the prince-bishop installed evangelical preachers in vacant parishes, wherever he could, throughout his temporal
and spiritual realms. Never admitted to the League, in spite of his
support of the campaign against the duke of Braunschweig-Wolfenbüttel,
he became a neutral party in the Schmalkald War—yet more evidence of Protestant disarray.[79] (But Franz von Waldeck also shows

---

[75] Hsia, *Society and Religion*, pp. 6–58. Behr, *Franz von Waldeck*, 1:78–209.

[76] Schindling, "Der Passauer Vertrag," p. 110. Waldeck had established an alliance
with the Protestant Philip of Hesse in 1532 but also played a central role in the
restoration of Catholicism in the diocese of Münster after the suppression of the
Anabaptist rebellion in the city. Behr, *Franz von Waldeck*, 1:271–326 for this and
the following. Also, Hans-Joachim Behr, "Waldeck, Franz Graf von," *Biographisch-
Bibliographisches Kirchenlexikon*, 13:193–5. May, *Die deutschen Bischöfe*, pp. 122–5, 135–7,
152–4.

[77] *Die Bischöfe des Heiligen Römischen Reiches*, pp. 190–2 for this and the following.

[78] Behr, *Franz von Waldeck*, p. 276.

[79] Behr, *Franz von Waldeck*, 1:279–326, 353–439.

us that, in 1543, the Protestant movement could threaten to secularize prince-bishoprics, in spite of earlier evangelical protestations
to the contrary and in spite of the lack of any organized plan in
the League against bishops.)

The religious controversy in Germany had always been a relatively low priority to the emperor.[80] Charles V was at war with the
French in 1536–1538, and he was planning since 1538 to attack the
Turks on several fronts, only to confront a new Turkish expansion
into Hungary in 1541 and another open conflict with France in
1542–1544.[81] When he concluded peace agreements with the king
of France and the Sultan in 1544, he was freer to treat Germany
than at any previous time in his reign. And so he did. He made
agreements with the papacy, the dukes of Bavaria, and the Protestant
Duke of Albertine Saxony.[82] When the long-awaited general church
council, summoned by the pope in 1544, opened at Trent the following year, the Protestants refused to participate. Since 1530, it was
agreed that a general council would resolve the religious controversy,
and this removed the contingency that permitted the emperor to
promise to leave Protestant churches temporarily in place.

In 1546–1547 the emperor and the king of the Romans, having
already divided the League, conquered it in a ten-month campaign.
The war began at the end of August 1546. By November it was
clear that the League could not raise the funds to complete the campaign, and defeat was certain.[83] By the end of December, the League's
southern members were either occupied or negotiating. By May 1547,
the Landgrave and the Elector of Saxony were in the emperor's
custody.

The defeat was traumatic. Four hundred evangelical pastors were
sent into exile from occupied lands.[84] Spanish soldiers were posted
in Württemberg, where all pastors were defrocked in 1548, in spite
of the absence of priests to replace them all. Duke Ulrich scram-
bled to reinstate some of the very canons and priests he had pen-
sioned over a decade before, who were still willing to celebrate

---

[80] Reinhard, "Die kirchenpolitischen Vorstellungen Karls V," p. 90.
[81] Gebhardt, *Handbuch*, 2:91–95.
[82] *Le temps des confessions*, pp. 355–66.
[83] Brady, *Protestant Politics*, pp. 297–8.
[84] *Le temps des confessions*, pp. 362–67 and the literature noted there.

Catholic liturgy.[85] When the city of Constance rejected the Interim of 1548, the response was swift. The city's territory was incorporated into Austrian domains, and citizens who refused to renounce the evangelical faith were expelled. But the war left the emperor's Protestant allies unmolested, and the Diet of Augsburg of 1547/8 and the Interim of 1548 hardly destroyed the religion of the Augsburg Confession in the lands of his enemies. The emperor, while trying to win acceptance of the primacy of his own military authority by the estates, hoped to facilitate a thorough Catholic reform that would quickly pull Protestants into its force field and draw them back to papal obedience.[86] Charles resisted calls from his theological advisors to hand all Protestant church property to their Catholic counterparts, although the same advisors meant to reform the old church, too. They had mapped out reforms of church offices and incomes to serve more narrowly the demands of pastoral care. The church unity that the emperor desired was partly frustrated by the continued Protestant refusal to submit to the general council, still technically in session, although it had been transferred from Trent to Bologna as the Schmalkald War came to an end, and there the council quickly fell dormant for four years. A religious reconciliation was partly frustrated by the estates themselves, a panel of whom tried in vain to formulate a settlement, while Catholic theologians repeated their demands for a restitution of all confiscated properties.[87] When the panel of estates failed, the matter went to a committee of theologians. Catholics dominated it, but one notable Protestant was there, the court preacher of Brandenburg, Johann Agricola.[88] After considerable debate, the Interim was accepted by most Protestants, chastened by the example of Constance and over the objections of Protestant clergy. The Interim reinstated the Catholic mass and returned churches to episcopal oversight, but the Protestant laity

---

[85] Ehmer, "Ende und Verwandlung," pp. 224–6.

[86] Horst Rabe, *Reichsbund und Interim. Die Verfassungs- und Religionspolitik Karls V. und der Reichstag von Augsburg 1547/1548* (Cologne: Böhlau, 1971), pp. 260–72 for this and the following. Also Luttenberger, *Glaubenseinheit und Reichsfriede*, pp. 425–501.

[87] Rabe, *Reichsbund und Interim*, pp. 413–424. In the face of the demands for restitution, Jacob Sturm insisted that such actions had been necessary for reform. Ibid., p. 422.

[88] Bucer also presented a recommendation to the panel of theologians. Ibid., pp. 424–49. For the elector of Brandenburg's role in promoting the Interim, Luttenberger, *Glaubenseinheit und Reichsfriede*, pp. 483–8.

were allowed to receive the host and the cup in the Eucharistic rite, and their married clergy were allowed to keep their wives. There was something here to alarm all parties. As was usual in German conflicts, all waited to renegotiate another day.

That day came quickly.[89] While Johann Friedrich and Philip of Hesse languished in imperial custody, resentments and fears of a Spanish servitude grew among the German princes. An emperor's success kindled anxieties among many. Where there was fear, there was opportunity. Moritz, who after the war received the prize of half of Johann Friederich's domains and his position as imperial elector, joined plans for an insurrection by the margrave of Brandenburg and forged an alliance with King Henry II of France. Henry was eager to take Burgundy, Artois, and Flanders. Moritz blandished him with promises of support for his imperial election. With the help of the margrave of Kulmbach[90] and Wilhelm, the son of the imprisoned Landgrave, and buttressed by non-aggression pacts with Bavaria and the archbishop-electors of the Rhineland, the Germans and the French king mobilized in March 1552. The Germans headed south to meet the emperor, and the French marched west across Lorraine. Five years before, Charles V was at the summit of his power, but now he was in Augsburg and unprepared. He fled to Austria, where he met a Ferdinand prepared to contract a peace with the Protestants. When the German troops reached Innsbruck, the emperor, as he reported to his sister Maria of Hungary in the Netherlands, left the Empire after prolonged discussions with his brother to allow Ferdinand to contract a peace with Moritz (the Treaty of Passau) without him.[91] The German phase of the war ended. The rebellion reignited the emperor's conflict with France, returned Johann Friedrich and Philip of Hesse to freedom, and most importantly, won the Protestants a promise of a permanent religious peace with guarantees of church properties previously confiscated.

The peace was fragile, how fragile was demonstrated in the next two years, when Albrecht Alcibiades, margrave of Kulmbach, undertook

---

[89] Gebhardt, *Handbuch*, 2:101 remains a useful brief summary, but see especially Brady, *Protestant Politics*, pp. 359–363.

[90] Ansbach and Kulmbach had been separated at the death of Georg the Pious. Georg's son received Ansbach, and Albrecht Alcibiades, Georg's nephew, received Kulmbach. The division of the inheritance came at Albrecht's expense.

[91] Führer, *Die Kirchen- und die antireformatorische Religionspolitik*, pp. 169–170. Schilling, "Charles V and Religion," pp. 302–3.

a second rebellion. Albrecht had supported the emperor in the Schmalkald War, but he also supported Moritz's rebellion in 1552: he helped negotiate the alliance between Moritz and the king of France. Now he tried to extend his territory along the Main river through the lands of the prince-bishops, at first by forcing concessions from the prince-bishops of Bamberg and Würzburg and from the emperor.[92] Had he succeeded, he would have controlled most of Franconia. Confronted and defeated by a coalition of the bishops, King Ferdinand, Duke Moritz (now the elector of Saxony), and the duke of Braunschweig, he was placed under imperial ban in 1554. None of this should be seen as a confessional war. The elector of Saxony and the duke of Braunschweig were, in this instance, defenders of prince-bishops, and like the rebel Albrecht Alcibiades himself, Protestants.

The terms agreed at Passau were confirmed and expanded at the Imperial Diet of Augsburg in 1555. The Diet recognized churches of the Augsburg Confession and granted the right to accept Lutheran churches to the rulers of the 390 territories and free cities of the Empire, but denied ecclesiastical princes the right to choose a confession (the Protestants did not subscribe to this last clause, but the emperor imposed it). The *churches* of the Augsburg Confession were legalized. But the faith of the Augsburg Confession, however tolerated, was not, not quite. The Peace protected the property and religious practice of imperial estates of the Augsburg Confession, including church properties that had previously passed to imperial subjects.[93] It suspended Catholic ecclesiastical jurisdiction over adherents of the Augsburg Confession and the application of heresy law to them. But the Peace did little to change the legal status of the church, including its property, and uses of church property continued to be debated as before.[94] The Lutheran faith remained a heresy in the eyes of the emperor and the Catholic estates, on the strength of papal and impe-

---

[92] Schindling, "Der Passauer Vertrag," p. 108 and the literature noted there.

[93] For this and the following, see Sieglerschmidt's review of unresolved issues in the 1555 Peace, *Territorialstaat*, pp. 160–7. He also notes that the terms of the peace pertained to imperial estates, their principalities, territories, and lordships, including their properties and subjects. But in the many regions, especially in the west and south of the Empire, where imperial subjection and definite governing authority often did not coincide, the peace "created more problems than it solved." Ibid., pp. 164, 173.

[94] Sieglerschmidt's point, *Territorialstaat*, pp. 165, 204–8, 286–7.

rial condemnations of Luther's doctrine, which were still valid. Protestants, for their part, alleged as vehemently the heresy of the old faith.

Between Jurisdictions and Purposes

In effect, this outcome merely restored and legitimized earlier facts on the ground, namely the facts created by the League of Schmalkalden in the early 1540's. The defeat of the League in 1547 only interrupted the trend toward imperial accommodation, the greatest achievement of which had been the suspension of the Imperial Chamber Court in 1543/4. In the long term, this may have been the League's most enduring accomplishment, which is strongly suggested by the 1555 peace agreement's adjustments to the Imperial Chamber Court, which the emperor had reactivated in 1548.[95] The court was now required to have an equal number of judges from the old church and the new one of the Augsburg Confession on its panel whenever it considered religious questions.[96] Evangelicals had demanded parity on the court since 1524, and now they achieved it. It was an important victory, in spite of the humiliations of the previous decade. The new rule answered the League's main complaint against the court, the complaint of religious bias, for the next four decades.[97] But again it was the League of Schmalkalden, not the Peace of Augsburg, that had taught the Empire how to accept churches of the Augsburg Confession. The key was not religious reconciliation, which only a general church council could have achieved (there was never any real chance of it), but legitimation of confiscations of

---

[95] His purpose, unsuccessful in the end, was to use it to step back princes' rights. For this and the following, Peter Schulz, *Die politische Einflussnahme auf die Entstehung der Reichskammergerichtsordnung 1548* (Cologne: Böhlau, 1980), p. 225; Duchhardt, "Oberste Gerichtsbarkeit," pp. 9, 219–27; Rabe, *Reichsbund und Interim*, pp. 303–321.

[96] Fuchs, "Supreme Court," p. 15 and the literature noted there.

[97] Heckel, "Die Reformationsprozesse," p. 14. Cases involved smaller estates (Catholic imperial cloisters and foundations or evangelical counts, imperial estates, imperial villages, and imperial knights) making complaints against large neighbors of the other confession. Most cases had to do with the removal or re-dedication of church property, change in forms of worship, occupation of clergy offices, assignment of building expenses, infringements on subjects of other lordships, protective measures against Calvinism, problems arising from inter-confessional marriages, and the distribution of church properties in bi-confessional imperial cities.

church property.

The Imperial Chamber Court did little to dam-up the fluid situation that produced a bi-confessional Empire, the situation of the
League of Schmalkalden from 1530 to 1543, the year of the court's
suspension. Its judgments varied according to the contingencies of a
case and the membership of the court, but the majority of the bench
always presupposed the illegality of Protestant reforms.[98] The court
was receptive to complaints by Catholic clergy alienated from their
benefices by Protestants, and the court was eager to trump other
jurisdictions.[99] Catholic priests, priors, prioresses, abbots, and abbesses
could expect a more sympathetic hearing here than before urban
judges. The court was generally less receptive to claims that implied
the validity of Protestant confiscations, although such cases did appear
before the court, for example, one brought by an evangelical pastor who sued the bishop of Constance for a benefice punitively withheld by his Catholic bishop.[100] However penultimate its decisions
were (the authority of any court in sixteenth-century Germany was
only as good as the readiness of communities to observe its will), the
court posed the main threat to Protestant reforms in Germany from
1530 to 1543, not because it could reverse changes to church property and personnel made by cities or princes, but because it could
underscore, propagate, and confirm their illegitimacy. That is what
the League neutralized three years before it fell.

As the court's achievements were limited, so too were the League's
goals. The court was one among several theaters of political action,
born as it was of a political purpose.[101] Accordingly, we might have
expected the League to answer the court with a political rationale
for lay dominion over the church, since confiscations and reorganizations of church property and personnel looked glaringly like just
such an exercise. But the League settled for much less than a definition
of lay dominion, as we will see.[102] The history of the League sug-

---

[98] Dolezalek, "Die juristische Argumentation," p. 30.
[99] For this and the following, ibid., pp. 27–28, and for attempts to negate the
prerogatives of lower courts, p. 41.
[100] This was reasonable enough for a Catholic bishop, one would think. Dolezalek,
"Juristische Argumentation," pp. 50–51. Individual clergy as plaintiffs were rare,
however. Ranieri, *Recht und Gesellschaft*, 1:228 n. 33.
[101] Duchhardt, "Das Reichskammergericht," p. 3. Ranieri, *Recht und Gesellschaft*,
1:171–2, for the court's importance in establishing and propagating norms among
the territories.
[102] Even Melanchthon's view of the magistrate's *cura religionis*, which asserted his

gests why.

First, the League relied on the traditional distinction between temporal and spiritual jurisdictions, even while they used their temporal authority to reorganize and manage church business. This circumstance was created at Nürnberg in 1532 when the emperor conceded to the Protestants the Imperial Chamber Court's incompetence in matters of faith. The League therefore had to define church property disputes as religious matters beyond the jurisdiction of lay courts, even while the League's members established their own authority to meddle in ecclesiastical affairs.[103] That is, the League's members needed both to encourage and discourage the exercise of lay power over church property. It may have been an inherently unstable position, but it fit the moment.

In addition, throughout the League's history, the coalition's political goal as a body was unclear. The League was supposed to create a political block within the Empire in which common interests were created by the religion of the Augsburg Confession. The only obvious thing about that purpose proved to be mutual defense in the event of a religious war and mutual support for church reforms, especially reorganizations of church property and administration. The League's goal was never secularization per se. Most importantly, the League did not, as a body, ever advocate an end to ecclesiastical principalities as such. When the League expanded its view of its mandate beyond the religious controversy, under the broad tent of religion, tension mounted until the League was shattered by the Schmalkald War. The desirability of a new view of dominion was just not agreeable to all members of the League. There was too much momentum behind an imperial peace pursued the normal way: in alliances that served mutual self-interest, while everyone tried to check Habsburg ambitions and avoid expensive armed conflicts with unpredictable outcomes.

The discussion of church property served the League's attempt to

---

position as foremost member of the church with oversight of both tables of the law, adapted the more expansive notion of the imperial *Kirchenvogtei*. Johannes Heckel, *Cura Religionis. Ius in Sacra. Ius circa Sacra* (Darmstadt: Wissenschaftliche Buchgesellschaft, 1962). James Estes noted his adaptation of a Catholic, specifically Erasmian, idea of the Christian prince or magistrate. Estes, *Peace, Order and the Glory of God*, p. 57.

[103] The Imperial Chamber Court itself had difficulty determining what a religious matter was between 1532 and 1544. Sieglerschmidt, *Territorialstaat*, p. 138.

assert and protect church reforms and confiscations, but it must also
have helped adjudicate competing forces within the League: the force
to expand princely authority and mobilize princes against the emperor,
to achieve imperial toleration for churches of the Augsburg Confession
while remaining faithful imperial subjects, or to avoid civil war.
Church property was an issue that had very much to do with the
nature and extent of ruling authority, yet unlike other issues debated
internally by Protestants (mutual defense, the right of rebellion, and
the right of reform),[104] it was a relatively safe topic. Whether the
League's members advocated an aggressive course or slipped into
the wing of the imperial peace party, its stance on church property
remained basically the same, namely: the League demanded acceptance of confiscations.

In other words, church property had to do with ruling authority
over religion, or the question of sovereignty, but this was never sys-
tematically theorized by the first generation of Protestant reformers.
Not a single Protestant treatise written during the history of the
League could be thought to compete with any of the medieval papal-
ist treatises in philosophical sophistication or with Marsiglio of Padua's
Defender of the Peace, still the best known defense of imperial authority in Germany at the time.[105] These works laid out terms of debate

---

[104] For these, Wolgast, *Die Wittenberger Theologie*, pp. 125–284, and Haug-Moritz,
Der Schmalkaldische Bund, pp. 511–29.

[105] Consider Ralph Keen's survey of them, in Ralph Keen, *Divine and Human
Authority in Reformation Thought. German Theologians and Political Order 1520–1555*
(Nieuwkoop: De Graaf, 1997), passim. Protestants treated issues of ruling authority
in biblical commentaries and polemical works, in moral and hortatory ways. They
focused on obedience to divine authority, the authority and limitations of law, obligations of subjects to rulers, and the morality of rulers—all with the intention of
motivating or reinforcing support of evangelical actions. Protestants produced admonitions to princes. The best known are Luther's letters to temporal rulers. There
also existed similar appeals to the estates of a territory, for example Antonius
Corvinus to the nobility of the Mark Brandenburg, Lüneburg, and Braunshweig,
an appeal to support reform on the basis of noble values regarding the government
of the household. Reinhard Lorichius' *De institutione principum loci communes* of 1538,
which I have been unable to examine, may also be aimed at territorial nobility. It
describes the difference between good and bad lords. Georg Geisenhof, *Bibliotheca
Corviniana. Eine bibliographische Studie* (Nieuwkoop: De Graaf, 1964 reprint of the 1900
edition), nr. 2, 111, 121, 127, 130, 132. *Melanchthon und die Marburger Professoren:
(1527–1627)*, ed. Barbara Bauer, 2 vols. (Marburg: Universitäts-Bibliothek, 2000),
1:303–6.

over dominion, political authority, and the church. It was all at hand and passed over. Yet Protestant reformers required the reorganization of church property, and a number of rulers did oblige them, while helping themselves to a substantial part of it. To justify these actions, theologians offered at least twenty recommendations treating church property before and during the history of the League.[106] To their history I now turn.

---

[106] Counting only official memoranda, that is *Gutachten, Bedencken,* or *Ratschläge* intended for official discussion and not personal letters or publications.

Lucas Cranach the Younger, *Martin Luther and the Wittenberg Reformers*, c. 1543 (anytime between 1532 and 1547, when Johann Friedrich was scarred in the face at the battle of Mühlberg),[1] oil on panel, 27 5/8 × 15 5/8 in. (72.8 × 39.7 cm), Toledo Museum of Art, Gift of Edward Drummond Libbey, 1926.55. Johann Friedrich of Saxony is surrounded by (from left to right) Luther, Georg Spalatin, Gregor Brück, and Melanchthon. He stands in a regal pose, his left hand resting on the hilt of his sword and his right on the hilt of a dagger, the dagger's pommel clearly visible.[2] The right hand appears to be placed outside the border of the cloak, which suggests that the dagger is supposed to be withdrawn from its sheath. Since a blade does not extend below the hand, the painting may be incomplete. Melanchthon's right index finger is raised instructively, while in his left hand he holds a rolled document. Luther and Melanchthon's expressions are satisfied; Johann Friedrich's presence, intrepid. The relatively small size together with the upward gazes of Spalatin and two of the unidentifiable men in the background suggest that this has been cut out of the lower lefthand corner of a crucifixion scene that most likely served as part of an altarpiece, where patron portraits sometimes appear. In an altarpiece, the directions of these gazes, determined, introspective, worried in the background, and admiring, create a kind of circuit between the prince, the reformers, and the grieving Virgin and John the Baptist at the foot of the cross and the suffering Christ hanging on it, who performs their redemption.

---

[1] Carl C. Christensen, *Princes and Propaganda. Electoral Saxon Art of the Reformation* (Kirksville, MO: Sixteenth Century Journal Publishers, 1992), pp. 69–71. *Glaube und Macht*, 2:148 nr. 201 and the literature noted there.

[2] For such a dagger in the Elector's possession at this time, with medallion portraits of himself and his wife Sibylle of Cleve on the top of the sheath, see *Glaube und Macht*, 2:191 nr. 287. It later came into the Albertine Elector's possession.

CHAPTER FOUR

THEOLOGICAL ADVICE

Soon after the recess of the 1530 Diet of Augsburg, Philip of Hesse said to a theologian, "Doctor, you all speak very well, but what if we don't follow you?"[1] In many things, rulers would. Theological advice was obviously crucial to the magistrates and princes of the League of Schmalkalden. The League defined itself as a coalition formed for the defense of religion, and theologians determined the teachings of the religion defended.

Luther heard and reported the comment to guests at his table. Recently coached by the elector's counselors to validate Protestant resistance to the emperor, he understood the Landgrave's warning.[2] He remarked that theologians who overextend imperial authority at the expense of princes—by thinking the emperor in Germany has rights like any king in a kingdom—risked being sidelined. "If we theologians think otherwise, for example, that such [a view] is not to be opposed as wrong, they'll say, like the Landgrave said, 'Doctor, you all speak very well, but what if we don't follow you?'" The

---

[1] WATisch 2:404–5, quoted by Luther between August and Christmas 1531. The comment reflects Luther's movement from an emphasis on imperial office before the 1530 Diet of Augsburg to a view of the emperor's strictly limited lordship within the political community of the Empire. Brecht, *Martin Luther*, 2: 411–15. See also Eike Wolgast, *Die Wittenberger Theologie und die Politik der evangelischen Stände. Studien zu Luthers Gutachten in politischen Fragen* (Gütersloh: Gerd Mohn, 1977), p. 299, and Wolfgang Günter, *Martin Luthers Vorstellung von der Reichsverfassung* (Münster: Aschendorff, 1976), pp. 176–9 and passim. Luther gives the interesting example of forestry rights (unlike kings, the emperor had no overarching right to wood, he says), which was, in fact, a matter increasingly subject to territorial regulation. Schubert, "Vom Gebot zur Landesordnung," pp. 35–7.

[2] The previous note. In the cited passage of the Table Talk, Luther defines the imperial infringement of princely rights as tyranny, and princely rights as an extension of the authority of the *paterfamilias*. Johannes Brenz had also rejected a right to resist the emperor among the imperial estates. Schneider, *Ius reformandi*, p. 127. The close association of reform with the emperor was later strongly promoted by Catholic theologians hoping to restore church unity after the defeat of the Schmalkald League, for example, Julius Pflug. See Heribert Smolinsky, "Julius Pflug (1499–1564)," *Katholische Theologen der Reformationszeit*, 6:27.

growth of Anabaptists and sacramentarians suggested to Luther that, in the absence of princely support, church reform would collapse into a sectarian morass. Convinced of their role as the learned interpreters of divine revelation and anxious to advise on public matters, theologians guarded their influence, as Luther taught his company to do on this occasion at his home in Wittenberg's Augustinian friary.

They exercised influence in two ways.[3] One was to inform official religious policies; the other, to influence the public. In German cities preachers helped create an evangelical groundswell among burghers sufficient to force reluctant magistrates to endorse and eventually promote reform.[4] Many of the leading Protestant theologians had helped muster the popular movement in cities before 1531, for example, Justus Jonas in Wittenberg in 1520/1, Andreas Osiander in Nürnberg, Oecolampadius in Basel, Ambrosius Blarer in Constance, Nikolaus Amsdorf in Magdeburg, Wolfgang Capito and Martin Bucer in Strasbourg; or they soon would, for example, Johannes Timan in Bremen and Wolfgang Musculus in Augsburg. In every instance, a stock set of caricatures, well known from the popular writings and sermons of Martin Luther and these men, aided the effort: the abomination of the mass, the futility of monasticism, the dishonesty of mendicant friars, the superstitions of traditional devotion, papal avarice, and the worldliness of prince-bishops. All caricatures had implications for property. They undermined the uses of chapels, chantries, and other religious shrines; altars and memorial endowments, every kind of monastery and their land holdings, incomes from public gifts spontaneous or planned (religious begging, bequests), annates and special church taxes, papal reservations of benefices, episcopal courts, and the judicial exemptions that helped protect all these things from lay encroachment. Since the new evangelical clergy were usually converted friars, priests, or holders of preaching benefices—and not bishops, abbots, or canons—they managed very

---

[3] Consider Hamm, *The Reformation of Faith*, pp. 228, 230.

[4] Heinz Schilling, *Religion, Political Culture, and the Emergence of Early Modern Society. Essays in German and Dutch History*, trans. Stephen Burnett (Leiden: E.J. Brill, 1992), pp. 135–201. Stephan Laux, *Reformationsversuche in Kurköln (1542–1548). Fallstudien zu einer Strukturgeschichte landstädtischer Reformation (Neuss, Kempen, Andernach, Linz)* (Münster: Aschendorff, 2001), passim. Dieter Fabricius, *Die theologischen Kontroversen in Lüneburg im Zusammenhang mit der Einführung der Reformation* (Lüneburg: Museumsverein für das Fürstentum Lüneburg, 1988), pp. 169–179.

little church property themselves, and in the cases of priests and preachers, bishops and Catholic patrons tried to replace them with orthodox pastors.[5] The preachers relied on magistrates and princes to reorganize the finances of the city's churches, in order to continue their work.

No comparable public role seems to have governed the progress of, at least, official confessional change in the countryside. Princes and estates appointed evangelicals to country parishes, a process eventually coopted from the estates by territorial administrations.[6] But in both cities and territories, the preachers tutored a city council or a prince on new ecclesiastical structures, which included counsel on church property. The rationale for confiscation was a matter for princes and city magistrates, to whom theologians provided the religious justifications for reforms and from whom they demanded firm support for evangelical ministry and culture. This was the context of the church property debate.

Their counsel reflected their professional culture. Theologians were educated in the schools of religious orders and university theology faculties and had experience teaching there (for example, Martin Luther, Martin Bucer, and Wolfgang Musculus), or they received instead an education in the universities' faculties of liberal arts (for example, Philip Melanchthon, one of the most influential intellectuals of sixteenth-century Europe). Most were deeply affected by humanism, which was transforming the study of logic and creating new energy behind the study of ancient texts and languages, which affected

[5] A notable exception to the rule of the absence of bishops in the evangelical movements was the bishop of Samland, whose 1524 Easter sermon in Königsberg helped provoke the riots of Easter Monday and Tuesday. Tschackert, *Urkundenbuch zur Reformationsgeschichte des Herzogthums Preußen*, 1:79–87. May, *Die deutschen Bischöfe*, p. 438.

[6] Peter Blickle, *Gemeindereformation. Die Menschen des 16. Jahrhunderts auf dem Weg zum Heil* (Munich: Oldenbourg, 1985), p. 14. Consider Bernd Hamm's suggestion that the distinction between urban and rural reforms and 1525 as a turning point not be exaggerated. He emphasizes theological continuities between Luther, Zwingli, and Bucer before and after the war. Hamm, *The Reformation of Faith*, 231–240. For rural conversion (the case of Ansbach-Kulmbach), Dixon, *Reformation of Rural Society*, pp. 66–202. For territorial organization and lordship, Schubert, "Vom Gebot zur Landesordnung," pp. 19–61. Idem, *Fürstliche Herrschaft und Territorium im späten Mittelalter* (Munich: Oldenbourg, 1996), pp. 61–108, and *Die evangelischen Kirchenordnungen des 16. Jahrhunderts*, edited by Emil Sehling and continued by the Institut für evangelisches Kirchenrecht der Evangelischen Kirche in Deutschland, 15 vols. (Leipzig: O.R. Reisland and Tübingen: J.C.B. Mohr, 1902–1977).

theologians of both confessions.[7] Jurists were more prominent at court, although some intellectuals crossed the boundary of theological and legal careers, for example, Georg Spalatin, who after completing his study of the liberal arts took a course in law. Leading clergy were part of the learned class of governmental advisors. Their advisory role had grown in late medieval Europe as an extension of the position of university professor, for most German universities were sponsored by princes, and rulers expected professors to serve a common welfare under their paternal care.[8] The most influential theologians occupied a stratum just below a prince's or city's high-level functionaries and ministers. They usually reached rulers through the upper tier.[9] The Landgrave's comment, "what if we don't follow you," reflects the dispensability of advice from the second tier of advisors and the relative demerit of theological advice on the topic of imperial authority, but not the expendability of theologians as such.

Their professional culture depended on informal communication rather than authority. Protestants eliminated the religious court of last instance, the papacy, and replaced it with no trans-regional organ, conciliar or otherwise. They replaced it with no single method to establish common premises, work-out agreed conclusions, enforce

---

[7] For the changing trend, see Ocker, *Biblical Poetics*, pp. 184–99 and the literature noted there.

[8] As such, theologians helped build the international Protestant networks that made Denmark an ally of the League, and they helped court England and France for the League. Brady, *Protestant Politics*, pp. 151–61. For the role of theologians in Protestant relations with France and England, consider Melanchthon, MBW 2:178, 179, 182, 183, 188, 189, 197, 198, 200, 201, 207, 208, 209, 228 and nr. 1552, 1555, 1563, 1564, 1578, 1579, 1604, 1606, 1607, 1611, 1612, 1613, 1631, 1635, 1637, 1681. A convenient presentation of documents relevant to the breakdown of English and Protestant-German negotiations in 1538 and 1539, as well as the French-Schmalkald negotiations of 1535, may be found in Martin Luther, *Sämmtliche Schriften*, ed. Johann Georg Walch, 23 vols. (St. Louis: Concordia, 1901), 17:209–82 nr. 1269–78 and 17:286–301 nr. 1282–87. For England, see also Diarmaid MacCulloch, *Thomas Cranmer* (New Haven: Yale, 1996), pp. 213–36. As an example of a medieval university master providing princely advice, consider Heinrich von Langenstein. Georg Kreuzer, *Heinrich von Langenstein unter besonderer Berücksichtigung der Epistola pacis und der Epistola concilii pacis* (Paderborn: Ferdinand Schöningh, 1987), pp. 93–101. For princes and their universities, see *Universities in the Middle Ages*, edited by Hilda De Ridder-Symoens, v. 1 of *A History of the University in Europe* (Cambridge University Press, 1992), pp. 102–6.

[9] Miriam Usher Chrisman, *Conflicting Visions of Reform. German Lay Propaganda Pamphlets, 1519–1530* (Atlantic Highlands: Humanities Press, 1996), pp. 34–5, 43–5. H.C. Erik Midelfort, *Mad Princes of Renaissance Germany* (Charlottesville: University Press of Virgina, 1994), p. 124.

them trans-regionally, and disqualify dissenting opinions. They relied, instead, on a shared presupposition: competent interpretation of scripture by believers, they presupposed, will produce common results among diverse scholars, a conviction dependent on the religious imaginary, the subjectivity of which is suggested by their belief in the agency of the Holy Spirit, the giver of the faith that allows correct religious understanding. At the same time, each theologian considered himself directly subject to Christ, whose will scripture revealed now until the final judgement. As their Catholic counterparts also believed, sacred learning was based on the interpretation of the bible, but this included the ability to represent and apply ecclesiastical tradition and canon law, evidence of a holy continuum in which Protestant clergy also believed, while they disputed the character of the church's holiness and the identity of its members.[10] Both bible and traditional sources characterized their discourse. Luther ceremoniously burned the canon law and ridiculed it when he was threatened with excommunication in 1520, but his arguments about papalism were tendentious and decontextualized,[11] and his position against law and tradition was softened by time and Melanchthon.[12]

Once an actual general church council threatened to materialize, at the ascent of Pope Paul III (1534–1549), their interpretation of church tradition increasingly alleged the independence of the continuum of doctrinal truth from church councils.[12a] In 1534, the League received a formal invitation to attend a general council at Mantua, which in fact never took place, but the new pope's resolve to convene a council was clear enough. Protestant theologians then emphasized non-conciliar continuities of the evangelical church with the Christian

[10] Ocker, *Biblical Poetics*, pp. 199–213. Pierre Fraenkel, *Testimonium patrum. The Function of Patristic Argument in the Theology of Philip Melanchthon* (Geneva: Droz, 1961). For Bucer, see Irene Backus' contribution to *The Reception of the Church Fathers in the West: From the Carolingians to the Maurists*, 2 vols., edited by Irene Backus (Leiden: E.J. Brill, 1997).

[11] Giles of Viterbo pointed this out in a 1521 brief rebutting Luther's *Warum des Papstes und seiner Jünger Bücher von D.M. Luther verbrannt sind*. Hermann Tüchle, "Des Papstes und seiner Jünger Bücher. Eine römische Verteidigung und Antwort auf Luthers Schrift 'Warum des Papstes und seiner Jünger Bücher von D.M. Luther verbrannt sind' aus dem Jahre 1521," *Lutherprozeß und Lutherbann*, pp. 48–68.

[12] For law and Luther, Melanchthon, Johannes Eisermann, and Johannes Oldendorp, see Witte, *Law and Protestantism*, pp. 119–175.

[12a] Thomas Brockmann, *Die Konzilsfrage in den Flug- und Streitschriften des deutschen Sprachraumes 1518–1563* (Göttingen: Vandenhoeck und Ruprecht, 1998), pp. 246–301.

past. Luther, in a letter addressed to Pope Paul and all the cardinals and prelates due to assemble at Mantua, mockingly observed:
it was nineteen years since his excommunication by Pope Leo X of
"unhappy memory." Luther admitted that he never abandoned his
appeal to a universal council. Unfortunately, he said, illness prevented him from attending the one now summoned, and poverty
kept him from sending a representative. He would respond in writing.[13] He produced a rash of anti-conciliar tractates that year.[14]
Antonius Corvinus, the Hessian theologian, responded to the council called in 1537 with a treatise explaining conciliar limitations.[15]
Two years later, Melanchthon published an account of the historical preservation of the articles of faith in the true church, in spite
of the obscuring opinions and errors of the church fathers.[16] After
the council convened at Trent, during preparations for the Schmalkald
War, he published a defense of Protestant obedience to God against
any contrary temporal authority, together with a rebuttal of the council's validity, citing ancient bishops, while discrediting those whose
obedience to the emperor ignored errors concerning doctrine, remis-
sion of sins, penance, devotion to saints and images, the prohibition
of marriage (i.e. clerical celibacy), and the preaching office.[17] Protestant
provisos and qualifications of conciliar authority mounted as soon as
a church council took shape.

Evangelical consensus was strongest when the preachers condemned
things. A corrupt and tyranical pope, together with his minions and
sympathizers, are the enemy. Monasticism and much if not all traditional devotion is futile. Religion cannot be bound to customs.
There are, strictly speaking, only two sacraments, baptism and the
eucharist, and the eucharist must be received by the laity in both
kinds, bread and wine. Beyond that, evangelical theologians could

---

[13] Announced in the preface to *Die Lügend von S. Johannes Chrysostomo* (1537), WA
50:52–4: "Denn freilich niemand unter euch sin wird, der meine sache und wort
fur ewrem schrecklichen feurigen Gott so wol fueren wurde oder kundte als ich
selbs, so mus ich komen, wie ich komen kan, wils nicht sein zu fus, ros oder wagen,
so sey es zu papyr und tinten."
[14] Collected in WA 50.
[15] Geisendorf, *Bibliotheca Corviniana*, nr. 106.
[16] *De ecclesia et de auctoritate verbi Dei*, CR 23:595–642.
[17] Philip Melanchthon, *Ursach, warumb die Stende, so der Augspurgischen Confession
anhangen, christliche lehr erstlich angenommen, und endlich dabey zu verharren gedenken: Auch:
Warumb des vermindte Trientische Concilium weder zu besuchen, noch darein zu willigen sey*
(Nürnberg: Vom Berg, 1546).

disagree alot, even on questions as central to Luther's criticism of the traditional church as the doctrine of justification by faith alone, the religious functions of divine law, or the correct interpretation of the sacraments.

The strongest points of contact between theologians may have been the courts of the League's two leading princes. In the decade following the 1530 Diet of Augsburg, Wittenberg enjoyed unprecedented religious influence. The opinions of Luther, Melanchthon, Justus Jonas, Georg Spalatin, Caspar Cruciger, and Johannes Bugenhagen affected virtually all religious discussions. Hessian theologians of Marburg's new university had comparable weight, but the Landgrave also relied on the advice of Martin Bucer, who was promoted by Jacob Sturm, the most influential urban magistrate in the League.

In the absence of a central religious authority, no single theologian (e.g. Martin Luther) dominated policy. To trace the influence of theological advice one must survey it as it happened, in letters and memoranda from just before the Peasants' War through the history of the League. Points of agreement gradually emerged and were soon exploited. This and the following two chapters examine the advice in chronological order. I begin with the inchoate opinions on church property that circulated before the League's formation and in its early years.

Premises

Martin Luther's 1517 criticisms of the practice of the sacrament of penance grew over the next three years into several rejections: of papal jurisdiction, of the binding authority of ecclesiastical tradition, of salvation by works, of the mediation of the saints on behalf of mortals before God, and of the necessity of the priesthood. Much of this implicated monasticism. An individual monk or nun could think of his or her life as concentrated penance, a life entirely committed to the salvation of oneself and others through the work of intercessory prayer for the living and the dead. The exact form of life was determined by a specific line of tradition centered around a religious order's rule, commentaries upon it, the order's liturgies, historical relationships with noble families, and/or papal privileges. Luther had opinions on all these things but centered his critique on the penitential quality of monastic life. In 1521 and 1522, he developed an argument that applied his interpretation of the gospel to monastic vows. This laid the foundation for a complex evangelical approach to monastic property.

The argument stands on the premise of Luther's concept of evangelical freedom. According to Luther, the sacrament of baptism included the vow to believe, ordinarily made by parents on behalf of their infant child. The baptized Christian was free to enjoy God with a clear conscience (that is, free of guilt over sin), by the exercise of faith, which is the only human prerequisite to salvation, and even so, it was given as a divine gift. Through faith, the conscience is freed from what Luther considered the oppression of the law and the tyranny of any notion that salvation must be earned by the performance of good deeds. Under the terms of this evangelical freedom there can be no such thing as a perpetual religious vow. Therefore, if monks and nuns recognize the futility of earning salvation by monastic prayer-regimens and wish to leave the cloister, they may freely do so. They are not bound by a permanent vow, since such a Christian vow cannot exist.[18] There is no aspect of monastic life divinely ordained. Those who think otherwise are deceived and the victims of a tyrannical human opinion, and the tyranny of the religious institutions that enforce the error. Should monks or nuns leave their monasteries, they are entitled to take back whatever dowries or donations they brought in, and the rest of the house's property should be used in accordance with the pious intentions of the donors.[19]

---

[18] Heinz Meinlof Stamm, *Luthers Stellung zum Ordensleben* (Wiesbaden: Franz Steiner, 1980), pp. 91–3 and passim, who traces the development of the rejection of perpetual vows in Luther, notes his indebtedness to the 1521 views of both Karstadt and Melanchthon, and gives evidence that Luther maintained this view throughout his life, up to a sermon preached 15 February 1546 at Eisleben, three days before his death. WA 51:187–194. See also Bernhard Lohse, *Mönchthum und Reformation. Luthers Auseinandersetzung zum Mönchsideal des Mittelalters* (Göttingen: Vandenhoeck und Ruprecht, 1963), passim, and Hinz, *Die Brüder vom Gemeinsamen Leben*, pp. 89–92.

[19] Respect for donors' pious intentions, as such, was demanded by canon law. The Ordinary Gloss to the *Decretum* went so far as to stipulate that a church patron must agree with a change in the use of a gift. Sieglerschmidt, *Territorialstaat*, p. 112. Catholics, likewise, appealed to donors' intentions against the Protestants, for example, in the recess of the imperial Diet of 1530. Sieglerschmidt, *Territorialstaat*, p. 133. The principle was applied to properties connected with foreign patrons in the church ordinance of Stralsund in 1525 and church visitations of Saxony in 1527 and Meissen and Vogtland in 1533. Sieglerschmidt, *Territorialstaat*, p. 232 n. 27. For Luther's role in prompting the Saxon visitation of 1527 and Melanchthon's role in executing and justifying it, Estes, *Peace, Order and the Glory of God*, pp. 49–50, 79–80.

To announce the freedom of the gospel and the danger of traditional monastic observances, rulers should install evangelical preachers and let the gospel run its course.

According to this, it remained possible for monks and nuns to convert to the evangelical faith without abandoning the cloister. Luther's criticism of monasticism from the perspective of evangelical freedom had the advantage that it could limit lay encroachment by restricting confiscation to cases of property freed by voluntary departures. After voluntary departures, the appropriate authority could redirect the property of an empty monastery, but its use must follow the religious intentions of the original donors, whose descendants might be doing the reassigning.

In 1525, Nürnberg threatened to close the monastery of Nürnberg's Holy Clares. Philip Melanchthon visited the nuns and advised the city council to exercise restraint. Caritas Pirkheimer, a patrician daughter and abbess, noted that when Melanchthon came, he

> said many things about the new doctrine, but since he heard that we based ourselves on God's grace and not on our own works, he said, we could as well become blessed in the cloister as in the world, if we don't merely hold to our vows. We on both sides agreed on all points, for only on account of vows were we disunited: he meant that they don't bind, one is not obligated to keep them; I meant, what one has vowed to God, one is obligated to hold with God's help. . . . He left with our friendship.[20]

The revocable character of monastic vows was, in fact, Luther and Melanchthon's central point against monasticism.

To this, Luther added an historical argument, which first appeared in his 1520 *Address to the Christian Nobility of the German Nation* and was repeated within a year by Andreas Bodenstein von Karlstadt and, for the rest of his life, by Melanchthon.[21] Monasteries, he said, originally functioned as schools but were diverted from their educational purpose over time by the encroaching superstitions of monks.

---

[20] *Die Denkwürdigkeiten der Äbtissin Caritas Pirkheimer*, pp. 131–2.

[21] WA 6:381–469. Schindling, "Der Passauer Vertrag," p. 114. Estes, *Peace, Order and the Glory of God*, p. 10. The first association of Melanchthon with this idea may have be when he signed Andreas Bodenstein von Karlstadt's recommendation on monasticism to the Elector. CR 1:493–510. Barge, *Andreas Bodenstein von Karlstadt*, 1:344. He also attributed the educational function to bishops. Estes, *Peace, Order and the Glory of God*, pp. 80–1.

Insofar as Luther and Melanchthon were concerned, confiscation depended upon these two premises, evangelical freedom and a particular view of the historic purpose of monasteries, and a third— the authority of rulers to reorganize church finances as a temporal matter. Luther's early writings frequently denied the right of a temporal power to interfere in spiritual affairs, a point expressed since 1522 in his famous distinction between the secular realm of law, in which temporal authority held ultimate power, and the spiritual realm of grace, which was subject to no earthly authority—often called the "two kingdoms" doctrine. James Estes has pointed out how, since 1521, Melanchthon insisted that the prince as a Christian must maintain true religion, and that beginning in the early 1530's to the end of his life, Luther also advocated this more positive view of a ruler's religious role, as did other theologians.[22] It corresponded to the common Catholic view. Melanchthon seems to have adapted it from Erasmus' concept of the Christian state, as it was summarized in the *Institutio principis christiani* of 1516.[23] Luther's own advice during the 1520's oscillated between encouraging temporal interference and preserving church rights.

Luther first advocated a particular reorganization of church property in 1523, when he endorsed an ecclesiastical ordinance for the small Saxon city of Leisnig.[24] In 1522, he had opposed the closure of cloisters in Wittenberg, but at Leisnig one year later he advocated the community's use of benefices, incomes, bequests, and other

---

[22] James M. Estes, "The Role of the Godly Magsitrates in the Church: Melanchthon as Luther's Interpreter and Collaborator," *Church History* 67(1998):463–483. Estes, *Peace, Order and the Glory of God*, pp. 1–52, here 26, who notes Luther's early use of "a difficult and cumbersome distinction" between a prince's routine authority "as political sovereign," as a Christian, as a Christian prince intervening in an emergency. By 1527, Melanchthon described this religious oversight as a divine office. See also Nicole Kuropka, *Philipp Melanchthon: Wissenchaft und Gesellschaft* (Tübingen: J.C.B. Mohr/Paul Siebeck, 2002), pp. 70–87.

[23] See Estes, *Peace, Order and the Glory of God*, pp. 54–61.

[24] H. Hermelink, "Zwei Aktenstücke über Behandlung der Kirchengüter in Württemberg zur Reformationszeit," *Blätter für württembergische Kirchengeschichte*, n.s. 7(1903):176–77, using older editions. Schilling, *Klöster und Mönche*, p. 210. Brecht, *Martin Luther*, 2:70–71. WA 11:401–16; 12:1–30. Karl Trüdinger, *Luthers Briefe und Gutachten an weltliche Obrigkeiten zur Durchführung der Reformation* (Münster: Aschendorff, 1975), pp. 60–67. WABr 3:594–96 nr. 937, esp. p. 505; WABr 4:133–34 nr. 1052. Many of the same points had been made by Andreas Bodenstein von Karlstadt at Wittenberg in 1520/21. Barge, *Andreas Bodenstein von Karlstadt*, 1:339–402. See also Estes, *Peace, Order and the Glory of God*, pp. 29–30, who notes that such princely intervention was justified by the *Address to the Christian Nobility* of 1520.

gifts controlled by the Cistercians of Buch to support an evangelical pastor and create a common chest for poor relief. After Leisnig, Luther promoted similar plans for Zerbst and Plauen, and by 1525 in Electoral Saxony overall, when he pointed the new electoral prince, Johann the Constant, to the monasteries of his realm and to the endowments of churches as the wellsprings from which to draw the stipends of evangelical preachers, should the prince hesitate to fund preachers out of his own fisc, which would have simply continued the expansion of princely patronage, but now in evangelical offices.[25] Luther's feelings about a ruler's interventions in the church were complicated. In spite of his ceremonious 1520 auto-da-fé of the papal bull threatening him with excommunication, alongside a copy of the *Corpus iuris canonici*, he upheld the application of canon law in Catholic places, when he answered a referral from Gregor Brück in April 1524 about an Eisenach benefice claimed by the Elector's government. The benefice holder, a certain Johann Pfister, abandoned the Augustinian Order. What was the prince to do with the vacant benefice?[26] "Oh, dear," Luther said, "Leave to the pastors what belongs to the pastors. I implore you, your honor. It is neither a joy nor a glory to me that these cases be referred from the jurists to the theologians. They ought not be tackled otherwise by us with the law of the pope, except when the reign of the pope had first been destroyed. For where he does not rule, there we may use the laws and the goods he left behind, not before." It is a complicated argument. He argues that the Elector's government has no claim to the benefice. The benefice must return to the Eisenach chapter, which did not support the new preaching. Luther accepts the chapter's canonical control of the benefice, on the paradoxical principle that papal law may apply once papal authority has been denied (i.e. the law, denatured of its spiritual claims, would no longer undermine faith). But his advice is also consistent with canon law, which the Eisenach chapter acknowledged still. This leaves the benefice unused by evangelicals until papal obedience ends in the Eisenach

---

[25] Sieglerschmidt, *Territorialstaat und Kirchenregiment*, pp. 223–54. WABr 3:594–96 nr. 937, esp. p. 505.
[26] WA Br 3:274–5 nr. 732.: "Obsecro te, vir optime, non est mihi gaudium nec gloria, istas causas a iureconsultis ad theologos referri; alias a nostris iura Papae non debent invadi, nisi prius regno Papae destructo; ubi enim non regnat, ibi sane iuribus et bonis eius relictis utamur, non ante."

chapter. Church law is respected while striving for the end of papal obedience.

A year and a half later, Luther suggested a more liberal approach to church property. On 31 October 1525 in a letter to Elector Johann, Luther bemoaned the neglect of parishes, whose laity were not providing the required support, neither in charitable gifts nor *Seelpfennige*, memorial gifts, nor were the rents from church properties sufficient to meet expenses.[27] Vicarages, schools, and appointments of teachers threatened to come to an end, he complained. The prince must intervene,

> your Electoral Grace will surely find the means. It's the cloisters, convents, land tenures, and donations and of things enough, where alone Your Electoral Grace is thrice encouraged: to inspect, appraise, and regulate (*ordenen*) them. God will bless you and prosper you, so that if God wills, the order (*ordenung*) that touches souls, like the university and divine worship, will not be hindered by the want and abandonment of a poor man's belly. That do we pray of his divine grace. Amen.[28]

Teachers and preachers, or candidates to these offices, should not be discouraged by a low standard of living. Incomes from church holdings could provide redress.

That same year, Philip Melanchthon answered the Elector of Saxony's concerns about tolerating evangelical preachers. In a recommendation to the prince, he defended the Elector's tolerance as obedience to God, in spite of his disobedience toward bishops.[29] For

---

[27] WABr 3:594–96 nr. 937, esp. p. 505.

[28] Ibid., "Euer Churfürstliche Gnade wird da wol mittel zu finden. Es sind kloster, stifft, lehen und spenden und des dings gnug, wo nur E.C.f.g. befehl sich dreyn begibt, die zu besehen, rechnen und ordenen. Got wird dazu seynen segen und gedeyen auch geben, das, ob gott will, die ordenung, so die seelen betrifft als die hohen schule und gotts dienst, nicht verhindert werde aus mangel und verlassung des armen bauchs. Das bitten wir auch seyne gottliche gnade, Amen."

[29] CR 1:763–770 nr. 355 (no specific date), answers to two questions posed by the Elector, whether it is right to teach the new doctrine and allow malpractice to end without the support of bishops and prelates, and whether princes were right not only personally to accept the new doctrine but to determine to end malpractice by cloisters and other foundations. In general, Luther and Melanchthon advocated princely intervention in the face of episcopal neglect, but also promoted the evangelical restoration of a bishop's pastoral office, while also admitting his temporal power. For the development of their views on emergency intervention in the face of episcopal neglect consider Estes, *Peace, Order and the Glory of God*, pp. 51, 67, 80–1, 130–1, 159, 166–172, 208 with n. 87.

each individual preacher must confess Christ and penalize malpractice, and each has been appointed to preach the truth by his bishop (by 1500 mendicant preachers were routinely required to hold episcopal licenses, and many of the first evangelical preachers came from their ranks). Since the bishop neglects and hinders the truth, the preachers are obliged to resist him. For his part, it is not enough for a prince personally to believe the new doctrine. Having done so, he must desist from persecuting those who teach it. Divine command obliges him to ignore imperial edicts to the contrary, that is, the edicts condemning Martin Luther, just as in the bible Jonathan not only failed to kill David, as his father King Saul commanded, but protected him instead.[30] Leopold von Ranke once counted Melancthon's advice as early evidence of evangelicals loosening themselves from the jurisdiction of prince-bishops, but Melanchthon's logic was much less ambitious.[31] To desist from persecuting evangelicals, the reformer argued, was to allow preachers to fulfill their episcopal, pastoral appointments, in spite of bad bishops.

A year later Luther claimed that confiscation should not be the first line of a prince's defense of the pastoral ministry.[32] Rather, the prince should compel communities to pay the salaries of evangelical preachers not covered by the incomes of church properties and compel them to support their schools, preaching offices, and pastors, as they are compelled to other territorial obligations. In poor places, cloister property should serve the purpose of the original donors, namely to support divine worship. The elector may employ what remains for his state's needs or for the poor.[33] Now, apparently for the first time, a Protestant suggested that a ruler possessed the right to confiscate church property for reason of state. But Luther's presupposition was still this: church property must first serve evangelical ministry. If a priest does not proclaim the word of God, he forfeits any right to church property.[34]

---

[30] 1 Samuel 19.
[31] Leopold von Ranke, *Deutsche Geschichte im Zeitalter der Reformation*, 6 vols. (München: Drei Masken Verlag, 1925–1926), 2:183.
[32] 22 November 1526, WABr 4:133–34 nr. 1052.
[33] Luther began to advocate princely use of oversupplies before the 1530 Diet of Augsburg demanded the restitution of monastic property. Compare Cohn, "Church Property," p. 165.
[34] Karl Holl, "Luther und das landesherrliche Kirchenregiment," *Luther*, vol. 1

The basis of lay intervention in church government, in this case a prince's, was the Christian obligation to support true religion. Luther's view of lay intervention presupposed the separate but complementary nature of spiritual and temporal powers in a good society. His well-known distinction between law and gospel reinforced this principle, strictly separating the power to govern from the church's ministry of preaching and sacraments. His view of temporal authority contrasted sharply with the revolutionary notions of divine law and godly commonwealth advocated before the Peasants' Revolt of 1524/5 by Karlstadt, Thomas Müntzer, Michael Gaismair, Balthasar Hubmaier, and Hans Hergot. Peter Blickle has called their idea of godly commonwealth "the total Christian state," and Luther's view of law posed an alternative to it.[35] The prevalence of these notions in the revolt and their continued presence among Anabaptists after the war encouraged Luther, Melanchthon, and others increasingly to emphasize the role of government in the promotion of true worship.[36]

This reaction to the revolutionaries and its implications for church incomes can also be observed in the year of the revolt in one of Luther's very influential followers, Johannes Brenz, the Lutheran preacher in Schwäbisch Hall and a former professor at Heidelberg. In a brief (*Rhattschlag*) offered to the Elector Palatine in June 1525, Brenz contrasted an evangelical, Lutheran distinction between law and gospel with revolutionary views. The elector had invited Brenz to answer the peasants' famous Twelve Articles, the most influential statement of the principles and aims of the revolt; the Palatine peasants' had accepted him as mediator.[37] His response to the elector's invitation proved to be the most extensive rebuttal of the Twelve Articles ever offered by an evangelical theologian.

The first article of the revolutionaries had insisted on the right of a community to elect its own pastor. The right of presentation of

---

of *Gesammelte Aufsätze zur Kirchengeschichte*, 6th ed., (Tübingen: J.C.B. Mohr, 1932), pp. 326–380, here 351–2.

[35] Blickle, *Revolution of 1525*, pp. 145–54.

[36] Estes, *Peace, Order and the Glory of God*, p. 69 for Melanchthon, pp. 184–7, 189 for Luther.

[37] For Brenz's advocacy of magisterial support for church reform in general during this period and, in reaction to appeals for tolerance of Anabaptist groups, his expansion of magisterial prerogatives in governing the affairs of the church, see James Martin Estes, *Christian Magistrate and State Church: the Reforming Career of Johannes Brenz* (University of Toronto Press, 1982), pp. 35–58.

candidates to church office belonged formerly to a bishop but also to lay or other spiritual patrons, namely the prince, nobleman, commune, or monastic community that established the benefice or acquired the benefactor's right.[38] The right of presentation tied the churches of a city or village to an intricate and far-flung web of spiritual and lay lordships, and this is exactly what the peasants meant to deny. Brenz countered by insisting that revelation did not dictate the manner of election. A Christian ruler was free to determine how the choice should occur, so long as *oberkait* gave subjects good, evangelical pastors.[39] Scripture was really concerned with the pastor's character and manner of life. Although the godly law left the manner of election open, election was not free. When the right of presentation belonged to a foreign prince or other lord, whether ecclesiastical or lay, it would be good to bring the candidate to the prince of the territory, so that his subjects need not respect two lords, the mayor appointed by the prince of the territory and the pastor appointed by the ruler with right of presentation. Lay intervention in ecclesiastical appointments should follow a ruler's protective and supportive role. Brenz raised, it seems for the first time in Protestant discussions of church property, the problem of foreign patronage rights. If a prince assumed control of all the churches in his realm, as an assertion of sovereignty, he would inevitably infringe on the rights of many patrons. Brenz's advice was tentative, but not necessarily realistic. He implied a preference for subordinating the rights of foreign patrons to local lordship.

Among evangelicals, there soon appeared, in tandem with the assertion of a ruler's responsibility to support religion and intervene in religious affairs accordingly, its opposite: an insistence that rulers could not intervene, seconded by Brenz himself. At the Swabian League's diet in Donauwörth in July 1527, the league sent a letter to its urban members instructing them to respect previous mandates and capture monastic runaways. The most principled evangelical

---

[38] That is, the right to present candidates retained by the creator of a church benefice, a patron.

[39] Johannes Brenz, *Rhattschalg und Guttbedunckhen herrn Johann Brentii über der Bauren gestelte und für Euangelische dargegebene Zwölf Articul Ahn Pfaltzgraff Ludwigen bey Rein, Churfursten*, in Johannes Brenz, *Werke*, ed. Martin Brecht, Gerhard Schäfer, 3 vols. (Tübingen: J.C.B. Mohr, 1970), 1/1:132–74, here 144–7.

program of monastic reform depended on runaways, who empty monasteries for princes and cities to harvest. The Donauwörth letter is a response to monastic attrition provoked by evangelical preaching. Protestant cities in the south reacted predictably. In September 1527, the cities of Nürnberg, Augsburg, and Ulm consulted with each other and published an appeal to evangelically sympathetic cities that declared the Swabian League's instruction an unlawful interference in spiritual affairs.[40] They insisted on the autonomy of ecclesiastical from lay jurisdiction (the Swabian League, in its 1522 charter, agreed to avoid church cases). An additional response to the Swabian League came from the city of Schwäbisch Hall, in the form of "Considerations on the League's Treaty" (*Bedencken über die Bundesvereinigung*) written by Johannes Brenz. He agreed that the League had no business in spiritual affairs, but he alleged that the emperor forced the League into them, illegally, against imperial law.[41] No one on earth had the power to bind or constrain the city council in matters of faith, the gospel, the soul, heavenly salvation—no superior, no lordship, no magisterium (*maisterschafft*), no law, no justification, no privilege (*freyhait*). It rather fell to the apostles and their successors, the bishops, whose office was to be seen not as a form of lordship, but as a form of service, a ministry.[42] According to Brenz, the division between spiritual and temporal jurisdictions was absolute. Temporal rulers had no jurisdiction in matters of faith.[43] The emperor and the Swabian League were equally incompetent in matters of faith.

It is difficult to reconcile the distinct views of temporal authority and church property that circulated among evangelical theologians before the Imperial Diet of Augsburg in 1530. One approach, suggested by Luther and Brenz, implied a degree of sovereign temporal authority over the church. Another, also suggested by Luther and Brenz, insisted on the separation of jurisdictions. The fact that this

---

[40] Brenz, *Werke*, 1/2:197–99. At the Swabian League's 11 November 1527 convention members agreed that the League had jurisdiction only in external matters, not matters of conscience. This was necessary to prevent Protestant cities from abandoning the alliance. Schlenck, *Die Reichstadt Memmingen und die Reformation*, p. 60. Karl Klupfel, *Urkunden zur Geschichte des Schwäbischen Bundes (1488–1533)* 2 vols. (Stuttgart: Litterarischer Verein, 1846–53), 2:314f.

[41] Brenz, *Werke* 1/2:200–10.

[42] Ibid., pp. 201–2.

[43] Estes, *Peace, Order and the Glory of God*, pp. 99, 189.

latter position characterized sacramentarians and Zwinglians encouraged Luther, Melanchthon, and others increasingly to emphasize the role of government in advancing religion.[44] By the beginning of the 1530 Diet, a number of princes and cities had taken control of ecclesiastical assets to support evangelical projects. These included Ansbach-Kulmbach, Hesse, Electoral Saxony, Lüneburg, Prussia, Nürnberg, Hamburg, Magdeburg, Memmingen, Strasbourg, and Ulm. When the 1530 Diet convened, the Catholic estates demanded restitution of things previously taken. The Landgrave of Hesse anticipated this demand and addressed the question of church property.

Philip of Hesse was still building the coalition of princes sympathetic to Luther. To support the endeavor, he now requested a brief on the religious controversy, which was provided by a Hessian official, which appears to have been written by urban theologians, for it is preoccupied with the mendicant orders.[45] Its polemic against the friars was presented among other standard evangelical topics and complaints: vows, councils, Luther, Christian life, and begging. At the Diet, another brief by the evangelical preachers of Nürnberg also circulated. It included a summary of evangelical doctrine and a statement of evangelical freedom, followed by these common Protestant assertions: the need to end the mass and allow pastors to marry; that "cloisters should be open and not a prison, so that the last will and testament of those who endowed them be fulfilled";[46] that cloisters do not honor God, but serve "bellies"; that monastic life is not a life of evangelical faith but opposed to it; that monks and nuns do not bring salvation to their donors; and finally that the poverty of cloisters is fraudulent, does not warrant support of their members from common property, and should therefore be closed.[47] These themes were common in popular print since the early 1520's, especially

---

[44] Estes in the previous note.

[45] Cahill, *Philipp of Hesse*, pp. 141–50, 152. Köhler, "Actenstücke der hessischen Reformationsgeschichte," *Zeitschrift für historische Theologie* 37(1867):217–247, here 217–20, 222–44.

[46] "Closter sollen darumb offen und kain gefenknus sein, damit der letzte will deren, die si gestift haben, verstreckt werde." *Quellen und Forschungen zur Geschichte des Augsburgischen Glaubensbekenntnisses*, ed. Wilhelm Gussmann, 2 vols. (Leipzig and Berlin: B.G. Teubner, 1911–30), 1/1:291–93.

[47] They added, "Und diß ist die ursach, darumb wir pillich und schuldiglich leren, das closterleben abzuthun und dises volk in ain rechte erbere christenliche ordnung zu pringen, dass si gleich andern ir aigene narung gewinnen, dieweil Got

in Luther's vernacular writings—from the anti-mendicant caricatures
to the appeal to donors' intentions.[48] But the friars had offered small
gains to a prince. Philip of Hesse needed a justification that relied
less on anti-mendicant caricatures.

In his warrant to the Hessian embassy to the Imperial Diet on
27 March 1530, the Landgrave included detailed instructions on
church property. When complaints arise against me regarding monastic property, he said, make oral or written report to put it in the
best possible light.[49] He recalled the settlement concluded at the
Speyer Diet of 1526, "that every *Obrigkeit* should rule and proceed
as it trusts and hopes to answer before God and the imperial majesty."[50]
He noted: so has he himself proceeded, as an obedient prince of the
Empire. In accordance with decisions of Diets of Nürnberg, Augsburg,
and Speyer, he ordered the clergy to preach the gospel without addition, and he appointed preachers to many cloisters.[51] He was, he
claimed, successful. The Landgrave recounted reform and reaction
to it. The adherents of the holy gospel preached, he said, against
many and diverse abuses among the clergy, monks, and the like, as
not only inconsistent with the Word of God but totally groundless.
The adherents of the old religion responded with a defense of papal
ceremonies and regulations, and they infiltrated the poor people and

---

kain mueßiggeen, Ez. 18 (7f), vil weniger pettlerei in seinem volk will leiden und
haben, Deut. 15 (4)." Ibid.

[48] Consider Ocker, "'Rechte Arme' und 'Bettler Orden,'" passim.

[49] *Quellen und Forschungen zur Geschichte des Augsburgischen Glaubensbekenntnisses*, ed.
Wilhelm Gussmann, 2 vols. (Leipzig and Berlin: B.G. Teubner, 1911–30), 1/1:327:
"Wan unter ader neben andern der closter ader closterperson, auch derselben guter
halb zu reden kompt, auch von jmants derowegen, sovil solichs uns belangte, geclagt
wurde, alsdan sollen die unsern nachvolgenden bericht thun, montlich oder in
schriften, wie sie solichs fur bequemest und gelegenest ansehen und gut sein bedunken
wurd."

[50] Ibid.: "daß jede obrigkeit also regiren und handelen solte, wie sie solichs gegen
Got, auch keis. Mt. getrawte und verhoffte zu verantworten." For the 1526 Diet
of Speyer and the origin of this clause in the Electoral Council (*Kurfürstenrat*) when
the electoral princes deadlocked on the extent to which to consider matters of faith,
see Kohnle, *Reichstag und Reformation*, pp. 266–9. The recess of Speyer 1526 was
taken as a legal basis for reform in the territories of Electoral Saxony, Hesse,
Ansbach-Kulmbach, and Braunschweig-Lüneburg. Ibid., pp. 278–97. Kohnle notes,
however, that the recess's article on religion was vague enough to be used by
Catholics and Protestants alike in support of their contrasting positions. Ibid., pp.
298–362, here 361.

[51] For this and the following, *Quellen und Forschungen zur Geschichte des Augsburgischen
Glaubensbekenntnisses*, 1/1:327–8.

taught them with tremendous zeal. Therefore, one of the parties had to yield. Meanwhile, the Landgrave insisted, many members of cloisters were coming to realize their errors and misunderstandings of the Word of God, and they abandoned the useless monastic life.[52] Philip made the same point in other words again, a little later, to claim that monks and nuns left cloisters in response to the gospel preaching he inaugurated in accordance with the imperial mandates of the Diet of Speyer in 1526.[53] He reviewed the meetings of Homberg and Marburg that preceded the closure of monasteries in his territory. He claimed that most monks and nuns have submitted themselves to the Word of God and entered the common Christian estate (*aus solichem closterlichen leben zu einem gemeinen christlichen stand begert*). He noted that those who left were handed a provision from monastic property and an *Abfertigung* (disclaimer) that prevented future claims, and lay guardians were installed in monasteries. All of this, he observed, followed the traditional rights and responsibilities of a prince.[54] The embassy was instructed to dispute any restoration of monks and nuns, images and religious objects, a non-evangelical eucharistic rite, or other traditional practices.[55]

The Landgrave argued as a servant of the church. He stressed the support he gave to evangelical preachers and his preservation of the religious uses of church property when monasteries were left empty. This may reflect the influence of Hessian theologians, who in another, undated brief for the Diet of 1530 treated the topic of monastic property. The authors included Balthasar Raid, Johannes Kymeus, and Antonius Corvinus, signatories a decade later to the Schmalkald Recommendation of 1540.[56] The brief discussed Christian freedom, episcopal authority (it is apostolic, not temporal, they said), the mass and sacraments, and the marriage of priests. Of monastic vows, the theologians insisted they could not be restored. Of the

---

[52] Ibid., 1/1:328.

[53] Ibid., 1/1:329–30.

[54] Ibid., 1/1:330: "Dan nachdem wir und unser voraltern, die fursten von Hessen selige loblicher gedechtnus, je und allweg uf solichen clostern als die landsfursten steure, dienst, volg und andere dergleichen gerechtigkait gehabt, so habe je uns ein insehens zu derselben herprachten gerechtigkeiten, wie obvermelt, zu haben gepurt."

[55] Ibid., 1/1:331.

[56] For their activities, Oskar Hütteroth and Hilmar Milbradt, *Die althessische Pfarrer*, pp. 47–49, 195–6, 269. For the 1540 recommendation and its importance, chapter 6 below.

empty monasteries, some should be made schools for men and women, noble and not noble. Preachers and pastors may then be recruited from these schools, but there, too, the elderly and the sick who are unable to work may hear the word of God. Monks and nuns should receive stipends to avoid (judicial?) complaints.[57] The Hessian theologians referred the matter of cloister property to the prince, who had in fact already converted much of it to evangelical uses and had already assigned stipends.[58] The document continues with treatments of fasts, feastdays, penance, prayer, processions, and ceremonies in general.

At the Diet itself, questions of church property were placed below questions of faith, but were not ignored altogether. From April to June, Melanchthon had prepared drafts of the Augsburg Confession, which "urge governmental action in support of true doctrine and worship" in obedience to God who orders kings and princes "to care for truth, the salvation of souls, and [God's] glory, and because he will exact retribution on the Last Day if they do not."[59] In August, in preparation for the Diet's theological dialogue, Melanchthon and Georg Spalatin drafted a list of non-negotiable points for the adherents of the Augsburg Confession. They listed the Confession's articles on faith, good works, Christian freedom, the lay reception of the cup in the sacrament of the Lord's Supper, clerical marriage, the non-sacrificial character of the eucharist, and the wording of the canon (the central liturgical portion) of the mass. By contrast, ceremonies, episcopal government, feasts and fasts were considered all negotiable. Cloister and church property was an issue surrendered, or surrenderable, to the emperor, who could decide what should be done with it.[60] The point should not be exaggerated. Rather than consign the material church to imperial sovereignty, which hardly existed in Germany, it recognized the emperor's supervening *Vogtei*, his obligation to protect the church. It was a traditional claim.

---

[57] Schilling, *Klöster und Mönche*, pp. 224–25. *Quellen und Forschungen*, 1/1:337–42 nr. 17: "Vor allen dingen aber begeren wir die exiticias [*leg* exitiosas] personas (monks and nuns who left cloisters) zu versehen, wo noch etwa mangel were. Den das genus hominum clagt vil and sulich gschrei kompt weit."

[58] *Quellen und Forschungen*, 1/1:337–42 nr. 17. "Wie man aber die closter guter, rent und gfelle in christlichen brauch weiter wenden soll, dweit wir hieruber, wie auch Christus von ime selbst zeugt, zu keinen richtern gsetzt, befehlen wir E.F.Gn. und andern gotforchtigen hern zu betrachten."

[59] Estes' summary, *Peace, Order and the Glory of God*, pp. 95–8, here 96–7.

[60] CR 2:280. Fuchs, *Konfession und Gespräch*, pp. 369–70.

Discussions then followed in the Diet's "committee of fourteen."[60a]
It was comprised of six theologians, Johann Cochlaeus, Johann Eck,
and the elderly Konrad Wimpina on the Catholic side and, on the
Protestant side, Melanchthon, Johannes Brenz, and Erhard Schnepf,
a theologian in the Landgrave's university at Marburg. Four princes
and four jurists accompanied them on the committee. The Protestants
agreed to respect the cloisters still standing until a general council.
They were ready, they said, to present an account of how cloister
incomes were being spent. But they could not surrender those incomes,
since the incomes supported many pastors, preachers, and schools.
They were also ready to concede a bishop's right to approve candidates for pastor and preacher (this was recognition of his role as
nominal patron of all diocesan benefices) and the bishop's spiritual
jurisdiction, including his use of ban and excommunication (this was
recognition of his penitential power). These concessions accompanied a set of formulae on the eucharist, original sin, penance, good
works, and the intercession of the saints, but the committee failed
to agree on the lay reception of the cup in the Lord's Supper, the
marriage of priests, or monastic vows and discipline.

These agreements showed how close the parties *could* be thought,
but when the formulae were presented to the Protestant and Catholic
parties at the Diet, both sides rejected them.[61] While the Lutherans
threatened to end negotiations and leave, Catholics arranged for
another committee of six, comprised of two theologians (Eck and
Melanchthon) and four jurists. By the time it met, Hesse and the
Protestant cities convinced the other Protestants to offer no further
concessions, and Luther also demanded by letter that the Protestants
remain intransigent on the Augsburg Confession's articles on the lay
cup, marriage of priests, the prohibition of private masses, the canon
of the mass, and monastic rules. The Catholic jurist, Hieronymus
Vehus, chancellor of Baden, suggested that the emperor decide the
matter of property from abandoned cloisters until a church council
should convene. The suggestion coincided with an earlier proposal
by Melanchthon and Spalatin.[62] But only Vehus and Melanchthon
remained willing to continue negotiations. The Protestant jurist,
Gregor Brück, chancellor of Electoral Saxony, announced that the

---

[60a] Fuchs, *Konfession und Gespräch*, pp. 370–380.
[61] Fuchs, *Konfession und Gespräch*, p. 379.
[62] Ibid., pp. 381–88, here 384.

Protestants would make no further compromises, and negotiations ended. Thus, the Augsburg Diet concluded with no agreements having been reached on cloisters, clerical marriage, the mass, or episcopal jurisdiction. It recessed with the lines between the parties more sharply drawn than ever.

Recommendations to Early Members of the League

Advice on church property during the first six years of the League of Schmalkalden, while the Protestants expanded in northern Germany and tightened their grip on several key imperial cities, remained occasional and inchoate. The need for a coordinated policy on church property only became clear when the League's clergy, in 1537, made formal supplication that the League protect the church from confiscations by its own members (Chapter Five, below).

The first recommendation after the formation of the League was a memorandum to the Elector of Saxony from Martin Luther, produced in early 1531, followed by another in August of that year. Both supported the Saxon sequestrations then underway.[63] In the first, Luther argued that the prince of Saxony may not restore or aid the restoration of the old worship among monks and pastors because it would be an offence to God. Luther offered this vacuous premise: canon law teaches that one should abolish abuses. Although no one is permitted to take church property, he admitted, the prince must prevent its robbery or destruction, and he could take abandoned property just as he has a right to the property of subjects who die without heirs. Nor could the prince permit the introduction of new monks, who would reestablish abuses. He should inventory monastic properties, as others have done. The property does not belong to the religious order but must remain at the place donated and be used for divine worship there. Likewise, Luther still believed that the use of the property must follow the intention of the donors, which was to establish divine worship: this, he said, was

---

[63] Walch incorrectly suggested the dates April and October 1532. *Martin Luthers Gesammelte Schriften*, 16:1829–35 nr. 1204, 1205. The two memoranda are published together in WABr 6:4–10 nr. 1766, the first with a brief Latin position piece produced by Melanchthon. For the correct dates, see the introduction to nr. 1766.

intended by the elector's ancestors when they made the donations. If the prince must use the major part of the property for pastoral care and schools, temporal government is entitled to use what remains, for temporal rule is a form of divine service, too. The property may be used to help impoverished nobility, which also, Luther alleged, conforms to the original establishment of cloisters and hospitals as places for poor noble children to be reared. Furthermore, since the prince now bears the costs of visitation, which church property is also intended to support, he is entitled to compensation from the church's assets. The elector is no thief, Luther explained, but popes, bishops, and monks are, who use the property for non-religious ends. Saint Ambrose sold chalice and church implements to free prisoners.[64] The electoral prince is equally obliged to perform such charitable labor, for which end, Luther commented, Christ gave him a cloister.

This last point is, to my knowledge, the most expansive statement of princely entitlement to church property made by any early German Protestant theologian, insofar as it connects a prince's entitlement to a share of church property to temporal rule, which is service to God. This identifies a portion of church holdings as subject to a prince's disposition. He implied a certain temporal agency far less contingent than his initial point, that abandoned church property must be put to appropriate uses.

The second memorandum of August 1531, according to the afterword by Justus Jonas, was hastily written in response to a demand by Electoral Saxony's Christian Beyer.[65] Beyer was a jurist who had been professor at the university of Wittenberg, burgomaster of the city, and the Elector's counselor during the troubles of 1520/1.[66] He had published the 21 January 1521 Wittenberg city-ordinance, an early example of reorganized church management. It consolidated incomes from benefices in a common chest for clergy salaries, poor relief, public loans, and citizen scholarships; closed satellite houses of external cloisters; and banned religious begging, confraternities, and other collectors of religious donations.[67] The removal of images

---

[64] C. 12 q. ii.70 CICan 1:710. Ambrose, *De officiis*, ii.140–141, edited and translated by Ivor J. Davidson, 2 vols., 1:347.

[65] *Martin Luthers gesammelte Schriften*, 16:1829–35 nr. 1205, MABr 6:4–10 nr. 1766, and Haug-Moritz, *Der Schmalkaldische Bund*, p. 649.

[66] Haug-Moritz, *Der Schmalkaldische Bund*, p. 649.

[67] Barge, *Andreas Bodenstein von Karlstadt*, pp. 354–402.

from Wittenberg churches followed within weeks, but the Elector, at the recommendation of Luther and the university's theologians, reversed these measures one month later. Now a decade after those events, Beyer advised that monks be restored to their cloisters and the properties of the church be returned again. The theological memorandum, in response, countered that church property must provide for parishes, ministers, schools, hospitals, a common chest, and poor students. It also allowed the prince a claim to oversupplies as compensation for his troubles. He might divert some of it to poor nobility or to public works, in spite of the prohibitions of canon law, it said. The prince is entitled, the document concluded, because he already supported the evangelical movement without compensation. A prince was entitled to compensation from the church, while oversupplies were subject to a prince's free disposition.

This document, like earlier pieces by the Landgrave and his theologians, retained the trappings of the inalienability of religious property, while stretching the reasons for a prince's intrusion, in connection with his protective and supportive role. It limited entitlement to oversupplies. Yet both memoranda rationalized political gifts that a prince might give from church assets (the support of "poor" nobles suggests the management of his network of subordinates). The portion of church incomes that paid for religious administration could cover visitations, salaries of clergy, repair of churches, and the like. In fact, between 1533 and 1543 Johann Friedrich used church property liberally, leasing most monastic lands to nobles and officials and using incomes to pay off debts, until, faced with his own empty treasury in his defense of Cleves, Jülich, and Berg in 1543, he revoked the leases to his own benefit.[68] In 1531, his predecessor the Elector Johann the Constant faced only a potential war.

The Wittenberg theologians rationalized Saxon sequestrations, then soon after scrupled over the entanglement of rights in the city of Bremen, an original member of the League. Urban conflicts added a new measure of pragmatism to the discussion of church property and made manifest the divergent concerns of theologians and princes.

----

[68] For this and the following, Cohn, "Church Property," p. 169 and A. Hilpert, "Die Sequestration der geistlichen Güter in den kursächsischen Landkreisen Meissen, Vogtland und Sachsen 1531 bis 1543," *Mitteilungen des Altertumsvereins zu Plauen im Vogtland* 22 (1912): 4–6.

By 1532, the citizens of the Hanseatic city had been exposed to ten years of evangelical preaching. In the last four years, the preachers labored against an impasse reached between a sympathetic city council and the oppositional canons of the archbishop's cathedral. Now, a year after the formation of the League of Schmalkalden, a citizens' committee tried to complete the town's conversion. At 7 am on Palm Sunday, 1532, a committee of 104 citizens, who had been elected the day after Epiphany, 2 January, gathered at the Church of St. Martin, proceeded to the home of Jacob Probst, led him to the cathedral, entered the chancel, silenced the priests about to say mass in the choir, put him in the pulpit, and listened to his sermon on the gospel reading for the day.[69] On Monday, another evangelical, Johannes Timan,[70] preached in the cathedral. Protestant sermons continued for the rest of Holy Week. Archbishop Christoph, travelling to the Imperial Diet at Regensburg, received news from the cathedral chapter, returned to his residence just upstream of the city on the river Aller, and dispatched a complaint to the Diet. His brother Heinrich, the Duke of Braunschweig-Wolfenbüttel, presented it at Regensburg on 1 May. The city council immediately began negotiations with the cathedral chapter, but refused to restore Catholic worship to the cathedral. Having joined the League of Schmalkalden the year before, they now asked it for advice. Should they return Catholic worship to the Cathedral? Their's was, we notice, as did the canons, a blunt invasion of the chapter's center of operations, not to mention the archbishop's church.

Philip of Hesse's theologians answered the council's search for advice, and so too did the theologians of Wittenberg (27 February 1533, Luther, Bugenhagen, Jonas, and Melanchthon). Both groups made the same points: insofar as the restitution of church property

---

[69] The events are summarized in WABr 6:428–29 nr. 1999, and in Otto Veeck, *Geschichte der Reformierten Kirche Bremens* (Bremen: Gustav Winter, 1909), pp. 1–7. For citizens' committees in north Germany and the Reformation, Schilling, *Religion, Political Culture, and the Emergence of Early Modern Society*, pp. 19, 73, 86–7, 88, 99, 121, 122 (examples of Lemgo, Braunschweig, Lüneburg, Hamburg, Göttingen). For a southern example of a citizens' committee pressuring a council for reform (Basel), Roth, *Durchbruch und Festsetzung*, pp. 36–79.

[70] Timan, still a leader of the church in Bremen in 1540, was also a subscriber to the 1540 Schmalkald memorandum on church property examined in chapter 6, below.

is concerned, Bremen is not obliged in cases in which they hold patronage, but insofar as churches with alien patrons are concerned (that is, non-citizens, such as the archbishop and, presumably, at least some members of the chapter) they cannot prevent restitution.[71] That is, to the city of Bremen they advised diplomacy. They differentiated between the limited cases in which the city might claim some jurisdiction and the rights of the archbishop and chapter. Bremen's city council eventually reached an agreement with the archbishop, on 22 September 1534.[72] Although the archbishop waived his right to restore Catholic ritual in the cathedral (the city payed a 1500 fl. compensation to him as the city's territorial lord) and although the city published an evangelical church order that year, evangelical control of the cathedral chapter was not accomplished until 1547, when an evangelical was elected as the chapter's prior.

The same question of alien rights and urban authority confronted other cathedral cities, for example, Basel, Augsburg, Strasbourg, Hamburg, and Magdeburg. It was necessary to compromise with cathedral chapters and other entrenched clerical groups. Chapters often held patronage rights in urban territory, not to mention the rents and tithes used to maintain buildings and personnel. Exactly how their intractability affected a city's efforts can be easily traced out in an example from the extreme south, the city of Basel, a well studied case of a town that assumed control of church assets in the immediate aftermath of an evangelical revolt.[73]

Basel's city council ended Catholic worship in 1529, in order to regain control over a populace driven to an iconoclastic frenzy by rebellious guildsmen. The council quickly took over the properties and incomes of cloisters within their temporal jurisdiction, aided by riots on 9 February, which drove many priests and monks from the city and destroyed furnishings and art in the cathedral's chancel and chapels and in other churches. The cathedral canons fled down the Rhine to Neuenburg and by summer relocated the cathedral chapter permanently to Freiburg. This presented a problem to the coun-

---

[71] MBW 2:90 nr. 1307, 1308, WABr 6:428–29 nr. 1999.
[72] Veeck, *Geschichte der Reformierten Kirche*, pp. 3–7.
[73] Roth, *Durchbruch und Festsetzung*, pp. 44–7, 71–9, which is nonetheless an incomplete account based on the documents gathered in *Aktensammlung zur Geschichte der Basler Reformation in den Jahren 1519 bis Anfang 1534*, ed. E. Dürr, P. Roth, 6 vols. (Basel: Verlag der Historischen und antiquarischen Gesellschaft, 1921–50).

cil, namely how to control foreign incomes owed to the cathedral. There was also the potential burden of whatever litigation the estranged canons might begin and whatever sanctions might follow. So, the city invited the chapter to return to town and offered guarantees of its properties. Instead, the chapter appealed to Ferdinand and the bishop of Constance. The Austrian government at Ensisheim viewed the conflict pragmatically. It advised the canons to bring their case to the Imperial Diet, negotiate with the city directly, or wait for the city to approach them. The bishop of Constance was also pragmatic. He advised them to take a reasonable compensation for their losses, no more than 8,000 pounds. Remember, the bishop said, the city needs to strike a deal: it needs those incomes, too.[74] In fact, the city needed to pay not only its own clergy but also Catholic priests in places outside the council's temporal jurisdiction, for example, Bussisheim, Enschingen, and Istein, where it proved impossible to install evangelical clergy.

As summer approached, both sides gave thought to the cathedral's rents and tithes.[75] Since the steward of the bishop's court remained in the city, the council instructed him to continue to take payments. They also informed the cathedral chapter's prior that tithes owed to him from within the city's jurisdiction were being collected in the usual manner. Meanwhile, Ferdinand instructed the Austrian government at Ensisheim to ensure the chapter's incomes. Its rents and tithes were to be sent nowhere but to the chapter relocated to Freiburg.

The council tried to collect tithes owed throughout the diocese to St. Alban's and the Carthusians. They were hindered in lands outside their jurisdiction by a contrary order published by the Ensisheim government at the cathedral chapter's request, even though this collection did not involve the chapter's property. Nevertheless, when it came time to collect taxes, the Austrians granted tacit recognition of the city's right to at least some ecclesiastical revenues from Austrian subjects. Ferdinand's special tax for the Turkish war was levied on tithes as well as other incomes. As a member of the Swiss Confederacy, the city considered its incomes from Austrian subjects exempt from the tax. The Ensisheim government disagreed. In late August they

[74] Roth, *Durchbruch*, pp. 36–47 for this and the following.
[75] Ibid., pp. 76–7.

informed the city that they expected rents and tithes owed to the
city's foundations and cloisters to be gathered there as usual, in the
expectation that the city fulfill the tax burden as prescribed.

In the meanwhile, the cathedral chapter rebuffed the city as much
as it could, ignoring overtures to negotiate, refusing to hand over
the keys to the cathedral's library and treasure, and answering the
city's threats with an imperial delegation whose jurisdiction Basel's
council denied.[76] As summer ended, the council grew confident. In
September, it ordered the break-in of the cathedral's sacristy. It
claimed the wine and grain tithes of the cathedral prior in Basel's
territory. It hauled away the sealed casks from the prior's cellar. And
it appointed its own people to the chapter's administrative offices.
The chapter was powerless to intervene. Eight months after February's
troubles, the city completed its takeover of the cathedral. But conflicts
with the cathedral canons over the chapter's assets continued—to
the end of the seventeenth century. Most contested incomes that fell
under other lordships, for example the bishop of Basel or the margrave of Baden, were lost to the town.

Most evangelical cities were forced to comprise. Strasbourg and
Magdeburg reached agreements with their cathedrals by 1534.[77]
Although Hamburg and Augsburg managed to force their chapters
out of the town walls, they could not control all cathedral assets,
however much they thought they should. In Hamburg, the controversy over the chapter's right to self-rule droned on to 1561, and
ended in compromise.[78] The city of Halberstadt's evangelically sympathetic council failed to control religious life in the town until 1539,
when it began its concerted effort, which lasted until the defeat of
the Schmalkald League.[79] Evangelical clergy in such cities must have
looked longingly to towns without cathedrals, for example Ulm,
Nürnberg, and Esslingen, where reform seemed to flow steadily toward
an open bay of Christian liberty and salvation by faith, from the
time of the city's first response to urban unrest, through the council's accommodation of evangelical preachers, to new church ordi-

---

[76] Ibid., pp. 46–7.
[77] Abray, *The People's Reformation*, p. 42.
[78] Immenkötter, "Die katholische Kirche in Augsburg," pp. 9–32. Otto Scheib,
Die Reformationsdiskussionen in der Hansestadt Hamburg, 1522–1528 (Münster: Aschendorff,
1975), pp. 180–8.
[79] Logemann, "Grundzüge der Geschichte der Stadt Halberstadt," pp. 128–138.

nances and an end to the mass; and the friars evaporated from urban society as their gift-incomes dried up, leaving empty cloisters for schools, hospitals, and poor relief.[80] The diplomatic position recommended to Bremen by Hessian and Wittenberg theologians acknowledged that it was necessary to compromise with the Catholic church. But princes and magistrates in 1533 were hardly ready to give up.

The Wittenberg theologians' response to Bremen in early 1533 was equitable. It reflected the delicate circumstances of the Protestant League—to make enemies only insofar as necessary. But the Protestant princes were emboldened by the Peace of Nürnberg (1532) to neglect alien rights. On 6 March 1533 Johann Friedrich complained to Duke Ernst of Braunschweig-Lüneburg that the Wittenberg theologians failed to consider how divine worship in Bremen's cathedral had fallen into neglect, how the cathedral chapter let worship decay. Besides, the Nürnberg Peace stipulated that the dispute should pass, as a matter of religion, to a general council (Duke Ernst was himself preoccuppied with women's houses that resisted conversion).[81] The advice of Wittenberg theologians arrived in Bremen with the Elector's letter on 15 March 1533. The city decided to try to follow the prince.

But the Hessian theologians stayed their earlier course. In 1533, Johannes Eisermann, rector of Marburg's university, published a treatise called *On the Common Good* (*Von dem Gemeinen nutze*), in which he argued that cloister property should be used according to the gospel.[82] Able-bodied monks are not entitled to its use, he protested. Its proper use is as alms for the worthy poor, that is those hindered by bodily

---

[80] Ulm, Brecht, Ehmer, *Südwestdeutsche Reformationsgeschichte*, pp. 70–73, 167–173. Esslingen, ibid., pp. 73–5, 174–7. In some cities, evangelical reforms culminated a process of growing urban control of local religious institutions. Ulm, for example, had long held control of the Hospital of the Holy Spirit, extended its prior's authority over the Augustinian canonry of St. Michael in 1446, enriched it with Franciscan properties when the Franciscans were subjected to observant reform in 1484 (and with Dominican properties in 1538 and 1580), and incorporated the city's two leprosaria (one for commoners and one for aristocrats) into it in 1522. The city had also appointed lay guardians over the city's single parish church of the Blessed Virgin in 1352, over the Augustinian canons in 1489, a convent of Franciscan tertiary women and the Holy Clares of Söflingen in the mid-fifteenth century. *Deutsches Städtebuch*, 4/2/2:275–7.
[81] MBW 2:90 nr. 1307, 1308, WABr 6:428–29 nr. 1999. For Lüneburg, Wolfgang Brandis, "Quellen zur Reformationsgeschichte," pp. 357–398.
[82] Schilling, *Klöster und Mönche*, pp. 213–16.

injury or deformity from working, as determined in the early 1520's by Martin Luther and Hans Sachs, among others, to exclude charity to friars.[83] Moreover, the *Obrigkeit* must destroy false religion and superstition. Eisermann appealed to the ruler's conscience, in the terms of the recess of the Diet of Speyer in 1526, as the basis for the Landgrave's redeployment of cloister property to evangelical uses: the prince is responsible to God and emperor to promote the common good.[84] But there was no suggestion that the prince had free disposition of the church's property or could use it for ends of state, no intimation that state sovereignty extended over the material church. The prince's actions in the church were mere acts of devotion and service, the piety of a man in power.

Princes seldom played a crucial role in advancing the evangelical movement in towns. Intimations of sovereignty were of little use to city councils. "In a walled city, where there was no secure place of refuge from internal rebellion, it was probably not difficult to convince all but the most militant Catholics that to fail to yield some would mean to lose all."[85] Riots helped build the momentum of reform in public places.[86] Urban conversion usually depended on popular pressure on councils. Preachers drove and rode matters to a point of crisis again and again. Then the preachers worked on magistrates to restore a post-Catholic stability that excluded the old clergy, the priests whose legitimacy they had been picking at in degrading sermons, usually for several years before the crisis came, and whose churches, benefices, and monasteries they hoped to harvest for the new church order.

An inflammatory technique that stoked the tinder of urban restiveness was the staged disputation. The staged disputation heated up

---

[83] Ocker, "'Rechte Arme' und 'Bettlerorden,'" pp. 130–141.

[84] An appeal to the common good is best known as a civic rationale for confiscation. Thomas A. Brady, "In Search of the Godly City: The Domestication of Religion in the German Urban Reformation," *The German People and the Reformation*, ed. Ronald Po-Chia Hsia (Ithaca: Cornell, 1987), pp. 14–31; idem, "Rites of Autonomy, Rites of Dependence: South German Civic Culture in the Age of Renaissance and Reformation," *Religion and Culture in the Renaissance and Reformation*, edited by Steven Ozment (Kirksville: Sixteenth Century Studies Society, 1989), pp. 9–23; for northern Germany, Schilling, *Religion, Political Culture, and the Emergence of Early Modern Society*, pp. 3–59, esp. 56–7.

[85] Brady, *Ruling Class, Regime and Reformation*, p. 207.

[86] Lee Palmer Wandel, *Voracious Idols*, p. 75, and passim for the role of popular unrest in forcing reform.

the rivalry between pulpits and allowed evangelical preachers to rake their rivals over bible verses in a great public display of evangelical dialectic, before magistrates and the public at large. The benefits were at least three. First, the preachers posed as competent, sure, and authoritative victors over incompetent priests. Second, their supporters could gather en masse and act like a menace to the old clergy and its supporters in the council. And third, Catholic councilmen could nervously observe the changing tide. Preachers used disputations to consolidate or confirm opposition to the old faith at Zürich in 1524, Nürnberg in 1525, Memmingen in 1525, and Hamburg in 1528.[87] Catholic interlocutors caught on. Evangelical preachers in Basel organized disputations several times in 1523 and 1524, but the city's attempt to do so, in late April 1525, failed.[88] At Magdeburg in 1525, lacking an actual staged confrontation between evangelicals and Franciscans, the evangelical clergy staged a literary one. The city council had asked the Franciscans to explain their order's religion, and the Francsicans, after a year's delay, complied. It was a warm defense of Franciscan evangelism written by the guardian, Johann Greuer, with a charming vernacular exposition of the Franciscan rule.[89] The council then gave the work to the new preachers for rebuttal. The evangelicals published it with their own commentary. They printed ridicule in the margins of their edition, which all resembles this example, found alongside Greuer's plain exposition of biblical verses in support of monastic vows: "how marvelously he argues here. Scripture confirms vows; therefore it confirms monastic vows. That is to say, Johann Greuer is a grey ass, therefore all human beings are grey asses," alluding to the undyed grey

[87] Bernd Moeller, "Zwinglis Disputationen. Studien zu den Anfängen der Kirchenbildung und des Synodalwesens im Protestantismus, *Zeitschrift zur Rechtsgeschichte, Kanonistische Abteilung* 60 (1974): 213–364. Wandel, *Voracious Idols*, p. 55. Schlenck, *Die Reichsstadt Memmingen und die Reformation*, pp. 38–70. Andreas Gäumann, *Reich Christi und Obrigkeit. Eine Studie zum reformatorischen Denken und Handeln Martin Bucers* (Bern: Peter Lang, 2001), pp. 113–148. Rainer Postel, *Die Reformation in Hamburg 1517–1528* (Gütersloh: Gerd Mohn, 1986), pp. 244–314.

[88] Hans R. Guggisberg, *Basel in the Sixteenth Century* (St. Louis: Center for Reformation Research, 1982), p. 81 with n. 20.

[89] *Der Barfußer zcu magdeburg grund yhres Ordens Nyderlegung desselbtigen ym wortte Gottes. Erstlich eyn sendebryff, wy sulchs den von Hamburg durch die von Magdeburg zu geschryben,* (Magdeburg: Heinrich Oettinger, 1526). Flugschriften des frühen 16. Jahrhunderts, Fiche 433–434 nr. 1174.

robes the Franciscans wore.[89a] The pamphlet includes the evangelicals' summary rebuttal at the end. In 1528, the Magdeburg council failed to draw the city's cathedral canons into a disputation, but the unflappable Nikolaus Amsdorf, chief evangelical preacher in the city at the time, rifled off pamphlets and thereby made this failure a public spectacle of the inferiority of the old faith.[90] Memmingen's council attempted a disputation in 1529, during a new effort to establish an evangelical church.[91] The previous year, a disciplinary ordinance reduced the number of Christian feastdays celebrated by the city and imposed evangelical rites of baptism and the eucharist, soon followed by an inventory of the Augustinian cloister and the creation of a welfare fund from some church property. In 1528, Ambrosius Blarer was brought in to preach, but the Holy Clares resisted his attempt to end the mass in their convent, and soon the bishop of Augsburg addressed a protest to the council, while the Ingolstadt theologian Johann Eck sent a treatise defending the mass. The council gave the treatise to Blarer for public rebuttal, which occurred 15 January 1529. But when the city invited Eck to defend his views in a public meeting, he declined for several reasons—the lack of an appropriate arbitrator in the city, the popular prejudice created by Blarer—offering to appear before the Swabian League or an imperial judge instead. By then, the uses of disputation were clear. Where public opinion allowed, or when it did not matter, a ruler wanted to prevent combustion between pulpits. A few years later in another region, when Göttingen attempted a disputation in 1531, the duke of Braunschweig-Calenberg scuttled it.[92]

In 1534, a disputation was attempted at Augsburg, too. As in many cities (for example, Basel), evangelical preaching began in a few of the city's seventeen cloisters, collegiate churches, and third-

---

[89a] Ibid., "we feyn arguirt ehr hie die schrift billichet gelubdte darumb billichet sie die closterlubdte, das ist eben soviel geredt Johann greuer ist eyn graw eßel darumb synd alle menschen grawe eßel."

[90] Friedrich Hülße, "Beiträge zur Geschichte der Buchdruckerkunst in Magdeburg," *Geschichts-Blätter für Stadt und Land Magdeburg* 15 (1880): 21–49, 164–198, 275–295, 331–374, here 339–341 nr. 19, 21, 22, p. 349 nr. 31, pp. 350–353 nr. 33, 34, 35, 36, pp. 366–367 nr. 47, 48.

[91] For Memmingen, Schlenck, *Die Reichsstadt Memmingen*, pp. 42–3, 64–6.

[92] Bernd Moeller, "Die Reformation," *Göttingen. Geschichte einer Universitätsstadt*, vol. 1, *Von den Anfängen bis zum Ende des Dreißigjährigen Krieges* (Göttingen: Vandenhoeck und Ruprecht, 1987), pp. 492–514.

order houses and was welcomed by the city's guilds, who happened to enjoy a particularly strong voice in this city's regime.[93] By 1533, monastic attrition had already depleted the membership of the Franciscan and Carmelite cloisters. The council sold the Franciscan cloister to the town's foundling hospital in 1533, and the Carmelite monastery was closed the following year. In 1533, the council also tried to draw out the town's priests, while it began to debate the limitations of the emperor's protective lordship over the church, the need for a clergy-controlled general council, and the responsibility of government to promote true religion.[94] The council approached the prince-bishop. They asked him to resolve the controversy raging between the city's evangelical and Catholic pulpits over such things as auditory confession, intercessory prayer for the dead, memorial masses, the eucharist, and various traditional religious customs. The bishop, who ruled from his palace at Dillingen, a small town on the Danube River a comfortable forty kilometers to the northwest, responded cooly. He explained that these rites could easily be demonstrated from ecclesiastical councils, once a judge acceptable to both sides is found.[95]

The council then tried to organize the disputation. One of the leading evangelical preachers, Wolfgang Musculus, in a letter to Ambrosius Blarer dated 29 March 1534, reported that on 6 March a delegation was sent by the city council to the canons of St. Mary's to challenge the validity of their religion.[96] The canons responded 24 March. Since their religion was well known from the councils of the church, they did not feel they needed to give any account of it. They didn't want to be drawn into a disputation, the canons said.

---

[93] Immenkötter, "Die katholische Kirche in Augsburg," pp. 9–32 for a summary of the events of 1533–1537.

[94] The city council sollicited some fourteen theological and legal briefs on these topics about this time, eight from 1533 alone. Immenkötter, "Die katholische Kirche in Augsburg," pp. 24–5. Their arguments are summarized in Karl Wolfart, *Die Augsburger Reformation in den Jahren 1533/34* (Aalen: Scientia Verlag, 1974 reprint of the Leipzig 1901 edition), pp. 45–60. See also Wilhelm Hans, "Gutachten und Streitschriften über das ius reformandi des Rates vor und während der Einführung der offiziellen Kirchenreform in Augsburg (1534–1537)," Ph.D. Dissertation, University of Leipzig, 1901.

[95] Immenkötter, "Die katholische Kirche in Augsburg," pp. 21–2.

[96] *Briefwechsel der Brüder Ambrosius und Thomas Blaurer, 1509–1548*, ed. Traugott Schiess, 3 vols. (Freiburg im Briesgau: F.E. Fehsenfeld, 1908–1912), 1:479–80 nr. 405.

Debates, they noted, had ambivalent outcomes at Leipzig, Zürich, Baden, Bern, even the Diet of Augsburg in 1530.[97] They might have remembered, too, that public disputations gave Philip of Hesse his pretext to confiscate monastic properties in 1527, which also happened at Zürich, Nürnberg, Memmingen, and Hamburg.[98]

Their own proposal was meant to be constructive. The conflict should be brought before the bishop of Augsburg, and *si supectus sit*, "if he be held suspect," before the bishops of Eichstätt or Freising.[99] If that didn't please the city council, the canons would accept a hearing before the universities of Freiburg, Tübingen, or Ingolstadt, or failing that, the arbitration of the dukes of Bavaria or King Ferdinand and Emperor Charles. Anyone but the Augsburg council. These alternatives also included tribunals that in the future could display the injustice of Protestant actions, which had to remind the council that a reformation would meet a wearying load of litigation. How it would turn out, Musculus did not venture to guess, for the priests, he noted, enjoyed the support of the principal merchants in the city, "who we should have won over first" (*die wir zuerst hätten gewinnen sollen*).[100] He had the information from "our people" (*ex nostris*) in the city council. The council, in fact, accepted the bishop of Augsburg as judge, in his capacity as prince, not bishop, they said.[101]

The disputation never took place. But the council nonetheless prohibited Catholic preaching in the city in July 1534, while limiting the performance of Catholic rites to the eight city churches under the bishop's or cathedral chapter's control. In the meanwhile, attrition and flight from the city's inhospitality devastated the city's monasteries (a begging ordinance removed the gift-incomes of the mendicant friars), and soon the Dominican friary, one of two Dominican nunneries, and one of three houses for Franciscan tertiary women were empty. The contest of pulpits continued, while Musculus and Bucer rallied support for the city council's interventions in the church, against the better advice of Luther, Melanchthon, and the united

[97] Immenkötter, "Die katholische Kirche in Augsburg," p. 22.
[98] See the literature in note 87, above.
[99] *Briefwechsel der Brüder Ambrosius und Thomas Blaurer*, 1:479–80 nr. 405.
[100] Ibid., and Lyndal Roper, *The Holy Household* (Oxford: Clarendon, 1991), pp. 12–16 and the literature cited there for the role of the guilds, especially in the Larger Council.
[101] Immenkötter, "Die katholische Kirche in Augsburg," p. 22.

Wittenberg theologians (they restricted the council's right to reform to cases in which it held patronage).[102] It took more than two years for the Protestant preachers to win the city council's full support. Finally, 17 January 1537, the remnant of Catholic clergy and nuns were given the choice of citizenship or expulsion with the loss of immovable property. The eight Catholic churches under the cathedral chapter were given to the Protestants; images and liturgical objects were removed from them in the next few days. The chapter transferred itself to the bishop's residence at Dillingen, together with the third order Dominican sisters of St. Ursula. Monks and nuns of three other foundations moved to holdings outside the city. The Benedictine nuns were relocated to the vacant St. Ursula, and their property outside the town was confiscated for the extension of battlements. But the remaining nunnery, St. Catherine's, became the center of the old faith for those Catholic citizens who resisted change. The council published an evangelical church order in July 1537, which marks the official conversion of the town. Soon after, Musculus co-authored one of the most sophisticated memoranda on church property ever brought to the League.

The Diplomatic View

How, then, to defend the transgression of the rights of patrons or possessors of tithes and rents, many belonging to entrenched corporations, such as cathedral chapters and collegiate churches, some of whose members often enjoyed blood ties to powerful families in and/or outside city walls? In 1534, the League for the first time indicated that this problem should be resolved by dissociating church property from individual rights. In 1534, when the League tried to recuse members of the Imperial Chamber Court from cases about church property, the League's jurists appealed for the first time to the legal maxim, *beneficium propter officium datur*, "the benefice is given on account of the office": the benefice belongs to the office, not the office-holder. The principle appears in a papal decree of Pope Boniface VIII (1294–1303) against absentee benefice-holders. The decree made

---

[102] Hans, "Gutachten und Streitschriften," passim.

its way into the *Corpus iuris canonici*.[103] *Beneficium datur propter officium* meant, first and foremost, that a benefice was to be treated as an income attached to an office and not as a gift that binds two individuals or as a property given to a benefice-holder as though it were a fief. This conformed to a good canonistic view of an ecclesiastical benefice. It contrasts with the Roman concept of *beneficium*, which was more ambiguous than an ecclesiastical benefice, closer to the medieval notion of gift, and closest to the ecclesiastical notion of *privilegium*: the ancient Roman *beneficium* referred to privileges personally given.[104] The League's theologians will soon appeal to the principle, *beneficium propter officium datur*, too, and I will return to it in due course.

The attempt to recuse members of the court amounted to a demand that the bench should accept Protestant infringements on the jurisdictions of Catholic bishops, clergy, and religious orders. It was a lot to ask. The year before, in 1533, the archbishop of Mainz had attempted to form a Protestant-Catholic peace coalition, building on the momentum of the 1532 Peace of Nürnberg, which he also had helped to negotiate.[105] In the spring of 1534, with the approval but

---

[103] In an attempt to encourage pastoral residency, Pope Boniface VIII revoked all incomes taken in abstentia from benefices given by his predecessors. He argued that because of the neglect of these absentee benefice-holders, worship is going downhill and "many an office, on account of which a benefice is given, is neglected" (*officium plerumque, propter quod beneficium ecclesiasticum datur, omittitur*). *Liber Sextus* I.iii.15 CICan 2:943. This one instance appears to be the maxim's only use in the *Corpus Iuris Canonici*. It does not appear in Gratian's *Decretum*. Timothy Reuter, Gabriel Silagi, *Wortkonkordanz zum Decretum Gratiani*, 5 vols. (Munich: Monumenta Germaniae Historica, 1990), 1:431–33. It does not, to my knowledge, appear in the *Corpus Iuris Civilis*. Haug-Moritz explains that this principle trumped the Catholic argument for the priority of donors' intentions, beginning with the League's 1534 attempt to recuse the court. "1534 war damit die juristische Legitimation gefunden, auf die protestantische Obrigkeiten zurückgreifen konnten, wann immer es zum öffentlichen Schlagabtausch mit den Katholiken über ihre reformatorische Politik und deren materiellen Folgen kam." Haug-Moritz, *Der Schmalkaldische Bund*, p. 512. See also ibid., pp. 277–87 for the failed 1534 recusation and subsequent discussions of recusal, and Sieglerschmidt, *Territorialstaat*, p. 141. Sieglerschmidt, and Haug-Mortiz following him, believe that the Catholic side, by contrast, based itself on the principle of donor's intention. Sieglerschmidt, *Territorialstaat*, pp. 130–38. This may exaggerate Protestant-Catholic differences, since Protestant theologians emphasized donors' intentions since at least 1521, although never exclusively, and both this principle and the priority of office (*beneficium propter officium*) were principles of canon law.

[104] Adolf Berger, *An Encyclopaedic Dictionary of Roman Law* (Philadelphia: American Philosophical Society, 1991 reprint), s.v. beneficium.

[105] Kohnle, *Reichstag und Reformation*, pp. 395–406 for his role in the Peace of Nürenberg. Fuchs, *Konfession und Gespräch*, pp. 392–95.

not the official sponsorship of the Catholic Duke Georg of Saxony, a group of Catholics and Protestants representing Electoral Saxony (Melanchthon and Brück), the collegiate church of Halle, the archbishop of Mainz (the chancellor Christoph Türck), the cathedral of Halberstadt (it was held by Albrecht, the archbishop of Mainz, as adminstrator, who was here represented by the auxiliary bishop, Heinrich Leucker), and the cathedral of Meißen held discussions on the articles of the Augsburg Confession for two days, 29–30 April, in the church of the Cloister of the Order of St. Paul the Hermit in Leipzig.[106] The Leipzig Colloquy, as this is known, was marred by disagreements over procedure as well as doctrine. It broke down over discussions on the mass. But it did produce an agreement on the doctrine of justification, and more importantly for my purpose, it did *not* discuss church property at all. This may have been the first sure indication that among Catholic reformers in Germany confiscations could be ignored.

Not too far away from Augsburg, Ulrich of Württemberg was organizing the confiscation of monastic lands. By the time the duke took advice from his theologians, in June or July 1535, most of the monasteries' documents had been confiscated, and lay officers had been assigned to take over the monasteries' business. His exchequer was told to decide how to use the property, while the duke's chamberlain booked the proceeds, according to the order sent to ducal "officers who have church property" (*Amptleut, so gaistliche guetter haben*).[107] Ambrosius Blarer probably wrote the subsequent theological *Memorandum, whether one may convert the convents of the ancients to the support of the evangelical church* (*Bedenken, ob man die Stifftungen der alten verendern und die clöstergüeter zu der evangelischen kirche underhaltung verwenden möge*). He remained influential at the duke's court until the following year.[108] The memorandum took the old Hessian position. It emphasized the intentions of donors, to endow worship; argued that the good intentions of their last wills are violated when their mistaken and childish notions of merit, et cetera, are entertained and respected; argued against purgatory, vigils, and masses; associated true worship with

[106] Fuchs, *Konfession und Gespräch*, pp. 392–95.
[107] Deetjen, *Studien*, pp. 183–84.
[108] H. Hermelink, "Zwei Aktenstücke über Behandlung der Kirchengüter in Württemberg zur Reformationszeit," *Blätter für württembergische Kirchengeschichte*, n.s. 7 (1903): 172–75. For the date and purpose, Deetjen, *Studien*, pp. 210–11, 419–20 n. 269.

charity; and concluded that the duke of Württemberg had to intervene against cloisters and foundations that follow old superstitions.
It did not appeal to Ulrich's prerogatives as patron. The memorandum quoted Roman law to establish the duke's duty to support
true religion.[109] There was no mention of reason of state, no suggestion that church property should strengthen bonds to aristocratic
friends and clients (a liberty theologians had suggested to the Saxon
Elector), no intimation of a ruler's sovereignty over the church. In
short, the document provided a minimal rationale for Ulrich's max-
imal confiscations. It stressed piety.

In late summer in Electoral Saxony, Johann Friedrich and the
theologians of Wittenberg worried over restitution as they discussed
an agenda for Catholic-Protestant negotiations.[110] On 12 or 13
September 1535 in a brief to Elector Johann Friedrich, Luther, Jonas,
Bugenhagen, Kaspar Cruciger, and Melanchthon noted that in peace
negotiations adherents of the Augsburg Confession would have to
refuse any prohibition of the further spread of evangelical teaching
and any limitation on accepting new members into the League of
Schmalkalden. They argued that the Imperial Chamber Court has
no right to meddle in church matters, and that a demand for the
restitution of church property should be countered by a proposal to
use such properties specifically for parishes, schools, and hospitals.[111]
Sometime that autumn of 1535, Melanchthon and Luther advised
Frankfurt am Main that in cases in which the city council holds
patronage, the city may resist opposition and could count on help
from the League. But in cases of foreign patronage, it could not hinder the restitution of properties.[112] This same solution was adapted
by the League's diet at Schmalkalden in December 1535 and pro-

---

[109] D 33.2.16, CICiv 1:502, on the maintenance of memorial legacies in cities.
[110] "Nach dem Scheitern des Leipziger Einigungsversuches 1534 war der
Gesprächsfaden im sächsischen Raum zunächst abgerissen," observed Thomas Fuchs.
Karlowitz did not seek dialogue with the Protestants again until over two years
later, in January 1537, which eventually led to the Leipzig Colloquy of 1539. Fuchs,
Konfession und Gespräch, pp. 395–6. This 1535 Wittenberg *Gutachten* shows, however,
that in Electoral Saxony there remained, in anticipation of future colloquies, a concern to clarify non-negotiable things.
[111] They also noted conditions for the recognition of a church council. MBW
2:205–6 nr. 1626 = CR 2:592–95, WABr 12:181–86 nr. 4258.
[112] October 1535 MBW 2:215 nr. 1653 and 5 November 1535 MBW 2:217 nr.
1658.

moted by the Landgrave: the diet confirmed a ruler's jurisdiction over property of clergy directly under him, but not over church property of clergy under foreign patrons.[113] It was the advice given to Bremen by Hessian and Wittenberg theologians in 1533.

Wittenberg now continued to promote this diplomatic view. On 23 May 1536 Luther, Bugenhagen, Cruciger, Jonas, and Melanchthon provided a recommendation to the city council of Augsburg on whether civil magistrates can abolish an impious cult and change religion in cathedrals.[114] The preacher is required to reform worship non-violently, they said, by teaching people and telling rulers their duties. After preaching has occurred, the civil authority must end godless rites, but only within the scope of their governing authority and patronage, as guardians of the first commandment, "you shall have no other gods." They must not meddle in the dominions of others, nor disregard the dominion and patronage rights of princes which the emperor had given them, thus shutting off the authority of popes.[115] The argument resurrected a theme from the first years of the Protestant movement, when it was alleged that the pope usurped the imperial system of ecclesiastical privileges.[116] All imperial estates

---

[113] Haug-Moritz, *Der Schmalkaldische Bund*, p. 517.

[114] MBW 2:252 nr. 1739, CR 3:224–29.

[115] Ibid.: "Iam enim secluditur autoritas Pontificis, sicut ipse Caesar in pacificationibus secludit, cum permittit Principibus ut in suis dominiis ordinent ecclesias. Hic enim omittit auctoritatem Pontificis, et significat se loqui de Ecclesiis, quarum dominium aut ius patronatus immediate pertinet ad ipsos principes."

[116] Heinrich von Gengenbach, the Observant Franciscan of Ulm who became an evangelical preacher in 1521, complained that clerical immunities from the many forms of taxation arose from the pope's theft of the emperor's prerogatives. But he argued that there was no imperial basis for clerical immunities, either, which he thought were in imitation of the privileges of ancient pagan priesthoods among the Egyptians and Babylonians. *Ein Gespräch mit einem frommen Altmütterlein von Ulm* (1523), and *Ein Sermon zu der löblichen Stadt Ulm zu einem Valete* (1523), *Flugschriften aus den ersten Jahren der Reformation*, ed. Otto Clemen, 4 vols. (Nieuwkoop: B. De Graaf, 1967), 2:74–75, 115 (article 27), 188–19. How imperial privilege was adapted to the case for Protestant reform is apparent in the city of Nürnberg, where in 1525 Andreas Osiander defended the city's imposition of oaths of citizenship on vicars of Nürnberg's churches by noting that the emperor gave clergy immunity so that they could serve the churches, but things have changed. "Die weyl aber yezo dieselben unnutzen kirchengebreuch alle gefallen—alls sie auch dem wort Gottes nit gemaß—so sey es gantz von notten, die vicarier und briesterschafft widerumb unter die welltlichen oberkeit zu bringen." Andreas Osiander der Ältere, *Gesamtausgabe*, 2:120. For imperial authority and urban church property, consider also Isenmann, *Die deutsche Stadt im Spätmittelalter*, p. 111.

agree with this opinion, the Wittenberg theologians said, but in such a difficult matter, the League should be consulted. The Peace of Nürnberg of 1532 guarantees the reform measures already concluded, they continued, but preachers must exercise restraint. The recommendation briskly denied that the new form of worship caused unrest ("we don't know these dangers," *agnoscimus haec pericula*). It insisted on the city's authority where it had patronage and on its lack of authority where it did not. Their advice was both apologetic and ecumenical: they denied that Protestant reform created instability and asserted that their view of patron's rights and obligations was shared by Catholic and Protestant estates.

A theologians' consensus was forming around the diplomatic view. It suited the delicacy of the League's situation as a coalition of cities and princes who needed to refigure their confiscations as the devout acts of good imperial subjects and good neighbors who respect others and are respected in turn. Theologians showed little interest in following the path suggested early on by Luther, when he entertained the idea that a prince's authority in temporal matters was absolute. In the early 1530's, urban conflicts forced the discussion of two practical questions, namely protection of the church and patronage. Protection implied the *ius reformandi*, the right and obligation to reform within one's domain, which each Christian shared at his or her station in life, in order that the property of the church serve the common good.[117] Equity required mutual, bi-confessional respect of this right. Patronage dictated a residual, partial dominion over gifts, but here, too, equity required mutual, bi-confessional respect. A prince might be the most prevalent patron in his realm, but he was certainly not the only one. He was one in a community of overlapping and layered powers.[118] Self-assertion implied the equivalent rights of others; a prince was no more king in his realm than the emperor.

---

[117] This would mean that the *ius reformandi* was neither an imperial right, nor did it merely express an obligation of rulers. This latter, internal right is what the Protestant estates presupposed through the 1530's. It was, according to their theologians, however, merely a ruler's expression of an obligation binding on all members of the church. Schneider, *Ius reformandi*, pp. 85–147, here 86, 138.

[118] Brady, *Protestant Politics*, 6–12.

CHAPTER FIVE

TOWARD A COMMON POSITION

The most divisive issue among Protestant preachers was the sacrament of the eucharist, the rite by which the faithful share a holy union with the resurrected Christ and the saints in heaven.[1] The rite expressed the bonds of a religiously imagined community. The church, as traditionally known, was a fraternity of people on earth united with the ordinary dead in a state of temporal remorse and healing by divine grace. The dead found relief in purgatory through the charity of their living relatives, until they are ready to enter the purified company of those free of sin and its damaging effects on the mind, will, and emotions. The sacrifice of the mass, its commutable merit, alleviated the sufferings of one's ancestors between earth and heaven. Outside the new clergy, these beliefs were tenacious.[2] Many

---

[1] Saints were perfectly sanctified souls who live in the presence of God. Protestants denied the ability of saints to intercede on behalf of people on earth, the existence of purgatory, and a post-mortem hierarchy of souls—not the existence of saints.

[2] Susan Karant-Nunn, *The Reformation of Ritual: An Interpretation of Early Modern Germany* (New York: Routledge, 1997), pp. 130–7. Karant-Nunn emphasizes popular attachment to traditional forms. For Protestant theology of the sacrament, Burkhard Neunheuser, *Eucharistie in Mittelalter und Neuzeit* (Freiburg: Herder, 1963), pp. 51–62, which only treats Luther, Zwingli, Calvin, and the Catholic response. See Thomas Kaufmann, *Die Abendmahlstheologie der Straßburger Reformatoren bis 1528* (Tübingen: J.C.B. Mohr/Paul Siebeck, 1992), pp. 420–437 for a summary of Bucer's assumption of the position of mediator between Wittenberg and the south in 1528, and pp. 444–7 for a convenient chronological chart comparing writings from Lutherans, Strasbourg, Basel and Zürich 1525–1528, when the north-south Protestant conflict over the sacrament materialized. For the Wittenberg Concord, the standard work remains Ernst Bizer, *Studien zur Geschichte des Abendmahlsstreits im 16. Jahrhunderts* (Darmstadt: Wissenschaftliche Buchgesellschaft, 1962). Heinz Schilling has pointed out that there was no link between the sacramental debate and regionally distinct outlooks on society (north vs. south, urban vs. territorial). Schilling, *Religion, Political Culture, and the Emergence of Early Modern Society*, pp. 189–201. Sacramentarians had no monopoly over urban reform. Lutherans also played an important role in communal reform in southern Germany in the 1520's, for example Andreas Osiander, Johannes Brenz, and Georg Gugy (a key figure in the Reformation in Memmingen for three years, he was expelled upon Ambrosius Blarer's advice in 1528). Schlenck, *Die Reichsstadt Memmingen*, p. 64. In the north, to name the two most prominent examples, Nikolaus Amsdorf and Johannes Bugenhagen were Lutherans active in urban reformations

people, perhaps most, would have felt the Protestant breach with a catholic (that is universal) spiritual society strongest here, in connection with this rite. In Ulrich of Württemberg's Stuttgart, when the last three masses were celebrated in the Church of the Holy Spirit on 2 February 1535, we are told, the church was full, the lamps and candles were plentiful, and the crowd wept.[3] In any town, the new preachers undermined gifts of influential clans who for generations used conspicuous memorial masses, in part, to publish their social status in benevolent terms.[4]

Protestant theologians promoted a different version of this life-afterlife fraternity, but it was also supernaturalistic. They emphatically presented the fraternity as the true representation of the fellowship between heaven and earth. Although the charity of human beings on earth could not alter the destiny of the souls of the dead, all who enjoyed the free gift of grace were united as the body of Christ, including the departed souls that live in Christ's presence. Human beings on earth experience that union most tangibly in the evangelical eucharist, it was said. The only proof that evangelicals had not abandoned souls in the intermediate state were theological arguments. In cities like Zürich, Constance, Magdeburg, Nürnberg, Strasbourg, Schwäbisch Hall, Basel, Hamburg, and Ulm, which ended public masses between 1525 and 1535 and participated in the internal Protestant eucharistic controversy, it was essential that the new preachers infallibly explain how their churches formed the true sacramental community, the united people of God. The new doctrine had to compensate for its own disruption of established church teaching and everyday memorialization of the dead. The theological argument between Wittenberg and the south German evangelicals was fueled by divergent readings of scripture, using the agreed tools of

---

through the course of their lives. Far more formative was the contrast between Protestant and Catholic positions.

[3] Auge, *Stiftsbiographien*, p. 97.

[4] This symbolic benefit may have been in decline. Memorial masses were increasingly offered in blocks, sometimes for the souls whose remains occupied an entire cemetery or for all the poor who could not afford to endow masses, omitting the names of individuals and, when endowed anonymously, ceasing to publish clan prestige in the old way. As anniversary endowments piled up through the years, it was imposible to say separately each mass that had been endowed. Staub, *Les paroisses et la cité*, pp. 269–270. Mireille Othenin-Girard, "'Helfer' und 'Gespenster.' Die Toten und der Tauschhandel mit den Lebenden," *Kulturelle Reformation. Sinnformationen im Umbruch, 1400–1600*, pp. 178–191.

scriptural interpretation, in order to minimize human and material mediations between the soul and God in the most reliable and convincing way.[5] But the professional culture of scholars was adversarial, disputational, to be exact, and theological disagreement was routine. The absence of a teaching magisterium increased the stakes of biblical argument.

The disagreement took shape after 1525 and persisted until 1536.[6] In 1536 evangelical theologians suspended the eucharistic debate. Since the ascension of Pope Paul III, Protestant unity became increasingly urgent. There was the threat of a conciliar answer to the Protestant appeal and the multiplication of property disputes as Protestantism expanded into new territories and cities. The conversion of Württemberg alone must have greatly intensified property dilemmas. The eucharistic debate remained suspended until the aftermath of the Schmalkald War. Since the Schmalkald League described its purpose as defense of the religion of the Augsburg Confession, and clergy defined that religion, theological differences among preachers and theologians had obstructed the coalition's early build-out, in spite the League's early, latitudinarian policy—to accept estates who merely tolerated preaching "of the true and pure Word of God" in their "principalities, cities, lands, and regions."[7] Luther's continued misgivings notwithstanding, theologians reached a eucharistic compromise soon after Duke Ulrich's restoration, then honed a broader doctrinal consensus and gave more determined attention to church property.

Duke Ulrich's reformation of the church in Württemberg was at first guided by Ambrosius Blarer, a preacher whose reputation was made in the cities of the southland and a sacramentarian by any account. The court of Philip of Hesse, with the support of the city of Strasbourg, had shaped Ulrich's religious sensibilities, such as they were, and the influence continued after the restoration. The Landgrave remained anxious to expand city members in the League. He pressured southern theologians to accommodate themselves to the Augsburg Confession. Duke Ulrich replaced Blarer in 1538, after Johannes

---

[5] Susan Karant-Nunn, *Reformation of Ritual*, passim, for the removal of sacral mediations as a central Protestant ambition.

[6] Kaufmann, *Abendmahlstheologie*, for the early development of the debate.

[7] Haug-Moritz, *Der Schmalkaldische Bund*, p. 113.

Brenz, the leading evangelical in Schwäbisch Hall, who opposed sacramentarian views, had already become influential at court.[8] The Landgrave, with the Strasbourg magistrate Jacob Sturm and the elector of Saxony, arranged for the theologians to negotiate at a conference at Wittenberg in 1536. The conference produced the formal agreement known as the Wittenberg Concord, which answered the eucharistic controversy by insisting on the spiritual oneness achieved when the eucharistic bread is consumed in faith as Christ's body.[9] It won the consent of Duke Ulrich and all the south German Protestant cities but Constance: Augsburg, Kempten, Esslingen, Frankfurt, Worms, Landau, Weissenburg, Memmingen, Kempten, and eventually Ulm.[10] The Swiss Protestant cities rejected the Concord, insisting on the eucharistic doctrine of the so-called "first" Helvetic Confession, composed at Basel that same year, but since 1531, they were of little significance to the Protestant League.

The Concord was largely the work of Strasbourg's Bucer and Wittenberg's Melanchthon. The Strasbourg city council and clergy sent official word of their acceptance of it to Wittenberg soon after negotiations ended, followed by a report of the Swiss refusal written by the Strasbourg theologians Bucer and Wolfgang Capito and addressed to Luther.[11] The Elector of Saxony then turned to the matter of complete doctrinal consensus in the League, in the expectation of a thoroughly united front against the established church (unity could serve the purposes of both resistance and negotiation, the alternative paths that lay before the League). If the difference of eucharistic theology was ever wedded by some religious logic to differing views of the church, political authority, and society, it had no effect on the internal Protestant discussions of church property. By 1536, the order of the day had become consensus, anyway. This eventually included a rationale for confiscations.

---

[8] Brenz was known for his controversy with the Basel theologian, Johannes Oecolampadius, over eucharistic doctrine, and he participated in the 1529 Marburg Colloquy. Estes, *Johannes Brenz*, pp. 8–10. Brecht, Ehmer, *Südwestdeutsche Reformationsgeschichte*, pp. 203–6.

[9] *Common Places of Martin Bucer*, translated by D.F. Wright (Appleford: Sutton Courtenay Press, 1972), pp. 255–379.

[10] MBW 2:284 nr. 1818. WABr 7:612–14 nr. 3116. Brady, *Protestant Politics*, p. 89. Brecht, *Martin Luther* 3:39–59.

[11] Two days after the Strasbourg city council sent a letter confirming the Wittenberg Concord, the Strasbourg clergy send notification to Wittenberg of their acceptance of it. WABr 8:6–17 nr. 3126–28.

In 1536, Johann Friedrich asked for a list of doctrinal articles to serve as a position piece, with regard to both the Protestant faith and related issues, for example the authority of church councils and marriage. Wittenberg theologians provided a text on the latter in December, and on articles of faith in January 1537, under the signatures of Luther, Jonas, Bugenhagen, Cruciger, Amsdorf, Spalatin, Melanchthon, and Agricola.[12] These articles bear the name of the place of their approval, at the League's diet in Schmalkalden, February 1537. There, the imperial chancellor Matthias Held appeared on his first mission to the League, in order to present the emperor's response to Protestant complaints against the Imperial Chamber Court made a few months earlier, and to sollict their participation in the church council summoned by the pope for Mantua.[13] The articles included a brief treatment of monasticism.

The Schmalkald Articles

The passage on monasticism (part 2 article 3) emphasizes the educational role of monasteries and opposes monastic religiosity. In former times, the article says, convents and monasteries were established for the education of learned people and decent women. They should be returned to such use, for the sake of educating pastors, preachers, and other servants of the church, as well as other necessary persons for earthly government. They should be used to rear young women to be mothers and housekeepers. Where monasteries and convents do not so function, it is better that they die of attrition, lest their blasphemous worship, instituted by human ingenuity, be thought to stand above the common vocation of all the baptized and above the offices and orders established by God. Monastic religion is contrary to the redemption of Jesus Christ (the first of the articles): it is not commanded by scripture, nor necessary, nor useful. It is dangerous and empty.

This was a very serviceable position, as circumstances before, during, and after the diet revealed. For one, Duke Georg of Saxony

---

[12] WABr 8:2–3 nr. 3124. Martin Luther, *Sämmtliche Schriften* 21:2141 and William R. Russel, *Luther's Theological Testament: the Schmalkald Articles* (Minneapolis: Fortress, 1994) for the articles.

[13] Haug-Moritz, *Der Schmalkaldische Bund*, p. 119.

was preparing his own sequestration, as a Catholic, and he must have warmed to some arguments for monastic correction. In 1535, he had ordered the inventory of properties of the Teutonic Order in Saxony, in order to reform their administration of church property, he said.[14] The Teutonic Master brought a complaint against this intrusion to the Imperial Chamber Court in February 1537. At first, the court's assessors seemed to accommodate the Catholic duke in terms faintly reminiscent of Protestant arguments. They admitted the necessity of a prince's preservation of monastic property, for example, by preventing overpayments to mother-houses in other lands (Konrad Braun's argument). Georg began confiscations later that year, when he seized the order's houses in Reichenbach and Adorf. The Imperial Chamber Court's tone immediately changed. The duke, it was said at court, is like a wolf commanded not to eat meat, so he catches a jackass, drops it in some water, and calls it a fish, and he was summoned to appear. It was a first indication that Catholic Saxony might follow the example of his Electoral neighbor, who was himself resisting, and helping others to resist, the assessors' interference in church affairs. At the same time a dilemma of succession further softened Duke Georg to the idea of a Protestant-Catholic rapprochement.[15]

Georg's son and heir, Prince Friedrich, was incompetent to rule. The duke nevertheless hoped to secure the succession for him at a meeting of his estates at Leipzig that year. He won their agreement, on the awkward condition that the prince be controlled by a team of regents—two counts, two prelates, two university professors, and sixteen knights—with a small contingent accompanying Friedrich at all times. Friedrich was eventually married-off to the daughter of the count of Mansfeld, but he died months later (1539), leaving the succession to Georg's brother Heinrich, whose evangelical sympathies were well known. Heinrich had already installed an evangelical court preacher in Freiberg in 1536.[16] The Elector of Saxony openly favored Heinrich's succession. When Georg's estates agreed to Friedrich, the Elector of Saxony threatened to install Heinrich by force. Now Georg hoped to reduce tensions, in part, by meliorating the differences

[14] Sprenger, *Viglius von Aytta*, pp. 77–80 for this and the following.
[15] Midelfort, *Mad Princes of Renaissance Germany*, pp. 53–54, for this and the following.
[16] Brecht, *Martin Luther*, 3:152–6.

between the confessions.[17] Church property was a point at which both parties could agree—that it did not religiously matter.

Duke Georg's counselor, Georg von Karlowitz, initiated a religious dialogue. Just days before the League opened its diet at Schmalkalden in early February 1537, he sent the Landgrave of Hesse a letter and suggested the parties find agreement around the articles of faith, overagainst disagreements about matters of rite.[18] The letter also expressed the opinion of the Schmalkald article on monasticism, which originated with Luther and Melanchthon in 1520 and 1521.[19] No one should drive people from cloisters or confiscate cloister property, he proposed, but the property of cloisters that have been freely abandoned should be turned into schools, in accord with the historical purpose of monasteries as schools of Christian piety: they should serve youth of 11–12 years.[20] Cloister property could provide salaries for preachers, doctors, magistrates, and youth-trainers (*Zuchtmeister der Jugend*), who all must be good and learned. Beyond that, people should pay for their own education. But the letter places this in the context of the preservation of the church by also insisting that endowments cannot be confiscated without injury to God and neighbor. Von Karlowitz continued to promote the use of monastic property for schools for the next decade. In the early 1540's, he advised Duke Moritz on the reassignment of church incomes to pension monks and nuns, fund schools, and provide poor relief.[21] In 1543 and 1546 he defended Protestant confiscations to the emperor, saying that Protestants only wanted to use endowments according to the intentions of donors, to fund schools.[22]

A stronger Catholic overture came to the Schmalkald diet in February 1537 from Matthias Held. The imperial chancellor conceded

---

[17] Fuchs, *Konfession und Gespräch*, p. 396.

[18] *Urkunden aus der Reformationszeit*, ed. Ch. Gotthold Neudecker (Kassel: J.C. Krieger, 1836), pp. 298–331 nr. 99. A letter of Georg von Carlowitz to Landgrave Philip of Hesse, Friday of the Purification of the Blessed Virgin (2 February 1537, and the diet opened 10 February, Haug-Moritz, *Der Schmalkaldische Bund*, p. 604), with two attachments. The first is a report of the correspondence between the emperor and Duke Georg of Saxony. The second consists of two *Bedencken*, one treating the correction of abuses in the church and church unity, and the second *Bedencken* arguing for unity around the articles of faith. The second *Bedencken* includes some discussion of church property.

[19] Chapter 4, above.

[20] *Urkunden aus der Reformationszeit*, pp. 307–8.

[21] Kühn, *Die Einziehung des geistlichen Gutes*, p. 112.

[22] Cohn, "Church Property," p. 167.

that negotiations over church property need not hold-up negotiations over the general right of rulers to promote religion by preventing its malpractice,[23] even though he dismissed threats by the
Landgrave and the Elector to act against the Imperial Chamber
Court.[24] The diet considered the rights of third parties over church
property. The League eventually recommended that Ulm, Esslingen,
and Frankurt retain monies owed from their churches to outsiders
in order to pay evangelical pastors, while conceding payments to
ecclesiastical lords owed in connection with their temporal dominion.[25] The possessions associated with *spiritualia*, the maintainence of
religious life, were proving to be the more mobile assets. The new
clergy should rely on these. Ulrich's fresh success in Württemberg
presented princes with an inspiring example, but unless endorsed by
clergy, it was all unjust seizure.

This new flexibility among the Protestant estates must have felt
like the threat of a frenzy on church property to evangelical theologians. Three weeks after von Karlowitz's letter to the Landgrave,
Philip Melanchthon, at the diet, wrote to the princes of the League
meeting at Schmalkalden, in the name of "the preachers, subjects
and willing servants, all assembled here" (*unterthaenige und willige Diener
Praedicanten allhier versammelt*).[26] The clergy had subscribed to the
Augsburg Confession the same day.[27] The letter reveals a new clar-
ity among the theologians. Liberties taken against the old confession
could also bankrupt the new. If reform were the purpose of confiscation,
a good portion of money, melted silver and gold, and wine and
grain stored in monastic farmsteads should have been enriching a
flourishing evangelical ministry, schools, and hospitals. In fact, churches
and schools were in severe need, Melanchthon observed. The gifts
are given for the support of religion, and rulers are obliged by God
to preserve and promote correct worship and to provide for ministers of the church, the letter insisted. Once the properties were scattered, it would be very difficult to replace them. Melanchthon then
presents a supplication. All the preachers gathered at the diet beg
the lords of the League to admonish the estates to preserve church

---

[23] Haug-Moritz, *Der Schmalkaldische Bund*, p. 510.
[24] Sprenger, *Viglius von Aytta*, p. 83.
[25] Haug-Moritz, *Der Schmalkaldische Bund*, pp. 524–5.
[26] 24 February 1537 Scheible MBW 2:297–98 nr. 1853=CR 3:288–90 nr. 1532.
[27] Scheible MBW 2:287–88 nr. 1852=CR 3:286 nr. 1530.

and cloister property for churches and schools (cities were known to appoint custodians to assure the preservation of church assets, a fact noted by the Imperial Chamber Court's protocol).[28] The clergy demanded a common policy on church property.[29]

Von Karlowitz and Melanchthon, the Leipzig initiative, and the preachers' supplication to the League suggest how tangled the problem of church property had become by February 1537. For one, the matter of princely control had not really been resolved. Was confiscation a right or a responsibility; was the church under some part of princely dominion or merely the beneficiary of the ruler's devout service? For another, there was pressure to expand evangelical reforms. Gabrielle Haug-Moritz has shown that after 1537, the Landgrave and the Elector of Saxony worked hard to promote confessionally homogeneous territories, and the League would pressure cities, for example Braunschweig in 1540, to carry the new church through the countryside by appointing evangelical pastors to their villages.[30] In addition to internal missionary pressure, the von Karlowitz overture now signaled both the readiness of Catholic princes to confiscate and the readiness of their advisors to contemplate reorganizations of church property upon a rationale shared by Protestants—the historical, educational purpose of monasteries.

For the moment, the estates promoted an aggressive stance on church property. They repeated the argument of 1534, based on the right of patrons to use material resources of the church, and they added that a burden of conscience forced the Protestant *Obrigkeit* to suppress worship that violated their confession.[31] Their position was based on the ruler's right to support and protect true and eliminate false religion (the *ius reformandi*, the right of reform) and the attachment of a benefice to a place, under the maxim *beneficium propter officium datur*.[32] Theologians—Johannes Eisermann in 1533 and the

---

[28] S. Seckendorf, *Commentarius hist. et apol. de Lutheranismo* (Leipzig 1694), lib. iii, p. 157. F. Roth, "Zur Kirchengüterfrage in der Zeit von 1538 bis 1540," ARG 1(1903):299–336, here 299. Also CR 3:288–90. The appointment of custodians was noted in the protocol of the court assessor Matthias Neser. Sieglerschmidt, *Territorialstaat*, p. 171 n. 103, and on the protocol's value, p. 50 n. 120 with p. 169 n. 99.

[29] Haug-Moritz, *Der Schmalkaldische Bund*, p. 530.

[30] Ibid., p. 526.

[31] Ibid., pp. 518–19.

[32] Ibid., p. 523. This use of the maxim implied that when a place converted from one confession to the other, the benefice converted with it, and the benefice remains under the dominion of the place. The Peace of Augsburg would later refine

authors of the Wittenberg memorandum of 1535—had advocated respect of foreign patrons, thereby limiting the authority of territorial or urban government. The attachment of a benefice to a place, the priority of locale, now threatened to cancel the claim of foreign patrons. The League was beginning to flex its muscle.

The League confirmed this position by recognizing the city of Augsburg's January 1537 prohibition of the mass, closure of monasteries, and creation of a disciplinary court, and they promised military support in defense of the reforms, should it become necessary.[33] Previously, the city only took over the property of cloisters surrendered by their last members. They had used the property to give monks and nuns pensions, provide poor relief, and establish a Latin school. The abbot of the imperial monastery of St. Ulrich fled Augsburg for Bavaria in 1537, but the cloister did not close. The city still needed to gain control of its rents and incomes. The League issued an admonition to the creditors, to no effect. At the League's diet at Schmalkalden in February and early March 1537, the Protestant estates pronounced themselves ready to support cities confiscating the incomes of extra-territorial church institutions, according to instructions sent to the cities of Ulm, Esslingen, and Frankfurt.[34] The advice

---

the rule to assert that the benefice goes to the *confession* of a place, which meant that an evangelical with patronage of a church in a Catholic territory would have to nominate a Catholic to the benefice. Paul Hinschius, *System des katholischen Kirchenrechts mit besonderer Rücksicht auf Deutschland*, 6 vols. (Graz: Akademische Druck- und Verlagsanstalt, 1959 reprint of the 1883 edition), 3:296–7, 5:62–3, 576–81. See also Sieglerschmidt, *Territorialstaat*, pp. 32, 141; 198–9 with n. 168 for examples from the later sixteenth century of a patron presenting candidates of the confession of the locale's governing authority. But consider also the provisions of the Saxon visitation of 1527, which stipulated that 1/3 of the assets of a benefice connected to a foreign patron be kept in a common chest, so that it may be used by the patron in the event of poverty or for the education of a son or daughter. Similar stipulations were made for Stralsund (1525), Meissen and Vogtland (1533), and Albertine Saxony (1527). Sieglerschmidt, *Territorialstaat*, p. 232, n. 27.

[33] Haug-Moritz, *Der Schmalkaldische Bund*, pp. 519–20, 525. Roper, *The Holy Household*, pp. 21–27, for the disciplinary court, and Gottfried Seebaß, "Die Augsburger Kirchenordnung von 1537 in ihrem historischen und theologischen Zusammenhang," *Die Augsburger Kirchenordnung von 1537 und ihr Umfeld*, pp. 33–58 for the church ordinance of 1537.

[34] Haug-Moritz, *Der Schmalkaldische Bund*, p. 524. The Imperial Chamber Court had already received a complaint against Esslingen the year before, from a priest who was imprisoned by the city for celebrating the mass and for actions against an adherent of Blarer in Württemberg. It later received another complaint from the Dominican and Carmelite provincials against Frankfurt in September 1537. Sprenger, *Viglius von Aytta*, pp. 64, 91.

of theologians in 1533 and 1535 had no apparent impact here. How they could promote mutual, bi-confessional recognition of rights was, at the moment, entirely unclear.

As the League's stance toward the confiscation of church property became more aggressive, it became more urgent to develop the common, religiously defensible rationale for which the clergy had called, in part because ministers were getting angry, and although they were not immediately relevant to politics, they bore the brunt of the culture war. In particular, they determined that the religion of the League was true and why, and that truth was the basis of the League's resistance to restitution suits. The theologians meant to use their leverage. At the League's diet at Braunschweig in March and April 1538, the city of Strasbourg asked the estates to give the matter of church property further consideration. The League's response acknowledged clerical anxieties. The estates noted with alarm that the properties of the church were disappearing to the church's harm, granting the main point of the 1537 preachers' supplication. In turn, the diet instructed the estates to take counsel of their lawyers and theologians regarding two questions: who has authority to reassign the use of the property and to administer it, and by what legal means were the interests and rents associated with church property and subject to foreign rulers to be used by the churches in question, to which the properties were originally given.[35] The theologians had re-insinuated themselves into the discussion of church property.

Two Recommendations for the 1538 Eisenach Diet of the League

Two theological recommendations were soon prepared for the next meeting of the League, in the summer of 1538, one for Strasbourg by Bucer and another for Augsburg by Wolfgang Musculus and Bonifacius Wolfahrt.

---

[35] Roth, "Kirchengüterfrage," pp. 299–300 n. 3, quoting from the original in the Augsburg city archive: "wem solche kirchengutter gepurn und zustehen solten, wohin und welcher gestalt, auch durch wen sie zu verordnen und zu gebrauchen, damit in dem, das cristlich und erberlich, furgenomen und solche gutter nicht unbillicher weis verschwendet oder von der kirchen alieniert werden möchten. Zum andern, mit was fug und rechtlichen mitlen die zins und rent der einigungsverwandten geistlichen guttern zustehenden, so under fremden herschafften gelegen, zu fordern und einzumanen, auff daß dieselbigen zu den kirchen, dahin sie gewidmet, gebraucht und erhalten werden möchten."

In the meanwhile, property conflicts only increased, as the Eisenach diet would soon be reminded. There came to the diet numerous reports of conflicts with the rulers of locales, and this complaint from a patrician named Wilhem Besserer of the city of Ulm.[36] Besserer's grandparents endowed benefices in the cloister of Memmingen. Now the reformed city of Memmingen refused to return the incomes, to which he held a right until his death, when they were scheduled to return to the cloister, which contract the city ignored, on the grounds that the Memmingen council was obligated to put the incomes to another Christian use.[37] This sort of thing was happening wherever Protestants were building their church.

Martin Bucer completed his recommendation and presented it to the estates 23 July 1538, the day before the opening of the Eisenach diet.[38] Augsburg's representatives quickly sent a copy home, where the city council had it hastily read out in Augsburg's Dominican church, 7 August, while the diet still continued its deliberations in Eisenach.[39] The head of Augsburg's evangelical clergy, Wolfgang Musculus, together with Bonifacius Wolfahrt, also produced a recommendation for the diet. Musculus and Wolfahrt's editor believed their recommendation derived from Bucer's.[40] It seems more likely that Musculus and Wolfahrt wrote their recommendation for Augsburg's own delegates, before Bucer's text came to town. In fact, Bucer's may well have been derivative, as I am inclined to think.[41]

---

[36] Sieglerschmidt, *Territorialstaat*, p. 27 n. 52, who notes several similar cases from Württemberg towns.

[37] The city balked when Besserer added a codicil to his demand, that an indicated friend be placed in the city's service when his studies were complete. Sieglerschmidt, *Territorialstaat*, p. 27 n. 52.

[38] It was published by Hortleder as an anonymous piece ascribed to 1538 or 1539. Hermelinck described the piece briefly from Hortleder but could not identify Bucer as the author. Roth identified it by means of a copy with Bucer's signature in Augsburg. Friedrich Hortleder, *Handlungen und Ausschreiben. Von den Ursachen des teutschen Kriegs*, book 5, chapter 8, (Gotha: Wolfgang Endters, 1645), 2:2002–14. Hermelink, "Zwei Aktenstücke," p. 179. The *Gutachten* is not included in *Martin Bucers Deutsche Schriften*, nor noted in its chronologies (6/2:9–14, 7:9). Brady found a copy in the Weimar Staatsarchiv, Reg. H, pagg. 167–70, no. 80, f. 201r–16r. Brady, *Protestant Politics*, pp. 198–9 n. 180. See also Seebaß, "Verwendung der Kirchengüter," p. 173.

[39] Roth, "Kirchengüterfrage," pp. 302–3.

[40] Roth emphasized Musculus' prior training in Strasbourg and his general debt to Bucer. Roth, "Zur Kirchengüterfrage," p. 313.

[41] Roth believed that Musculus provided advice on a previous occassion, basing this on this reference in instructions given to the Augsburg delegation to Eisenach:

The two recommendations attempted comprehensive answers to the questions posed at Braunschweig, but they also give a distinct view of Protestant theology not easily won elsewhere. I wish to review them carefully, for the recommendations accomplished two very useful things. First, they presented the League with canonistic arguments. Although the League's diet would not discuss the matter until 1539 and 1540,[42] these briefs thoroughly documented a clerical defense of restricted Protestant confiscations from the canon law. Later theological briefs make only vague reference to the canon law and seem to presuppose these earlier formulations.

Second, both documents tried to reinforce the crucial impression that Protestants acted within the established boundaries of Christian tradition, crucial to the League's posture of piety and churchly devotion. Wolfahrt and Musculus cited numerous passages of the Bible and canon law in a Gatling-gun manner that was (and is) utterly familiar to readers of late medieval theological manuscripts, right down to the standard method of citation.[43] They presupposed readers with canon and Roman lawbooks opened on their tables. If one looks up their references along the way, as the authors intended, the impression is unmistakable, that theirs was simply an argument within tradition, a discriminating argument to be sure, but there is nothing unusual or un-Catholic about canonistic discrimination. I note and summarize the legal citations in my footnotes. For his part, Bucer applied a particular conception of divine law and its relation to other legal sources, added more exposition to his legal references,

---

"wo der ratschlag begert wurde, was von ainem erbarn rath bedacht were der gaistlichen gutter halben, inhalt des Braunschweigischen abschids, in dem sollen die gesandten den ratschlag, so hievor deßhalben gestellt und demselbigen, auch dem abschid zu Schmalkalden im 37. jar vergangen, gemes, zum peßten handeln und beschließen." "Zur Kirchengüterfrage," p. 313 n. 2. The instructions could, however, just as easily refer to the Musculus-Wolfahrt text, conveyed to the delegates before this was written. The instruction says, in effect, negotiate church property in a way consistent with the advice and the 1537 recess of the League's diet. The Musculus-Wolfahrt text is simply an answer to the questions posed at the previous meeting in Braunschweig.

[42] Haug-Moritz, *Der Schmalkaldische Bund*, pp. 532–33.

[43] The first citation, for example, appears as distinction 63, canon *nullus*, the gloss at *ecclesia*, which is *Decretum* D. 63 c 1, CICan 1:234–5, and the standard gloss, *Decretum Gratiani emendatum et notationibus una cum glossis Gregorii XIII iusu editum* (Rome: In aedibus populi Romani, 1582), col. 418. Roth's edition reproduces the citations in their original, incomplete format. I provide them in modern format with reference to the standard critical editions.

and stressed his own theoretical framework. In one place, on the division of church property, Bucer argued against the view offered by Wolfahrt and Musculus, encouraging the impression that he wrote his brief to improve upon the Augsburg document. Let us consider each brief in detail.

Musculus and Wolfahrt aimed for what one might call a purely religious view of church property. The temporal authority of bishops and "great prelatures" (such as abbacies) was a matter for the lawyers, they said.[44] The spiritual community of the church was the preachers' concern. But how does church property fit a spiritual community? *Kirchengüter*, church properties, are not the true property (*waren gueter*) of the church, they said. Its real possessions are the spiritual goods of faith, hope, love, "and other gifts of the Spirit."[45] Its material things are not even "possessions" (*gueter*) in the strict sense, but *commoda*, "conveniences." They are called property as a figure of speech.[46] But Musculus and Wolfahrt then define church property in a way that includes both the spiritual traits they named and the conveniences that support the ministry: "everything the church has or has had for the worship of God and to promote the honor of Christ" (*alles was die kirch gibt oder geben hat zum dienst gottes und zu erweitern die eere Christi*). The authors describe four basic features of church property—its religious purpose, the diversity of its managers, the variety of its sources, and its immunity from lay interference. The preachers' supplication of 1537 raised the last matter.

Wolfahrt and Musculus turned to history. The name *Kirchengut* came early to refer to the property assembled by the church for its poorer members, the authors noted. Its original purpose was superseded when power over the property grew complex. After the deaths of the apostles, it was dispersed, some of it held by bishops and chapters, some by parishes, some by cloisters, some by *spitalen* (hospitals), and some used for alms. Likewise the sources of church property had diversified—imperial, princely, noble, civic—yet all was still

---

[44] Roth, "Kirchengüterfrage," p. 315.

[45] Musculus and Wolfahrt add the crucial conclusion that this qualified the nature of dominion of such property. It should be treated as something like budget salary lines and not as gifts having been given and received as a personal possession.

[46] Roth, "Kirchengüterfrage," p. 317: "das ist bequembliche ding . . . darumb solche per catarhresin [*leg.* katharesin] in aim misprauch den namen kirchengueter in der kirchen erlangt haben." *Per katharesin* means "as a matter of good style (a figure of speech)."

given for divine worship and poor relief.[47] Imperial immunities rendered the property non-inheritable, a point that Musculus and Wolfahrt
supported from canon and Roman law.[48] They note that the name
Kirchengut refers comprehensively to the material things of any and
all ecclesiastical institutions.[49] The church could claim ownership,
insofar as the term, church, refers to the community of believers
(Mt. 18.15–17), not the buildings and not the clergy (they cite canon
law as a source of confusion here).[50] The property is the common
possession of the people of God, given to honor Christ and support
ministers of the Word, the poor, sick, widows, and needy people, a
claim they supported with New Testament references.[51]

Protestants had earlier unearthed this claim—that church property is communal and not possessed by individual benefice holders—
in a case brought by the cathedral chapter of Speyer against the
city of Esslingen before the Imperial Chamber Court.[52] It was implied
by the maxim, *beneficium propter officium datur*, to which Musculus and
Wolfahrt also will appeal in due course. They assumed that gospel
ministers had the same right to charity as the worthy poor, an association of ministry and poverty long promoted in cities by another
clerical group, the mendicant orders, and denied to the friars in early
Protestant polemics.[53] Communal ownership is demonstrated from
the church fathers. Augustine's famous letter to Count Boniface "on
coercing heretics with restraint" (*de moderate coercendis hereticis*), cited
from the canon law,[54] shows that church property belongs not to

[47] Roth, "Kirchengüterfrage," p. 317.
[48] *Novellae* 7, CICiv 3:48–63. *Decretales Gregorii* III.xiii.1–12 and III.xlix.1–4, CICan
2:512–16, 654–5.
[49] Roth, "Kirchengüterfrage," p. 318.
[50] Ibid., p. 319. The canon law is here cited as the source of the opposing view.
Decretum D 63 c 1, CICan 1:234–5 says no layman may insert himself in an ecclesiastical office nor overthrow a common, harmonious, and canonical election. The
gloss says that here the church refers to churchmen, *Ecclesiam hic vocat viros ecclesi-
asticos. Decretum Gratiani emendatum et notationibus una cum glossis Gregorii XIII iusu editum*
(Rome: In aedibus populi Romani, 1582), col. 418. Nicholas of Cusa discussed the
same passage when he argued that metropolitans should perform their pastoral functions and not be distracted by secular concerns. *The Catholic Concordance*, ii.29, paragraph 221, p. 171.
[51] Roth, "Kirchengüterfrage," pp. 319–20. Mt. 10, 1 Cor. 9, Acts 2, 4, 6, 11,
Ro. 12, 15, 1 Cor. 16, 2 Cor. 8.9.
[52] Dolezalek, "Juristische Argumentation," pp. 48–49.
[53] Ocker, "'Rechte Arme' und 'Bettler Orden.'"
[54] C 23 q. vii.3, CICan 1:951–52, quoting Augustine's Ep. 50, a 417 letter noting:

the bishop but to the community.[55] Jerome's letter to Nepotianus, cited from the *Decretum*,[56] calls it *Kirchenraub*, church robbery, when ecclesiastical property is used for oneself and not for the poor.[57] Ambrose agrees in book 2 of his *De officiis*: the church has neither silver nor gold for any purpose other than poor relief (also cited from the canon law).[58] Papists, the authors allege, were guilty of embezzlement when they neglected the poor.[59]

Who, they then asked, might distribute the property, and who can spend it (*Von wem die kirchengueter sollen außgespendet werden?*)?[60] In the New Testament (Acts 6.1–6), we are told, the appointed managers were the apostles and the deacons they delegated. Just as the deacons were godly people chosen from the community, so too, godly people should be chosen for the task today. The care of the poor, in addition to preaching, followed the apostolic example, which the authors proved from the New Testament (Gal. 2.10) and the canon law.[61]

Who might correct the misuses of church property?[62] In answer, Wolfahrt and Musculus repeat common Protestant accusations of church corruption and add canon law citations, apparently in order to deny that the church can be trusted to correct itself. Nine abuses are named. 1) Clergy consume church property for their own benefit and neglect the poor. 2) They add elaborate devices, some of them

---

because of the imperial laws transferring Donatist property to Catholic use, the property enters that of common Catholic society and is governed as such.

[55] Roth, "Kirchengüterfrage," p. 319. In the case of the Speyer cathedral chapter against Esslingen, the Assessor Mor quoted Augustine to argue that church property could be taken from Donatists and given to Catholic clergy. Dolezalek, "Juristische Argumentation," p. 50.

[56] C 12 q. ii.71, CICan 1:710–711. Jerome, Ep. 52.6. CSEL 54:413ff. Jerome argues that care for the poor, rather than beautifully appointed churches, is the glory of bishops. And he does indeed call it theft not to use it for the poor.

[57] Roth, "Kirchengüterfrage," 320–21.

[58] C 12 q. ii.70 CICan 1:710, which quotes Ambrose's argument for the sale of sacred vessels to redeem captives. *De officiis* ii.140–141 offers also the example of St. Lawrence. Ambrose, *De officiis*, edited and translated by Ivor J. Davidson, 2 vols., 1:347

[59] Roth, "Kirchengüterfrage," p. 321.

[60] Ibid., pp. 321–22.

[61] D 82, c. 1–2, CICan 1:289–91 (bishops must provide for the needy, quoting the Council of Arles in 511, and Pope Innovent I on the ministry of deacons from 405). D 86 c. 6–20, CICan 1:299–302. C 12, q. i.5–11, CICan 1:677–681 (various prohibitions of clergy owning individual property).

[62] Roth, "Kirchengüterfrage," pp. 322–28.

made of precious materials, to aid worship—from clocks and images to vigils, organ music, and singing. 3) They create benefices out of church property against canon law, for *beneficium datur propter officium*, "the benefice is given on account of the office," while the canon law roundly condemns the sale of church office (in effect, they complained that church property was used to create a clerical job market).[63] 4) They embezzle cloister donations intended to fund hostels to bring up poor children in godliness (quoting a letter of Jerome from the canon law) and create canonries, and they justify the misuse with canon law.[64] 5) They accumulate legacies and incorporate patronage rights and tithes but neglect to preach the Word of God. Jerome had predicted this in a letter to Pope Damasus; the passage was taken up in the canon law (the recommendation adds a brief exposition to the effect that pastors should be servants of the church, not lords over it).[65] 6) They fail to work. Masses, prayers, chants, and liturgical reading do not count as labor because these deeds are neither of apostolic foundation nor necessary. The reader is referred to Bernhard of Clairvaux.[66] The ancient Christian practice was a weekly Lord's Supper, prayer, and singing, and it required few ministers. But since then, the number of clergy have increased beyond all proportion, not to mention cloister personnel, all of whom the authors accuse of wasting church property, which was true, if one agreed with the early Protestants that the tasks of votive masses, intercessory prayers, and the hearing of confessions were wrong and useless. 7) Furthermore, some individuals take in huge incomes even when they receive adequate support from family inheritances or are

---

[63] C 1, q. i, CICan 1:357 is cited, which treats abuse of office. Causa 1, at "quidam" begins with Gratian telling a story that establishes the importance of the subject. There was a son whose father tried to buy him a place in a monastery. He was turned down by the abbot. The boy grew, was ordained, and unknown to him, his father payed off an archiepiscopal counselor, and the son was made a bishop. The payoff came to light, and the son was accused before his metropolitan and found guilty of simony. The story includes no citation of, paraphrase of, or allusion to the maxim *beneficium datur propter officium*.

[64] Jerome to Eustochius, Ep. 22, *De custodia virginitatis*, *Decretum* C 11, q. i.3 or 47, CICan 1:627, 641; both say that clergy may not be brought before secular judges. C 17, q. iv.29, CICan 1:822, against secular violence toward clergy.

[65] C 16, q. i.67, CICan 1:784–5: it is sacrilege for those priests who can be supported by their families to take what belongs to the poor.

[66] Bernard of Clairvaux, *Opera* ed. Jean Leclercq et al., 9 vols. (Louvain : Brepols, 1957–1998), 4:485–92.

fit to earn a living by labor, in contradiction of canon law and scripture.[67] 8) The clergy use the superabundance of church property for
themselves.[68] 9) Finally, the recommendation alleges, almost all clergy
entered their estate through simony, which is equal to lèse-majesté
according to canon law.[69]

These were *Catholic* moralisms, applied in canon law to the highly
differentiated society the church had become, a society of clergy and
religious, those distinguished from the laity by vows of chastity, governed hierarchically by bishops and monastic superiors, and devoted
to the work of spiritual regeneration. Their use by Musculus and
Wolfahrt is sophisticated: to justify an economized church, a reduction of clergy, offices, and functions. The common work of ordinary
priests, monks, and nuns is simply dismissed: votive masses, administration of penance, and intercessory prayers—most of this tied to
the memorialization of the dead. So, too, is the market of religious
services that a differentiated clergy expanded and exploited, and
careerist priests pursuing benefice incomes and desirable offices; but
anyone who had read and enjoyed dialogues by Erasmus might concede these allegations. The allegations aimed for a narrow goal, not
just a smaller clergy on the Protestant model, but a clergy corrected
from without when it failed to correct itself.

The charge of simony seems to cap the list as a summary indictment. Musculus and Wolfahrt then noted how according to canon
law, simony required five progressive penalties: excommunication,
confiscation of all property, dismissal from all offices and honors,
infamy, and restoration of property.[70] The authors recalled that in
1522, 100 articles complained of these things to the Nürnberg Diet
to no effect. It was the Diet that helped position the Lutheran movement within the rising chorus of German complaint against church
corruption, papal greed to be extact.[71]

---

[67] C 1, q. ii.7, CICan 1:409–10: pastors with means should not be supported by
the church. Gratian adds the comment that those who join the clergy should abandon their property like Peter, Matthew, and Paul; and like Zacheus, they should
distribute it to the poor.
[68] Bernard of Clairvaux, *De consideratione ad Eugenium Papam*, III.iii.19, III.v.19–20,
IV.i.1–IV.ii.5. *Opera* 3:439–41, 446–53.
[69] C 1, qq. i, ii. CICan 1:357–411. Question 2 mainly treats simony.
[70] *Decretum Gratiani emendatum et notationibus una cum glossis*, col. 649–50.
[71] Anonymous, *Was Bebstliche heyligkeyt auß Teütscher nation järlicher Annata, und eyn
yeder Bistum und Ebbtey, besondern taxirt* (no place: no publisher, 1523), Flugschriften
des frühen 16. Jahrhunderts, Fiche 6 nr. 16.

They next turned to the correct distribution of church property.[72] According to the New Testament (Acts 4.12) the goal of *ausspendung*, "paying out," is to alleviate need, and this requires a professional ministry. Three types of people may use church properties: the ministers, the poor, and pilgrims. The authors defined ministers as those who preach and give sacraments, while deacons or others are supported by the church, if not supported by their families, freeing them from the distractions of additional labor. They defined the poor and the needy as the homeless (*hausarmen*), widows and other elderly (those too old and weak to work), poor daughters and boys, and foreigners and pilgrims (*die, so von der warhait wegen anderswo her vertriben weren*, victims of religious persecution). To support these groups, the ancients established cloisters as training schools (*zuchtschuel*), not only at cathedrals but also in parishes and alongside houses of instruction (they cite canon law),[73] where needy children could be raised. Scripture[74] and Augustine determine the educational purpose of gifts and incomes. Augustine named the education of needy children as the purpose of tithes.[75] Canon law, they continued, also determines that the bishop should provide for those who cannot work.[76] To this end, the law of the church divides church property into four parts: one to the bishop, one to the clergy, one to the poor, and one to the church building. The same charitable purposes apply to the silver and gold implements of churches,[77] on the examples of Augustine, Ambrose, and St. Lawrence. In addition, the authors pointed out, Jerome criticized costly expenses in God's temple in a passage preserved in the canon law.[78] Church property, in short, can only legitimately support religiosity.

---

[72] Roth, "Kirchengüterfrage," pp. 328–31.

[73] D 37, c. 12, CICan 1:139, from an 826 synod of Pope Eugenius II. The canon calls for the creation of schools of liberal arts and dogma.

[74] Deuteronomy chapters 14, 24 ; 2 Corinthians 8, 9; Acts 2, 4; 1 Timothy 5.

[75] Actually C 16, q. i.66, 68, CICan 1:784, 784–5, from a letter of Jerome to Pope Damasus, Ep. 36, CSEL 54:268 (everything held by the clergy belongs to the poor).

[76] C 12, q. ii.23, 26–28, 30, CICan 1:694–7, all arguing for the four-fold division of church incomes between bishop, clergy, the poor, and buildings. For D 82, c. 1–2, note 61, above.

[77] C 12, q. ii.71, CICan 1:710–1. C 12, q. ii.13–14, CICan 1:690, from an 869 Roman synod, alleging that church property may only be alienated to redeem captives, and Pope Gregory the Great saying the same.

[78] C 12, q. ii.71, CICan 1:710–1.

Who, then, should administer and distribute church property?[79]
Those to whom it belonged, the recommendation says, namely the
community, which was governed by *oberkait*. The bishop's office, they
alleged, has usurped oversight on the mistaken grounds of an apostolic calling. The bishop claims to be a successor of the apostles,
and just as the soul is superior to the body, so bishops say they
stand above temporal things: "since souls, which are more precious
than property, are committed to the bishop, so much the more does
the care of money pertain to him," goes the argument of canon
law.[80] This was a mainstay of medieval views of the bishop's office
and, by extension, the papacy.[81] Musculus and Wolfahrt objected to
both any claim to dominion based on apostolic succession and any
claim that spiritual authority subsumes temporal authority. As to
apostolic appointment, bishops were not the only ones appointed.
The apostles, they said, established deacons (*diakonos, diener*) when the
church grew, leaving the bishop to focus on his spiritual tasks, preaching and pastoral care. Moreover, spiritual authority cannot imply
temporal power, although the authors seem to concede the superi-
ority of spiritual to temporal, if the hierarchy is seen as impersonal:
the material things of the church must serve spiritual purposes. This
was the authors' early premise, and they determined from canon law
that such purposes were fulfilled by targeted acts of charity toward
ministers, the poor, and exiles. Since bishops fail to distribute church
property to the poor as canon law prescribes,[82] the community must
step in and reform the church. The established ruling authority (*orden-
liche oberkait*) must carry out the community's responsibility. Biblical
kings set the precedent. Kings David and Solomon appointed ministers to perform temple worship;[83] Solomon deposed the high priest

---

[79] Roth, "Kirchengüterfrage," pp. 331–36.

[80] C 12, q. i.24, CICan 1:685–6, from the apostolic canons: "Si enim animae
hominum preciosae illi sunt creditae, multo magis oportet eum curam de pecuniis
agere, ita ut potestate eius indigentibus omnia dispensentur per presbiteros et dia-
cones, et cum timore et omni sollicitudine ministrentur." Musculus and Wolfahrt
translate the passage: "dann so die seelen der menschen, welche köstlicher seind
denn das guet, dem bischof vertraut seind, vil mer stat im zu, daß er auch des
gelts sorg trage etc."

[81] Karlfried Froehlich, "Saint Peter, Papal Primacy, and the Exegetical Tradition,
1150–1300," *The Religious Roles of the Papacy: Ideas and Realities, 1150–1300*, ed.
C. Ryan (Toronto: Pontifical Institute of Mediaeval Studies, 1989), pp. 3–44.

[82] C 12, q. i.23, CICan 1:684–5, from a council of Antioch.

[83] 1 Chron. 16, 23, 24, 25, 26.

Sadoch;[84] King Asa of Judah and king Jehoshaphat renewed divine worship,[85] and king Hezekiah reestablished the priesthood and exercised authority over church property, with which he purchased peace from the king of Assyria.[86] King Josiah exercised power over worship, ministers, and the temple with its treasury and property.[87] These were commonplaces of Melanchthon's doctrine of the *cura religionis*, the temporal ruler's protection of the church.[88] The reorganization of the church is an emergency response to the failure of bishops to exercise their pastoral office.

Musculus and Wolfahrt then turned to current events. In their day, they complained, the Catholic party denies that church property is a matter of religion, and therefore they sue Protestants before the Imperial Chamber Court.[89] Did Musculus and Wolfahrt mean to disqualify temporal authority from spiritual affairs in general? No. They took particular aim at this court. For at the same place, they conceded the administration of church properties to *oberkait*, and temporal authority, they went on, is obliged to appoint appropriate people to perform it, as the apostles themselves had done when they appointed deacons. Imperial law forbids the misdistribution of property, they observed,[90] and to prevent it, stewards (*schaffner*) should give an annual account (this had been Philip of Hesse's arrangement). Any customary claim made from the sheer antiquity of possession is groundless. The years of clerical possession are meaningless because clergy never had rightful possession to begin with, according to canon law: "disposition of property does not support what is

---

[84] Actually, Sadoch was the one who Solomon put in place of Abjathar, 1 Reg. 2, 2 Par. 3, 4, 5, 6, 7.

[85] 2 Chronicles 15, 2 Chronicles 17.

[86] 2 Kings 8, 2 Chronicles 29, 30, 31.

[87] The authors also answer a counter-example: Jeroboam's crime was not the confiscation of temple property but the fact that he used it against the Word of God. Cf. 1 Kings 11.26–14.20.

[88] Estes, *Peace, Order and the Glory of God*, pp. 60, 70, 75, 116, 152, 154 (and in Luther, p. 192).

[89] Roth, "Kirchengüterfrage," p. 334: "und auch jetzund die gaistlichen hierzu sich des kaiserlichen gewalts geprauchen und ausgeben wider die protestirenden stend, die gueter der kirchen horen nit in die religionssachen; und das wider ir aigne recht, nur darumb, daß sie sie pringen mögen in die erkanndtnus und gewaldt des kaiserlichen camergerichts, in welchem sie vermeinen den lang besessen raub noch lenger zu erhalten."

[90] C 1.2.14. CICiv 2:13.

invalid," (*preaescriptio non defendit invalidum*)[91] and "a possessor in bad
faith can never dispose" (*possessor male fidei ullo tempore non praescribit*).[92]
Dominion belongs to neither the prince nor the clergy exercising
office, or in other words, neither patrons nor benefice-holders. Likewise,
no imperial privilege contrary to the church of Christ is valid, a
point the authors defend by a small pile of legal citations.[93] It was
also a point of contention in Augsburg the year before, when the
bishop and canons argued that the city was prevented from removing Catholic clergy by their obligation to obey the emperor.[94] Wolfahrt
and Musculus excluded this claim. They have also reached and documented the broad conclusion needed by the League of Schmalkalden:
the law of the church, like scripture itself, gives no reason to restore
church properties.

   The recital of Protestant commonplaces—the brief's list of corruptions, its anti-papalism, the New Testament characterization of
reformed churches, etc.—may obscure the originality and importance
of this document. Musculus and Wolfahrt exploited the fact that
canon law sees bishops as pastors, not princes, which Catholic reformers recognized, too. It was easy to portray prince-bishops as delin-
quent pastors. This allowed the authors to present confiscations as
an emergency action in defense of the public character of church
property. The property was subject to a community represented by
its government. Of equal importance to this decidedly urban view
of government was the claim that government exercises no dominion over the church. This conceded the formal autonomy of the
church from secular jurisdiction, the issue raised by the preachers'
supplication to the League's diet in 1537. When it came to ecclesiastical property, government merely served religion.

   Martin Bucer's recommendation used a similar format to the same
end, namely the defense of *restricted* secular interference.[95] He answered

---

   [91] C 12, q. v.4, CICan 1:1251–2, Augustine's Ep. 199 to Editia, saying a man
cannot rescind a vow of chastity made with the consent of his wife (see also the
maxim among the epigrams to this book).
   [92] Cf. *Gregorii Decretales*, V.xli.1–11, CICan 2:927–8.
   [93] C 7.33.4 et passim. CICiv. 2:308. C 25, q. ii.25, CICan 1:1018–9, where Pope
Gelasius, at the end of the fifth century, says that episcopal dignity suborns to the
city that looses its leaders. C 11, q. ii.63, CICan 1:660: "Privilegium omnino mere-
tur amittere qui permissa sibi potestate." *Gregorii Decretales*, V.xxxiii.4, CICan 2:850.
Musculus and Wolfahrt translate the sentence: *der ist wirdig, sein freihait gar zu ver-
lieren, der sich seines gewalts darin mispraucht.*
   [94] Haug-Moritz, *Der Schmalkaldische Bund*, p. 520.
   [95] Hortleder, *Handlungen und Ausschreiben*, 2:2002–14. The following summary further

the Braunschweig questions in five articles that determined 1) to whom church property belongs, 2) how it is to be used, 3) expanding upon the second point, who the true ministers of the church are, 4) who is responsible to restore church property to its correct use, and 5) the integrity of patronage rights. The argument is simple. It begins with the premise that the property belongs to the particular Christian community to which it was given; oversupplies in richer communities should serve poorer churches, by providing villages with preachers. There are only three legitimate uses, he said, to which there corresponds a three-fold distribution: 1) to support ministers, 2) to provide alms for the needy, and 3) to supply the material and worship needs of churches.[96] Bucer called any other use *Kirchenraub*, church robbery. Ruling authorities could assume pastoral care themselves but must assign it to others, he alleged. Like Musculus and Wolfahrt, Bucer set his argument in an historical frame, which reflects a certain consensus (we have seen that Melanchthon and even von Karlowitz had argued similarly): that over the years church property accumulated far beyond the needs of the church. Therefore, Bucer observed, pope Gregory I gave church property to the (Frankish) king to fight the Lombards, and he used it to relieve the inflation crisis in Rome, which Bucer compared to the campaign against the Turks and the preservation of noble lineages in his own day. Bucer did not say *Obrigkeit* should be *compensated* from church property, as though they had a claim to it. He complained that it could only be used to support true ministers, not benefice hunters or vicars infected by superstition. *Obrigkeit* should administer it. His recommendation stresses the necessity of assigning the property a religious use and the premise of communal rights and obligations, both of which touch on a broad view of public welfare (charity could support the defense of Christendom and the survival of impoverished nobility). But a government's jurisdiction is limited, Bucer explained in his fifth article.[97] The rights of evangelical churches under a non-evangelical lordship must be respected (Friedrich

---

cites Hortleder only when it departs from the original's order of argument or quotes the original. For the edition, see note 38 of this chapter.

[96] Bucer is probably taking this as a fair summary of *Decretum* C 11, q. i and C 12, q. ii. CICan 626–42, 687–712. Berthold Pürstiger's *Onus ecclesiae* of 1519 argued that this was the division of property modelled by the primitive church. Schmuck, *Die Prophetie*, p. 204.

[97] Hortleder, *Handlungen* 2:2014.

Hortleder, the seventeenth-century jurist, noted that in 1555 the Peace of Augsburg asserted the same). Likewise, Protestants must respect the same rights of Catholic patrons in Protestant lands. Bucer, in effect, restated the diplomatic view offered to Bremen by Hessian and Wittenberg theologians in 1533.

Bucer intended to show that his view was consistent with the practice of the early church, as evident in scripture and the canons of early councils and popes. Biblical evidence was complemented by explanations of imperial and canon law, a method Bucer later preserved in his 1540 dialogue on *On Church Property*, as Gottfried Seebaß has recently pointed out.[98] Legal texts, in Bucer's view, derive their validity from a divine archetype revealed in scripture. Divine law is found in scripture but also in many laws issued by councils, emperors, and popes.[99] In the present case, divine law dictates the proper uses of church property, and it determines who may use it. Bucer cited several passages of canon and Roman law to confirm the communal ownership of church property.[100] But, Bucer added, temporal rulers are flatly prohibited from confiscating tithes or church incomes.[101]

Bucer then questioned whether distribution should be according to three or four uses of property, a fastidious matter of no particular significance except, perhaps, as a correction to the Augsburg recommendation. He argued that church incomes should be divided three ways, and according to Roman law, the third part should go to church buildings.[102] He then reviewed the four-fold division suggested by canon law and by Musculus and Wolfahrt, without referring to the Augsburgers by name. The "church rules" (*Kirchen Reguln* is a phrase that nicely reflects his view of the canon law, as something that offers contestable guidance) divide the uses into four, he noted, but it should be three, as is said in the canons.[103] The portion

---

[98] Gottfried Seebaß, "Martin Bucers Beitrag zu den Diskussionen über die Verwendung der Kirchengüter," *Martin Bucer und das Recht. Beiträge zum internationalem Symposium vom 1. bis 3. März 2001 in der Johannes a Lasco Bibliothek Emden*, ed. by Christoph Strohm (Geneva: Librairie Droz, 2002), pp. 167–83.

[99] Hortleder, *Handlungen*, 2:2003.

[100] C 12, q. ii.13, CICan 1:690. C 12, q. ii.30, CICan 1:697. C 16, q. i.60, CICan 1:781. C I.ii.14, CICiv 2:13. *Novellae* 7, CICiv 3:45–59. C 12, q. ii.3, 4, 21, 23, 43, CICan 1:687, 693, 694–5, 701, "und an anderen Orten mehr," Bucer added.

[101] Hortleder, *Handlungen*, 2:2004. *Novellae* 120, CICiv 3:526–537.

[102] *Novellae* 7 and 120, CICiv 3:45–59, 526–537.

[103] He refers the reader to C 12, q. ii.25–31, CICan 1:695–97. Hortleder, *Handlungen*, 2:2005–6.

for the ministry is sometimes divided into two (one for bishops and one for clergy) or the portion for the poor into two, one for pilgrims and one for the needy, making four portions out of three. Since imperial law poses even more divisions, the number four is arbitrary.[104] But three parts is the most ancient practice, and according to Roman law, ancient precent stands.[105]

Bucer then expounded passages of both imperial and canon law to conclude that church property must be used exclusively for the ministry and the poor.[106] Church ministers who do not do their duty should not get church incomes, he said.[107] Rather, true ministers should receive them. "Therefore, when the Lord will help accomplish a well ordered Reformation of the church, one will no longer allow our government, land, and people, and the care of souls and ministry of the church to rest upon this or that person, but rather on such a person as one wants and can use in episcopal and other church ministries."[108] Bucer's statement applies the maxim, *beneficium datur propter officium*. Incomes are not tied to individuals, as though they were gifts or personal privileges. They are rather tied to specific church jobs. Bucer noted that the offices must go to suitable people, according to Gratian's *Decretum*.[109] He then used the canon law to document the history of church offices and the growth of prerogatives among bishops, archbishops, and patriarchs. The offices multiplied as church property increased, he explained. Yet the law

---

[104] He discussed C 1.2, CICiv 2:12–18, C 1.3, CICiv 2:19–39, and *Novellae* 3, 58, CICiv 17–23, 293–5.

[105] C 1.2.12 and C 1.2.16, CICiv 2:13–14.

[106] *Novellae* 3 *sub fine*, Bucer said, which would be chapter 3, CICiv 3:22, where Justinian commends the ancient practice of appointing *oeconomi* to manage ecclesiastical accounts. He also referred to C 1, q. ii.6 (clergy who can be supported by their families rob churches if they take church incomes, Bucer explains), C 1, q. ii.10. C 12 q. ii.25. C. 12. q. ii.21. CICan 1:409, 411, 693–4, 695–6.

[107] *Novellae* 67, 123, CICiv 321–23, 539–66. C 7, q. i.24, CICan 1:576. C 7, q. i.43, CICan 1:583. *Decretales Gregorii* III.iv.4, 9, 10, 16 (these all treat the withdrawl of benefices from absentee office holders. Bucer mistakenly referred the reader to *Extravagantes, De clericis non residentibus*, which has no such title).

[108] Hortleder, *Handlungen*, 2:2007. C 1.2.3, CICiv 2 :19–39. *Novellae* 123.4–5? CICiv 3:544. "Der halben wann uns der Herr zu rechtschaffner Reformation der Kirchen helffen wird, so wird man die unsere Regierung, Land und Leute, und die Seelsorg und Kirchendienst nit mehr uff einerley Personen ligen lassen, sondern diejenigen, die man zu den Bischofflich und andern Kirchendiensten brauchen wil und kan."

[109] D 89, c. 5, CICan 1:312. C 16, q. vii.13, CICan 1:804. Hortleder, *Handlungen*, 2:2008–9.

says that ministers of defective skill and character should be deposed, according to ancient conciliar and episcopal decrees presented in the church and imperial law.[110] Augustine and Cyprian said that officers who do not preach the Word of God or care for the poor should be removed by the community.[111] Ruling authority must intervene to correct religious malpractice, according to scripture and the *Decretum*.[112] But not the emperor. Imperial power, Bucer explained, no longer sufficed to the task of reform, because imperial authority had declined. The emperor was no longer absolute, as he had been in Frankish times, because since the tenth-century Saxon dynasty, imperial office was acquired by election and through decrees, pacts, and other ways. Governing authority comes from God, but imperial power was degraded by imperial law and the councils of the estates.[113] This historically conditioned limitation left the Protestants free to resist the imperial will, when they depose papist clergy and convert church property to its correct use.[114]

Bucer, in short, argued that just as *Obrigkeit* is responsible to end religious malpractice, church property is to support religion.[115] The

---

[110] Bucer appeals sweepingly to *Decretum* D 25–50, 81–92 and *Novellae* 16, 58, 85, 123. CICan 1:89–203, CICiv 3:104–5, 293–5, 386–9, 539–66.

[111] Cf. Augustine, *Contra Cresconium* ii.11, PS 43:474, where Augustine discusses briefly a bishop's obligation to the community.

[112] D 8, c. 1, CICan 1:12–14. Hortleder, *Handlungen*, 2:2010–12.

[113] Hortleder, *Handlungen*, 2:2012.

[114] According to C 1.5, CICiv 2:50–60. C 1.8.1–8, CICiv 2:5–12. *Novellae* 308, CICiv 3:227–34; *Decretum* C 23, q. v.20, CICan 1:936–7.

[115] Since 1527, Bucer began to develop a view of magisterial authority in religion distinct from Luther's. His position informed the development of Strasbourg's church organization between 1532 and 1535. In place of Luther's distinction between secular and spiritual realms, he distinguished between two forms of the church, territorial and confessional. Secular magistrates, he argued, had the responsibility to govern the external, territorial church, on the example of the kings of the Old Testament, in order to promote the confessional church. Church discipline was exercised by clergy and lay representatives of the magistrates and the congregation, who together served on a disciplinary commission and possessed the power to excommunicate. To form this commission and carry out its judgments was the responsibility of secular government. The commission belonged to the external, territorial church. Hammann, *Martin Bucer*, pp. 251–73, following Wendel, *L'Eglise de Strasbourg*, pp. 162–87. Bucer defined deacons as ecclesiastical officers appointed to oversee the management of the church's external affairs, such as property (church order produced for the city of Ulm in 1531 and in a proposal to the Strasbourg's reforming synod of 1533). The Strasbourg church order of 1534 placed oversight and control of deacons under magistrates. Hammann, *Martin Bucer*, pp. 59–60, 240. Musculus and Wolfahrt followed the Strasbourg model.

advice made explicit what the early Hessian justification for confiscations implied (only religious uses are permissible), and it reinforced the preachers' supplication of 1537 and Strasbourg's concern that church property was rapidly disappearing into princely fiscs or sold. Bucer may have had Württemberg in mind, maybe England and Denmark, too. The effect of Bucer's argument was identical with that of Musculus and Wolfahrt. The confiscation of church property was a corrective measure that preserves the historical, religious purposes of church property. Was this a unique point of view? Does it reveal a religious view of society at odds with Wittenberg? Bucer and Musculus and Wolfahrt all saw civil polity as an extension of the spiritual community of the church. But all believed that divine law stood at the basis of political authority and social order. They may have disagreed on the redemptive significance of law, but this did not affect discussions of church property in any way.

In an apparent gesture to a vulnerable church, the recess of the Eisenach diet declared that the property of churches and monasteries should be kept together, territorial boundaries and confessions regardless.[116] That fall, Bucer's recommendation made the rounds. He sent a Latin copy to Ambrosius Blarer in October.[117] The Strasbourg city council sent Bucer to Marburg in early November to share it with the Landgrave's theologians and jurists (he was told to show them how to use the decisions of ancient councils to support evangelical property claims). From Marburg, he went to Wittenberg, where he brought another memorandum by his colleague Capito to Martin Luther. Luther assigned it to Justus Jonas for a response (20 or 21 November 1538). Jonas said he admired Capito's piece and noted its general agreement with Bucer's, sympathizing with their rebuttal of what he called the Satanic temptation confronting the church. He promised to say more later. Luther's own position was ambivalent. In mid-November while in Wittenberg, Bucer had appeared as a Sunday guest preacher in Wittenberg's city church. Luther met with him afterward and gave a verbal response to Bucer's recommendation. Luther later summarized his response

---

[116] Sieglerschmidt, *Territorialstaat*, p. 158.

[117] For this and the following, including Jonas' letter, *Der Briefwechsel des Justus Jonas*, ed. Gustav Kawerau, 2 vols. (Hildesheim: Georg Olms, 1964 reprint of the Halle, 1884–5 edition), 1:305.

in a letter to the Strasbourg war council (20 November 1538). It was typically aloof, but not entirely unrealistic. These days, he said, it is best to let matters rest.[118] Those who "have church property but do not perform pastoral care" should be admonished. The sources, i.e. legal texts, Strasbourg (that is, Bucer) has noted can be used to pressure, in writing and publicly, those who stubbornly remain in cloisters, he observed. This wasn't Bucer's point at all, which Luther apparently simply ignored, suggesting Bucer's sourcework be deployed to support his own view of the evangelization of monks and nuns: help monks and nuns get over monastic vows. The real issues to anyone who cared about the progress of confiscations or knew anything about confiscations since 1535 had become far more complex, and they had not been resolved: the question of patronage rights, the dispersion of church property, public property, the definition of religious purposes, and church custodianship.

But Melancthon gives the impression that in autumn 1538 theologians had not completely resolved a difference of approach, one argued from the common good and another argued from princely patronage. He sent a letter that same day (20 November) to the Strasbourg city council with a brief memorandum on church property.[119] Bucer later shared it with Philip of Hesse.[120]

Melanchthon's memorandum broadly agreed with the texts of Bucer and Musculus/Wolfahrt. He alleged that church property should, first, provide for the ministers of the gospel, and second, provide for theology students. Third, it should be used to support the poor. The property always belonged to the true church and not to the emperor, Melanchthon noted, and he appealed to the example of St. Lawrence, who rightly refused to give the emperor Decius

---

[118] WA Br 8:325–6 nr. 3275: ". . . in dieser Zeit (so kürzlich sich viel eräugen) de facto stil zu stehen sei. Aber indes die Personen, so der Kirchengüter haben und der Seelsorge nicht achten, anzusprechen sind, damit sie re vera Personen werden. Alsdann, wo sie nicht fort wollen, können sie mit solchen Schriften und Rechte, durch Euch angezeigt, erstlich durch öffentlich Schrift ersucht und endlich zurecht bracht werden, oder anders geschehen, dass ihn doch ihr Mutwill nicht folgen muss."

[119] 20 November 1538, CR 3:608–9 nr. 1752.

[120] Lenz, *Briefwechsel Landgraf Philipp's des Grossmüthigen von Hessen mit Bucer*, 1:54–55 nr. 21, letter of Martin Bucer to Simon Bing written at Homberg in Hesse asking him to send Melanchthon's *responsum . . . de bonis ecclesiasticis*, on church property, to him at Kassel, *quod illustrissimo principi nuper tradideram vesperi et repetere mane obliviscebar. Mittendum illud est senatui nostro cum aliis literis.*

gifts previously given to the church. The point, he said, was clearly taught by Paul, Augustine, Leviticus, the canons, and the civil law, which he named seriatim, apparently content with the case Bucer had made (which had been more thoroughly documented by Musculus and Wolfahrt). Persecutors of the gospel and true doctrine had no legitimate claim to church property. He added this concession to Bucer, with a codicil: patrons have their entitlements. Christian rulers in each church should administer and protect such property and appoint ministers. But patrons may use some of it, both for the common benefit (*zu gemeinem Nutz Hülf thun*) and to cover expenses born on account of the churches.

This was the sole point at which Melanchthon departed from the argument Bucer had made. He did not emphasize this difference, but the implication must have been transparent. His reference to patronage cast the matter of church property in an entirely different light. A prince's entitlement arose from a residual, partial dominion over gifts, recognized in the patron's "honor," which included the right to present candidates for office and church relief in times of emergency need.[121] But bishops, as Musculus, Wolfahrt, and Bucer have reminded us, were obliged by the example of Augustine, Ambrose, and St. Lawrence to see church property as the patrimony of the poor. Melanchthon's view put church property in the context of princely property rights, a degree of princely disposition of church property, as semi-private property. By contrast, the urban theologians stressed the semi-public character of church property. The reform of it could include confiscations by reason of state, including defense and noble poor relief, but not as a matter of entitlement. According to the urban view, redeployment of church property was an extension of charity, the use of the property for its original purpose of contributing to welfare. Both views could be argued from canon law. Both views justify confiscations by princes or city councils. In his 1538 memorandum, Melanchthon concluded that counsel should be taken on how to help the churches, where they need support, so that no one part of the estates should pose a burden to another.[122] The cautionary implication was: cities should not burden princes with their communal ideas.

---

[121] Sieglerschmidt, *Territorialstaat*, p. 92 n. 117.
[122] CR 3:608–9 nr. 1752.

A 1539 Anonymous

More theological recommendations circulated among cities. Nothing
is known about the content of one of them, from the city of
Braunschweig, by their preachers. It was sent to Frankfurt, where
the League's diet met from February to April 1539.[123] Although the
council kept a copy in their archive, it is not, to my knowledge,
extant. But we know from a Braunschweig letter that they were also
in contact with Goslar and Magdeburg.

The city of Ulm preserved a more advanced memorandum. It
was issued by the Frankfurt diet (April 1539) under the seal of the
diet and two imperial negotiators, the electoral princes of Brandenburg
and the Palatinate.[124] This reminder of the peace negotiations kindled
the previous year with the Palatine prince's assistance points to the
changing context of the League's discussions of church property. It

---

[123] Stadtarchiv Braunschweig, B III 5:5, f. 415, from the letter of the Braunschweig
city council dated Thursday after Invocavit Sunday 1539 (in early March), addressed
to the *Rat* and secretary of Frankfurt: "...Juwer E(rsame) thogesanthe schriffte
hebben wy entfangen und wider gelesen, und horen hertlick gerne, dat juwe E.
gesunt und wol syn thor stede komen staen ok in trostliker guder vorhopeninge
Bodt de almechtige werde vordan syne gnade und seghen vorlegnen. De heren
predicanten hyr mit uns hebben ohr bedenckent by de kercken goider, wo id dar
mede scholde werden geholden, schrifftlick gestellet und ouer gegeuen, dat wy iro
der instruction na, hyr by vorwaret und under unsern secret vorsloten thoschicken,
dewile dat bedenckent der predicanten mer vasthe lang gestellet willen juwe E. in
deme und ok sunst in andern saken twiuels fry de notorfft und gelegenheit wol
bedencken. Dho deme moghen wy juwen E. nicht unangetzeiget lathen dat uns
kort na juwem affreisende von den erbarn von Gosslar unsen vorwanthen frunden
ohrer uplage und beswerung haluen de ohnen mit vorstoppung der straten und
sunst schal beiegenen schriffte syn tho gekomen und vormarken dat in geliker gestalt
de andern erbarn stede disses ordes schrifflick schullen syn ersocht, dewile wy id
ouers dar vor holden wolgemelte von Gosslar werden ohre geschickten ok wol
benueen jro thor stede hebben, und up anbringent dusser und anderer uplage und
beswerung widers rades plegen, so hebben wy ok in dusser saken so entlik tho
antworden und sunst allerleie uordenckent gehat und noch und schicken jwren E.
dersuluen schriffte und ok unses antwordes copien hyr inne vorsloten, und vormarken dat de van Magdeborg de Gosslarschen schrifft gelick alse wy in effectu
hebben vorantwordet, wor nu dusser saken dorch de Enigunges vorwanten wert
gedacht werden jwre E. sick in deme wol weten tho holden."
[124] Stadtarchiv Ulm, A1214, ff. 576–618. An archivist gave it the title *Ratschlag
über die geistlich guetter zu Franckfurt ubergeben* (f. 579r). The scribe who wrote or copied
the document gave it this more elaborate, dated title (f. 578v): "19 April Anno 39.
Bekantnus aller steend beschwerden, am Camer unnd anndern gerichten, von den
beeden unnderhandelen churf(ürsten) Pfalz unnd Brandenburg unns den stennden
unnder irm siguln zugestellt." For the electoral princes at the diet, Haug-Moritz,
Der Schmalkaldische Bund, pp. 113, 193, 531 n. 11.

was no longer merely the internal affair born of clergy concerns in 1537.

To my knowledge, this recommendation has never been edited. Martin Frecht, the head of the Ulm clergy since 1533, may have been the first to read it at Ulm.[125] It began not with ecclesiology but with the *ius reformandi*, "God has roused and called us to serve him to Reformation of his church, to the end that his church will be returned to her right shape and form, that is, reformed."[126] It then presented a defense of this obligation in 129 paragraphs,[127] followed by a brief outline of practical measures.[128] Another scribe added a précis crammed onto a single folio.[129] The document took a broad view of the obligation to reform, advocated secular uses of church property as an extension of reform, and promoted the replacement of prince-bishops with lay officers.

How wrong are the men who accuse Protestant rulers of avarice, the anonymous complained. They say Protestants destroy, not reform churches, taking the property to become rich and powerful. This is unfair. The accusation belongs to the many who hate church discipline and oppose it, "the example: England, Denmark, and certain other principalities" (*das exempel, Engellandt, Denmarck, unnd ettlicher annderer fürstenthumben*). Yet there are also people of good will who put us in the same category of church destroyers.[130] The estates therefore clarified their intention to return their church to the true apostolic sacraments and observances, as they believed holy scripture to require; their's was simply a commitment to holy discipline (*hailsame zucht der kirchen*) both with regard to church ministers and the community, for church property has been restored to its correct use according to scripture and the canon law (*zu irem rechtenn brauch denn das göttlich wort unnd die canones fördenn behalt, angelegt, unnd ussgespendet wurdenn*).[131]

---

[125] The document identifies no author(s). For Frecht, Brecht and Ehmer, *Südwestdeutsche Reformationsgeschichte*, p. 171.

[126] Ibid., f. 580r: "Gott hatt unns erweckt, unnd berufft, im zu diennen zuo reformation seiner kirchen, das ist darzu, das seine kirchen wider zu irer rechten form, unnd gestalt pracht werdenn, hoc est reformentir."

[127] Ibid., ff. 580r–611v.

[128] *Vom wege zu sollcher reformation zukomen*, Ibid., ff. 611v–615v.

[129] *Summarischer ausszug auss dem ratschlag von kurchengutter zu Frankfurt ubergeben*, ibid. f. 617r–v.

[130] Ibid., f. 580r–v.

[131] Ibid., ff. 580v–581r.

We now arrive at the beginning of the argument. As in the Augsburg and Bucer recommendations, its core is an evangelical ecclesiology. The true form of the church consists of three things: correct doctrine, correct performance of the sacraments, and correct performance of "the other church practices."[132] Church property must be used, according to scripture and canon law, to the best advantage of the religion of Christ and of the needs of all Christians.[133] The opponents try to prevent the restoration of church discipline.[134]

The anonymous notes that in their territory church properties have not been depleted as in some principalities (one might easily think of Duke Ulrich's domains), although church property may be used by rulers for the community, even for the maintenance of public order (*nottwendige pollicey unnd gemeinenn friden oder recht*), repeating a concession to temporal uses that Musculus, Wolfahrt, and Bucer had earlier made, as an extension of the *ius reformandi*.[135] King Hezekiah, the ancient king of Judah, redeemed his people from the king of the Assyrians by selling all the temple silver and gold, even stripping the gildwork from the doors.[136] "Our princes" (*unnsern fürstenn*) confiscated the property for their "dear churches" (*ire lieben kirchenn*), for holy religion and for the peace and good government (*gutte policey*)

---

[132] Ibid., f. 181r–v: "Dann in disenn dreien stucke stehen die rechte form unnd wesen der kirchen Christi, das nemblich die war christliche leher unnd die seligenn sacrament sampt den anndern kirchenübungen sowil deren die rechte unnd besser-liche usspenndung, der leer unnd sacramennten ermordert, rein ordennlich, unnd mit warem christennlichem Ernst gefiert, ussgespenndet unnd gelobet."

[133] Ibid., ff. 581v–582r: "Item die Kirchenguettter den gemeinden Christi trewlich behalten, unnd zu waren uffbawen der kirchen, wie das die hailig schrifft unnd all-tenn canones, außweisen, angelegt unnd ußgespenndet werden, dartzu das die haili-genn religion Christi zum bösstenn gefürdert, unnd aller notturfft der Christen inn gemein unnd besonnder uffs aller fluegtlichest rath beshehe."

[134] Ibid., f. 582v: ". . . zu dem ist alles ire fechtenn unnd strittenn wider unns allein darumb das sie die reformation der christlichenn zucht nicht geduldenn mögen, unnd sich gern in irer unzucht unnd unordnunget halltenn wöllenn."

[135] Ibid., ff. 583v–584r. Also f. 583r: "Der kirchenn guetter halbenn ists auch gott seie lob minder manngel bey unns dann uff dem gegentheil, dann ob wol inn ettlichenn furstennthumben, dess eintheil also angewanndet, daß sich daran vil gütherziger stossenn, unnd inen die bößwilligenn daher gar nahe, den pöstenn schein, ires klagenns, wider unns shöpffen, noch wo man den kirchenn diennst shuben unnd die durfftigenn zur notturfft verlehen unnd dann shon auch ettwas vonn kirchen-guottern, uff die gemeine notturfft Land unnd lewt zu regierenn, unnd schutzenn unnd nemblich die kirchen bey der gesundenn leere und warer Religion zu han-ndthaben unnd schirmen, angeköret, hatt man sollichs, uß den göttlichen rechten unnd den canonibus noch wol zuueranntwortenn."

[136] Ibid., f. 583v. 2 Kg. 18.14–15.

of their subjects.[137] Thus "our" opponents sought to destroy Christian order in the Empire, when they imposed the edict of Worms, against which "we" appealed to a council (*an ein recht, fray christlich concilium*).[138] The preachers explained that according to the canons and laws, the improvement of the church should be accomplished through provincial or national councils, but when the imperial estates, with emperor, commissar, and stateholder (*statthalter*) tried to arrange one in 1525 (it was actually discussed and scuttled at the Imperial Diet of Speyer in 1526), the opponents intervened and brought it to naught. Since, they have continued to prevent a free council.[139] The anonymous then accuses their opponents of ignoring imperial decisions that favor the Protestants. Instead, the opponents undertake a campaign of provocation that causes greater dissension within the Empire than between the Empire and the Turks.[140]

The memorandum continues in this plaintive manner, stating the correctness of the League's members' resistance to restitution suits, primarily on the basis of the right of reform. The document is most preoccupied with the wrongness of the opponents, who undermine ecclesiastical renewal—*böſerung* (improvement) by the reformed clergy.[141] Perhaps on the strength of the earlier Bucer and Augsburg pieces, the author(s) invoke canon law as much as or more than scripture, but in name—not one specific decree, decretal, or canonistic commentary is cited. Someone else had documented the legal case. It would appear to have been the Augsburg and/or Bucer recommendations of the previous year.

The memorandum favored aggressive confiscation by carefully reinterpreting it. Intrusions by ruling authorities are justified, the anonymous insists. They recognize how conventional this is. King Ferdinand of Spain, in response to the threat of the Turks, used ecclesiastical properties to fund a military order that conducts royal business to this day, and it provides annual incomes to certain high ministers, such as Nicholas Perrenot de Granvelle, the imperial

---

[137] Ibid., f. 584r, 589v–599v.
[138] Ibid., ff. 484v–485v. The anonymous advocates a national council. See f. 611v.
[139] Ibid., f. 586r–v.
[140] Ibid., f. 587r.
[141] Ibid., f. 588r–v.

chancellor.[142] The anonymous failed to mention that these actions were negotiated with Rome; they were papally approved. In addition, the text continues, in France and Germany the two military orders, the Hospitalers of St. John and the Teutonic Knights, accumulated property, neglected parish needs, and provided little service to the community or to rulers, whether in day-to-day government or warfare. Not so "with our estate" (*mit unserer stennd*). For unlike the kings of Spain, England, and France, the League uses church property to serve the needs of defense and government—to be exact, the defense of religion, the maintenance of good government, and the preservation of peace—while the opponents dole out (actually *lehen*, give as fiefs) prelatures, bishoprics, abbacies, and priories to favorite ministers, or they simply convert the prelatures into government ministries in violation of the rights of collegiate chapters.[143] The anonymous drew a fine distinction here. Confiscation as such was licit in their minds, whether Catholic or Protestant, as the examples of military orders and Spanish royalty show, but Catholic purposes are corrupt. Evangelical ones are religious. They wanted to make property *usage* the difference between Catholics and Protestants. They believed that Protestants used the church's things to strengthen a government that supported religious reform.[144] The illicit confiscators—the English,

---

[142] Ibid., f. 589r–v. The *Bekantnus* names three such officers: *herr Franzen von Canaser, item herr Niclausenn vonn Gravwel, dem herren vonn Newkilchen, unnd vilen anndern.* At the 1476 national council of Seville, Ferdinand and Isabella began to seek royal control over the three Spanish military orders, eventually becoming grandmaster of each and retaining for their own disposition a number of their highest offices. The process of control was confirmed by the papacy and made permanent during the reign of Charles. Joseph F. O'Callaghan, *A History of Medieval Spain* (Ithaca: Cornell, 1975), pp. 661–2. The Spanish expansion of such royal prerogatives in the church appears nearly a century later in the Lutheran jurist Matthias Stephanus' discussion of patronage law, when he describes temporal government's *potestas circa ecclesiastica* as *custos utriusque tabulae*, the custodian of both tables of the Ten Commandments, referring to Luther's division of the commandments into those pertaining to God and those pertaining to neighbor. Stephanus insists that the ruler's actions vis-à-vis church property require theological consultation. Sieglerschmidt, *Territorialstaat*, p. 258.

[143] Ibid., ff. 589v–591r.

[144] Ibid., f. 591r: "derhalbenn auch unnsere kirchen unnd obern disem exempel, mit nicht nachuolgen sollen, wie wir dann auch sie eingriffen, inn die kirchennguotter, mit solchem exempel nicht verthaidingenn wöllen, sonnder allein mit der entsthuldigung der notturfft die heilige religion, unnd dann auch mit policey unnd friden zu bestöllenn, erhalten unnd shützenn."

the French, and the Spanish—squandered church property on favorites.[145]

The commitment to mutual defense, so central to the League's existence, was presented as the mere defense of religious reform. "As said, the canons themselves and natural law determine that church property should serve the protection of religion and also common need."[146] In those places where more was confiscated than the defense of the church required, the oversupplies serve the "necessary government and common protection of subjects," which the memorandum earlier established as legitimate uses of church property.[147] But even so, the anonymous pointed out that Protestants used most property for schools, true church ministers, and support of the needy.[148] It contrasted evangelical uses with what they described as the sacrilegious simony prevailing among bishops, prelates, and other church ministers before the reform of the church. They expected bishops to guarantee and participate in the teaching of good doctrine and the maintenance of church discipline, or be found guilty of simony and removed.[149] Since cathedral and collegiate canons failed to contribute to pastoral care, and their singing (of the divine office) was useless, it was equally sacrilegious to support such activities with church property.[150] Ancient decisions of the Council of Chalcedon (451) determine that abbots, priors, and monks should support themselves by physical labor, while the accumulation of property from god-fearing people and the monastic incorporation of churches, burial services, and business interests defrauded parishes of their necessities and contradict the canon law. Consider the Protestants, the anonymous said. They returned defrauding monks to work, as Augustine said they

---

[145] Ibid., f. 590r.

[146] Ibid., f. 591r: "Dann diß wie gesagt, die canones selb, und das nattürlich recht vermögen, das das kirchengut zu shutz der religion, unnd auch gemeine notturfft diennen solle."

[147] Ibid., f. 591v: "Unnd ob es an ettlichenn orttenn sheinet, das vonn kirchennguottern, mehr einzogen were dann die defension der kirchen, unnd religion eruorderte, so wurt doch, an denselbigen orten darzuthun sein, das die nottwenndige regierung unnd gemeiner schutz der unnderthanen, an zugriff, inn die kirchennguetter nit wol habenn mögenn versehen, unnd erhaltenn werdenn, nun sole aber wie vor anzeiget, das kirchenngut auch zu diser notturfft der mennschen ankeret warden." Also ff. 600r–601r.

[148] Ibid., ff. 591v–592r, 599r–600r.

[149] Ibid., ff. 592r–594r.

[150] Ibid., f. 594r–v.

should be returned, in his *On the Work of Monks*.[151] The mendicant orders originally compensated for the failures of bishops and parish priests. They were meant to teach in urban churches and in the countryside among the peasants, but they too have fallen into the useless deeds of "singing and reading," that is, the divine office and votive masses.[152] Women's cloisters consumed resources that should go to divine worship and the needy, which the authors also counted as sacrilege.[153]

But the failures of Christian ministry were not necessarily Catholic alone. Unfortunately, the authors now added, many of "our mentioned clergy" live like the mob (*unnsere genannten geistlichenn, wie der gemein hauff ist*). Princes and rulers are obliged to see that all church property is returned to its correct use (*rechten brauch*) according to the canons and laws.[154] The anonymous claims it would be easy for the imperial estates to correct the abuse of church property: in addition to the support of worship and poor relief, the property would benefit the Empire.[155] Money may go to necessary governmental officers (*vil personen die die regierung, unnd andere nottwendige geshefftenn verrichtenn*).[156] The authors advised the appointment of vice-lords, majordomos, advocates, and managers (*vicedominos, maiores domus, defensoren, oeconomen*), which had been stipulated by Roman law.[157] Vice-lords are to take

---

[151] Ibid., f. 595r–v, f. 597v–598r. Augustine, *De opere monachorum* xxix.37. PL 40:576–77.

[152] Ibid., ff. 595v–596r: "So seind die Bettelordenn allein uffkomen, die saumnus der bishouen und pfarrerer inn christlicher leere, bey den volck zu erstattenn, weil dann auch dise sollchem ampt ußnemettenn, after, das sie inn jedem closter einigen prediger habenn, zuerhalltenn ir ansehenn, unnd die kirchen zu fürdern, unnd dann uff das lanndt shickenn, den armenn baueren das ir abzugingen, senndet haben sich auch gegeben uffs singenn unnd lessen, unnd messenn damit sie irenn brauch zuerhalten die hailige christliche religion zum shweresten verderbann, so seindt sie auch dem bann des h. Paulen gegen denen die nit allain eruordennlich sonnder auch shädlich wandeln erkennet unnd erwerffenn, wie auch dass anathemato dess h. Gregorii und aller altenn concilien, derhalben das sie ires ordennlichen diennsts, inn der kirchen nicht ußwarttenn, unnd dagegen allen aberglaübenn, unnd verderbenn der religion fürdern, derhalbenn auch inenn kain halber vonn kirchennguettern an ein iugens sacrilegium zu messen geburen mag."

[153] Ibid., f. 596r–v.

[154] Ibid., ff. 601r–602v.

[155] Ibid., f. 602v: "das zu bestellenn, das dem reich dauon merckliche diennst gelaistet und allerlay lewten, die iren ehrlich uffzuziehen unnd zu erhaltenn, grosse und gottselige vortheil widerfaren mögen." See also f. 610v.

[156] Ibid., ff. 602v–604r.

[157] Fourneret, "Biens ecclésiastiques," *Dictionnaire de theologie catholique*, 2/1:859.

over the temporal rule of bishops.[158] The Council of Chalcedon in
451 ordered the appointment of a *defensor*, "advocate," and *oeconomen*,
"manager" in each diocese to administer and defend its temporal
possessions. The memorandum discussed various ways to keep these
church offices and related properties non-heritable.[159] Church property could also be used to establish institutions to raise noble children.[160] The resources consumed by canons, vicars, chaplains, monks,
and friars were sufficient to establish schools to educate youth in
divine worship and to provide for the poor and exiles, the authors
said.[161]

This document differs from the two earlier urban answers to the
League. For one, it is more rhetorical and serves entirely as a defense
of the *ius reformandi* and the actions taken upon that obligation. For
another, it presents the Protestant case as part of a recapitulation of
ancient Christian forms of organization. It emphasizes two points of
consensus between evangelical cities and princes: the defense of religion and the religious legitimacy of applying some church property
to public uses. The examples of England, Denmark, and Spain underscore the urgency of an evangelical policy that preserved the church's
patrimony.

A Saxon Experiment

For early January 1539 in Saxony, Georg von Karlowitz arranged,
with the Landgrave of Hesse, a colloquy that involved Bucer and
Melanchthon. At the end of 1538, the Landgrave sent Bucer, who

---

Norman P. Tanner, ed. *Decrees of the Ecumenical Councils*, 2 vols. (Washington, DC:
Georgetown University Press, 1990), 1:99 (the twenty-sixth decree of the Council
of Chalcedon). *Codex* 1.3. 42 and *Novellae* 123.23. Pope Gregory the Great included
the *vicedominus*, "vicelord," and majordomo among diocesan administrators. Ep. 45,
PL 77:1294. Fourneret, "Biens ecclésiastique," 2/1:859.

[158] Ibid., ff. 604r–606v treats the replacement of temporal government of bishops (*Stifte*) by the *vicedom ampt*.

[159] *Bekanntnus*, ff. 607r–608v, emphasizing also the advantage of making children
of canons legitimate.

[160] Ibid., f. 609r–v.

[161] Ibid., ff. 609v–610r: "Das überig dann von den kirchenguettern, so diser zeit
allein vonn den allermenigelich unnutzen, chorherren, vicarien, caplanen, mönchen,
unnd brüdern heimbracht würdt, wurde noch genugsam sein, die shulen zubestöllen,
zum kirchenndiennst jungen uffzuziehen die disen diennst verrichtenn, zuerhallten,
unnd für die armen, haunthen (?) unnd frömbden versehung zuuerordnen."

was in Hesse at the time, to Wittenberg in order to join the Electoral Saxon participants. Melanchthon had declared himself ready to join a colloquy the previous November, if Luther approved.[162] The Protestant delegates arrived at Leipzig on 1 January—Bucer and Johann Feige, the Landgrave's chancellor, with Melanchthon and Gregor Brück, the electoral prince's chancellor. Karlowitz and Ludwig Fachs, another counselor at the Saxon court in Dresden, represented the Catholic side. Conspicuously, Karlowitz did not include a theologian in his entourage.[163] The official dialogue quickly foundered. Karlowitz suggested an historical gauge to resolve religious disagreements, which could have seemed a friendly gesture to evangelicals, namely that each side accept only things practiced by the apostolic church up to the time of Pope Gregory the Great. Had he known of the anonymous, he might have been encouraged by its appeal to Gregory's example. The Schmalkald articles, Melanchthon, Muscuslus and Wolfahrt, and Bucer had put their arguments in similar historical frameworks. Apparently, von Karlowitz hoped to establish a common opposition to ecclesiastical princes as the common ground between the two Saxonies. Von Karlowitz said the norm of antiquity would let bishops save face when renouncing their temporal authority, since the emperor could not force bishops to do it. He conceded that clerical lordships would easily destroy any reforms.[164] The Protestant theologians either missed the convergence of interests or distrusted this political move and objected on a technicality: the normative timeframe extended too late. By the year 600, numerous abuses were already in place, they said. Karlowitz responded by asking both sides to address the normative timeframe in briefs treating the apostolic church, but he was less than sanguine, for the reigning court theologian at Dresden, Cochlaeus, was, in his opinion, unlikely to help. The official colloquy ended with the disagreement about the date of the church's decline. But discussions between the principals continued over the next days. They included Georg Witzel, a Protestant who returned to Catholicism in 1530, who was since 1538 active in the duke of Saxony's territory. A friend of von Karlowitz, he agreed that the model for Catholic reform was the

---

[162] Fuchs, *Konfession und Gespräch*, p. 401.
[163] Ibid., p. 402.
[164] Fuchs, *Konfession und Gespräch*, pp. 403–7 for this and the following.

early church.[165] Bucer and Witzel produced a reunion proposal that included a doctrine of justification very close to the Lutheran position. It also suggested modest reforms in the doctrines of the eucharist, monasticism, the adoration of the saints, feast days, the sacrament of holy anointing, fasts, and the place of temporal government. It ignored the problem of church property. It advocated a common faith.

The Frankfurt diet of the League followed in the month after these discussions. There the princes, in response to the imperial Chancellor Held and the imperial commissar (the exiled archbishop of Lund, Johann of Lieze), declared that church property could only be used for divine service and church or charitable ends.[166] The princes could do this because charity was a wide-open virtue, after all. Even Bucer could pity the impoverished nobleman and allow church property to be used to prop up a fading bloodline. It qualified as a religious use.

Meanwhile, Ulrich of Württemberg was learning to assume a plaintive, pious tone. He must have wondered whether theologians could possibly understand a prince's burdens.[167] In a lengthy instruction to his counselors of 23 March 1539 for the convention of the Schmalkald League at Frankfurt, he complained that as prince he is unable ever to renounce feeding, traveling in retinue, appraisal, common territorial tax, serfdom and other legal matters, which he and his ancestors have taken over from the cloisters, and he cannot relinquish the responsibilities of patron, benefactor (*Stiftherr*), and caretaker (*collator*) assigned by common spiritual and temporal rights. It was therefore all the more burdensome, he alleged, that he should provide for preaching offices, pastors, church ministers, stipendiaries, university, hospitals, and the poor chest with ecclesiastical benefices (*geistliche Gefällen*). He took nothing for his own uses, he said, but did it for the benefit of his subjects and his downtrodden land. His temporal purposes as a ruler, in other words, served religion and social welfare. The boundary between affairs of state and matters of religion

---

[165] Henze, *Aus Liebe zur Kirche Reform*, pp. 152–208. Witzel was ridiculed for his conversion, and his advocacy of reform was declared a sham, for example in *Flugschriften des späteren 16. Jahrhunderts*, Fiche 1093 nr. 1876.

[166] Hermelink, "Zwei Aktenstücke," p. 180. Also summarized by Sieglerschmidt, *Territorialstaat*, p. 144.

[167] Hermelink, "Zwei Aktenstücke," p. 180.

may seem conveniently porous, but should we dismiss Ulrich as insin-
cere? He preferred to think of himself as a reformer, not an embezzler.
He instructs us not to overemphasize the difference between urban
theologians and Wittenberg—communal powers and personal, princely
ones; semi-public views of property or semi-private ones (the property exists to benefit the church versus the residual rights of donors).
Such different viewpoints existed, but played little role now.

CHAPTER SIX

THE SCHMALKALD RECOMMENDATION OF 1540

On 19 April 1539, emperor Charles V and King Ferdinand, with the adherents of the Augsburg Confession, agreed to conclude the Truce of Frankfurt, a fifteen-month armistice.[1] The agreement prohibited the League of Schmalkalden and the Nürnberg League from admitting new members during the truce, prohibited any further confiscation of ecclesiastical rents or incomes, and called for a religious colloquy to take place at Frankfurt, 1 August 1539, to resolve the religious controversy. The colloquy would turn into three, and they would not take place until 1540 and 1541, at Hagenau, Worms, and Regensburg.

The gathering momentum of negotiation soon overcame the memory of the Diet of Augsburg's failed dialogue in 1530. During the 1530 Diet, agreements of theological spokesmen satisfied colleagues in neither party and resulted in greater Protestant intransigence.[2] The Leipzig colloquy and the Truce of Frankfurt opened a new path. The renewed possibility of negotiating matters of faith to the point of a permanent imperial peace promised to elevate the importance of the League's discussion of church property. What began in 1537 as an internal debate provoked by theological advisors now touched high imperial politics. The Protestant rulers reacted to this development by trying to remove the subject from consideration, as we will see in the next chapter. King Ferdinand of Austria supported a negotiated settlement out of his abiding need to enlist German troops against the Turks. The emperor now agreed to negotiate the religious controversy under the auspices of the Imperial Diet and

---

[1] Signed by Johann Friedrich of Saxony, Philip of Hesse, and the burgomaster and council of Frankfurt "im Namen unser selbst und aller unserer Fürsten, Grafen, Herren, Städte und Stände unserer Augsburgischen Confession und derselben Einungsverwandten." Martin Luther, *Sämmtliche Schriften*, 17:308–15 nr. 1292. Hortleder, *Handlungen*, i.32, 1:120–24.

[2] Fuchs, *Konfession und Gespräch*, pp. 367–88, esp. 381–88. Kohnle, *Reichstag und Reformation*, pp. 381–94.

not an ecclesiastical council. The Imperial Diet was a venue pretty
close to the League's most current demand, that the controversy be
resolved by a national synod.[3] The concession raised a papal-princely
reaction. Pope Paul III and several Catholic princes, most especially
the dukes of Bavaria, insisted that any final resolution could only
happen in a council convened by the pope. Meanwhile, the Protestant
clergy continued to worry over the preservation of the church's
patrimony.

It may be well meaning, but it is premature to take the Truce of
Frankfurt and the religious colloquies that followed as a rising chorus of ecumenical good will, the unity of the body of Christ reassert-
ing itself over an unnatural schism. That thought seems to have
occurred to no one, at first. The Truce of Frankfurt alarmed Catholics
and Protestants alike. Times were bad in this year of the truce,
Melanchthon noted in a letter to his friend and colleague Joachim
Camerarius that spring, with a sickened Landgrave, a bad harvest,
and "huge, hard, odious debates" in Wittenberg.[4] All Protestant
princes must have felt like the Landgrave, who in his 5 November
1539 instruction to his delegates to the next diet of the League worried over the danger posed by *Protestant* theologians. Philip of Hesse
told his emissaries that he was certain that if Martin Bucer insisted
temporal uses (*was die obern dorvon haben solten*) must be controlled by
appointed administrators (*die obern nit allein dormit umbgingen*), he would
split the League and prevent others from joining "our religion" (*so
wirdet er die puntnus mit der zeit trennen und vilen den weg verschliessen, unser*

<hr />

[3] The demand was composed and sent from the League's Schmalkald diet in
1540. *Akten der deutschen Reichsreligionsgespräche*, 1/1:70–81 nr. 19. The option of a
national council had also been discussed, and dismissed by Charles V, in 1528, just
before the Diet of Speyer. Reinhard, "Die kirchenpolitischen Vorstellungen Karls
V," p. 74.

[4] 20 April 1539. MBW 2:432 nr. 2190, CR 3:697 nr. 1799: "Etsi autem quales
sint voluntates τόν δυναστόν non ignoras, tamen induciae sunt huius anni. Princeps
Hassiae aegrotat, ut nuper tibi scripsi. Etiam malum quoddam ut videtur bono fuit,
difficultas annonae, quae maior est apud nos, quam apud vos. Magnae hic et
difficiles et odiosae contentiones fuerunt, quarum argumenta tibi scribam, cum
rediero domum, ut integram et veram teneas historiam. Non dubito Drum haec
gubernare, propterea te tranquilliare animo esse volo." An imperial offer of a general peace had arrived at Wittenberg a month before, and in early April it was
given to the Schmalkald League, which Luther regarded skeptically, and the controversy over Johann Agricola of the law continued, while his doctrine seemed to
spread. Brecht, *Martin Luther*, 3:167, 201–3.

religion anzunemen).[5] It should be left to the conscience of individual rulers, the Landgrave instructed his people to say. A truly evangelical ruler would do the right thing and guarantee necessary provisions to parishes, churches, offices, and the poor. He recognized the League's internal sticking point, a reluctance of urban theologians and magistrates to recognize princely property claims in the church, and he found it ludicrous. Do the promoters of Bucer's view, he wondered, mean that emperors and kings, who have enjoyed great advantages from church property in the past, should just hand it over to others now? The Landgrave conceded that the property should not be torn away from the hospitals, rectors, schools, etc. to which it belongs (*den spitälern, pharherren, schulen etc., was idem gehorte. So wurden auch deiselben gutter nit so usgebeten und zerrissen*). But there was a difference between noble and free foundations (Philip meant that noble lineages have a customary bond to these monasteries). He told his counselors to ask the League's diet if noble and free foundations should be handled the same way. He knew that a legal discussion of noble monasteries could establish the residual rights of donors.

At the next diet of the League, which met at Arnstadt in early December 1539, the Hessians introduced the subject, and the Elector of Saxony called on the estates to talk about accelerating reforms before all efforts are frozen by a final settlement; the Elector was himself worried about his plans to control the succession of a bishop in Naumburg.[6] Duke Ulrich of Württemberg instructed his delegates to push for a strong view of princely rights.[7] Strasbourg's concern to restrict the uses of church incomes was checked by other cities, like Ulm, who complained that the support of clergy was costing them thousands of florin.[8] There was, too, this point, made by the Landgrave: amplifying princely rights could strengthen and attract new members to the Protestant coalition (in late 1539, the boom of new members had just passed).[9] Bucer conceded to *Obrigkeit* a right to ecclesiastical oversupplies in emergencies of war, inflation, or the like.[10] During

---

[5] Günther Franz, *Urkundliche Quellen zur hessischen Reformationsgeschichte*, 3 vols. (Marburg: N.G. Elwert, 1954), 2:322–3 nr. 399 for this and the following.

[6] Haug-Moritz, *Der Schmalkaldische Bund*, pp. 520–21.

[7] Hermelink, "Zwei Aktenstücke," p. 180.

[8] Haug-Moritz, *Der Schmalkaldische Bund*, p. 523.

[9] Franz, *Urkundliche Quellen*, 2:322–3 nr. 399.

[10] Haug-Moritz, *Der Schmalkaldische Bund*, p. 532.

discussions on 3 December 1539, Celle, Hesse, and Württemberg
pleaded to leave church property to the conscience of the relevant
government. Jacob Sturm insisted on the need for a common position. The city of Esslingen said oversupplies should serve the common good.[11] These voices were not quite as discordant as they may
at first seem. The difficulty was whether princes would view the common good as a sufficient rationale, when they could also pursue their
ends as patrons who retain some obligations and rights over donated
properties. The representatives of Electoral Saxony summarized the
discussion like this: the cities want "a decision once and for all" (*dz
einmal ein ordnung gemacht*).[12] The League accepted a rank order of
uses: first, the support of pastors, schools, and church ministers; second, the preservation of the nobility, especially the daughters of poor
nobility; and third, promotion of the common good. The rank order
was repeated a week later in the diet's recess. Everyone agreed on
the first use. The second acknowledged princely interests, the third,
urban convictions. This juxtaposition of princely and urban viewpoints
would not do, and the question of church property was still unsettled.

As the religious colloquies approached, it was necessary to clarify
talking points and non-negotiable items. Bucer and Witzel had already
begun to clear the ground. Now Johann Friedrich instructed the Wittenberg theologians to prepare defenses of the Augsburg Confession.[13] On
18 January 1540, Luther, Jonas, Bugenhagen, and Cruciger provided
Johann Friedrich with a brief treating 1) themes to be discussed,[14]

---

[11] Haug-Moritz, *Der Schmalkaldische Bund*, p. 534.

[12] Haug-Moritz, *Der Schmalkaldische Bund*, pp. 534–5. *Akten der deutschen Reichsreligionsgespräche* 1/2:1127–8 nr. 395.

[13] December 1539 Johann Friedrich of Saxony told Luther, Jonas, Bugenhagen,
Cruciger, and Melanchthon in Wittenberg to prepare for a religious colloquy. They
with the princes of the Schamlkald convention of 1 March were instructed to prepare to defend the Augsburg Confession. The Elector promised to send the acts of
the Leipzig dialogue between Bucer and Georg Witzel. MBW 2:486 nr. 2332, CR
3:868–71 nr. 1872, WABr 8:647–50 nr. 3425. 7 January 1540 at Wittenberg, Luther,
Jonas, Bugenhagen, and Melanchthon told Johann Friedrich that they received the
previous letter with the Reformation of Georg von Carlowitz (from the 1539 religious colloquy at Leipzig). They then recounted some of the points made in a brief
given to Johann Friedrich on 18 January 1540. MBW 3:19 nr. 2346, CR 3:920–22
nr. 1913, WABr 9:8–11 nr. 3431.

[14] The themes identified for the colloquy were named as justification by faith,
merit, sins of the saints (the Lutheran view was that complete freedom from sin,
even after justification, was impossible outside of heaven), ecclesiology, penance,
food laws, the cult of saints, monastic vows, purgatory. MBW 3:22 nr. 2352, CR
3:926–45 nr. 1918, WABr 9:19–35 nr. 3436, Philipp Melanchthon, *Epistolae, iudi-*

2) necessary external matters,[15] 3) matters indifferent,[16] and 4) cloisters. In the fourth item, they advocated the use of monastic properties to establish schools and hospitals, functions associated with
early monasticism in both Protestant and Catholic sources, as we've
seen. Attrition after evangelical preaching might purge cloisters of
all but the elderly, since new recruits were usually prohibited, transforming monasteries into homes for pensioners. That undermined
their purpose as schools. The Wittemberg theologians therefore recommended the establishment of new schools and universities in cities,
so that monastic property would serve its original purposes of education and poor relief for the nobility and others. They required the
dissolution of men's and women's cloisters alike, but not as an act
of sovereignty, rather as an act of religious restoration. For the
Wittenberg theologians worried that the problem of church property
would push the articles of faith off the agenda at the forthcoming
religious colloquy.[17]

Bucer reacted to this document with mistrust, but not on account
of its specific proposals, which reflected changes that had already
taken place in Saxony. In a letter to Philip of Hesse, he worried
that the Wittenbergers intended to preempt an open discussion.[18] His
suspicion was misplaced. The 18 January brief avoided the only real
disagreement, which was a difference of approach to the rationale

---

cia, consilia, testimonia aliorumque ad eum epsitolae quae in Corpore Reformatorum desiderantur,
ed. Heinrich Ernst Bindseil (Halle, 1874, and reprinted Hildesheim: Georg Olms,
1975), pp. 146–47 nr. 194. The same text is reproduced from an edition of the
Schmalkald Articles published in Wittenberg in 1575 by Walch in Martin Luther,
Sämmtliche Schriften 17:319–34, where the signatories are expanded to include
Melanchthon, Myconius, Amsdorf, Sarcerius, Timan, Scheubel, Tardus, Bucer,
Corvinus, and Kymeus. That is, the 1575 Wittenberg edition presents this piece as
more broadly representative of theologians from the Schmalkald League, not just
Wittenberg, which is probably incorrect, given the origin of the text in Wittenberg.
Akten der deutschen Reichsreligionsgespräche 1/2:116–29 nr. 395 has the long version.

[15] That there may not be private masses, not even for the mere memorialization of the dead, any cult of saints, or processions of the eucharistic chalice.

[16] They said that religiously indifferent matters may only be considered when
bishops cease their persecution of evangelicals, and there is no recognition of papal
authority. Only after Catholic bishops and princes recognize evangelical doctrine
and necessary rites can agreements be reached over communion, sung masses, private absolution, daily worship, feast days, saints' days, and fasts. Compromises on
ecclesiastical jurisdiction of bishops and cathedral chapters must require the participation of lay *Obrigkeit*, they added.

[17] Haug-Moritz, *Der Schmalkaldische Bund*, p. 535.

[18] *Martin Bucers Deutsche Schriften*, 9/1:81.

for confiscations. The approach advocated by Bucer had stressed communal needs; the one favored by Wittenberg stressed princely entitlement. These corresponded to differences traceable to canon law, which treated church property as both a semi-public and a semi-private thing. But just as Bucer had already proved willing to concede some subordinate degree of princely rights, so too, the Wittenberg theologians conceded communal uses. All agreed that the faith of the Augsburg Confession was the proper subject of Protestant-Catholic debate, not church property. When, soon after, attention turned to the religious colloquy, Bucer reported to Strasbourg that the theologians enjoyed consensus.[19]

In the meanwhile, an assessor of the Imperial Chamber Court, Konrad Braun, attacked the League's view of restitution suits, and he called for a complete rejection of the Truce of Frankfurt. Braun currently represented the electorate of Mainz on the court. He was already deeply troubled by the League's complaint to the emperor the year before, of the court's alleged bias. Accordingly, his objections to the Truce began the day its text was read out to the assessors, 26 April 1539: since the emperor lacked power to decide religious matters, this truce, he felt, may be invalid.[20] When his colleagues proved ready to accept the Truce's terms, with its temporary freeze of church property cases, Braun published his complaint. Before the end of October, when the Truce was originally due to expire, he published a combative *Dialogue of a Court Counselor with two Learned Men, a Theologian and a Jurist, and then with a Scribe.*[21] In it, he argued that church property was not a religious matter at all but clearly fell under the competence of the imperial appeals court, while warning against the poison of Lutheran heresy.[22] All of this put him at odds with Albrecht of Mainz, a member of the imperial peace party; the

---

[19] Ibid., 9/1:81–82.

[20] Maria Barbara Rößner, *Konrad Braun (ca. 1495–1563): ein katholischer Jurist, Politiker, Kontroverstheologe und Kirchenreformer im konfessionellen Zeitalter* (Münster: Aschendorf, 1991), pp. 58–62.

[21] *Ain Gesprech aines Hoffraths mit zwaien Gelerten, ainem Theologen und ainem Juristen, und dann ainem Schreiber, so zu letzt auch von ongeschicht dartzu kummen, von dem Nurnbergischen Fridstandt Regenspurgischen Kayserlichen Mandat der Protestierenden Stendt ausschreiben wider das Kaiserlich Camergericht und dem Abschide jüngst zu Franckenfurt bethaidingt* (n.pl.: n.publ., 1539) and printed in Hortleder, 1:124–157. See Rößner, *Konrad Braun*, p. 345.

[22] Gottfried Seebaß, "Martin Bucers," pp. 169, 174–5. Heckel, "Die Reformation-sprozesse," pp. 13–14. Sprenger, *Viglius von Aytta*, p. 34.

archbishop of Lund, the architect of the Truce, dispatched a complaint to Matthias Held.[23] The exchange launched Braun into his future vocation as a publicist against the Protestants.[24]

Bucer had written his own defense of the Truce of Frankfurt that summer under the pseudonym Chünradt Trew von Fridesleuffen, "Conrad True of the March of Peace," and after Braun's attack, he published another three dialogues under the title *Von Kirchengütern, On Church Property*, on 3 February 1540, under the same name.[25] The third dialogue provided Bucer's recommendations. More than answer Braun, the book clarified his views to his Protestant peers, elaborating ideas of his 1538 recommendation, including a narrow restatement of princely entitlement to church property, but an entitlement subordinated to the rule of charity. The Protestants, he said, took nothing from the church, for the church's property belongs to true Christians, and Protestant uses of it have been consistent with the truth of canon law. What is true in canon law, littered as it is with contradictions, are those things that are also clearly taught in scripture (he relied on the *Decretum* and Justinian's *Corpus Iuris Civilis*; he avoided the later *Decretales*).[26] Bucer conceded the right of princes to confiscate church property for their own use, for some princes are so poor, such confiscation was merely poor relief. Furthermore, he argued, since most of the property was given by high noble families, the heirs are entitled to take some of it back in time of necessity. Pope Gregory the Great set a precedent for temporal use long ago

---

[23] Rößner, *Konrad Braun*, p. 63.

[24] Ibid., pp. 66, 92–159.

[25] Roth, "Kirchengüterfrage," pp. 310–11. Haug-Moritz, *Der Schmalkaldische Bund*, p. 522, who notes the relation of Bucer's work to the Schmalkald discussion of Johann Friedrich's more aggressive postion on church property. Brady believes that Johann Friedrich's position stands between the extremes of Bucer's defense of limited episcopal jurisdiction and Duke Ulrich's opposition to bishops. Brady, *Protestant Politics*, p. 173. For the date of writing, Rößner, *Konrad Braun*, p. 61 with n. 233.

[26] Seebaß, "Bucers Beitrag," pp. 169–72, 175–77 for this and the following. Seebaß notes that Bucer's argument relies on Justinian's *Codex* 2, 3, 14 and especially Justinian's *Novellae* 3, 5, 6, 7, 46, 67, 123, 133. The Decretals insist that church property can only be "alienated" with consent of cathedral chapter and pope. *Liber Sextus* III.ix.2. CICan 2:1042–3. The *Decretum* emphasizes the communal nature of church property and the bishop's responsibility to dispense it to the needy, drawing heavily on the fathers and councils of the early church. *Decretum* C 12 q. i.22–26. CICan 1:684–86.

when he sold church property to barter a peace agreement with the
Lombards. Pope and emperor use it for particular tasks and defense
against the Turks. The Spanish knights' orders use it similarly. The
evangelical princes likewise use it to protect religion. To that end,
government may also use part of it to defray the costs of negotiations, meetings, and defense. This was not secularization, in Bucer's
mind, but a broad view of religious uses. Nor can any substantial
difference between his view and Wittenberg's be said to remain. As
in the theological recommendations of 1538 and 1539, these arguments
also suggested a kind of bi-confessional civility. Temporal authority
was defined by its religious obligations, regardless of confession.

Bucer, who had won his reputation as the reformer of an urban
church in the early 1530's, now turned to the question of prince-
bishops. The first step was to accommodate princely entitlement to
communal notions of public welfare, to recognize the semi-private
and semi-public character of church property at once, as he just did.
The next step was to accommodate prince-bishops.[27] Bucer recognized, first, that it was unrealistic to view them as occupying a spiritual office. They were unwilling to return to the true pastoral form
of episcopacy represented by bishops like Ambrose, Augustine, Martin
of Tours, and others. Those who embrace the Reformation, he said,
should accept the mere title of arch-prince or prince. Cathedral chapters should be divided into two colleges, a younger and an older
one, and these should elect bishops. The new bishops should have
no spiritual powers,[28] but they should retain the rights and responsibilities associated with church administration. They could call syn-
ods and oversee ministers and poor relief (these were functions Bucer
had earlier invested in deacons).[29] Confiscated incomes of cloisters
and endowments for memorial masses and other obsequies should
support the poor and students. The proposal separated pastoral from
princely offices, but preserved prince-bishops as temporal powers with
a particular position in the temporal church, preventing their passage to lay dynasties.[30] His propsal preserved church property.

---

[27] Roth, "Kirchengüterfrage," pp. 310–11. Gäumann, *Reich Christi und Obrigkeit*,
pp. 232–5.
[28] Their spiritual power was sacramental and included the diocesan administration of penance, and by implication the use of ecclesiastical censures, and the distribution of sacramental power to priests through ordination. It is a huge restriction.
[29] Hammann, *Martin Bucer*, pp. 251–73.
[30] Gäumann, *Reich Christi und Obrigkeit*, p. 234.

To the effort at accommodation of the League's faith within the Empire, Bucer's book contributed arguments for the qualified acceptance of an imperial order in which ecclesiastical princes played a prominent role, both in the college of electors and in the college of princes. More important for the League's internal debate was this. Even before the 1540 diet of Schmalkalden, Bucer indicated a way to overcome the internal disagreement on church property. He conceded princely entitlements while stressing priorities of use, putting charity above princely entitlement. This did not end worry over the prince's abuse of the church. As the League's diet drew near, a commission of Hessian theologians, including Corvinus and Raid (they would later sign the 1540 recommendation) presented a brief to the Landgrave that included an article on church property.[31] They tried to limit princely claims upon it. They insisted that it be used to support pastors, schools, and hospitals, as ecclesiastical canons and Justinian's *Institutes* taught. The fact that they provided no citations of law may suggest familiarity with the Musculus/Wolfahrt or Bucer documents of 1538. They warned that if learned pastors lacked material support, they might leave for the newly converted territories of Brandenburg and Albertine Saxony, depleting Hessian parishes and schools of their ministers and leading to the decline of the Word of God and the liberal arts, with society regressing to godless barbarity. After parishes, schools, and hospitals have been supplied, the Hessian theologians continued, whatever church property remained should go to a common chest and be held inviolable until time of emergency ("until the fatherland falls into unavoidable need or religion is assaulted or attacked," *bis das das vaterland in unvermeidliche not keme oder der religion angegriffen oder bekriegt würde*). In the absence of such emergency, they concluded, divine and secular laws alike determined that the property could not be alienated from the church.

The Landgrave of Hesse must have bristled at these claims. To be sure, he granted the priorities on which theologians insisted: to support churches, schools, universities, and hospitals. But a prince should get what he wants, and he had a particular man in mind, as he explained to his delegates to the diet of Schmalkalden.[32]

---

[31] *Akten der deutschen Reichsreligionsgespräche* 1/2:1134 nr. 396.

[32] *Instruction auff den tag zu Smalkalden prima Marcy Anno 1540* (another hand added the date 27 February in the margin), Hessisches Staatsarchiv Marburg, Bestand 3,

222   CHAPTER SIX

One needs among particular estates to make distinctions on church property, and our counselor should just say openly: in the case of Duke Ulrich of Württemberg, he came into a devastated land, and church property could not be spared. Again, the duke of Lüneburg confronts massive debt, their land is also devastated; that church property should be restored would be to them very onerous and not at all opportune. From their church property, parishes and advanced schools, also hospitals, were provisioned. Again, since cloister personnel are provided for, one must allow these estates [the princes] more than the others. So may one maintain with the other estates with regard to church property, once their parishes, schools, and hospitals have been provisioned. If something remains there, one may seize it afterward as a lowest matter of religion and use it. For all that, the counselor should report that our cloister property just brought in—once the parishes, universities, and schools were provisioned, as we set out to do—left little or really nothing leftover.

With special burdens come special prerogatives. But "other estates," that is cities, faced pretty much the same dilemma, namely, having taken on added fiscal burdens, they needed more income. Philip may have learned from Bucer that clarifying priorities, putting princely entitlement at the end of the list, could appease the clergy. Confiscation of oversupplies was "a lowest matter of religion," acceptable as a lowest priority, after the provisioning of parishes, schools, and poor

---

Nr. 540, ff. 1r–12v, here ff. 7v–8r: "[mg. Geistliche gůter] Der Geistlichenn guther halben wie mans da ordnet rund macht das Christlich unnd gůt ist, das man solche gůter wennde, das die kirchenn, schulen und hohen schulenn darvonn unnderhaltenn werdenn. Item das die geordneten spittal In wesenn pleiben das lassenn wir uns nit misfallenn. [mg. underschul nit etzlichen gehalten der geistlichen guter halbe] Doch mus man mit etlichenn stennden unntherschidt inn denn geistlichenn gůternn habenn: und das sollenn unnsere Rethe offenntlich freÿ herauss sagenn: Als nemblich mit herzog Ulrichenn zů wirteennberg hatt es die gestalt, das er in ein verdorben lannd ist kommen, unnd der geistlichenn guther nit kann entberen. Item so steckt der herzog zů lenneburg in grossen schulden, ist Ir lannd auch verderbt, das die die geistlichenn guter solten widdergebenn were Irenn hoch beschwerlich unnd gar nit gelegenn. Vann Ire pfarren unnd hohe schülenn aůch spittal versehen weren. Item das denn closter personenn zimbliche aůsserer unnd unnter haltunng verordnet were, Mŭste man diessen stenden etzwas mehr nachlassenn dan andernn. So mochte mans mit denn annderen stenden der geistlichen guter halbenn also halten wann Ire pharren schulen unnd spittal versehen weren. Vere dann was uberig da, nachdem dann ist ein untest der religion sachen halbenn ufgehet mochte man: das so uberig were: zů solchem untestenn gebrauchen. [mg. bericht bey s .b. closter gůtern geschrifhen] Dabeÿ sollenn unns der Rethe berichtenn das unnsere closter gůter sogar ingevirnn, wann die pfarren hohen schulen unnd schulen darvonn bestelt werdenn als wir Jzo jm furhabenn ein das wir thun wollenn, das wenig oder gar nichts uberig pleibenn werde."

relief. Lest anyone think much leftover property was at issue, he reported that the provisioning of parishes, schools, and hospitals in his territory consumed almost everything. Bucer had conceded the right of a prince in an emergency—to pay for negotiations, meetings, and defense. The Landgrave said the state of emergency had arrived. Dukes like those of Württemberg and Lüneburg already faced financially ruined administrations. But Philip was careful to point out that he stood above reproach. *His* monastic property went to parishes, a university, and other schools.

Before the League's meeting in Schmalkalden, Philip also tested the Catholic peace advocates' ability to accept confiscations. He sent Heinrich Lersener, Hessian Chamber Secretary and Minister, his chief agent in the 1540's, to the archbishop Johann of Lund in Cologne, and they met on 5–6 March 1540. Lund was not likely to sympathize. Four years earlier king Christian III had removed him and his suffragan bishops, confiscated monasteries, and secularized the properties of the Danish church. In exile the archbishop became a senior imperial diplomat: he mediated the Truce of Frankfurt (April 1539). The Landgrave's overtures accomplished nothing.[33] Heinrich gave the archbishop articles from Philip that justified confiscations.[34] The archbishop said he is not a theologian and did not intend to be dragged into a theological disputation, then he demanded that the Landgrave had to restore the church's properties in full.

The League's diet at Schmalkalden convened in early March 1540. When the theologians arrived, they wondered if they would be taken seriously.[35] Philip of Hesse, 8 or 9 March 1540, told Bucer and Melanchthon that although the archbishops of Mainz and Trier, the Electoral Prince Palatine, and the Duke of Bavaria want peace, they are not interested in reformation. But there is good will at the imperial court and with the imperial chancellor, Nicholas Perrenot de Granvelle, he reported. They should therefore write a summary of

---

[33] Seebaß, "Verwendung der Kirchengüter," p. 180. Haug-Moritz, *Der Schmalkaldische Bund*, p. 65.

[34] Lenz, *Briefwechsel*, 1:475–89, here 486.

[35] 7 March 1540, Melanchthon wrote from Schmalkalden to Myconius to say that the theologians do not yet see why they have been summoned, and he complained that, as always, doctrine will be handled last. MBW 3:38 nr. 2389, CR 3:976 nr. 1938. *Martin Bucers Deutsche Schriften*, 9/1:79.

religion (the Wittenberg theologians already had, at Johann Friedrich's request, on 18 January),[36] and a position-piece on church property, to be sent with a formal request for a religious colloquy.[37] Melanchthon must have been pleased to see the theologians thrust to the center of the League's attention. They met, discussed a recommendation composed by Melancthon, and on 9 March 1540 signed it (one in absentia), as representatives of the two Saxonies, Hesse, Nassau, Strasbourg, Magdeburg, and Bremen.[38] Then on 11 March 1540, Bugenhagen presented two documents to the League's estates.[39] One was the Wittenberg recommendation in defense of the Augsburg Confession of 18 January.[40] The other was the common recommendation on church property of 9 March. A day after the documents were submitted, Bucer reported the broad representation of theologians at the diet to Strasbourg.[41]

The recommendation of 9 March is the only theological document of the German rebellion against the papacy to record a formal consensus of evangelical theologians on church property. The theologians' advice consisted of six brief points that synthesized ideas already in circulation, and they acknowledged both urban and princely views in the way basically mapped out by Martin Bucer, as we can see in the third and fourth articles.

First comes the obligation to reform. It belongs to *oberkeit* to restore correct worship, install pastors, establish schools, and provide for the needy, the theologians said.[42] This hardly required proof: it "is clear in many of our writings and irrefutably demonstrated." It is soci-

---

[36] See note 14, above.

[37] MBW 3:38 nr. 2390. *Martin Bucers Deutsche Schriften*, 9/1:80–81 n. 9.

[38] The date, according to Scheible, and Bindseil before him, is evident from Cruciger's letter to Friedrich Myconius, 10 March 1540. In that letter Cruciger reports among other things, "Yesterday a writing was composed by Phlipp with common consent on ecclesiastical property. Today, God willing, our opinion will be offered to the League's members" (*Heri compositum est a Philippo communi consensu scriptum de bonis Ecclesiasticis. Hodie deo volente nostrae sententiae offerentur foederatis*). Melanchthon, *Epistolae, iudicia, consilia, testimonia aliorumque*, pp. 147–48 nr. 195.

[39] Haug-Moritz, *Der Schmalkaldische Bund*, p. 536.

[40] Note 14, above.

[41] 12 March 1540, Bucer in a letter from Schmalkalden to his colleagues at Strasbourg, noted "Hic sunt a Saxone Philippus, Pomeranus, Ionas, Crucigerus, ab Hesso tres, ab inferioribus civitatibus duo, unus a duce Henrico Saxone." *Martin Bucers Deutsche Schriften*, 9/1:79 n. 2.

[42] Text and translation may be found in Appendix 1.

ety's divine order; the absence of divine order in pagan society pro-
duces chaos and hell. Second, church property must remain stable.
Where the *oberkeit* ended the malpractice of religion, the parish property stays, for if it didn't, the ruler would have to make new endowments to support pastors. Dominion over it belongs to the church.
Lacking a singular form of church government, however, this claim
says almost nothing. Who exercises this dominion and by what authority? Temporal government, the theologians claim, *oberkeit*, as protector. By saying it this way, they have excluded any temporal ruler's
dominion over church property. Government serves, not rules religion. Third, incomes must remain stable. When an incompetent
preacher or pastor is removed and the office given to a competent
one, the income stays with the office and goes to the replacement,
according to the rule, "the benefice is given on account of the office,"
beneficium datur propter officium, which was "expressed openly in many
places in laws," again, a matter requiring no proof. A benefice is
not like a fief given to a knight, for life. It is a stipend for an office,
not a gift freely given, as some presume. That is, it is not a gift
given on exchange for service and did not establish clientage; it was
entirely separate from the system by which lords controlled lands
and peoples in Germany still, to speak in only the most general
terms about lordship.[43]

Fourth, dominion of church property arises from communal ownership. The property belongs to the community, according to Augustine,
who said as much with regard to the property of Donatist heretics:
it became public property protected by *oberkeit*. The same holds for
the property of convents and monasteries. Princes and cities alike
took control of church property to end improper worship, "For there
can be no doubt that they are responsible for both, to abolish incorrect worship, as the first and second commandments teach, and to
take up the administration as patrons and protectors of common
property, and especially of church properties. Thus no one should
have governing power (*imperia*) other than the temporal ruler." This
subtle distinction describes protection, not any external dominion
over the church.

Fifth, church property is inalienable, yet it cannot simply be left
to enrich the church itself or its personnel. It has to be used, and

---

[43] For the variety of forms, their geographical distinctions, and the literature, see
Scott, *Society and Economy*, pp. 153–97, here 195–6.

this conditions the government's responsibility to preserve it. It is preserved not for its own sake but for the good of the community. Accordingly, governing authority must ensure that the superabundance of church property serves the common good. The first obligation is to support preachers and schools, second to help the poor. After that, it could support a variety of causes: the studies of noble and non-noble youth, clergy pensions, and a poor chest for relief at times of inflation. Finally, any remaining surplus could be used by the *oberkeit* as *patroni* to compensate for religious expenses, insofar as patrons already provide for parishes, schools, studies, and the poor. The theologians called confiscators of parishes and hospitals—those not content with the properties of convents and cloisters—simply reprehensible. They admonished such rulers to use the property according to the rank-order of parishes, schools, and the poor. The entitlements of governing authority must be confined to last place in the list of uses. The theologians call for the appointment of territorial "managers" (*oeconimi*) to give regular account of the properties and their use, borrowing the term from Roman law, that had appeared in the memoranda of Bucer and the anonymous of 1539.[44] But with this stipulation, the League's clergy had agreed that princely entitlements could be granted, if put in the last place of a pecking order and restricted to oversupplies.

Sixth, conflicts between cities and princes should be avoided. Urban churches and monasteries have only one purpose: to serve parish ministry. Yet urban church property is mostly controlled by cathedral churches and chapters, collegiate churches, or other monasteries. Different Protestant cities have different relationships with their cathedrals. At Strasbourg, Augsburg, Constance, Bremen, and Magdeburg, cathedral canons deny the authority of city governments. At Frankfurt, Esslingen, Hamburg, and Braunschweig, canons simply remain independent of the city, and the cities have no supremacy over them. In both cases, city councils are obliged to correct historical mistakes, such as the incorporation of parish churches by collegiate foundations or monasteries or the failures of cathedral chapters to provide pastoral care. When cities control assets and incomes of

---

[44] Note 157 chapter 5.

the cathedral chapter, collegiate churches, or monasteries, they are simply returning the property to local religious uses, for example by providing incomes to evangelical preachers. In the case of cities, oversupplies should go to churches of the neighboring countryside and to poor noble lineages. Presumably, this point also followed the principle that gifts must remain with the community, if we may assume that the theologians saw the community as a series of devolving social spheres, with the urban commune at the center and the parishes and noble lineages of its region spreading to the periphery. The theologians granted that these things should be negotiated with bishops and chapters, but cities also had a right to expel "pagan" pastors and persecutors of true doctrine. They encouraged cities to take control of as much church property as possible, as the cities of Hamburg and Minden had done, ignoring any imperial rights or claim, since the emperor had already failed by protecting incompetent priests. St. Lawrence resisted the ancient Roman Emperor Decius, mid-second century persecutor of Christians, when Decius demanded the church treasury from him. Ambrose told the emperor Theodosius I that although everything may be the emperor's, the church is Christ's. The theologians dismissed an unnamed accuser at the Imperial Chamber Court (Konrad Braun was surely meant) as a poisonous snake.[45] The matter of urban foundations was religious. It was beyond the court's jurisdiction.

The Schmalkald recommendation of 1540 resolved the conflict among the League's theologians. What uncertainty had existed over the tension between communal need versus princely entitlement, semi-public versus semi-private views of church property, was now gone. By adding their names to this document, the urban theologians conceded entitlement as an extension of patronage rights, while the Wittenberg theologians accepted the strict subordination of any such exercise to religious uses. The matter now had to be discussed by the League's estates.

The estates discussed church property on 13 and 14 March. All agreed that reform was expensive. The princes down-played the surplus in question, and the cities noted that the Reformation cost

---

[45] Bucer had described him to the Landgrave as the court's most poisonous speaker in early 1540. Rößner, *Konrad Braun*, p. 62 n. 239.

more than it brought in.[46] Jacob Sturm argued that the property must first be used to fulfill the purpose for which it was given, as the conventions of Schmalkalden 1537 and Arnstadt 1539 determined. But oversupplies were for the common good and defense, at the discretion of government, he insisted. It has been said that Sturm hereby put to rest Bucer's endeavor to limit lay control.[47] But as we have seen, Bucer had been moving in this direction for two years. Sturm was stating Bucer's modified point of view. Nothing in the discussion seems to have departed from the path agreed by the theologians four days before. The estates then agreed to form a committee of learned men and lawyers.

On 16 March 1540, the theologians composed and signed a memorandum against Sebastian Franck and Caspar von Schwenckfeld, who still drew adherents in Protestant lands of south Germany to their radically personalistic faith.[48] Apparently at the same time, a draft of a church property clause for the diet's recess was prepared and soon after revised, probably by the aforementioned committee of learned men and lawyers.[49] The revision appears to have been

---

[46] Haug-Moritz, *Der Schmalkaldische Bund*, pp. 536–7.

[47] "Mit dieser Äuserung, welche die Verwaltung des Kirchenguts dem Ermessen der Obrigkeiten überantwortete, hatte sich Jacob Sturm explizit von der Bucerschen Konzeption verabschiedet." Haug-Moritz, *Der Schmalkaldische Bund*, p. 537.

[48] CR 3:983–86 nr. 1945, MBW 3:41 nr. 2396. *Martin Bucers Deutsche Schriften*, 9/1:80.

[49] Staatsarchiv Marburg Beistand 3 Nr. 538, ff. 59r–60v, *Verordnung der Kirchengueter* (a title given in a note on the fold at the end, f. 60v). The actual final recess of the diet, dated 15 April, did not include the first paragraph of the draft (the final version may be found in Roth, "Kirchengüterfrage," pp. 301–2, printed from the copy received by the city of Augsburg). The title at the beginning (for the italicized passages, see the following note): *Von Kirchen guthern*. An archivist dated this March 16 in the margin. The text: "Nachdem auch uff dem tage zů arnnstedt der kirchen unnd closter guter halbenn wie die christlich und unerweiselich zugebrauchen unnd anngelegt, auch damit solle gehaltenn werdenn, geredt, auch ezliche wege unnd mittel bedacht, unnd furgeschlagen werdenn unnd aber aůs mangell, das nitt alle stennde, zů demselbenn mahll beschlisslich zůreden, beuelch gehabt biß uff diese jizige zusamenn kunfft der stennde, fernner dawonn zuredenn zu ratschlagenn unnd zuschliessenn auffgeschobenn werdenn, jnnhalts des artickels jnn bemeltem arnstettischem abschiedt begriffen.

"So habenn der stennde Bottschafften unnd geschicktenn, solichenn artikell jzo fur die hannd genomen, denn mit vleis bewegenn und berathschlaget, unnd dieweil diese stennde, Gott lobe, zufürderünge der ehre des almachtigenn, unnd zů erhaltůng seins ewigen unnd allein seligmachende worts, dahin sich auch der christliche aÿnůng unnd verstenndnůs thut erstrecken zum hochstenn geneigt, unnd solchs zůthůn, sich schuldig erkennenn, unnd es am tage, das die hohe notturfft erfordert, damit darůff

made 20 March. Three minor changes suggest that disagreement had been reduced to diction, and the revision is virtually identical to the text included in the recess. First, where the original wished to support the ministers who provide for preaching and dissemination of the divine word from church property in "the most stately and best manner," the revision even more modestly said "as necessary and well."[50] Second, where the original listed charitable uses of

---

gewachtet, wie die kirchenn mit gelerthenn geschickten unnd Gots furchtigenn leûthenn bestelt, auch zû erziehung der jûgenndt, so künfftig zû pfar unnd kirchen [f. 59v] dinstenn unnd anndern christlichenn amptenn, gebraucht werdenn sollenn, desgleichen zû notturfft der armenn furder versehûng geschehen moge. Unnd dann den wider wertigenn Jre unnpilliche aûfflage unnd nachrede dieser gûter halbenn, welche sie doch selbst vilfeltig gannz unnbillicher weise, denn rechtenn kirchen brâuchs, entwenndenn unnd verschwenden: abgewandt unnd jdermeniglich sehen, spuren, unnd inn dere thatt vermerckenn moge, das es diesem teil, nit umb das zeitlich, sonnder vill mehr um das ewige, unnd also die recht schaffene christliche religion, davonn aûch das zeitlich gût, unnd sonderlich das jhenige, so bereithenn, zur kirchenn verordenet dienenn soll: zuthun ist.

"Als habenn sie diesenn artikell, die kirchen gûter betreffennd vonn Jrenn vornembstenn geler[ten] der hailigenn schrifft mit hochstem vleis erwegen unnd berathschlagenn lassenn, unnd demselbigen nach aûs christlichem gutenn bedennckenn unnd versachenn jnnhalts des arnstettischenn abschieds, eintreghtiglich bedacht, unnd enndtschlossenn, das erstlich unnd fur allenn dingenn von solchen geistlichen oder kirchenn gûtern, die weill es inn alle wege pillich unnd loblich, das furnemblich die selbenn zu recht geschaffenenn, christlichen mildenn kirchen, unnd gemeinen nutz sachen [f. 60r] gewanndt unnd gebraucht, unnd unnunnuzlich umbracht oder verschwenndertt werdenn, die pfarrer, prediger unnd anndere kirchen diener zuverkundigung unnd ausbreitûng des gotlichen wortts, *zum stattlichstenn unnd bestenn* darûn underhaltenn. Zum anndernn das die schulenn zûr zücht der jûgendt, damit kunfftiger zeit geschikte gelerthe, unnd tûgennliche leûthe, zu christlichenn ampternn erzogenn, nottûrfftiglich darvon bestelt und versehenn.

"Zum drittenn denn armen unûermogennden gebrachlichenn, auch haûsarmenn leûthen, geholfenn dieselbenn zûûnderhalten, hospitall und gemeine oder Gots kestenn, auffgericht werdenn, unnd der armenn jugenndt, edlenn unnd uneldenn, jm lannde unnd stetten nach gelegennheit, hilff zum studio geschehenn unnd denn kirchen dienernn, so schwach unnd alt werdenn, unnd emeritj sindt, unnderhaltung gereicht, auch *vorredt verschafft, das man inn thewrenn zeithen, denn armen unuermûgenden helffen moge,* unnd dergleichen milde christliche gûte verordnûng unnd versehûng bedacht, unnd inns werck bracht werdenn, wie solchs ein jede obrigkeit nach gelegennheit, zubedenncken, zûûerordenen und mit solchen guthern, unnd was doran uber die ausgabe unnd ufwenndung der jztgemeltenn milden werckenn unnd verordnûng [f. 60v] uberig sein also zuhanndlen, zugeparen, unnd umbzûgehenn wissenn wirdet, wie sie das jegenn Got *Kais. Mt.* unnd mennniglichen unpartheischen getrawt zuveranthwortten unnd aine christliche obrigkait schuldig unnd jr unverweislich ist."

[50] I've marked the places of the three changes in italics in the previous note. Staatsarchiv Marburg Bestand 3 Nr. 538, ff. 74r–75v, *Von Kirchengüternn*, dated 20 March according to the same archival hand, f. 60r and underscored in the manuscript: "Notturffliglich und woll."

church property, it included the provision, "that in times of inflation,
the poor un-propertied may be aided," but the revision named widows and orphans in place of the un-propertied poor.[51] The new
wording was taken from the New Testament (James 1.27), which
calls the care of widows and orphans a mark of true religion. Third,
where the original concluded with a statement of the League's unpar-
tisan commitment to God and the imperial majesty, the revision
replaced "imperial majesty" with "all *oberkeit*."[52] The new wording
may reflect the denial of a special imperial relationship to urban
church property in the 11 March theological recommendation. The
diet's actual recess (15 April) replaced *oberkeit* with the more princely
ehrbarkeit, honor (titular, as in "your honors").[53]

At the diet, preparations for a religious colloquy continued, and
the theologians worried that the allure of peace might compromise
religious confession. A day after the theologians signed the recommendation on church property, Bucer, in the presence of the theologians assembled at Schmalkalden, related to Wolfgang Capito by
letter that the whole world should know there can be no agreement
on religion and church property apart from those who agree on
justification by faith, the correct use of the sacraments, and the correct exercise of penitential power.[54] By 25 March, Bucer had completed a brief report of the Protestant faith, requested privately by
Philip of Hesse.[55] Philip may have worried earlier over tensions
between Bucer and Wittenberg, but there was little danger at the
moment. If an anonymous undated document placed among the
Landgrave's materials for the 1540 Schmalkald diet is to be believed,
the estates as a whole considered the 1539 Peace of Frankfurt's article on church property unacceptably restrictive and unobservable,

---

[51] Ibid, marked with a vertical line in the original's margin: "auch do die ver-
storbenn, unnd sich jnn christlichen etlichen unnd gutem wanndel erhaltenn habenn
jre weibe unnd kinder, jnn armuot verlasshen auch bequeme hůlff unnd steuer geth-
ann, jre kinder so darzů geschickt, zů der lehre gehaltenn unnd jre dochter zu
ehrlichenn stannde destobaß aůsgestatt můgenn werdenn."

[52] Ibid, f. 60v: "aller oberkeit."

[53] Roth, "Kirchengüterfrage," p. 302.

[54] 10 March 1540. Olivier Millet, *Correspondance de Wolfgang Capito (1478–1541).*
Analyse et index (Strasbourg: Mission de la Recherche du Ministère des Universités,
1982), p. 258 nr. 725.

[55] *Martin Bucers Deutsche Schriften*, 9/1:81 n. 9 (the editors argue that Scheible con-
fused this private summary with the official Schmalkald answer to Granvelle. Cf.
MBW 3:38 nr. 2390).

but the real question at this point was simply this: what would the emperor concede?[56] The League's purpose was, the anonymous comment on the Peace of Frankfurt said, to provide for the widest, unfettered dissemination of the Word of God.

This was, yet again, a statement of the obligation to reform, and it reflects the voice of Protestant clergy. It was their job, after all, to disseminate the Word of God. If their influence fell short of today's Council of Guardians in the Islamic Republic of Iran, the body of theologians and lawyers who check all Iranian parliamentary decisions for conformity to Islamic principles, they nonetheless intended to keep the matter of faith, as they understood it, on the League's agenda, the faith of the Augsburg Confession to be exact. Property was a distraction to them. The princes were easily wedded to this cause of faith, as we can see in the League's official response to the

---

[56] Staatsarchiv Marburg Bestand 3 Nr. 538, f. 79r–v, a brief, undated piece with the title, *Betreffennde die beschwerlichenn artikell jn frannckfurdischen anstanndt als nemblich die geistlichenn guotter, unnd die einnemüng, jnn die christliche verstenndnus.* The text refers to a clause in the recess of the League's Arnstadt diet that worries whether objectionable clauses of the Truce of Frankfurt will remain negotiable, a concern because the League was violating the Truce by trying to bring in new members, as was the Catholic League of Nürnberg (*Akten der deutschen Reichsreligionsgespräche im 16. Jahrhundert* 1/2:1100 nr. 392). "Nachdem zů arnnstedt bedacht, dieweill Kais. Mt. gemeinenn stennden denn frankfurdischenn anstanndt, nicht zůgeschriebenn noch raufinirt, das mann pillig frei sehe, hinfůro denn selbigenn annstandt jnn seinem clauseln, zuhaltenn oder nicht, das mann auch die begerenndenn, jnn die verstenndnůs woll einnemenn mochte, unnd aber danebenn fur gůt anngesehen, das uff jziger zusammenkunfft, davonn solte geredt werdenn, was hinfarther züthůn, ob solche claůseln des anstandt, wilche die vnnstennden beschwerlich jnn kunfftiger hanndlůng einzureůmenn sein soltenn oder nit. So habenn die stennde nachgehabter vleissiger erregůng unnd unnd [*sic*] errede darůff abemals unnd ferrner jzt alhie, beschlossen das mann der obgedachten zweiter artikell, als der kirchen gůter, und der einnemüng halten, jnn der christliche verstenndnůs, aus oberzelten ursachen nůmehr freistehe, unnd unůerpundenn seien. Vas aber hinfuro jnn kunftigenn furfallenden fridshanndlungenn, zůthůn unnd einzugehen achten sie jziger zeit unnfruchtbar sein, weil unngewis, was jnn kůnfftigen hanndlůngen furfallenn mochte, wie dann aůshieůor gepflogener hanndlungen erfaren, davonn zůredenn und zurathschlagen, unnd sonderlich weil mann nit wissenn kann, was die Kay. Mt. aůf die bscheheůe schikůng, zůr anthwort gebenn wirdet. Zu dem, das aůch vill stennde nicht alhie, unnd es besser noch zur zeit, sich daruff nit zůerrlerenn und zuschliessen, dieweill solche dinge wie woll jnn geheim pleibenn mochten. Sonnder das man solcher der Kay. Mt. anntwort errarttenn solle, dan hette mann sich daraůff, ferner uff den fahll zůunnterredenn unnd zůschliessenn, aber jn allwege bedencken die stennde, wie sich kůnfftig die furfallendenn fridhanndlungen zů wagenn mochten, das es dahin gericht, dan in dem hailigenn euangelio unnd gottlichen wortt, sein laufft und aůsbreitung nicht benomen noch verhundertt, sonnder frej unnd unngejret gelassenn werde."

imperial invitation to a colloquy: the clergy taught them the rich
tone of moral offense. They used it to exclude church property from
the coming negotiations.

The answer to the imperial invitation was given on 11 April 1540,
four days before the diet's recess, under the name of the Landgrave
and the Elector of Saxony. It was sent on behalf of the League to
the emperor's ambassador, the imperial minister Granvelle, and published in pamphlets in German, Latin, and French, the German
under the coats of arms of the Saxon Electoral Prince and the
Landgrave of Hesse. John Calvin, approaching the last year of his
Strasbourg residency, translated a copy for the emperor into French,
the emperor's mother tongue.[57]

They began with the irenic tone one might expect—committed to
peace, aiming to bring peace to the Empire through the honor of
Christ, against religious abuses—and then quickly digressed to a
defensive polemic on church property.[58] We are, they said, accused
before the emperor of chasing after church property or other things,
unconcerned with God's honor and the improvement and salvation
of souls. Granvelle should defend the Protestants before the emperor,
for the public is being affected by these accusations. The League's
opponents fall on these accusations in desperation, Granvelle was
told, because they cannot defeat Protestant arguments. The opponents are the avaricious ones, who seek to preserve church wealth
rather than correct the glaring vices that afflict the church. They
care more for principalities, government, kingdom, and comfort than
godly doctrine. They know well that the League's members were not
after temporal goods. After all, the Landgrave and the Elector say,
"not one of us has removed and taken into his administration a single bishop in Germany. Indeed, they cannot rightly compel us to a
spiritual court. The bishoprics have their revenues, rents, and incomes
still."[59] The opponents, by contrast, take the property of Protestant

[57] *Martin Bucers Deutsche Schriften*, 9/1:80. Johannes Calvin, Ep. 218, CR 38/2:39.
[58] A shortened version was first printed at Granvelle's request. It is reproduced
in Hortleder, *Ursachen*, I.v.9, p. 1124. The longer, original version may be found
in modern German translation in Luther, *Sämmtliche Schriften*, 17:338–53. *Akten der
deutschen Reichsreligionsgespräche* 1/1:81–89 nr. 21 (the Latin version). See also CR
3:989. The pamphlet: Johann Friedrich I, Philipp Landgraf, *Responsio, quam in causa
religionis dedimus ad instructionen, quae allata est Smalcaldiam* (Wittenberg: Georg Rhau,
1540), Flugschriften des späteren 16. Jahrhunderts, Fiche 1007 nr. 1766.
[59] *Sämmtliche Schriften*, 17:340: "Niemand auch von uns hat einem einigen Bischof

churches, the two princes complained. They refuse to pay incomes and rents owed to Protestant churches. While bishops neglected to pay out incomes for pastors and schoolmasters in the cities (Protestant cities are meant), the cities support pastors, preachers, chaplains, schoolmasters, and other ministers from communal property, to their own disadvantage, and the expenses were huge.[60] The Landgrave and Elector added that they use cloister property, incomes, and rents to cover annual expenses, but over the sixteen years since this began (this brings us to the beginning of the Peasants' Revolt in 1524), they have spent more than those properties brought in, and the expenses keep growing. The point is by now obvious: German Catholics, not Protestants, are church robbers.

Why, then, had the administration of cloisters been changed in Protestant places?[61] The two princes answered with a careful statement of Lutheran doctrine and evangelical policy. Since the light of the holy gospel shone out of true worship in Protestant lands, many monks and nuns of their own accord abandon monastic hypocrisy and pretense (*Heuchelei und Gleißnerei*). In order that monks might study or enter another estate and establish a household, they are given a sum of money. Where monks remained, evangelical preachers were installed, who demanded an end to un-Christian worship. The monks or nuns who wanted to remain were supported. The Protestants, out of charity, made monasteries hostels for the poor. Both actions belong to the princely office, to correct false doctrine and religious malpractice (*Mißglauben*) and to protect monastic property, "that such common property would not be completely lost, which the monks already either left or neglected, or be perniciously destroyed. For this is clearly the case, that the princes are guardians of common property that was donated to support pastors, preachers, churches, and school ministers, and poor people."[62] The Landgrave and Elector

---

in Deutschland an seiner Obrigkeit entzogen und genommen. Ja, sie können auch den geistlichen Gerichtszwang nicht recht führen. Die bischöflichen Stifte haben ihre Rente, Zinse und Einkommen noch."

[60] Ibid., pp. 340–41.

[61] Ibid., p. 342.

[62] Ibid., p. 342: ". . . und also daß solche gemeine Güter nicht gar umkommen, welche bereits die Mönche entweder verließen oder verachteten, oder übel umbrachten. Denn das ist je am Tag, daß die Fürsten sind Bewahrer gemeiner Güter, die zu Unterhaltung Pfarrer, Prediger, Kirchen und Schuldiener und armer Leute gestiftet sind."

constructed their argument around the set of religious priorities advocated by the League's theologians. Moreover, they continued, the cloisters also failed to administer themselves adequately, and so Protestants appointed administrators (*Verwalter*) and overseers (*Vorsteher*) to tend monastic households, agriculture, and other offices. With this statement, the two princes put the League's actions in the context of reforming ancestors. Princes and cities used such appointments to reform monasteries for over a century.[63]

The changed administration was entirely protective, the Landgrave and Elector concluded.[64] Who can deny that it was for the good? Protestants, they explained, used the incomes first to support pastors in the neighborhood, then other churches, and hospitals and schools. To provide the support, the Protestants rectified the uneven distribution of monastic revenues, rents, and incomes. Surplus fell into the prince's hand, but in many lands it was hardly anything at all. The remainder went to support poor priests and provide stipends for poor students. If a council or other assembly discusses the unity of the church, the League would insist that such property be used to support churches, schools, and other public uses. "For church property is for the support of preaching offices and pastorates, schools and churches and public necessity," according to divine law, the ancient councils, and the canons.[65] Consider the neglect of urban parishes by bishops and cathedral chapters, who fail to provide for them, and their neglect of education. God established *Polizei und Weltregiment*, temporal government, for only one reason, to preserve religion, faith, doctrine, and scripture. Since the League committed itself to use church property only for such Christian purpose, it expects the same of the other side.[66]

If these actions were correct, the Imperial Chamber Court was unjust.[67] To oppose the League on church property, as the Elector

---

[63] Ocker, "Religious Reform and Social Cohesion," pp. 69–94 and the literature noted there.

[64] *Sämtliche Schriften*, 17:343.

[65] Ibid., "Denn der Kirchen Güter gehören zu Unterhaltung des Predigt- und Pfarramts, der Schulen und Kirchen und gemeinen Nutzens Nothdurft."

[66] Ibid., pp. 343–44: "Wir erbieten uns auch, als dann einen Vorstand zu machen, daß die geistlichen Güter zu solchen christlichen Gebrauch und milden Sachen gebraucht sollen werden, wie oben bemeldt, wo unsere Widersacher auch wiederum einen Vorstand machen."

[67] Ibid., pp. 344–45.

and the Landgrave have outlined it, is to oppose religious reform. Attempts to use the court to force restitution would amount to an attempted confiscation of evangelical churches. This contradicts the Imperial Chamber Court's purpose as an instrument of imperial peace: it would encourage war by bleeding evangelical churches, at a time when many parishes already lacked pastors and many monasteries were already impoverished: for a well-run church, the Elector and the Landgrave assumed, made for a well-ordered society. The degradation of churches would cause a rapid reversion to social wilderness: the common man would stray into a pagan, wild, raw life; the next generation of rulers would inherit a barbaric people. They called on Granvelle to bring the League's complaint against the superior court to the emperor.

The rest of the document rehearses doctrinal disagreements: the eucharist, celibacy, penance, etc., the proper menu of any future colloquy, according to the theologians and the League's estates. In their answer to the emperor, the two princes gave pride of place to church property. They must have shocked Catholic theologians, for they simply returned the accusation of church robbery. Beware of crafty Lutherans, Pope Paul III and his closest advisors would soon warn their legate to the religious colloquy of 1541.[68] To dismis Lutherans as crafty overlooked the actual merit of their case, but it was good advice. The members of the League believed in themselves; they believed that their confiscations were religious and just. In fact, they had to assume the truth of their premises and ignore all reasonable objections. For Protestant ambitions had progressed steadily over the previous decade. They had tried to freeze ecclesiastical proceedings against Lutheran heresy by appeal to a general council. Then they denied the competence of lay courts, in particular the Imperial Chamber Court, to treat their reorganizations of church property, since they were purely a religious matter. Now they insisted all the more on their religious intentions. Without those intentions, they had no case.

In other words, the League's purpose on 11 April 1540 was to declare the non-negotiable status of church property in the forthcoming colloquies, by emphasizing the unwillingness of the Protestant

---

[68] Elisabeth Gleason, *Gasparo Contarini. Venice, Rome, and Reform* (Berkeley: University of California Press, 1993), p. 206, quoting the papal instruction to Gasparo Contarini for the Regensburg Colloquy.

estates to compromise their religious motives. A case for confiscation
argued from princely entitlements could have undermined this virtuous self-presentation. The theologians, although preoccupied with
the protection of pastors' incomes and the survival of schools and
charities, had, in fact, served the League well.

The recess of the diet of Schmalkalden was published four days
later, on 15 April 1540.[69] Pomerania, Hesse, and Württemberg agreed
with the chancellor of electoral Saxony, who opened the deliberations, that the matter of church property needed resolution, and they
defended their ecclesiastical confiscations.[70] Jacob Sturm noted that
after fulfilling the purposes for which donations were made, the oversupplies should serve the common good, including defense. The other
cities agreed with Strasbourg, and only Marburg claimed that the use
of oversupplies should still be treated in greater detail. Like the
answer to the emperor's invitation, the final document avoided the
matter of princely entitlements (or private property rights) and stuck
to religion, as the theologians had taught them to do. The estates
said, there was great need to appoint learned and God-fearing, appropriate men, to churches, a great need to educate youth, to tend to
the poor, and to promote correct church practices. They had taken
advice from those learned in holy scripture. The recess reported the
decision that church property was to be used for correctly organized,
that is evangelical churches, and for common use. Rather than waste
church property, it should be used for parishes, schools, and poor
relief, or as the recess said: for pastors, preachers, and ministers, that
they may preach and spread the divine Word; to prepare youth for
church offices; to help the poor.[71] To that end, members of the

---

[69] Haug-Moritz, *Der Schmalkaldische Bund*, p. 537. For much of the text of the
recess (with subject descriptions of the parts left out) edited from the copy in Ulm,
Akten der deutschen Reichsreligionsgespräche 2:1102–12 nr. 393. Roth, "Kirchengüterfrage,"
pp. 301–2 reproduces the article on church property from the copy in Augsburg.
Gottfried Seebaß, following Robert Stupperich, observed that Pomerania and
Wittenberg did not subscribe, suggesting division in the League on the article.
Seebaß, "Verwendung der Kirchengüter," p. 173. Robert Stupperich, "Bucer und
die Kirchengüter," *Martin Bucer and Sixteenth Century Europe. Actes du colloque de Strasbourg
(28–31 août 1991)*, ed. Christian Krieger, March Lienhard, 2 vols. (Leiden: E.J.
Brill, 1993), 1:166–9. This appears to be incorrect. *Akten der deutschen Reichsreligionsgespräche*
1/2:1111 nr. 393.
[70] For this and the following, Haug-Moritz, *Der Schmalkaldische Bund*, p. 537.
[71] Roth, "Kirchengüterfrage," pp. 301–2. *Akten der deutschen Reichsreligionsgespräche*
2:1105–6 nr. 393.

League agreed to establish hospitals and common chests, offer aid to poor students, noble and otherwise, from cities and the country-side, and offer pensions to retired church ministers and to the fam-ilies of deceased ministers. Oversupplies, the recess concluded, should be used in a way that was accountable to government and to God.

Again, the League's princes described their actions as religiously as they could. Even Ulrich of Württemberg, who tried to sell what-ever church ornaments remained in his realm that very year, expected his counselors at the religious colloquy soon to take place at Hagenau (June 1540) to appeal directly to the diet's recess.[72] The League again complained about the Imperial Chamber Court, which recently revived cases against Minden, Strasbourg, and others, as the Schmalkald recess of 1540 observed.[73] The princes could expect more litigation, as places like Halberstadt, Magdeburg, and the territory of Ansbach-Kulmbach, places less successfully converted over the past decade (not to mention the newly converted territories), prepared to take greater control of city churches in the early 1540's. But there was, too, the allure of a permanent peace.

---

[72] Deetjen, *Studien zur Württembergischen Kirchenordnung*, pp. 144–5. *Akten der deutschen Reichsreligionsgespräche* 1/2:767–9 nr. 285 (here p. 768), 1/2:775–6 nr. 288A, 1/2:776–8 nr. 289.

[73] *Akten der deutschen Reichsreligionsgespräche* 1/2:1109 393.

CHAPTER SEVEN

THE COLLOQUIES, THE WAR, AND THE PEACE

The Schmalkald diet of March/April 1540 ended the League's internal debate over the extent, manner, and rationales for the temporal uses of church property. Even when charity and social welfare covered obvious princely ambition, it had apparent public benefits. It aided troubled noble lineages and helped pay for urban battlements, as well as pastors' incomes, student bursaries, and relief to the worthy poor. Urban governments and princes had the same obligations to promote true worship and end abuse, to ensure that church property served God and the godly intentions of donors, not the avarice of ecclesiastical careerists (that is how they framed the matter). The estates must have left Schmalkalden with a renewed sense of outrage at the Imperial Chamber Court. Suspension of cases before the court was the precondition of any true peace, the city of Ulm now said.[1] No one in the League could disagree: no acceptance of confiscations, no peace. Or as Duke Ulrich of Württemberg said to his embassy to the Hagenau colloquy in June, he wished to negotiate a peace in the absence of a resolution to the religious controversy.[2] The Schmalkald diet of that spring had also determined to focus Protestant-Catholic dialogue on the Augsburg Confession and on the Apology Melanchthon wrote for it at the Diet of Augsburg in 1530 (he revised it for publication in May 1531).[3] In effect, they had said yet again, the controversy was about religion, not property.

This feat of rhetorical engineering matched the religious sensibilities of rulers, the hopes of their clergy, and the need of the hour. It also won a predictable Catholic response. Before the first colloquy at Hagenau (June 1540), the bishop of Vienna, Johannes Fabri, in his notes on how to handle Protestants, wondered at their pre-

---

[1] According to the draft of a *Gutachten* to the Landgrave. *Akten der deutschen Reichsreligionsgespräche* 1/2:1011–12 nr. 364. Philip of Hesse kept the matter alive in preparations for the Worms colloquy. Consider ibid., 2/2:723–4 nr. 227.

[2] Sieglerschmidt, *Territorialstaat*, p. 154 with n. 56a.

[3] Brecht, *Martin Luther*, 2:451. Johann Friedrich was particularly concerned that Protestant delegates make a common defense of the Confession and Apology. *Akten der deutschen Reichsreligionsgespräche* 2/2:741, 800, 801, 838 nr. 236, 261, 280.

sumption. How many male and female monasteries, bishoprics, and other benefices had been established of old by devout Christians, often by Roman emperors, kings, and princes? The emperor is their protector. The expulsion of monks and nuns, the expropriation and sale of monastic property and church treasures, all fall to imperial justice.[4] To Fabri, restitution suits were valid and important. Similarly, the dukes of Bavaria told their counselors at Hagenau to demand restitution, along with the restoration of the mass and an end to all abusive sermons, and to resist Protestant attempts to receive incomes from outlying properties, in Catholic lands, of monstaries under Protestant control.[5] During the colloquy of Hagenau itself, Friedrich Nausea, deputy bishop in Vienna, responded to the Augsburg Confession's article on monasteries by insisting that the monastic profession was irrevocable and government was required to protect the profession and the properties that support it.[6] When Johannes Cochlaeus composed a memorandum on the twenty-eight articles of the Augsburg Confession for King Ferdinand, presented to him during the Hagenau colloquy on 17 June 1540, he was alarmed by the degree of readiness in imperial circles to allow the League's evasive maneuver.[7] Article 27, on monastic vows, was totally wrong, he said, according to scripture and patristic literature. He denied the Protestant claim that monks and nuns should be free to remain in their cloisters until a future council or leave as they wish, even if Protestants promised to tolerate monastic rites and dress and to protect monasteries from violence and injustice. "How they hold to all this stands before everyone's eyes."[8] "They chase after the temporal properties, rather than inquire after the faith or piety of the same people [monks and nuns]."[9] Visitations were how Catholic governments began monastic reforms. To Cochlaeus, Protestant visitations were only the pretense to secularize properties. "We can't be so . . . soft-headed!," he insisted.[10]

---

[4] *Akten der deutschen Reichsreligionsgespräche* 1/2:1227 nr. 409.

[5] Ibid., 1/2:583 nr. 222

[6] Ibid., 1/2:1159–77 nr. 402, here pp. 1174–5.

[7] Martin Luther, *Sämmtliche Werke*, 17:372–89, here 386–7. *Akten der deutschen Reichsreligionsgespräche* 1/2:1143–56 nr. 400.

[8] Luther, *Sämmtliche Werke*, loc. cit., "Wie sie aber das alles indessen gehalten, liegt jedermann vor Augen."

[9] Ibid., "Daher ich besorge, daß sie mehr nach den zeitlichen Gütern trachten, als nach dem Glauben oder Andacht derselben Personen fragen."

[10] "Wir aber können nicht so überhinfahren und leichtsinnigen Gemüths sein." Martin Luther, *Sämmtliche Werke*, 17:372–89, here 386–7. *Akten der deutschen Reichsreligionsgespräche* 1/2:1143–56 nr. 400.

"If they [the Protestants] were not so blinded and possessed by stinginess and godless mammon," the matter might have been negotiable.[11]

At Hagenau and Worms (November 1540), to which the Hagenau colloquy was moved, Catholic theologians struck this discordant note. Although Gasparo Contarini came at the emperor's request and was appointed papal legate to the colloquy in May 1540, he was not sent to Germany until the next January. Giovanni Marone, papal nuncio to King Ferdinand, who represented the papacy at Hagenau and Worms and who favored Contarini's conciliatory approach to the Protestants but not, at first, religious colloquies, worried that all of Germany was about to be lost.[12] To keep Germany, Contarini, with Ferdinand and Charles V, were willing to concede Protestant confiscations. The emperor omitted the property problem in his invitation to Johann Friedrich and Philip of Hesse to the first religious colloquy of 1540. The emperor struck instead a strong chord of paternal reconciliation.[13] In response, yet again, the League reasserted the legitimacy of their confiscations, and they included a copy of the 11 April 1540 response to the imperial proposal for a religious colloquy.[14] Held did not rebut them. Pope Paul III provides further evidence of the emperor's deliberate omission of church property. The pope worried that Protestants took advantage of the emperor's desperation to build an anti-Turkish army with German troops.[15] And there was no question, in the pope's mind, of the justice of restitution cases brought to the Imperial Chamber Court. The ecclesiastical electors seemed to agree.[16]

Philip of Hesse answered this Catholic reaction with a relatively gregarious proposal. He explained to his counselors that in each territory the properties could be put in escrow for the period of negotiations at Hagenau, and the princes of each land could assume support of the monks who had left them.[17] The proposal must have been

---

[11] Martin Luther, *Sämmtliche Werke*, 17:387: "Wenn sie nun der Geiz und gottlose Mammon nicht ganz verblendet und besessen hat, so könnte man auch in diesem Stück wegen leidlicher Mittel und Wege handeln und sich vergleichen."

[12] Gleason, *Gasparo Contarini*, p. 203.

[13] Luther, *Sämmtliche Schriften* 17:355–57 nr. 1301. *Akten der deutschen Reichsreligionsgespräche* 1/1:25–28 nr. 5. The colloquy was planned first for Frankfurt, then Speyer, and took place at Hagenau.

[14] Luther, *Sämmtliche Schriften*, 17:360 nr. 1302. *Akten der deutschen Reichsreligionsgespräche* 1/1:65–70 nr. 18, here p. 68.

[15] For this and the following, Luther, *Sämmtliche Schriften*, 17:364–72.

[16] Consider the report of Hessian counselors from Hagenau, *Akten der deutschen Reichsreligionsgespräche* 1/2:684 nr. 255.

[17] Ibid., 1/2:686–88 nr. 256.

discussed at Hagenau because Johannes Eck included a version of it in a list of points of agreement.[18] According to his notes, cloisters that had not been closed would be left alone, and monks who had abandoned them would be returned, while lay patrons and advocates would preserve the cloisters that were not committed to either party ("unattached," *ledig*). Rulers would provide for the abandoned cloisters, preaching offices, parishes, and schools, and then whatever was left-over could be "put aside" (*beigelegt*) until a future council. This plan could go nowhere. It was inconsistent with the League's current policy, to exclude church property from negotiation; moreover, there was really no Catholic church authority with whom to negotiate. When Contarini was finally sent to Germany as papal legate, he came with the papal empowerment to conclude nothing.[19]

The key to the confiscator's case was, as strange as it may seem, integrity, a point now emphasized by Philip of Hesse. Philip, whose bigamy recently had shown him far too sincere about his most intimate affections, approached the colloquy at Worms insisting on his religious motives for confiscation. In his *Instruktion* for the religious colloquy at Worms in 1540, he reminded his delegates, among other things, that he forced no one from cloisters but allowed those who wished to remain, and those who wanted to leave to take wives or husbands and work for a living. He established two hospitals for the poor from the properties, two more for the nobility, used others for the university, and salaried pastors with the rest. He said calmly, "It is our view that one should let ecclesiastical property go to things for which they were given, like to schools, hospitals, stipends, pastoral salaries, support of the poor, etc, for long ago it was the intention of donors to offer their gifts to the honor of God."[20] Philip could only approve Bucer's movement toward a position that accepted princely entitlements and ecclesiastical princes (he likely had something to do with the development of Bucer's opinion). In a letter to his chancellor Johann Feige of 6 December 1540, he summarized Bucer's position

---

[18] Ibid., 1/2:1140–43 nr. 399, here p. 1142.
[19] Gleason, *Contarini*, pp. 205–6.
[20] Schilling, *Klöster und Mönche*, p. 225. *Akten der deutschen Reichsreligionsgespräche*, 2/2:861–62 nr. 286; *Urkundliche Quellen zur hessischen Reformationsgeschichte*, 2:345. "Es ist unser mainung, das man billich die gaistlichen guter zu den dingen, darzu sie geben, solt kommen lassen, als zu schulen, spitaln, stipendien, pfarr zu versehen und armen zu erhalten etc., dann einmal ist der stifter mainung gewesen, ire gaben zu gots ehr zu wenden."

in this striking way: as long as ecclesiastical property provides for parishes and church ministry, the rest can remain "in the hands of the bishops, the lords, or whatever one should call them" (*in Handen der Bischove, Herren, oder wi man di nennen wolte*).[21] The Landgrave thought Granvelle might be impressed.

Ulrich of Württemberg also emphasized his integrity. In the instruction to his delegates to the Worms colloquy, he relied on the position annunciated by the Schmalkald recess of that spring. He took it as a statement of princely service to the church. At Hagenau, he noted, it was decided that the priority would be the Augsburg Confession and Melanchthon's Apology, but if the Confession should get tabled for a discussion of church property, he wanted his delegates to insist on his obligation as a Christian ruler. He had to guarantee that churches perform correct worship, which he considered the purpose of church property, namely to provide for pastors, ministers, preachers, schools, and poor relief; temporal authority managed and distributed (*usstaln*) the property.[22] He expected his counselors to correct accusations that he despoiled churches. They should explain that the property belongs to the church of a place. He merely restored it to its correct us. Prebends withheld (by bishops and chapters) from (evangelical) preachers and pastors of a place had to be restored. Restitution and sequestration raised the same questions, he suggested by using the nouns interchangeably (*restitution oder sequestration*, he says repeatedly). In short, he simply asserted the points agreed at the Schmalkald diet that spring.

Regensburg

Granvelle arrived late to the colloquy at Worms, before watchful eyes (a delegate from Protestant Bremen counted out his train, sixty horse and twelve mule strong).[23] Once settled, the colloquy quickly bogged down in negotiations over presidency and procedure, in disagreements about the precedence of the general council called by

---

[21] Roth, "Kirchengüterfrage," p. 312, quoted from Lenz, *Briefwechsel Landgraf Philipp's des Grossmüthigen von Hessen mit Bucer*, 1:281, of Granvelle: "es solte bei im nitt ein wenig thuen."

[22] *Akten der deutschen Reichsreligionsgespräche* 2/2:976–78 nr. 333.

[23] According to Daniel von Büren's account, emissary of the city of Bremen. *Akten der deutschen Reichsreligionsgespräche* 2/2:1083 nr. 373.

Paul III, which Protestants now disputed, and in disagreements over the agenda. All of this was accompanied by speeches on the unity of the church and the dangers of superstition and religious abuses. The colloquy culminated in a four-day dialogue between Melanchthon and Johannes Eck (14–18 January 1541). It produced a formula on the doctrine of original sin.[24] The colloquy never reached the topic of church property.

After the conclusion of the colloquy at Worms, Bucer, his associate in Strasbourg Wolfgang Capito, Granvelle, and the imperial secretary Gerhard Veltwyk produced articles to serve as the basis of the next dialogue.[25] The articles were circulated to the Landgrave (he had it translated into German) and to Joachim the Elector of Brandenburg, and from the latter an anonymous copy went to Martin Luther and Melanchthon in Wittenberg. Bucer was anxious that Luther not identify him with the articles, so convinced was he of Luther's animosity.[26] Luther rejected the articles nonetheless, and he, like a number of old-guard evangelicals, denounced the entire effort to achieve confessional unity.[27] Gasparo Contarini arrived in March as papal legate to the next dialogue, to take place during the Imperial Diet at Regensburg in spring and early summer. He was an adherent of the Italian "evangelism." He was also an experienced Venetian ambassador, a bishop, and a cardinal renowned for his promotion of reform at the papal court in recent years. His presence showed the extent to which Pope Paul III would back the emperor's plans to achieve a religious

---

[24] Documents relevant to this colloquy are conveniently gathered in *Akten der deutschen Reichsreligionsgespräche* 2/1:212–261 and Martin Luther, *Sämmtliche Schriften* 17:389–557.

[25] For the composition of the book, Lenz, *Briefwechsel*, 3:33–38. The document in its original form, before the Regensburg revisions (the original form is known as the *Wormser Buch*) may be found, in Latin and German, in the *Akten der deutschen Reichsreligionsgespräche* 2/1:574–701. The best edition of the Regensburg Book may be found in *Acta Reformationis Catholicae Ecclesiam Germaniae Concernentia*, 6 vols. (Regensburg: Friedrich Pustet, 1959–74), 6:21–88, the apparatus to which marks the original articles and compares the four versions published subsequent to the colloquy by Bucer, Eck, Melanchthon, and the Cologne theologian Johann Gropper. Another edition may be found in Martin Luther, *Sämmtliche Schriften* 17:556–805, here 587–666 nr. 1369. See also Fuchs, *Konfession und Gespräch*, pp. 423–29.

[26] Fuchs, *Konfession und Gespräch*, p. 430.

[27] WABr 9:333–4 nr. 3578. Fuchs, *Konfession und Gespräch*, pp. 430–31. Others opposed to dialogue included Nürnberg's Wenzeslaus Linck and Andreas Osiander. Although present and sceptical at the colloquy of Worms, Nürnberg's city council replaced Linck and Osiander with the more moderate Veit Dietrich for the Regensburg Colloquy. Lorz, *Das reformatorische Wirken Dr. Wenzeslaus Lincks*, p. 121.

peace. That is, the pope would do it in appearance only. The emperor
made his readiness to accommodate the League unmistakable before
the Diet began, when he suspended cases against its members before
the Imperial Chamber Court.[28] By contrast, Pope Paul III had explicitly instructed Contarini that he went with no plenipotentiary powers.[29]

The basis of negotiation at Regensburg was a revised version of
the articles produced after the conclusion of the colloquy of Worms.
Contarini made some twenty changes to the articles just days before
the beginning of the Regensburg discussions. At the Diet, after the
colloquy's conclusion, imperial scribes copied the document, and four
distinct versions were subsequently published.[30] It came to be known
as the Regensburg Book. The previous dialogues at Augsburg (1530),
Leipzig (1539), and Worms (1540) had focused on the Augsburg
Confession, and we have seen how the League favored that approach.
Bucer and Melanchthon, the League's preeminent theologians at
Regensburg, now quietly took another course. The Regensburg Book
represented a new approach to bi-confessional dialogue, in that it
incorporated agreements reached in preliminary discussions, namely
those that took place just after the Worms colloquy had ended. As
Contarini revised the articles, the Protestant estates and their theologians
reviewed their own ground rules and doctrinal articles, and the theologians insisted that they would not be sidelined by the princes.

The religious colloquy took place between 28 April and 22 May
1541. The Catholics were represented by Johannes Gropper, Julius
Pflug, and Johannes Eck; the Protestants by Melanchthon, Bucer,
and Johannes Pistorius. Melanchthon and Eck dominated the proceedings. Contarini was not a direct participant. He gave directions
to the Catholic delegation and later enthusiastically endorsed the colloquy's most remarkable achievement, its agreed statement on the
doctrine of justification.[31] But the colloquy was a frustrating affair.
Melanchthon and Eck, for all their differences, were equally skeptical,
disappointing those, like Bucer and the Protestant princes, eager to
pursue accommodation with the Empire. By the end of the colloquy,
Contarini also cooled to an imperially endorsed settlement. Accordingly,
the colloquy ended with more articles disagreed than agreed.

---

[28] Brady, *Protestant Politics*, p. 223.
[29] Gleason, *Gasparo Contarini*, pp. 201–24.
[30] Lenz, *Briefwechsel*, 3:33–38 for this and the following and note 25, above.
[31] Gleason, *Gasparo Contarini*, pp. 201–56 for this and the following. See also
Fuchs, *Konfession und Gespräch*, pp. 429–56.

The emperor conveyed the Regensburg Book to the estates of the Diet with the recommendation that its religion be tolerated in the Empire in the interim, that is, before a final resolution to the religious controversy.[32] The estates of both confessions rejected it. Building off the formula of Worms, the discussions produced consensus around doctrines of original sin, human will, and justification. Contarini strongly supported the colloquy's article on "inherent" and "imputed" justification, and the doctrine had made its impression on Protestant theologians, as well.[33] In Rome, these accomplishments raised suspicions about Contarini's orthodoxy. The colloquy's greatest theological accomplishment, the doctrine of double justification, had no impact on Catholic theologians, nor could it supplant the Augsburg Confession's article on justification among the Protestants.

We could have expected more. The 1537 report of Contarini's reform commission to Pope Paul III, *A Resolution on Fixing the Church* (*Concilium de emendanda ecclesiae*), had lamented a depressing list of corruptions: bad priests, the benefice trade, the accumulation of bishoprics by cardinals, absentee cardinals and bishops, ineffective ecclesiastical courts, indiscipline in religious orders, the superstitious preaching of pardoners, mendicant purveyors of cheap absolution, and the tolerance of celebrity prostitutes by bishops in Italian cities.[34] These sentiments spread far beyond the circles of elite, humanistically educated churchmen in Rome. They were soon to be attributed to Bartholomaeus Latomus, an established critic of Luther's doctrines, by Martin Bucer.[35] They were shared by the Cologne theologian

---

[32] Fuchs, *Konfession und Gespräch*, p. 451 for this and the following.

[33] For example, John Calvin, *Institutes of the Christian Religion* III.xi.1, III.xvii.4–5, in passages that appear for the first time in the 1539 edition. *Opera selecta*, edited by Peter Barth, Wilhelm Niesel, 5 vols. (Munich: C. Kaiser, 1926–62), 3:182; translated and edited by Ford Lewis Battles and John T. McNeill, 2 vols. (Philadelphia: Westminster, 1960), 1:725–6, 806–7.

[34] Gleason, *Gasparo Contarini*, pp. 129–76. *Concilium Tridentinum*, 13 vols. (Freiburg im Breisgau: Herder, 1901–38), 12:134–45. Elizabeth Gleason, ed. *Reform Thought in Sixteenth-Century Italy* (Chico: Scholars Press, 1981), pp. 85–100, and John C. Olin, *Catholic Reform from Cardinal Ximenes to the Council of Trent, 1495–1563* (New York: Fordham, 1990), pp. 65–79 for English translations.

[35] Latomus, in reply to Bucer, admitted that he has often decried the indiscipline, moral corruption, doctrinal neglect, inept preaching, competition for benefices and church offices in the church, which in his view precipitated the ignorance of the Gospel, rejection of discipline, impiety, contempt for authority, and crimes of the Protestants. The exchange took place in 1543. Bucer hoped to move Latomus from making allegations of church robbery. William Stanon Barron, "The Controversy between Martin Bucer and Bartholomew Latomus," (Ph.D. Dissertation, The Catholic University of America, 1966), pp. 61, 67–8, 77.

Johannes Gropper and by Julius Pflug, for example, both of whom
had to contend with an encroaching Protestantism, Gropper because
of his archbishop's flirtation with Protestant reform and the League,
Pflug because of Saxon intentions for the see of Naumburg. Pflug
had long served as an advisor to Duke Georg.[36] He took refuge in
Mainz after the introduction of the Reformation in Albertine Saxony,
but in early 1541 he had just been named the bishop of Naumburg.
It was Pflug's election that Johann Friedrich contested, when he
installed the evangelical Nikolaus Amsdorf in his place in 1542. To
Bucer's overtures to Latomus during the attempt to reform the archbishopric of Cologne, Latomus returned charges of church robbery
and the complaint that Protestants weakened the church at lay hands.[37]
Neither Latomus, Gropper, nor Pflug could avoid such exchanges
with Protestants in the next decade, as they hoped to draw Lutherans
into a reformed Catholic church.

Gropper's *Handbook of Christian Instruction* (*Enchiridion christianae insti-*
tutionis) served as a guide to Catholic spiritual renewal. It had been
published as an addendum to canons of the provincial church council
of Cologne in 1538, and the archbishop of Mainz commended it to
his counselors at the first religious colloquy of 1540. "The reformation
of our friend the archbishop of Cologne," he called it.[38] Then and after
the Diet, Gropper, with like-minded churchmen, promoted monastic
renewal. Prayer and discipline, not financial security, were the substance
of their reforms. It was the position they would later take at the
inconsequential religious colloquy at the Imperial Diet of Regensburg
in 1546.[39] By contrast, Protestants had spent the last twenty years
ridiculing monastic discipline. The first Regensburg Colloquy (1541)
could have rescued a religious peace by fanning the embers of common discontents. That, however, is precisely what did not happen.

After the colloquy, the Imperial Diet continued for two more
months. There, Protestants presented a proposal on the correction

---

[36] May, *Die deutschen Bischöfe*, pp. 224–9. Heribert Smolinsky, "Julius Pflug
(1499–1564)," *Katholische Theologen der Reformationszeit* 6:13–32.

[37] Stanton, "Controversy," pp. 90–2.

[38] *Akten der deutschen Reichsreligionsgespräche* 1/2:817 nr. 305.

[39] Consider the *Gutachten* Gropper produced for Charles V at the Second Regensburg
Colloquy in 1546, Julius Pflug's draft of reform proposals, and Pflug and Helding's
draft of an agreement. *Acta Reformationis Catholicae* 6:156–255 nr. 13–15, esp. pp.
168–9, 239–40, 253–54. For the more strictly anti-Protestant adaptation of Pflug
by the imperial court preacher Pedro de Malvenda in discussions of a religious
peace after the Schmalkald War, see Rabe, *Reichsbund und Interim*, pp. 267–9.

of abuses and the improvement of lay and ecclesiastical estates. It included two memoranda, one anonymous and another under Melanchthon's name. Both embedded the case for Protestant confiscations within appeals for reform.[40] Given the failure of the colloquy, all the Protestants could do is assert the purity of their intentions and build sympathy for their actions. This was the burden of the two theological memoranda. Let us consider each in turn.

The anonymous memorandum emphasized the historical regression in the church from charitable giving to greed, elaborating an idea that appeared in the 1537 Schmalkald article on monasticism, the 1538 recommendations by Musculus/Wolfahrt and Bucer, and the 1539 Leipzig colloquy. Its presuppositions were canonical and uncontroversial: that no one of the Christian community should be left in need, that the emperor and princes endowed the church to support ministers and the poor, that the property grew to a super-abundance, that its correct uses were determined by canon law,[41] and that surplus belongs to the poor. Any other use is sacrilege, the memorandum alleged. Antiquity commends distribution of church resources by deacons, subdeacons, and *Oeconomen*, administrators. Cloisters originally cared for the poor, especially the elderly, widows, and the sick; and *collegia*, collegiate churches, were formed for those who served. But these roles were degraded over time. Canonries and hospitals of the Holy Spirit eventually appeared. Abuses multiplied, for the part of church property owed to the poor and students preparing for church ministry was withheld from them, just as the property of hospitals and collegiate foundations, originally donated for the same purposes, was divided into benefices and used to support the least necessary ministries of the church, like singing the divine office and reading the mass. To hinder priests and deacons who would abandon such unnecessary functions is to hinder the distribution of alms, church discipline, and the care of souls. The need

---

[40] Luther, *Sämmtliche Schriften*, 17:707–30 nr. 1384, esp. pp. 714–16 and 728–30. They were originally published in Martin Bucer's version of the acts of the Regensburg colloquy, from which Hortleder took them up. Another German version of the first piece may be found in CR 4:529. The second piece, by Melanchthon, is also published in a slightly different version in CR 4:541, where it is dated 17 or 18 July.

[41] It should be, the memorandum said, divided into four parts, one for the bishop to shelter pilgrims and the needy, another for the clergy under the bishop to serve the churches, a third to maintain church buildings and the instruments of religion, and a fourth to provide for the poor and needy, including foreigners.

to restore property to its correct use was urgent: there are too few educated clergy, and most are "good for nothing" (*die zu keinem Dienst in der Welt weniger taugen*). How bizarre it seemed to the anonymous that those who try to restore property to its proper use should be accused of sacrilege and *Kirchenraub*, church robbery. The property must support pastorates and schools.[42]

The second memorandum, which bears Melanchthon's name, made a different appeal to the Imperial Diet. He pleaded that monasteries be used to fund schools, ornaments of the state, seeds of the Christian church: "in short, prestigious schools are the font of all virtuous character in human life."[43] When they fall, blindness follows, in religion, and in the arts, and people are reduced to animals. Wise rulers always support learning. He then traced the decline of learning to the success of Christianity in the Roman Empire. He said, in ancient Israel the temple functioned as a kind of university for the education of prophets, and in the early church, schools and *collegia* were established to raise youth in divine doctrine, from which discipline and virtue follow. But as the convents got rich and bishops were burdened with temporal government, schools and studies declined, when alien peoples from Asia invaded Greece and Italy (the Germanic tribes). Since then, Melanchthon alleged, many errors and superstitions arose. Monastic theology came along, mixed with philosophy and dissembling, *Heuchelei*, and so corruption progressed to the present day. Rulers had to act, Melanchthon said, to restore Christian doctrine in schools and universities. A thousand years ago as parishes multiplied it became necessary to support students who would later take parishes. He, too, accused the Protestants' enemies of failure to observe the ancient order. He defended government action to educate future pastors as the preservation of the Word of God. He called for the improvement of existing universities in doctrine and morals, which included a stipulation that all students be required to study some theology, and the curriculum be cleared of all but useful knowledge. He claimed that the Reformation could not be accomplished without the support of *Obrigkeit* and a public regimen of discipline and penalties. And he defended the use of Church endowments for the appointment of ministers, courts, and schools. He considered these three uses consistent with the purposes for which the endow-

---

[42] Luther, *Sämmtliche Schriften*, 17:716.
[43] Ibid., 17:727–30 for this and the following.

ments were made. Any surplus should be used to improve pastors already in office, to support judicial personnel, and to fund visitations. It would be better to end monasticism altogether, since Christian rectors (*Pfarrherren*) should live with a pious wife and children, rather than that zealous students should suffer hunger, churches be without pastors, and learning fade away. Cloisters for women were useful, Melanchthon thought, to protect their weak nature, but in cities, it would also be good to convert some into women's schools, without burdening the women with monastic vows.

Of these proposals, only the use of church property to fund territorial courts is new. It reflects not only Melanchthon's confidence in the role of courts as an institution that preserves the moral fabric of society, but his perception that they, together with schools and churches, are regarded by all the imperial estates, Catholic and Protestant, as instruments of social welfare. In other words, he explained again the readiness of evangelicals to embrace a bi-confessional equity among the imperial community of estates.

These pleas could only hope to show Protestants at their most benignly Christian, as rulers whose leading clergy shared an abiding desire to restore religious nurture and social order. There was no chance after the failure of the colloquy for a settlement on the articles of faith. The theological agreements on original sin, human will, and justification did not overcome Protestant suspicions of a general council, and Pope Paul III would settle for nothing less than a conciliar settlement achieved under his own watchful presidency.[44] But while doctrinal reconciliation foundered, efforts to win acceptance of confiscations of church property carried on.

The advice seems to have had the desired effect. For one, Contarini accepted Melanchthon's definition of religious purpose. It was necessary to promote schools, he said on 12 July 1541, as the Diet drew to a close, thereby admitting the validity of schools as a religious use of church property.[45] As it happens, monastic property would increasingly be used by Catholic rulers to fund schools, usually Jesuit and Capuchin schools, and charitable foundations.[46] What were the Protestant schools in 1541 that drew their sustenance from confiscated church property? The most famous were the universities of Marburg

---

[44] Gleason, *Gasparo Contarini*, pp. 227, 248.
[45] Luther, *Sämtliche Schriften*, 17:734–36 nr. 1387. CR 4:507.
[46] Henze, "Orden und ihre Klöster," pp. 99–102 and the literature noted there.

and Wittenberg, the new city school of Strasbourg (its master Jean
Sturm was among Europe's most influential Latin dialecticians in the
1530's), the princes' schools of Saxony, and the cloister schools of
Württem-berg.[47] Contarini was complimenting some very prominent
redeployments of church materials and incomes accomplished over
the previous fifteen years. Five days earlier Contarini had called upon
German bishops to imitate the Protestant example. They should build
schools for noble children, he said (the archbishop of Mainz had
reported to him their quality and distribution among the Protestants).[48]

The emperor then made concessions better than the Protestants
had ever seen. The Diet's recess was published 29 July. It stipulated
that the doctrines of the Regensburg Book would be tolerated until
a council, a national synod, or an Imperial Diet issued a conclusive
decision. The emperor extended the Peace of Nürnberg until such
a meeting. The city of Strasbourg had been negotiating a suspension
of the Imperial Chamber Court, and a set of cases had already been
suspended before the beginning of the Diet.[49] The emperor now
offered to suspend the Protestant cases altogether. A secret communication promised to respect Protestant property.[50] Charles V's purpose was to freeze the current status quo. He determined that cloisters
and churches undamaged and not dissolved should remain as they
are. The emperor's desire was surely to protect Catholic monasteries that survived in Protestant territories: "the cloisters and convents
thus far not destroyed and abolished should remain; not sold by any
Obrigkeit under which they lie, to seize the same for Christian reformation."[51] The recess declared that clergy, i.e. Protestant and Catholic,
must be given whatever incomes owed to them, which the emperor
clarified: including clergy and incomes from endowments, cloisters,
and convents that adhere to the Augsburg Confession.[52] The needs

<hr/>

[47] Anton Schindling pointed out the status and recognition enjoyed by model
evangelical schools. Schindling, "Der Passauer Vertrag," pp. 114–5. For Jean Sturm,
Olivier Millet, *Calvin et la dynamique de la parole* (Geneva: Éditions Slatkine, 1992),
pp. 117–122. Sturm won his reputation at Paris, to which he came from Louvain
in 1529. He was active there as a teacher, editor of classical texts, writer of classical
commentaries, and humanist in the service of the Cardinal Jean du Bellay, leader
of the anti-Habsburg faction at the French court. In the latter capacity, he helped
forge attempts at rapprochement between the German Protestants and king Francis
I. See also Brady, *Protestant Politics*, p. 156.
[48] Gleason, *Gasparo Contarini*, p. 255.
[49] For this see Brady, *Protestant Politics*, p. 168.
[50] Fuchs, *Konfession und Gespräch*, p. 452.
[51] Luther, *Sämmtliche Schriften*, 17:799–801 nr. 1404. CR 4:623–25 nr. 3252.
[52] Luther, *Sämmtliche Schriften*, ibid.

of ministries and schools, of whichever religion, were to be supplied as they were before conversion.[53] These were answers to the *Protestant* charge of church robbery against Catholics. The emperor, in effect, conceded the charge.

Aftermath

It took three more years for cases against the League before the Imperial Chamber Court to end altogether, in spite of Charles V's suspension of Protestant church-property cases, but as we have seen (chapter 2, above), this success came just as the League's internal divisions began to reveal how great its vulnerabilities were. The case of Goslar rekindled the League's debate over recusal, which led to the recusation of 1542 and the suspension of the Imperial Chamber Court in 1543/4 (the recess of the 1544 Diet of Speyer incorporated the League's principle that church property must remain at its locale), while at the same time the extension of the League's defense mandate beyond the religious controversy, and the vulnerabilities this manifested in the alliance, begged for imperial exploitation.[54]

The war came at the end of August 1546 and ended with the imprisonment of the Philip of Hesse and Johann Friedrich the following spring. But the defeat of the League in 1547 and the Augsburg Interim of 1548 created nothing more than a temporary interlude to the League's accomplishment in 1541.

The theologians, including Martin Bucer, had contributed much to the post-war settlements—practical, then official acceptance of the churches of the Augsburg Confession—by adapting themselves to the requirements of the League's princes between 1538 and 1540.[55] A century ago, Kurt Körber, the author of the first modern monograph on the confiscation of church property in Reformation Germany, concluded that the League failed to discover a unified principle, a

---

[53] Ibid.
[54] Chapter 2, above, and Brady, *Protestant Politics*, pp. 249–327. Sieglerschmidt, *Territorialstaat*, pp. 156, 159 for the imperial recess and its anticipation of the terms of the 1555 peace and their divergent interpretations.
[55] Haug-Moritz may overstate the differences between theologians and lawyers, on the matter of the three uses of property, which is an adaptation of Bucer's threefold use: the ministries of the church, schools, and the poor, leaving the *Obrigkeit* to decide what to do with whatever remains. Haug-Mauritz, *Der Schmalkaldischer Bund*, pp. 537–38.

legal basis for confiscation.[56] They had employed several: benefice as office and income rather than gift, the local stability of benefices, social welfare (the common good, poor relief, and education), donors' religious intentions, the rights and responsibilities of patrons, and most especially the obligation to protect religion. Once Catholic victory in the war allowed the reinstatement of the Imperial Chamber Court in 1548 and after the Treaty of Passau in 1552 and the Peace of Augsburg in 1555 legalized toleration in a way identical with that achieved earlier, de facto, by the League, the court became again the venue in which both the redistribution of church property by Protestants and demands for restitution occurred, with this added evangelical benefit: it was determined that religious questions would only be settled by a panel of judges evenly divided between the two confessions, which meant suits over church property were likely to end in deadlock.[57] Nevertheless the court remained, as it had become in the 1530's, the principal venue for the pursuit of conflicts over church property. Why did such disputes continue at all?

One reason was the ambiguity of the Peace of Augsburg. Paragraph 19, section 7 says this about church property seized before 1552:[58]

> Since some estates and their ancestors seized certain foundations, cloisters, and other goods and employed them for schools, charity, and other things, so also should such confiscated properties (which do not belong to those who are immediately subject to the Empire and are imperial estates and the possession of which the clergy did not have at the time of the Passau Treaty [the 1552 agreement] or since) be included in this peace and, according to the decree (about each estate with the above treated confiscated and employed property), they should be left standing and should not be discussed nor contested with regard to the same estates whose rights are neither included nor excluded [herein], for the preservation of a lasting, eternal peace. For that reason, and by the power of this agreement, we hereby order and command the chamber judges and assessors of the imperial majesty that they should not recognize and settle any citation, order, or process about these confiscated and employed properties.

Property seized before 1552 was exempt from prosecution. As Bernhard Ruthmann pointed out, the article does not stipulate what should be done with properties confiscated after 1552, and consequently

---

[56] Körber, *Kirchengüterfrage*, pp. 188–89.
[57] Bernhard Ruthmann, *Die Religionsprozesse am Reichskammergericht (1555–1648)* (Köln: Böhlau, 1996), 484–580. Fuchs, "Supreme Court," p. 16.
[58] Ruthmann, *Die Religionsprozesse*, p. 484.

Protestants and Catholics interpreted the clause each to one's own advantage.[59] Catho-lic jurists took the passage as an amnesty, an exceptional ruling that applied only to properties in Protestant pos-scssion in 1555. An amnesty implied that the prohibition of further confiscations nevertheless remained in force. Catholic jurists also assumed that ecclesiastical immunity, as determined by canon law, also remained valid, in which case a prince could have no legal claim or title to any church property. The Protestant interpretation presupposed parity between the two confessions and a prince's right of reform (*ius reformandi*). According to this view, the Peace of Augsburg prohibited the confiscation of church property from religious founda-tions that enjoyed imperial privileges, but it allowed the confiscation of property in all other cases (e.g. noble foundations rather than imperial ones). Or in other words, the terms of debate had hardly changed since 1540, except in this. The Protestant submission to impe-rial power and jurisdiction, in matters of church property, had become more explicit, and conflicts over such property settled into something like a routine. No longer did it have to do with the life or death of the Protestant movement. But that is beyond my present subject.

It must have been difficult to foresee a Protestant future at the end of the League's history. In 1547, both sides approached the war exchanging recriminations. The League blamed the Catholics for fail-ing to reform. The emperor determined to treat the League as rebels.[60] The civil war seemed to herald the end of imperial order, the delicate balance between imperial and princely rights, which upset could result ultimately, Germans worried, in a hereditary, Habsburg German monarchy. Strasbourg's Jacob Sturm, clearly the League's most important diplomat, had declared achievement of a religious peace impossible before hostilities broke out, and he lamented the division of the Empire when they began.[61] Sturm expected apocalyptic doom but took solace in the example of the early church, which thrived under oppression. During the war, Philip Melanchthon felt the same despondent certainty. He had a dream-vision on the night of 2 January 1547. By then, the cities of the Upper Danube had fallen, Duke Ulrich of Württemberg was negotiating a settlement with the emperor, Ulm had surrendered, Frankfurt had fallen, and

---

[59] Ruthmann, *Die Religionsprozesse*, pp. 484–87 for this and the following.
[60] Brady, *Protestant Politics*, p. 138.
[61] Ibid., pp. 294, 297.

Strasbourg, Hesse, and Electoral Saxony were contemplating their
next move. Strasbourg soon began negotiations with Charles V. The
Landgrave and the Elector took their more stubborn course. The
Elector was defeated at the battle of Mühlberg 24 April. The Landgrave
and their remaining supporters surrendered soon after.

Lucas Cranach the Younger prepared a woodblock image of
Melanchthon's dream, and Melanchthon added verses that were published alongside it on 6 January 1547.[62] The text and image were
composed during a flurry of religious pamphleteering during the war,
contributing to a crescendo of Protestant self-assertion in the face of
sure defeat and likely ruination (pamphleteering and apocalyptic
doom continued over the five years between the end of the war and
the Treaty of Passau, and periodically thereafter).[63] The dream-image's
prevailing figure is a German Ajax, the Greek hero of the Trojan
War, clothed like Hercules in the impenetrable armor of a lion's
cloak. Ajax made the victory at Troy but killed himself in the end
rather than endure an insult, when the armor of the slain Achilles
was given to Odysseus and not to him. His suicide points to the
heroic desperation Melanchthon must have hoped to enflame in this
current tragic war. His preacherly message was that even in the face
of defeat, the gospel assured the warring Protestants. The church of
Christ, the high mountain rising over the warrior's head, would pre-
vail, even while they clung to the ruins of their shipwreck.

Strangely enough, Sturm and Melanchthon were right, in a way.
In spite of the defeat, the churches of the Augsburg Confession did
survive and in the next generation flourished in the Protestant lands
most cooperative with the policies of the Empire. Melanchthon attributed it to divine providence and evangelical devotion. They owed it
to their success with church property.

---

[62] Max Geisberg, *Der deutsche Einblattsholzschnitt in der ersten Hälfte des 16. Jahrhunderts*,
40 vols. (Munich: H. Schmidt, 1923–9), vol. 28, nr. 13.

[63] For the pamphleteering, Brady, *Protestant Politics*, pp. 306–7, p. 323 nn. 97–100
and the literature noted there, and Haug-Moritz, "Holy Roman Empire," section 3;
for after the war, Thomas Kaufmann, *Das Ende der Reformation. Magdeburgs 'Herrgotts
Kanzlei' (1548–1551/2)* (Tübingen: J.C.B. Mohr/Paul Siebeck, 2003), pp. 488–9. For
apocalypticism after the Peace of Augsburg, consider Peter Starenko, "In Luther's
Wake: Duke John Friedrich II of Saxony, Angelic Prophecy, and the Gotha Rebellion
of 1567," Ph.D. Dissertation, The University of California at Berkeley, 2002, and
for the popularity of Luther's prophecies, Robin Bruce Barnes, *Prophecy and Gnosis:
Apocalypticism in the Wake of the Lutheran Reformation* (Palo Alto, California: Stanford
University Press, 1988), pp. 60–99.

The Image of a Dream (Wittenberg: Nicolaus Schirlentz, 1547), with verses by Philip Melanchthon and an image by Lucas Cranach the Younger.

I saw an Ajax of youthful limb standing,
  Who with a tawny lion's pelt was clothed.
As the strong right hand grasped an ash-wood lance,
  And the shield's broad knob plaited his left;
On which the great hardened hides of seven oxen
  By an expert's hand had been carefully fixed.
But over Ajax's head rose a high mountain,
  With flowers and lush grass blooming over all,
At its summit stood Christ, the victor, upright,
  The Only from the Father forever born,
Bearing signs, triumph's advent and death vanquished,
  Such are the things peers' soldiers hardly see.
Under his feet in the mountain a trophy,
  The golden cross was set by angelic hand.

Terrified minds see many fleeting images,
  Which through the dim bare night do fly,
But this image, if not lying shadows mimick,
  Maybe this one warns disquieted men:
Though the raging generals conduct dismal battles,
  They feel it in their flesh how, as they go,
By now the fatherland with civil blood was polluted,
  So we, guilty, by a just God's anger are crushed:
While yet amidst the waves a shipwrecked survivor
  Gathers to himself some torn-up planks:
So Christ might rescue from the swelling ocean someone,
  He from the Father eternally seeded,
Who already has acted among the doubtful,
  That He the victor at the mount's crest might stand.

Turn, I pray, O Christ, the angry Parent from us,
  You, the power for us at entreaty's place
Disperse that anger from the mind of the Parent,
  End it, so to suffer the sound of your voice.
The study of Your doctrine, the little Sarepta,[64]
  The home of Your teaching, shield it, I pray.
Do grant us, You merciful, a peaceful serenity,
  The minds of the generals and the people to rule,
Your voice pleads, "Could anyone from me be snatched knowing
  the words to My hands sure to be tooled?"

---

[64] Sarepta or Zarephath was the obscure city where the prophet Elijah fed a poor widow and her son through a drought from a miraculous jar of meal. 1 Kings 17.8–16. Luke 4.26.

The voice pledges deeds, and our bossom moves us,
  That from You our hearts might dare demand aid.
That You would save us, with burning vows I beg You,
  Us and our armies of Your law zealous,
So recognition among mortals will keep shining,
  How your truth will stand steadfast forevermore.

Printed at Wittenberg by Nicolaus Schirlentz, 1547

IMAGO SOMNII
PHILIP. MELANTHO.

A tacem u ti ſtantem, iuuenilia membra
    Qu ſolù indutis pelle Leonis erat.
Fraxineamq; h ſtans cum fortis dextra teneret,
    Leuum ip, deſpri texerat umbo latus,
In quo magna num deruntur tergora ſeptem
    Artificis doc a iuncta fuiſſe manus,
Sed ſupra capu Aiacis mons eminet altus,
    Floribus & leto gramine ubiq; uirent,
Cuius in excelſo uictor ſtat uertice CHRISTVS
    Vincit æte no de genitore ſatus,
Signa gerens.r. ducens ſuperata morte,triumphi,
    Qualia tun ccernitum ferre cæterus uidet,
Huius ſub pedibus ,medioq, in monte, trophæum,
    Angelica,& ex eſt aurea fixa,manu.

M Vlta quiaé p uid æ ſimulachra fugacia mētes
    Quæ cæca uolitant irrita nocte, uidēt,
Sed tamen hæc ſi non luſit fallacibus umbris,
    Talia ſollicitos forſan imago monet!
Quantus irati mouerunt triſtia bella,
    In ſua graſſantur uiſcera tamq, Duces,
Et tam ciuili patria eſt polluta cruore,
    ſullaiq, nos ſontes opprimet ira Dei:
Vt tamen in medijs lacerat æ naufragus undis,
    Qui ſupereſt,tabulas colligit ipſe ſibi,
Sic aliquem eripiet cætum de fluctibus iſtis
    Æterno CHRISTVS de genitore ſatus,
Eſtq, inter dubios manſura Eccleſia motus,
    Vt uictor CHRISTVS montis in arce ſtetit.

F Lecte precor nobis iratum CHRISTE parens
    Qui uis pro nobis ſupplicis eſſe loco   (tem,
Et quem ſparſiſti prolatam e mente parentis,
    Deleri uocem ne patiare tuam.
Doctrinæ; tuæ ſtudium,paruamq, Sareptam.
    Doctrinæ hoſpitium,protege queſo,tuæ.
Et placidam clemens nobis concedito pacem,
    Tuaq, ducum mentes,tu populoq, regas,
Nemo meis manibus cætum mea dicta colentem,
    Sic inquit tua uox, eripuiſſe poteſt.
Hæc promittit opem nobis, & pectora,ut à te
    Auſint auxilium poſcere, noſtra monet.
Vt ſeruet igitur,uotu te ardentibus oro,
    Agmina,quæ legis ſunt ſtudioſa tuæ,
Semper ut agnitio mortales luceat inter,
    Manſura æterno tempore,uera tui.

Impreſſum Vuittebergæ,per Nicolaum
          Schirlentz.
        1547

The Image of a Dream (1547)

CHAPTER EIGHT

DOMINIONS

If the evangelical movement began by accident, it coalesced as a bold experiment. After the imperial sentence of 1521, Luther spent less than a year in hiding, then lived, preached, lectured, and polemicized with impunity in Wittenberg. The season of uprisings soon came. It was a clarifying event for the evangelical movement: most of Luther's followers with any established religious or political authority were determined not to be rebels. The uprisings also clarified the role of evangelical magistrates and princes as protectors of the church: they would defend and promote the new religion, but the church should pay its own way from its property. The conversion of monasteries and the redeployment of monastic wealth might have seemed blatantly criminal had the revolt of 1524/5 not left various rulers, great and small, urban and territorial, most of whom were still Catholic and many of whom would so remain, in control of scattered church properties in trust. As the evangelical movement took shape in Germany, theologians had to redefine the confiscation and redeployment of church incomes and lands as something more permanent than an emergency action. They defined it as the protection of religious reform.

The preceding chapters have shown how the first generation of Protestant theologians provided lay rulers in Germany with a limited rationale for the confiscation of church property. Notably lacking was a definite and clearly articulated theory of sovereignty that subordinated the church to temporal dominion. Theologians had hinted at such an idea. It was suggested by Brenz's recommendation to the Elector Palatine in 1525 that territorial ruling authority should be singular and by Luther's early advice to the electoral prince of Saxony in 1526 that church property could be used to meet the expenses of state. But Protestant cities (for example, Nürnberg, Augsburg, and Ulm) soon found themselves defending the traditional separation of secular and spiritual jurisdictions in response to the interference of the Swabian League. By the time of the 1530 Augsburg Diet, theological advice to Protestant rulers approached the matter of church

property in three ways: by suggesting territorial sovereignty, by insisting on the separation of jurisdictions, or by justifying state uses of
church property.

In the first years of the Schmalkald League's short history, Protestants
making claims on church property were confronted by the rights of
foreign patrons again and again. The previous chapters have shown
how theologians eventually advised cities to respect those rights, for
example at Bremen, Frankfurt, and Augsburg. The League's estates
took a different approach. They discussed the rights and obligations
of Catholic third parties over property in Protesant cities repeatedly
and opportunistically from 1537 to 1540.[1] In several instances, they
said, the rights of Catholics should be ignored, and the rights of
evangelicals, for example as patrons of churches within Catholic lordships, should be used indiscrimately.[2] The question was whether to
set confessional uniformity above property rights in territories or
respect property rights at the expense of the religious coherence of
a region. It is tempting to presuppose the former as the main Protestant
ambition. This would seem to have plunged the estates headlong
into the consolidation of territorial state-churches—small-scale nation-
alizations of the church.[3] Did it?

From 1538 to 1547, the League aggressively debated, pursued,
and failed to implement policies that would lead in the direction of
territorial sovereignty, with one exception: the de facto legitimation
of confiscations of church property. Their rationale was limited in
such a way that the religious self-consciousness of the early Protestant
movement had nothing to do with secularization. The worried theologians on the second tier of courtly advisors invented Protestantism.
They also tried to preserve the privileged position of the church, but
as a trimmer organization restricted to pastoral ministry and its corollaries in education and poor relief. Fortunately for them, their rulers
needed to pose as defenders of religion.

Although it seemed duplicitous to their Catholic opponents, the
League relied on an image of the integrity of their churches, insofar as integrity was associated with the separation of ecclesiastical

---

[1] Haug-Moritz, *Der Schmalkaldische Bund*, pp. 522–9 and chapters 5 and 6, above.
[2] Haug-Moritz, *Der Schmalkaldische Bund*, pp. 526–7, the example of advice to
Kempten and Memmingen in 1538.
[3] Haug-Moritz, *Der Schmalkaldische Bund*, p. 527. Sieglerschmidt, *Territorialstaat*,
passim.

and lay jurisdictions. Only by defining its actions against the established church as the defense and promotion of religion could the
League deny the power of lay courts, in particular the Imperial
Chamber Court, to demand restitution. When between 1537 and
1540 the League finally developed a common position on church
property, the only sacred assets consistently and freely granted to
rulers were deemed to be oversupplies after a religiously defined
order of priorities—first the ministry, then schools, then poor relief.
Rulers, the League's theologians said in 1540, could use oversupplies for public ends, which they associated with the religious responsibilities and expenses of rulers. This satisfied the desire of Protestant
clergy to protect parishes and schools. It also allowed city magistrates and princes to describe their confiscations as religious deeds,
for by the time they got to oversupplies, the rulers complained, they
were merely recovering a small part of the onerous financial burden of the church, as the Landgrave and the duke of Württemberg,
for example, insisted.[4] The threat of a religious war encouraged rulers
to connect princely debt-relief to the protection of their religion. The
religious rationale circumvented the redefinition of ruling authority
and its relationship to the church. Yet it served a political purpose,
namely, the exclusion of property from Catholic-Protestant negotiations in 1540 and 1541. It eventually helped neutralize the Imperial
Chamber Court. It allowed acceptance of estates of the Augsburg
Confession in the Empire. The emperor accepted this rationale in
1541. The suspension of the Imperial Chamber Court in 1543/4
further legitimized it.

This political achievement was not primarily the result of a reformist
plan. The evangelical party took shape around anti-Catholic polemic
and actions, not around national aspirations. The movement of the
religious controversy into the community of imperial estates played
the predominant role. The most effective rationale for the confiscation
of church property was an evangelical adaptation of the traditional
conviction that a ruler must protect religion. The rationale was conservative. The League's theologians reinforced this appeal to tradition
when they used ecclesiastical and Roman law with scripture to show
that confiscation merely responded to religious malpractice and
defended true worship. Theologians relied on sweeping generalizations
(Luther in 1531, the Schmalkald recommendation of 1540) or insisted

---

[4] Chapter 6, above.

on patristic and papal-reform texts in the canon law (Musculus and Wolfahrt, Bucer).

The *Decretum* helped establish the church as an autonomous juris-diction alongside temporal power in the twelfth century and defended the church's much disputed legal supremacy.[5] Times had changed, but the practical authority of canonical tradition survived Martin Luther's early attacks. Musculus, Wolfahrt, Bucer, the anonymous of 1539, and the theologians assembled at the Schmalkald diet of 1540, like their medieval predecessors, assumed a selective doctrinal con-tinuity between scripture, imperial law, and ecclesiastical law. The moral tone of the medieval reform papacy's decrees served them well—complaining against corruption and simony, harping on the spiritual character of the priesthood and monasticism. But they applied canon law in a new way.[6] They made a substitution. Whereas the medieval reform papacy traced corruption to the infiltration of lay rulers into the church, the Protestants traced it to a corrupt clergy. They ex-changed the reform papacy's spiritual priesthood for reforming laity.

This substitution presents a telling close-up within the panorama of western Christianity. The first generation of the Protestant move-ment was mired in a secular-ecclesiastical conflict.[7] The advice given by Protestant theologians over the course of the 1530's oscillated between incompatible positions, namely the possibility of secular uses of church property versus the inviolability of the church. In recent history and in the near future, rulers approached this ancient prob-lem incrementally. The kings of England, France, and most recently Habsburg Spain were, for two centuries prior to the Protestant rebel-lion against the papacy, adept at restricting papal power while confirming the validity of the papal court, which they did by acquir-ing papal privileges that increased their access to church incomes.[8] They could do it in the name of reform and reinforce their religious credentials. Charles V was among the most succesful in this generation.

---

[5] Gratian, *The Treatise on Laws (Decretum dd. 1–20)*, trans. Augustine Thompson (Washington: Catholic University of America Press, 1993), D. 9, pp. 28–32.

[6] For earlier uses, consider Ocker, "The Fusion of Papal Ideology and Biblical Exegesis in the Fourteenth Century," *Biblical Hermeneutics in Historical Perspective*, ed. Mark S. Burrows, Paul Rorem (Grand Rapids: Eerdmans, 1991), pp. 131–51, also Ocker, *Biblical Poetics*, pp. 149–83, 199–213, and the literature noted there.

[7] Bernd Hamm has made a similar point on the evidence of church discipline. Hamm, *The Reformation of Faith*, p. 250.

[8] In general, Paolo Prodi, *The Papal Prince*, translated by Susan Haskins (Cambridge University Press, 1987).

We have seen him at work in the Netherlands (Chapter 2, above).
As king of Spain and following a long history of crown intervention
on behalf of preferred candidates to bishoprics, he won a special
monopoly of nominations to vacant Spanish sees from the papacy
in 1523. The crown proceded to lay claim to 1/4 to 1/3 of each
new appointee's incomes, while determining that candidates be not
only of high birth, as we might expect, but also well educated and
suited to office.[9] In another typical infringement widely known in
Italy and France after the Council of Trent, Catholic rulers appointed
commendatory abbots over monasteries, who in many instances were
non-ordained favorites. Commendatory abbots enjoyed the community's wealth while the community lived more spiritually from a minimal budget under a prior.[10] There were myriad ways that a Catholic
ruler coopted the property-holding church. Church dominions belonged
to a stable system of capital and exchange, in which episcopal appointments and the papal court played a useful role. The fundamental
difference between Catholic and early Protestant infringement on the
church was not its basic rationale. Ruling authorities of both confessions posed as protectors of religion. Reform was based upon this
one point of agreement between the theologians and the estates: it
was the responsibility of lordship to protect religion and guarantee
that church gifts served religious purposes. One hardly needed to be
a Protestant to believe that.[11] The difference between Protestants and
Catholics had to do with the definition of religious purposes, whether
the definition involved Luther's view of the sacraments or one informed
by Luther to some degree. The difference was also the papacy.

---

[9] This extended privileges granted for the sees of Grenada in 1486 and the new
world in 1508. H.E. Rawlings, "The Secularisation of Castilian Episcopal Office
under the Habsburgs, c. 1516–1700," *Journal of Ecclesiastical History* 38(1987):53–79,
here 55, 57, and passim.

[10] For this and other uses of monastic property by Catholic rulers, Beales, *Prosperity
and Plunder*, p. 33.

[11] Protestant jurists before and after 1555 sometimes excluded the possibility of
the secularization of church property, allowing only its reassignment to another religious purpose, while differing with Catholic jurists over what such a purpose could
be. Hieronymus Schurpff (d. 1554), in a well known opinion, argued that the abbot
and monks of a cloister did not possess authority to cede the cloister to a temporal
lord, since a change of use must be approved by the pope or a general council,
and only a future council can determine whether monastic life is consistent with
godly law. If a council were to decide against monasticism, a prince and emperor
would still have no claim to the property. But Schurpff conceded the lord's right
in emergency to redeploy the property for the sake of *cura religionis*. Sieglerschmidt,
Territorialstaat, pp. 217–8 and n. 214 for additional authors on the same theme.

Catholic infringement on the church was legal, insofar as it manipulated the established system of papal governance. The Protestants had the burden of evading the charge of church robbery without the *benefit* of the papal court. That the German Protestants eventually succeeded is amazing.

It is amazing because they lacked territorial sovereignty in a truly meaningful sense. German confiscations therefore look complicated and reluctant when compared, even briefly, to England, Denmark, and Sweden. In England, King Henry VIII's principal secretary and chancellor of the exchequer, Thomas Cromwell, devised a plan for the nationalization of the English church in 1534. It included the dissolution of all English monasteries.[12] Cromwell then superintended the process. The closures began with smaller houses in 1535. They were followed by a wave of voluntary departures of monks and nuns and the complete secularization of all monastic houses and properties between 1537 and 1540. Although the king may not at first have intended to end monasticism in his kingdom, that is what he accomplished. Only chantries, chapels, some collegiate foundations, hospitals, fraternities, and guilds were left standing. These were secularized later: Henry won an act of Parliament in 1545 to that end, and the Duke of Somerset, Protector of Henry's successor, the young Edward VI, carried it out in 1548. The restoration of Catholicism under Mary Tudor (1553–1558) did not reverse the nationalization of the church. Yet church properties did little to strengthen royal government in the long term. Most of the monastic property was soon sold to English gentry, the properties dissipating while the proceeds paid the costs of wars with Scotland and France in 1542 and 1543.

In Sweden the king won more lasting benefits. Gustav Vasa came to the Swedish throne in 1523 by leading a rebellion against the Danish king, Fredrik I.[13] Through the rest of the 1520's, he increased

---

[12] For this and the following, A.G. Dickens, *The English Reformation*, 2nd edition (University Park: Pennsylvania State University Press, 1989), pp. 170–72, 230; George W.O. Woodward, *The Dissolution of the Monasteries* (New York: Walker, 1967), pp. 122–38. For women's houses, consider Marilyn Oliva, *The Convent and the Community in Late Medieval England: Female Monasteries in the Diocese of Norwich, 1350–1540* (Woodbridge: The Boydell Press, 1998), pp. 185–207.

[13] Michael F. Metcalf, "Scandinavia, 1397–1560," *Handbook of European History, 1400–1600*, 1:523–42. Ole Peter Grell, "Introduction," *The Scandinavian Reformation from Evangelical Movement to Institutionalisation of Reform*, edited idem (Cambridge Unversity Press, 1995), pp. 1–5. E.I. Kouri, "The Early Reformation in Sweden and Finland, c. 1520–1560, ibid., pp. 42–69, esp. 50–1.

his control of church tithes, a traditional enough endeavor, but in
1527 he placed all the church's temporal domains under royal administration (a tidy 21 percent of Sweden's arable land), deprived bishops of their castles and forts, and eliminated them from Sweden's
national diet. To guarantee cooperation, he promised the nobility the
right to reclaim all properties donated to the church by their lineages
since 1454. These actions contributed the lion's share to the increase
of royal holdings during the course of Gustav's long reign (1523–1560),
from some 5.5 percent to 28 percent of Sweden's farmlands—even
though conversion to the new faith was otherwise slow. The archbishop of Upssala gradually assumed control of the national church,
but the first Protestant church order was not introduced until 1571.

Denmark experienced an even more drastic secularization than
Sweden. During the reign of Fredrik I (1523–1533), Lutheran preachers had established themselves in a number of urban churches, having
been encouraged by the king and by his son, the future King Christian
III.[14] Christian was educated by Lutheran tutors in Wittenberg, and
when he received the small fief of Haderslev/Tørning, he undertook
a reform experiment that began with the dismissal of the Catholic
dean of a collegiate church, progressed by means of Lutheran appointments to parishes and the creation of an evangelical school, and culminated in the expulsion of friars from Haderslev and the confiscation
of precious objects. The new preachers set-off a wave of rapid attrition
from urban monasteries. Most mendicant cloisters were abandoned,
then confiscated between 1527 and 1532, a few holding out until as
late as 1541.[15] By Fredrik's death in 1533, one third of Danish
monastaries had been taken over by nobles as lay administrators.[16]

The friars had much less property than bishops. The Danish bishoprics were held by a handful of aristocratic lineages, who together
with their ecclesiastical relatives dominated the royal diet, and they
ran the kingdom until the civil war of 1535–1536. The war ended
with Christian III as king. His military ascent was given a constitutional veneer by an election in the royal diet, after purging the diet.

[14] His father's uncle, Christian II, was the Danish king supplanted in Sweden by
Gustav Vasa thirteen years before. Grell in the previous note and Martin Schwarz
Lausten, "The Early Reformation in Denmark and Norway, 1520–1539," *The
Scandinavian Reformation*, pp. 12–41.
[15] Lausten, "Early Reformation," pp. 14–5, 18–27. E.H. Dunkley, *The Reformation
in Denmark* (London: S.P.C.K., 1948), pp. 57–60.
[16] Martin Schwarz Lausten, *A Church History of Denmark*, trans. Frederick H. Cryer
(Burlington: Ashgate, 2002), p. 95.

Christian III took Copenhagen in July 1536, then imprisoned all the Danish bishops, declared the monarchy hereditary, summoned the estates to the diet at Copenhagen without the clergy, there replaced the bishops with Lutheran superintendents, and declared the episcopal properties his own.[17] And so it was. Unlike England, the treasuries of King Christian III of Denmark and King Gustav Vasa of Sweden swelled with ecclesiastical incomes, helping to set both monarchies on a course that could best be described as absolute.

In Germany, a community of strident rulers reluctant to defer to anyone, excepting perhaps God, confiscated church properties, yet they always confronted at least some religious communities whose patrons and privileges were impossible to ignore. Their success should prevent anyone from rhapsodizing their devotion to religious liberty. Princes were good at thinking on a relatively short term, a vital skill given the volatility of political life in the Empire. To one extent or another, many wanted to use church property for emergency infusions of capital. The theologians had reason to worry that the property might quickly disappear from the church's accounts. To restrict princely demands in the years to come, the administration of Protestant church property in Germany often fell under the aegis of an ecclesiastical council, a consistory, as it did, for example, in Saxony since 1539 and in Württemberg a decade later, where Johannes Brenz designed a council for Duke Ulrich's son and successor, Duke Christoph, a system of oversight later introduced in Braunschweig-Wolfenbüttel and other territories.[18] But princes continued to draw on state-church funds to cover emergency expenses right down to the Peace of Westphalia.[19] After 1555, princes behaved like Philip of Hesse in 1527. They redirected incomes while calmly articulating the evangelical discourse of reform. In the League of Schmalkalden there was a certain distance between the religious discourse of princely or magisterial conduct and actual fiscal management. The early Protestant discourse harped on spiritual renewal; the actual fiscal policy used

---

[17] Lausten, "Early Reformation," pp. 29–32.
[18] Estes, *Christian Magistrate*, pp. 59–80. Idem, *Peace, Order and the Glory of God*, pp. 175–6. Dixon, *The Reformation and Rural Society*, p. 55. Sieglerschmidt, *Territorialstaat*, pp. 235–245, which surveys the varieties of institutions of territorial, clergy oversight and the variety of methods in such fundamental matters of church management as the appointment of pastors, and the relation of these to (and their subversion of) traditional patronage rights.
[19] Cohn, "Church Property," pp. 170–71.

properties to relieve debts, induce nobility, or renovate battlements. The theologians hoped to appease princes by permitting transfers from, as it were, the arguable ledger of oversupplies to meet expenses of government. Martin Bucer, no less than theologians of Marburg or Wittenberg, obliged government by coming to agree that, with the priority of church needs freely conceded, government had a claim to surplus church property. This was where ruling authority was tested, and the very crucial question now becomes: how did the League articulate its right to use church property? That they *could* use it is important enough. Conceding the rights of foreign patrons helped position the Protestant estates as rulers committed merely to religious reform, and this stated motivation, in turn, helped them resist courts hearing cases against the confiscations they did make. That is, Protestant rulers could acquire sacred assets because they could resist the charge of church robbery. How did they justify their actions?

Not by appealing to a ruler's sovereignty. This neglect is important and not to be taken for granted. Why did the League not claim that its princely and city members possessed the sovereign right to seize church properties and use them as they would? The king of England did. The kings of Sweden and Denmark did.[20] Why did they not simply assert a hierocratic authority, itself holy, expanding upon their position as *caput ecclesiae membrorum*, head of the territorial church's members?

Although theologians asserted something approaching a sovereign right periodically in the 1530's in cases where rulers held patronage, claims to this right receded beneath the self-presentation of religious devotion, charity to be exact, a matter of social well being and not property. Charity was considered a divine gift, a grace-caused activity. The predominant reason for the failure of arguments for sovereignty to take hold appears to have been a practical one: the Imperial Chamber Court. The secular use of church assets undermined the League's definition of property disputes as *Religionssachen*, as matters

---

[20] In Sweden, the rationale first suggested by the court theologian Laurentius Andreae was based on a concept of the church's property as the common property of the community of the faithful. By 1539, Gustav Vasa demanded that he teach greater obedience to temporal authority. In 1539, the king assumed administration of the temporal church. Kouri, "The Early Reformation in Sweden and Finland," in *The Scandinavial Reformation from Evangelical Movement to Institutionalisation of Reform*, pp. 48, 62.

of religion exempt from imperial jurisdiction. For, to say that property was subject to *secular* rule would concede the court's jurisdiction. Lacking a clear political defense of their *imperium*, they defined the purposes of state religiously. A cynic might wonder, how different was that from the much-lamented political uses of ecclesiastical power by prince-bishops, or by popes, who did not hesitate to describe and execute purposes of state as matters of religion? It differed only in the status of the actor. Protestant rulers were laymen who had found a new way to define their political purposes as religious, apart from prince-bishops and popes.

From the standpoint of ruling authority, a new concept of dominion was required, some particular explanation of the right of lay rulers to control, not just promote, religious affairs: an ideology for the princely *summus episcopus*, as the electors of Brandenburg would call themselves in the seventeenth-century.[21] Not in this generation. As the Protestant position on church property emerged over the League's first decade, the luster of sovereign claims dimmed. The theological memorandum of 1540 insisted on the independence of church dominion ("the church has dominon over . . . properties [of the church in a place]," it says), consigning to rulers the protective role. Nor did the League come to depend upon a particular reformer's view of governing authority, for example Bucer's, Musculus's, or Luther's. It relied on a conventional view: government, ordained by God, was regulated by customary and imperial laws and obliged to defend religion. With a modest rationale for confiscations the League and its theologians skirted the question of the distinction between secular and religious dominions.

This much was clear by 1540. By that year, the League's membership dominated the north of the Empire. But evangelical intellectuals clung to a traditional image of imperial authority and adapted it to their rhetoric of reform. This was interestingly displayed in Wittenberg, 1540, by a student of Philip Melanchthon. Heinrich Smedenstedt of Lüneburg delivered a discourse upon the occasion of his promotion to Master of Arts that year. He dedicated its published version to two people, Duke Franz-Otto of Braunschweig-Lüneburg,

---

[21] Cohn, "Church Property," p. 179. The seventeenth-century Protestant jurist Sigismundus Finckelthaus argued that the bishop's power went to the Protestant prince or magistrate after the Peace of 1555, but by necessity of expanding and conserving the church. Sieglerschmidt, *Territorialstaat*, pp. 260–1.

heir to the duchy and son of Duke Ernst.[22] Franz-Otto's father had
long supported the evangelical party and was an early member of
the Schmalkald League. He confiscated precious objects from churches
in 1531.[23] But a territorial visitation had yet to occur (1543), and
an evangelical church order had yet to be implemented (1564). To
date, some religious orders in the duchy stubbornly resisted evangelical efforts.[24] The flattering theme of Smedenstedt's declamation
was Otto I, the tenth-century Saxon emperor who established the
imperial church system. But his oration on this ideologically promising
subject tells us little about fantasies of Empire in this politically aus-
picious year. Take Otto as your example, he urges the duke in his
dedication, an example of a king born to an age of corrupt popes,
who determined to free the church of papal tyranny. Otto acted out
of his own imperial dominion. His dominion measured the extent of
the emperor's power, which in turn opened up his religious opportunities. Otto was, to Smedenstedt, a foremost example of true piety,
a viewpoint so traditional it had appeared in Leo X's summons, in
1521, before the Diet of Worms took place, to the new emperor
Charles V, that he follow the examples of Otto and Charlemagne
and add his own condemnation of Luther to the papal one.[25]
Smedenstedt leaves so much unclear: whether Otto set a precedent
for the devolution of imperial authority to princes, whether Smedenstedt
meant to promote the Saxon Elector as heir to Otto's imperial legacy,
or whether he meant to erect a norm against which Charles V's
policies may be followed or resisted. His politically apprehensive oration cared more about the continuity between evangelical reform
and the historical Saxon example of church betterment at the hands
of the temporal ruler.

This might seem unremarkable in this oratory genre, used by a
new master whose hopes for future employment could preclude bold
ideas as well as provoke them, except that Smedenstedt's seniors,
too, deliberately avoided the specifics of dominion's exercise and

---

[22] CR 11:509–530.

[23] *Die Territorien des Reichs im Zeitalter der Reformation*, 3:18–21 for this and the
following

[24] A 1542 treatise by Erasmus Alberus, more famous for his translation of Aesop's
fables, hoped to mobilize the reigning Duke Ernst the Confessor against the Franciscans
of Lüneburg. Luther added a preface. *Der Barfuser Muenche Eulenspiegel und Alcoran*
(Wittenberg: Hans Lufft, 1542).

[25] The same analogy had been made by Giles of Viterbo. Tüchle, "Des Papstes
und seiner Jünger Bücher," in *Lutherprozeß und Lutherbann*, p. 65.

pursued moral rhetoric instead. A conventional appeal to prayer, gentle law-enforcement, Christian selflessness, and the punishment of evil by princes has been traced back to Martin Luther's *On Secular Authority*, written late in 1522, which sharply distinguished between temporal and spiritual authority.[26] The distinction was eventually adapted to insist, by 1534, that princes promote religion and protect authentic pastors.[27] Luther's 1534 commentary on Psalm 101 presents "a long, rambling, and logically untidy portrait of a 'real' king [namely David]" as a royal model of service to the Word of God.[28] He had advocated princely intervention in religious emergencies since 1520.[29] Philip Melanchthon's brief 1539 treatise *On the Office of Princes*, carried a similar hortatory tone. It exhorted the prince to end religious abuses as an obedient confessor of Christ, custodian of the moral law in external discipline, head of a noble household and father to his subjects, and a foremost member of the church who shuns the persecution of godly people and recognizes that the purpose of human society is to make God known.[30] In 1543, Melanchthon repeated the religious duties of princes in two declamations written for the two sons of the Elector, which were then warmly endorsed by Luther in his preface to the published version.[31] This moral reasoning—the prince's responsibility to promote religion—culminated Melanchthon's progressive clarification of governmental authority in the promotion of reform, in collusion with Luther, as James M. Estes has explained in careful detail. It hardly represented a novel approach to ruling power and religion. Traditions provide for good order, Melanchthon had said early on.[32] The gospel is about spiritual renewal; it leaves (noble) household and (urban) republic in place.[33] The gospel, in fact, demands that existing governments be preserved and obeyed.[34]

[26] Estes, *Peace, Order and the Glory of God*, pp. 37–41, here 41.
[27] Ibid., pp. 201–3, 206, 211.
[28] Ibid., pp. 193–205.
[29] Ibid., pp. 10–11 (and p. 209 for Melanchthon in 1543).
[30] Ibid., pp. 152–164.
[31] Ibid., p. 209.
[32] Said of liturgical chants and calendar in his commentary on Colosians written in 1527. Ibid., p. 77.
[33] Said in the mature statement of his position on ruling authority and reform in the *Loci communes* of 1535. See ibid., p. 122 I take Melanchthon's terms *oeconomia* and *politia* to imply the noble household (as in medieval usage) and the urban republic.
[34] Ibid., p. 124, and CR 21:549–551.

Moral continuity was the order of the day, together with its imperial pieties.[35] The emperor's office stood at the center of the prevailing image of German nation.[36] There it remained, with Protestants
attaching their faith to it in a peculiar way, as Smedenstedt's famous
contemporary Johann Sleidan suggests. The Schmalkald League commissioned Sleidan's history of the religious controversy. He finished
it in 1555 with a dedication to the now Albertine Elector of Saxony.
There he considered Charles V with astonishment. The emperor's
inheritance exceeded that of all earlier German emperors, he observed.
It was the basis of his unprecedented power, but not really the basis
of his historical position. His place in history came from the religious
controversy. It is no coincidence, Sleidan explained, that Martin Luther's
disputation with Johannes Eck, after which "the parties of both sides
arose" (die Parteien beider seits erhuben), took place just after Charles
succeeded Maximillian. Religion was the chronometric of great kings.
The controversy placed Charles at the end of a line extending from
the biblical Cyrus through Alexander, Julius Caesar, Constantine,
Charlemagne, and the Saxon Ottonians.[37] Charles' enduring opposition
to Luther mattered not at all. His importance to history came from
the coincidence that the evangelical party arose on his watch.

These people were not theorizing power. They were limiting it.
Consider their omissions. A fund of religious and political ideas about
dominion existed and was widely known. In Europe, the disposition
of church property had long been associated with the definition of

---

[35] Alexandra H. Kess has noted that Johann Carion's *Chronicon* (1532) had earlier presented a continuum of adherents to the true church throughout history,
which later became the guiding principle of Matthias Flacius Illyricus' *Catalogus
testium veritatis* (1552) and served as a "Protestant counterpart to the Catholic notion
of an apostolic succession." Clarion and Melanchthon both adapted a division of
history into four periods, rather than the prevalent scheme of six or seven periods,
that corresponded to the prophet Daniel's four empires of Babylonia, Persia, Greece,
and Rome. Alexandra H. Kess, *Johann Sleidan and the Protestant Vision of History*, Ph.D.
Dissertation, University of St. Andrews, 2004, pp. 104–8 (the quotation is from
p. 107).

[36] Schubert, *König und Reich*, passim, emphasizing the hierocratic character of the
office. Haug-Moritz, "Holy Roman Empire," for its restricted use among the
Protestants and by the League, and the literature noted there.

[37] Johannes Sleidan, *Warhaffte eigentliche und kurze Beschreibung aller fuernemer Haendel
so sich in Glaubens und anderen weltlichen Sachen bey Regierung und großmaechtigen Keyser Carls
dises Namens deß fuenfften mehrerntheyls in Teutscher Nation zugetragen und haben verlauffen*,
trans. Michael Beuther von Carlstatt (Frankfurt: Johann Feyerabendt, 1583), f. ii
(verso). I'm indebted to Dr. Michael Printy's forthcoming article on Sleidan's four-
monarchy scheme for bringing this to my attention.

dominion, both ecclesiastical and lay, as we have seen.[38] It had a place in the debate between the king of France, Philip the Fair, and Pope Boniface VIII at the dawn of the fourteenth century, and it was debated soon after at the court of Pope John XXII in his conflict with the Franciscans as he attempted to rout the last remnant of the Spiritual Franciscans and their sympathizers from the Order. It was debated at the court of Emperor Ludwig of Bavaria in his conflict with the same pope. Richard FitzRalph adapted ideas of evangelical dominion to argue for the dissolution of the mendicant orders. Eventually, his definition of dominion was adapted by John Wyclif in arguments for royal authority and the divestment of church property. Wyclif influenced early Hussites. Their arguments were noted and rebutted in the theological textbooks and lectures of the fifteenth and early sixteenth centuries. One might have expected fourteenth-century debates to prepare the way for a broad reconsideration of sovereignty, but by 1400, the best known innovations in concepts of dominion were associated with Wyclif's heresy. The association seems to have muted theological discussions of sovereignty in the century before Luther, but some still considered the possibility of lay intervention in the church, and they wrote about it. Cardinal Nicholas of Cusa said that moving the administration of church properties and non-religious jurisprudence to lay administrators could reduce the temporal entanglements of bishops. The anonymous *Reformation of the Emperor Sigismund* called for an end to the temporal authority of bishops. At the end of the fifteenth century the so-called *Revolutionary of the Upper Rhine* insisted that church property was the emperor's to take back.[39] A 1519 pamphlet by the very orthodox bishop of Chiemsee, Berthold Pürstiger, shows us how remarkable such intellectual experiments could be. His *Onus ecclesiae (The Church's Burden)* adapted a Joachite, Spiritual-Franciscan view of history and argued that the restoration of a pure church around a property-less clergy would occur by stages, first in the reform of the mendicant orders, then in the church overall, by means of a future angelic pastor.[40]

---

[38] Chapter 1.
[39] Wolgast, *Hochstift und Reformation*, pp. 57–58. Nicholas of Cusa, *The Catholic Concordance*, ed. and trans. by Paul E. Sigmund (Cambridge University Press, 1991), ii.29, paragraphs 221–224, pp. 171–4. *Reformation Kaiser Siegmunds*, ed. Heinrich Koller (Stuttgart: Anton Hiersemann, 1964), pp. 116–68, esp. 126–134, 230–37.
[40] Wolgast, *Hochstift und Reformation*, p. 56. Josef Schmuck, *Die Prophetie 'Onus Ecclesiae' des Bischofs Berthold Pürstinger* (Vienna: Verband der Wissenschaflichen Gesellschaften Österreichs, 1973), pp. 13, 204, 222, 259.

Berthold's daring proposal (the heretical ancestry of his ideas of a
property-less church delivered by an angelic pope was unmistakable)
stood upon a century's insistence by unquestionably orthodox thinkers
and pundits that the church's power in temporal affairs should some-
how be restrained. Most of this thinking appears to have been ignored
by the first generation of Protestant theologians.

Reformation Germany was missing either a theory that defined
the church's control of property and the conditions under which that
right is forfeited, to allow someone else, for example a temporal
ruler, to control it, or a theory that defined power over property as
belonging ultimately to a temporal ruler, who might delegate it to
or withdraw it from the church's use. Let us consider each in turn.

The first is a theory of church dominion. Luther seemed to deny
that church dominion could exist at all, while his contemporaries
would normally presuppose that it did. He distinguished sharply
between the church as a temporal organization and a spiritual one,
especially in his early writings. His position was adapted by others
of the most influential evangelical theologians, for example, Melancthon
and Bucer.[41] The church was most properly a spiritual body, governed
by the preaching of the Word of God, while its faith was also nurtured
by the sacraments. The external church was a ruler's domain, and
the ruler's government was a personal endowment from God. Ruling
authority had a theological basis; it was a calling. Its exercise was
entirely personal, not an abstract power of state over both rulers
and subjects, yet its authority was independent of the individual
ruler's character, since governing office as a divine endowment was
not affected by the corruptibility of the office holder. The exercise
of this power belonged entirely to the earthly kingdom, was utterly
distinct from spiritual governance, and had its authority directly from
the divine source, not through the church.[42] The obligations of

---

[41] Schneider, *Ius reformandi*, pp. 129, 130–1. Bernd Hamm has recently noted the
close proximity of the positions of Luther, Zwingli, Bucer, and other major reformers on society and civil authority. Hamm, *The Reformation of Faith*, pp. 234, 248.
John Witte has argued that Melancthon and the jurists Johannes Eisermann and
Johannes Oldendorp "were less reserved than Luther about building bridges between
the two kingdoms." Witte, *Law and Protestantism*, pp. 119–175, here 172, and 105–117
for a summary of Luther's doctrines and its legal implications. Estes argues the
essential agreement and symbiotic development of their ideas of temporal authority. *Peace, Order and the Glory of God*, pp. 205–212 and passim.
[42] Wolgast, *Die Wittenberger Theologie*, pp. 44–45.

Obrigkeit, according to Luther, were to preserve the peace, conduct war, and maintain justice and social order, matters that Luther characterized as external, non-spiritual life.[43] But such obligations came to include the defense of religion, together with the right to remove and prevent religious malpractice when necessary, a position that Luther developed in tandem with Philip Melanchthon and which came to be widely held by evangelical reformers.[44] It was a negative power. To correct religious abuses was properly the business of the church, supported by a temporal government that manages external things in a complementary way.

Luther gave frequent advice on political affairs, especially during the early reign of the Elector Johann Friedrich. He attempted to reconcile the prince's policy and his own theology (an exception to this accommodation was his opposition to the election of Ferdinand as king).[45] By 1536, the Elector expected his theologians to be increasingly compliant, for example, by subjecting their religious articles to his judgement and approval. Eike Wolgast observed, "here is apparent the beginning of the way that leads in the second half of the sixteenth century to the concept of princely office as lords also over the church with judgment of last instance (*Entscheidungsrecht*) in theological questions."[46] Bernd Christian Schneider has noted how the way to princely authority over the church was paved by the attempts of evangelical imperial estates to defend their reforms as a protected right, an extension of the Melanchthonian *cura religionis*, the protection of religion.[47] This may have softened the boundary between the temporal and spiritual churches, but it hardly established the right of reform as an imperially guaranteed right (the *ius reformandi*) in Luther's generation.[48]

By Eike Wolgast's account, the origin of the prince as *summus episcopus* was the absence of church dominion, for that is what the

---

[43] Ibid., pp. 53–64.

[44] Wolgast, *Die Wittenberger Theologie,* pp. 64–75. Estes, *Peace, Order and the Glory of God,* pp. 10–11, 13, 21, 43–4, 177, 180–212, and 210 with n. 99.

[45] Wolgast, *Die Wittenberger Theologie,* p. 293 and passim for this and the following.

[46] Wolgast, *Die Wittenberger Theologie,* p. 298.

[47] Schneider, *Ius reformandi,* pp. 80–1, 86, 130–3, 138. Estes has traced Melanchthon's own expansion of the obligation of *cura religionis* from the months preceding the 1530 Diet of Augsburg to Melanchthon's *Loci communes* of 1535 and his *De officio principum* of 1539. See Estes, "The Role of the Godly Magistrates," pp. 463–48, and idem, *Peace, Order and the Glory of God,* pp. 92, 94–8, 116–9, 126.

[48] This is Schneider's point.

Wittenbergers implied: the church has no dominion over material things. It exercises an exclusively spiritual government. An early Protestant alternative is usually ascribed to Huldrych Zwingli and other southern reformers, for example, Ambrosius Blarer and Wolfgang Musculus, although in many points they agreed with the Wittenbergers. According to them, there was no distinction between the temporal community and the church, and this was the basis of a government's intervention in religious affairs: as a member of the community of faith, government must end abuse and promote true religion whenever and to the full extent that it can. Ruling authority could also be described as issuing from a natural power, as Wolfgang Musculus said, with the care for the church an extension of the magistrate's paternal authority over subjects, to whom Musculus also ascribed exclusive juridical power in external affairs.[49] The fact that these reformers often appealed to divine law as a basis for positive legislation gave this approach to ecclesiology a revolutionary hue, and a potentially theocratic one. But like Luther, they assumed a duality of spheres, a point we observed at the beginning of the Augsburg recommendation by Musculus and Wolfahrt, and one that Martin Bucer emphasized as he, among others, tried to protect church property and define temporal obligations in a way that would seem compatible in Wittenberg. Upon the wide frame of European political and economic thought, it is more important that they, too, during the time of the League of Schmalkalden, did not rest their case for the confiscation of church property on the nature of dominion per se.

Since 1527 Bucer began to develop a view of magisterial authority in religion distinct from Luther's early position.[50] His position informed the development of Strasbourg's church organization between 1532 and 1535. In place of Luther's distinction between temporal and spiritual realms, Bucer distinguished between two forms of the church, territorial and confessional. Lay magistrates, he argued, had the responsibility to govern the external, territorial church, on the

---

[49] Ruth Wesel-Roth, *Thomas Erastus: Ein Beitrag zur Geschichte der reformierten Kirche und zur Lehre von der Staatssouveränität* (Lahr: Moritz Schauenburg, 1954), pp. 107–8.

[50] Hammann, *Martin Bucer*, pp. 251–73, following Wendel, *L'Eglise de Strasbourg*, pp. 162–87. Gäumann, *Reich Christi und Obrigkeit*, pp. 159–243, stressing the primacy of the kingdom of God and Christ's rule for Bucer, which subordinates all temporal authority to the service of religion. Estes has pointed out that Melanchthon communicated his developed view of the *cura religionis* to Bucer in 1534, *Peace, Order and the Glory of God*, pp. 116–9.

example of the kings of the Old Testament, in order to promote the confessional body. Church discipline was exercised by clergy and lay representatives of the magistrates and the congregation, who together served on a disciplinary commission and possessed the power to excommunicate. To form this commission and carry out its judgments was the responsibility of temporal government. Thus church discipline belonged to the external, territorial body. But as we have seen, Bucer did not intend for this view to undermine church prerogatives or priorities. Magistrates may have had the oversight of church properties, but the use of them had to be religiously, that is theologically and clerically defined. Their dominion was strictly limited.

Let us take Luther and Bucer as representatives of two prevalent, alternative evangelical concepts of Christian society—Luther's two realms and Bucer's two churches. Something was missing from both. It was Thomas Erastus, who in the 1570's developed a Protestant theory of absolute temporal authority. Although born in Switzerland, Erastus spent most of his career as professor of medicine in the Palatine Elector's University of Heidelberg, where he helped establish the reformed church between 1559 and 1564, while serving on the count's church council. [51] In the council, he opposed attempts, briefly successful (until the restoration of Lutheranism in the Palatinate in 1576), to introduce a Genevan model of moral discipline under the ultimate jurisdiction of clergy rather than magistrates and princes. In place of a mere separation of jurisdictions, ecclesiastical and temporal, Erastus posed the strict separation of a spiritual and an external church.[52] An internal communion with the Holy Spirit constituted the spiritual church, while everything else, from the masonry of church buildings to the pastor standing at the head of the congregation, belonged to the external church. The external church was used by God to actualize his spiritual reign through external means, which included such traditionally spiritual activities as preaching and the sacraments.[53] In his view, the external was entirely under the authority of temporal rulers, including preaching and the sacraments; it enjoyed no immunities from secular jurisdiction. Likewise,

---

[51] Wesel-Roth, *Thomas Erastus*, pp. 43–82.
[52] Compare Luther's distinction of the internal and external churches. Estes, *Peace, Order and the Glory of God*, pp. 15–16.
[53] For this and the following, Wesel-Roth, *Thomas Erastus*, pp. 96–102.

government, *gubernatio*, was either internal or external. The internal
governor was God. The external was the magistrate, a singular
authority, whether individual or corporate, who exercised a single
jurisdiction over the social body. To Erastus, there was no question
of a prince's control of church property and personnel, no question
that both were secular, no essential difference between the sources
of a pastor's salary or a bailiff's.

Erastus' doctrine of the church overcomes the early Protestant
deficit in political theory. He went where no one in the first generation would go, although an ideologically driven confiscation of
churches could have benefitted greatly from his ideas. He was no
clergyman and lacked a personal stake in clerical privileges. But
some, for example Martin Chemnitz, the most prominent Lutheran
theologian of Erastus' generation and personally involved with reforms
in Braunschweig-Wolfenbüttel, maintained the Melanchthonian position: a prince intervened in the church for the care of religion, as
"foremost of the church's members" (*praecipuum membrum ecclesiae*).[54]
Others consigned the oversight of the material church to a clerical
estate, for example Erastus' contemporary, the Herford professor
Johannes Althusius.[55] A prince's obligation differed from that of other
Christians by degree, not kind—by virtue of his temporal office. He
had no intrinsic right to church property. This corresponded to
prevalent Lutheran views of society. Scholars of the new faith still
imagined society as a body of three estates (clergy, ruler, and people), which Luther had adapted from the famous medieval triad,
with the intention of balancing communal rights and ruling power.[56]
Princely officers represented each status, an eloquent display of the
emerging administrative monopoly, but jurists still restricted rulers'
rights in the church, a century after Luther's rebellion against the
papacy and in spite of the integration of clerical management structures into territorial administrations.[57]

---

[54] Schneider, *Ius reformandi*, pp. 173–82. Schneider points out that Johann Gerhard,
the most prominent professor of the next generation, associated the right of reform
with a ruler's sovereignty. For the development of the idea in Melanchthon, see
Estes, *Peace, Order and the Glory of God*, pp. 60, 63.

[55] *Politica methodice digesta* viii.6. *The Politics of Johannes Althusius*, translated by
Frederick S. Carney (Indianapolis: Liberty Fund, 1995).

[56] Sieglerschmidt called it a theological "ornament" added to communal rights
in the jurists' discussion of the appointment of ministers. Sieglerschmidt, *Territorialstaat*,
pp. 263–4, 280.

[57] Sieglerschmidt, *Territorialstaat*, p. 268.

Between the Peace of Augsburg and the Peace of Westphalia a territorial right of reform among the imperial estates became fixed.[58] Yet during this time, views of church and political authority fell between the extremes of princely sovereignty and ecclesiastical autonomy. Luther's generation left many unresolved questions for their successors to ponder, who struggled to reconcile growing princely power to the traditional assumptions that passed through the Reformation to them. The Lutheran prince depended on the administration of the church by ecclesiastical bodies, whether or not they included lay members in the fashion of Geneva or the French and Dutch Calvinists. Lutheran church orders preserved some legal exemptions from lay courts enjoyed by clergy in the Middle Ages, and they left in place the medieval method of paying clergy from tithes, endowments, and other church property.[59] Protestant jurists repeated canonical assumptions and doctrines. Lutheran jurists refused to concede the prince's monopoly over the church. When they addressed the question of episcopal authority in the absence of bishops, they entertained three possibilities. It could pass to a prince, to his clerical superintendent, or to both in different capacities, since German bishops had exercised both temporal and spiritual authority, which were now divided between different personnel.[60] Where episcopal jurisdiction had been suspended, the jurists argued that lay rulers must intervene, on the conditions of medieval patronage law, which determined that the government of churches could not revert to their lay patrons, since patrons lacked the power to manage ecclesiastical life. Lordship, on the other hand, carried the obligation to reform.[61] Princely government, but through clerical officers, dominated appointments to churches after 1555, while imperial law required foreign church patrons to present candidates who belonged to the confession of the ruler of the place.[62] Both were important moves toward territorial uniformity. Yet all rulers posed as opponents of clerical malpractice and as restorers of church property to its proper use, traditionally

---

[58] Schneider, *Ius reformandi*, pp. 173–321, and 322–414 for the Peace of Westphalia.

[59] Ernst Walter Zeeden, *Konfessionsbildung. Studien zur Reformation, Gegenreformation und katholischen Reform* (Stuttgart: Klett-Cotta, 1985), pp. 160–70.

[60] Consider the discussion of the Protestant jurists Matthias Stephan, Sigismundus Finckelthaus, and Zacharias Hermann in Sieglerschmidt, *Territorialstaat*, pp. 255–275.

[61] The jurist Matthias Stephan's point. Sieglerschmidt, *Territorialstaat*, p. 220.

[62] Sieglerschmidt, *Territorialstaat*, p. 269.

Catholic responsibilities.[63] Patronage rights post-1555 have been called
a fossil of earlier law, eccentric among the emerging institutions of
the territorial church,[64] but would the traditional really have seemed
eccentric? Church patrons were still said to possess, as they had in
the medieval church, the canonical rights of honor, obligation, and
insurance—the "honor" to present candidates, the obligation to protect the church, and emergency relief when the patron faced misfortune—a century after the controversy over Martin Luther.[65]
Protestant church orders adapted traditional clerical immunities, which
included tax protections and exemption from temporal courts in certain cases.[66]

It was entirely natural for any clergyman in the sixteenth century
to insist that the church was a self-governing entity whose sanctified
purpose must be undergirded, as it had long been, by the privileges
given to its properties and personnel. These remnants of church privilege reflect, at the least, the strength of a social imaginary, according to which rulers simply restored religious hygiene after papal
corruption.[67] Insofar as the church's formal property rights were concerned, matters stood not very far from where they had been 250
years before, when publicists debated the organization of the world
in two societies: one of the church and the other of lay dominion.

---

[63] Sieglerschmidt, *Territorialstaat*, p. 226.

[64] Sieglerschmidt, *Territorialstaat*, pp. 253, 290.

[65] Ibid., pp. 268, 271. Modestinus Pistor held that the Augsburg Confession did
not intend to completely remove all canon and Roman law. Ibid., p. 219.

[66] In the case of a clergyman *actiones reales* (a claim to property) went to the ordinary court; *actiones personales* (a claim to a contractual or owed obligation) went
to the superintendent for arbitration, then to the consistory or church council.
Sieglerschmidt, *Territorialstaat*, pp. 248-9.

[67] Consider Matthias Stephan, Sigsimundus Finckelthaus, and Zacharias Hermann
on the validity of patronage law, which Finckelthaus and Stephanus traced to clientage in classical Rome, as cited and described by Sieglerschmidt, *Territorialstaat*, pp.
256-7. Witte, *Law and Protestantism*, pp. 53-85, examines the recovery of canon law
among the Lutherans before the 1550's.

CONCLUSION: PROSPECT/RETROSPECT

The Holy Roman Empire was a community of imperial estates shaped by common endeavors.[1] It was a peculiar society. The community's individual members used the Empire's structures to govern their interactions. Its Diet functioned reasonably well as a forum for complaint and as a mechanism for mutual endeavor. The Diet helped moderate conflicts. It made decisions, but required cooperation to implement them. Lordship expressed a personal power coexisting with that of other lordships. Moreover, each state was the living product of an aristocratic society. The prominence of a prince or lord was enhanced by the prestige and privileges of birth-rank and ascribed status. Spheres of influence sprawled. The territorial borders of lordships could be very unclear in the period 1525–1547 (the clearest geographically defined authority in Germany belonged to a rector over his tiny parish).[2] These conditions had begun to change before the Luther controversy and continued to change for over a century after, as the norms governing society within territories became more uniform across the Empire, gradually replacing personal command, and as borders increasingly demarcated lordships.

The religious controversy fit this dynamic environment naturally. Did the controversy accelerate the rise of the territorial state within or alongside the Empire? The case of church property suggests the controversy's contribution was indirect and partial, at best.

The trend of territorialization has often been described as a constitutional process,[3] through which state sovereignty grew in principalities, eventually to flow into the nineteenth-century state—like water from the rivulets of medieval dominions passing through the rivers of territorial governments into the great ocean of modern nationhood. In the classical version of the national narrative, Luther occuppied a prominent but complex position. It's best known promoter

---

[1] Ernst Schubert has described the Empire as a *Leistungsgemeinschaft.* Schubert, "Vom Gebot zur Landesordnung," p. 61 and passim, for this and the following.

[2] Sieglerschmidt, *Territorialstaat,* p. 185.

[3] Consider Sieglerschmidt, *Territorialstaat,* p. 175 n. 111 for a concise statement of the view in the context of church property rights.

is probably Leopold von Ranke, who explained that state power was mixed from two ingredients, Roman universalism and national particularity. The German nation could only be born by leeching out the universal claims of a foreign authority, the authority of popes, such as Martin Luther's rebellion might have done, in order to fortify the nation-state.[4] To von Ranke, the experiment of state-building in Germany was ruined by the success of sixteenth-century popes and their Counter-Reformation, or one could say, it was ruined by Catholic Reform, until Prussia came to dominate Germany in the nineteenth century. The best known *cultural* interpretation of this historical sequence may be Jacob Burckhardt's, who believed that while the dogmatism and property acquisition of the medieval church frustrated the centralization of state power, the rise of Protestantism did not free the state from religious domination, since the new state-churches fell into their own cultural sclerosis.[5] Rather, he concluded in 1868/9, the separation of church and state had become "the problem of our time." Protestant theologians and historians frequently repeated or adapted a similar outline of the Reformation's long-term cultural and political impact: a partial advance toward the Enlightenment (an anticipation of the modern state) in the early sixteenth century, thwarted by conservative intellectuals, extended by the growth of a philosophy unencumbered by dogma, then ending with either the fusion of a Protestant social ethic to the state or the political and cultural liberation of the state from religion.[6] They debated

---

[4] Thomas A. Brady, "Ranke, Rom und die Reformation: Leopold von Rankes Entdeckung des Katholizismus," *Jahrbuch des Historischen Kollegs 1999* (Munich: Oldenbourg, 2000), pp. 43–60, here 54–55. Also, Haug-Moritz, "The Holy Roman Empire, the Schmalkald League, and the Idea of Confessional State-Building."

[5] Jacob Burckhardt, *Weltgeschichtliche Betrachtungen* (Leipzig: Alfred Kröner, no year), pp. 116–120.

[6] For my purpose, the following examples, who in one way or another associated the Reformation with nineteenth-century secularizations, may suffice. An eventual fusion of state and religion (albeit with strikingly different chronologies and outcomes): Richard Rothe, Ernst Troeltsch, Karl Holl, and Emanuel Hirsch. Kurt Leese, *Die Religion des protestantischen Menschen* (Munich: J. and S. Federmann, 1948), pp. 80–100. Karl Holl, "Die Kulturbedeutung der Reformation," a lecture held in Berlin in 1911, in *Gesammelte Aufsätze zur Kirchengeschichte*, 2 vols. (Tübingen: J.C.B. Mohr, 1932), 1:468–543. Ernst Troeltsch, "Die Bedeutung des Protestantismus für die Entstehung der modernen Welt" (1906), translated as *Protestantism and Progress: the Significance of Protestantism for the Rise of the Modern World* (Philadelphia: Fortress, 1986). Christian Albrecht, "Zwischen Kriegstheologie und Krisentheologie. Zur Lutherrezeption im Reformationsjubiläum 1917," *Luther zwischen den Kulturen*, pp. 482–499. The separation of religion and politics: Gerhard Ritter, Klaus Deppermann.

Luther's place in the outline. Accordingly, modernizing attributes have been variously ascribed to early Protestant movements. One approach stressed Luther's contribution to authoritarian rule,[7] while others identified Protestantism as a "vulgarization of the Renaissance" and a source of progressive secularity.[8]

Gerhard Ritter, *Luther. Gestalt und Symbol* (Munich: F. Bruckmann, 1925), pp. 114, 159. Klaus Deppermann, *Protestantische Profile von Luther bis Francke* (Göttingen: Vandenhoeck und Ruprecht, 1992), pp. 9–10, 16–29 (separation of religion and politics alongside the freedom of the individual and equality). For the place of Enlightenment philosophy in the traditional narrative, and its origin in the thought of the Enlightened pietist Friedrich August Tholuck (d. 1877), see John Stroup, *The Struggle for Identity in the Clerical Estate: Northwest German Protestant Opposition to Absolutist Policy in the Eighteenth Century* (Leiden: E.J. Brill, 1984), pp. 3–6. Johann Gottfried Herder asked this rhetorical question, with regard to reformers who in recent centuries had advanced progress but left "gaping holes, commotion, and dust" behind. "Luther! Gustav Adolf! Peter der Große! Welche drei haben in den neuern Zeiten mehr verändert? Edleren sinnes geändert?—und sind ihre, zumal unvorhergesehene Folgen, allemal zugleich unwidersprüchliche Zunahmen des Glücks ihrer Nachkommen gewesen? Wer die spätere Geschichte kennt, wird er nicht manchmal sehr zweifeln?" Heinrich Bornkamm, *Luther im Spiegel der deutschen Geistesgeschichte*, 2nd edition (Göttingen: Vandenhoeck und Ruprecht, 1970), p. 270. Cf. Eric W. Gritsch, "Luther and the State: Post-Reformation Ramifications," *Luther and the Modern State in Germany*, pp. 54–5.

[7] William Montgomery McGovern, *From Luther to Hitler* (New York: Houghton Mifflin, 1941), seen as one of several English and American writers adapting Troeltsch's view of Luther by Thomas Kaufmann, "Luther zwischen Wissenschaftskulturen," *Luther zwischen den Kulturen*, pp. 475–8. Herbert Marcuse, *Ideen zur einer kritischen Theorie der Gesellschaft* (Frankfurt: Suhrkamp, 1969), pp. 57–8, judged harshly by Deppermann, *Protestantische Profile*, p. 14. Carlton J.H. Hayes, *Christianity and Western Civilization* (Stanford University Press, 1954), pp. 32–36, which depicts Luther as, like the Renaissance, "reactionary in essence" and helping to give rise to absolute states that challenged "the principles of plural authority and constitutional government which emanated from Christian teaching and found special expression in Western Europe in the Middle Ages." See also Tracy, "Luther and the Modern State," in *Luther and the Modern State in Germany*, pp. 9–19. Others have contrasted Luther as an opponent of princely authority with Melanchthon, as the promoter of territorial churches. See James Estes' discussion of this view and its problems, *Peace, Order and the Glory of God*, p. xii with n. 7.

[8] Preserved Smith, *The Age of the Reformation* (New York: Henry Holt and Co., 1920), p. 749. Robert L. Heilbronner, *The Worldly Philosophers*, 7th edition (New York: Simon and Schuster, 1999), p. 35. Luther's iconic position in the rise of the state is more or less absent from recent histories of European nationalism, which tend to see the state emerge as a response to desacralized monarchy or as an adaptation of religious or quasi-religious collective identities that may or may not have medieval and early modern origins. For nationalism and desacralization, Hans Kohn, *The Idea of Nationalism: A Study in Its Origins and Background* (New York: Macmillan, 1944, reprinted 1961). For nationalism as religion, Carlton J.H. Hayes, *Nationalism: A Religion* (New York: Macmillan, 1960), and another view, emphasizing England as the first nation-state, Adrian Hastings, *The Construction of Nationhood. Ethnicity, Religion and Nationalism* (Cambridge University Press, 1997). For the variety of views and approaches toward nationalism, Lloyd Kramer, "Historical Narratives and the Meaning of Nationalism," *Journal of the History of Ideas* 58 (1997): 525–545, here 527–8.

It is tempting to set the early Lutherans marching toward a post-Napoleonic nineteenth-century, when German theologians could predict the consummation of the church in the Prussian state, the fulfillment of the Reformation in a final secularization.[9] Through the course of the 1530's, the Protestant estates came to downplay the uniqueness of their view of Christian society, emphasizing the continuity of their church with the past, even while their theologians emphasized the corruption of traditional religion.[10] This was a pragmatic move, meant to counter charges brought against Protestant rulers before the imperial appeals court. Gabriele Haug-Moritz has rightly emphasized the role of legal scholars in the development of the pragmatic policy. This need not imply a juxtaposition of pragmatic lawyers and confessional theologians, nor need it reinforce the assumption that church property was a political and economic matter that tells us nothing about the religion of sixteenth-century Germany, a view that has its origin in early Protesant polemic, which obscures the role of property in the building of an empire of two churches.

Any attempt to place Europe in a progressively secular chronology falters on post-Reformation Catholic strength, and with regard to the Protestant states of Germany, it falters on the clergy who continued to insist on at least some traditional rights and protections through the eighteenth century and into the Napoleonic Era.[11] To compensate for the fact, the national narrative has often relied on allegations of political and cultural recidivism in the later sixteenth and seventeenth centuries, as did Burckhardt. The less tendentious approach accepts broader continuities in religion. For the Catholic church was hardly in retreat. Its revival in the seventeenth and eighteenth centuries saw some fifty-one German princes convert to the old faith,

---

[9] So taught Richard Rothe. Gabriele Schroeder, "Speculation, History, and Politics: Richard Rothe's Negative Ecclesiology as a Response to the Transformation of Nineteenth-Century German Society," Ph.D. Dissertation, Graduate Theological Union at Berkeley, 1997. See also Heckel, "Das Problem der Säkularisation."

[10] In his study of polemical literature from 1538 to 1541, the period of religious colloquies and intense negotiation between imperial and papal representatives and the Protestant League of Schmalkalden, Georg Kuhaupt concluded that Protestant truth-claims lost their unique theological dimension, being subsumed to political concerns, like the rejection of the Imperial Chamber Court's jursidiction. Kuhaupt, *Veröffentlichte Kirchenpolitik*, pp. 317–18.

[11] For Catholic strength, Beales in the following note. For Protestant anti-particularists and anti-secularists during the Enlightenment, Stroup, *Struggle for Identity*, pp. 187–8, 227–8, 234 and passim.

while great monasteries functioned then, as they did in the Middle Ages, as "virtually independent principalities."[12] The secularizers of the late eighteenth and early nineteenth centuries confronted a wealthy church that by then held about twenty percent of Europe's real property, half of it possessed by monasteries. German Catholics, approximately one-third of all Germans, belonged to a thriving, continental organization. As to German Protestants, their clergy did not form a secularizing avant guarde. Rather than help facilitate the unrestricted secularization once thought to stand at the core of absolutist polities, they seem to have been anti-secularists and generally opposed to centralizations of state power.[13] So too, there is little reason to contrast post-Reformation politics with a progressive Luther. The political consequences of Luther's social teachings were neither so definite nor so clear that he should stand as an avatar of modern society, culture, or religiosity.[14] Moreover, there was little in Luther's day to suggest widespread disestablishments of the Catholic church in the early nineteenth century or the secularity typical of European societies today, however much the religious geography of Europe changed in the sixteenth century.

More recent scholarship on Germany avoids the ascription of political change to Martin Luther—be it decisive, temporary, or mere potential change. Yet all agree on three closely related points. Rulers stood behind Protestant successes. The new church could only establish itself by the imposition of state power. And the efforts of German rulers to control churches belonged to a general, long-term growth of princely government in territories, the princes competing with each other and guarding against dynastic ambitions of the Habsburg Emperor Charles V and his brother Archduke Ferdinand of Austria, who, since 1531, also held the title of Roman king.[15]

Then German historians divide. Some believe the religious controversy over Martin Luther was more or less incidental to these

---

[12] For this and the following, Beales, *Prosperity and Plunder*, pp. 5–6, 27, 39–83, esp. 58–60.

[13] Stroup, *Struggle for Identity*, pp. 3, 187–8.

[14] He was neither a Machiavelli nor a Bellarmine, a Vitoria nor a Molina, a Seyssel nor a Hotman, a Buchanan nor a Hobbes, Thomas A. Brady once observed. Brady, "The Reformer's Teaching in Its Social Setting," *Luther and the Modern State in Germany*, pp. 42–3.

[15] This designated Ferdinand as presumptive emperor-elect. He held the crowns of Bohemia and Hungary since 1526.

political developments (for example, Karlheinz Blaschke and Ernst Schubert).[16] Confiscation, when it did occur, followed traditional patterns, not new ones, Walter Ziegler has pointed out.[17] Martin Heckel argued that after 1555 there developed a confessionally neutral state-law for the church, while the common law absorbed canonical norms.[18] Others insist that the confessional divide, and a ruler's confession, became a—or *the*—motivating force in state-building by encouraging the development of centralized organs of government, the solidification of ideas and sentiments of social unity within territories, and the assertion of ruling authority (for example, Heinz Schilling and, with particular stress on the development of cultural norms, Bernd Hamm).[19]

The case of church property suggests that the truth lies in the combination of these views. While the religious controversy played a central role in imperial politics for specific political reasons, a traditional view of society was required in the first generation of the Protestant movement. This was, ironically enough, the contribution of the new theologians. They defined the religious purposes that protected the property gains of the League's members. Confessional identity helped the League assume a conservative posture.[20] Devotion

---

[16] Blaschke argued that the Reformation provided an opportunity for increased bureaucratic control of society by the state, but a state in transition from "the territorial dominion of the Middle Ages to the territorial state of the early modern era." He concluded, "The Reformation tied these together. It advanced the construction of the territorial state, while the rising territorial state fostered—not to say, made possible—the victory of the Reformation." Blaschke, "The Reformation and the Rise of the Territorial State," pp. 74–5. Schubert has pointed out that the transition from medieval dominion to state in fact took place in a much longer timeframe, and it was not very far advanced in the first half of the sixteenth century. Schubert, "Vom Gebot zur Landesordnung," pp. 19–61. The religious controversy was a squabble between Dominicans and Augustinian Hermits, the religious orders of Tetzel and Luther, thought Voltaire, Diderot, and Hume. See A.G. Dickens, John M. Tonkin, *The Reformation in Historical Thought* (Cambridge: Harvard University Press, 1985), pp. 112, 128, 138.

[17] Ziegler, "Reformation und Klosterauflösung," pp. 597–8.

[18] Martin Heckel, *Staat und Kirche*, pp. 71–2. Sieglerschmidt, *Territorialstaat*, pp. 126–9, 283–5.

[19] Heinz Schilling, "Confessional Europe," *Handbook of European History*, 2:641–681. For Hamm, see his, *The Reformation of Faith in the Context of Late Medieval Theology and Piety*, pp. 1–49, 217–253.

[20] The League's clerical advisors might have agreed with Edmund Burke, who decried the "philosophic spoilers" of monasteries in the French Revolution and their "spendthrift sale" of monastic properties. "A disposition to preserve, and an ability to improve, taken together, would be my standard of a statesman. Every thing else is vulgar in the conception, perilous in the execution." Edmund Burke, *Reflections on*

was the main ingredient of the League of Schmalkalden's successful defense of confiscations of church property. It was the moral basis of the League's resistance to demands for restitution. The theologians helped show how everything Protestant rulers seemed to do against the church was in fact for it, in fulfillment of the obligation to protect religion. They defined the religious emergency that invited cities and princes to intervene.

Their piety contributed little that was new to the state. Sixteenth-century territorialization occurred in a strikingly late-medieval way. It required the negotiation and propagation of rights and obligations between parties and the assertion of norms; when state power did grow, it was by moderating the estates' interactions through territorial statutes, courts, and diets.[21] The myriad legal *consilia* of sixteenth-century jurists and the hundreds of urban and territorial ordinances were tools of negotiation.[22] It is best to see the *consilia* in the dynamic social context of the imperial community at work, rather than as the basis of constitutional government in a modern sense. The Protestant movement began and established itself in Germany well before the members of that community knew territorial supremacy. An abundance of "influences or foci for loyalty and identity" continued to characterize Germany for centuries to come.[23]

By 1555, there seemed to be no place in Germany like Geneva, so completely subject to the discipline of a single confession. *Cuius regio, eius religio*, the famous formula associated with the Peace of Augsburg, enshrined the pragmatic settlements of the 1540's. The Peace could not prescribe the confessional state, simply because rule in very many places had yet to be concentrated in the integrated, territorial administrations of singular authorities. The new church

---

the Revolution in France (New York: Anchor, 1973), pp. 172, 176 and Beales, *Prosperity and Plunder*, p. 314.

[21] Schubert, "Vom Gebot zur Landesordnung," p. 30.

[22] To think of them as the laws of 300+ "polities" may imply how incoherent the judicial system was. Witte, *Law and Protestantism*, pp. 177–196, for a summary of laws, their absorption of canon law, and their rejection of the church "at least in theory, as the primary object and subject of charity and social welfare." For this last matter, see also Sebastian Kreiker, *Armut, Schule, Obrigkeit. Armenversorgung und Schulwesen in den evangelischen Kirchenordnungen des 16. Jahrhunderts* (Bielefeld: Verlag für Regionalsgeschichte, 1997), p. 234 and passim, who explains "die ungenügende administrative Reichweite obrigkeitlicher Verordnungstätigkeit."

[23] N.R. Reagin, "Recent Work on German National Identity: Regional? Imperial? Gendered? Imaginary?," *Central European History* 37 (2004) 273–289.

established itself by accommodating this fissiparous arrangement of power and the measure of diversity that came with it. Conflicts over church property between 1525 and 1547 set the stage for continued debate through the ninety-three years that followed the Augsburg Peace. That debate was further complicated by the church property upheavals of the Dutch Revolt in the northwest and the Thirty-Years War throughout the Empire.

The early debate over church property reveals the expanded role of a canon-law assumption about the relation of property to society. It may be the only conceptual innovation in the controversy over church property, and it is a subtle one. Just as acceptance of confiscations depended upon a traditional conviction (a ruler's obligation to protect the church), so also the reformers' defense of confiscation and church property implied a socialization of material things. The reformers defined the church's material goods not according to anyone's dominion but according to use and purpose. The purpose of sacred things was ultimately the experience of grace in a place. This was the sense of dominion in the theological advice to the League in 1540: "the church has dominion over . . . properties [of the church in a place]."[24] By "dominion" the theologians meant to restrict the purpose of property to the welfare of a particular locale. The church was in their minds a spiritual fellowship of baptized people ideally coterminus with cities and territories. For Protestants to say the church possessed dominion left all relevant questions unanswered, in particular, who had the right to use, consume, and destroy its material things? The theologians wanted to say, insofar as the raw power to control was concerned, everyone, and therefore no one. Church property had to be administered for the benefit of each Christian populace. Later in the 1540 advice, the theologians complained that the properties of the church are not "free fiefs that one should give to such an awful, godless lot [that is, non-reformed clergy], to waste uselessly and without discipline." The property is not really subject to the disposition of any particular power. It is subject to correct use, its moral and religious profitability. With this assertion, even Ulrich of Württemberg could think of himself as the church's most devoted defender. The precedent was taken from the semi-public character of church property in canon law. The theologians subor-

---

[24] Appendix 1.

dinated the property rights retained by patrons to this socialized
view. It was a strictly religious notion associated with an order of
priorities, with the work of reformed clergy always in first place, then
schools that embrace correct doctrine, then poor relief, and finally
those other things that preserved the common good, including temporal government. As territorial administrations grew in the decades
to come, to the particular advantage of the imperial princes, they
increasingly managed common properties, which coincided with the
absorption of canonical norms by public law and a gradual transfer
of personal dominion (the material control of private properties) to
public power (the power of state).[25] But the prince remained one
person within a hierarchically arranged body of faithful who were
all obliged to preserve this common good. His was a prerogative
based on the coincidence of his social position, which is what sep-
arates him, for example, from Edmund Burke's state: "in a question
of reformation," concluded Burke at the end of his discussion of the
sale of monasteries in Revolutionary France, "I always consider corporate bodies, whether sole or consisting of many, to be much more
susceptible of a public direction by the power of the state, in the
use of their property, and in the regulation of modes and habits of
life in their members, than private citizens ever can be, or perhaps
ought to be."[26]

The theologians' socialized view of property belonged to a different
world than modern debates over common ownership, social welfare,
or the natural rights of individuals. The reformers did not link common property to the state as its most correct administrator, as the
representative of a collective will, or as a guarantor of the individual's
natural powers. Rather, they adapted a medieval social imaginary,
a concept of the church. All Christians bore the responsibility to
promote and protect the proper use of common property—religious
assets—according to one's own station in life. This fact must prevent
us from attributing the origins of modern liberal or social republics—
conceptualized around individual moral responsibility, social welfare,
or some combination of both—to Protestant reformers, however central the memory of Protestant rebellion may have been among some
theorists of liberal republics or welfare states a century ago. The

---

[25] Sieglerschmidt, *Territorialstaat*, pp. 145, 273, 285 and passim.
[26] Burke, *Reflections on the Revolution in France*, p. 178.

CONCLUSION: PROSPECT/RETROSPECT

issue was something else. It was the absence of an encompasing, collective umbrella in Protestant Germany apart from Christendom, since Christendom no longer corresponded to government by the hierarchical church. Christianity was, in the evangelical imagination, simply the universal religion of congregations tutored by biblical preachers and organized in several ways territorially, while secret believers were scattered throughout Catholic realms, where their faith was oppressed by the tyranny of papal government and idolatry. Together, all who had faith comprised a single imagined community, to borrow Benedict Anderson's famous phrase,[27] which they imagined as the community of saints, whose worldly features were reduced to a new practice of sacraments and a body of selectively traditional convictions. In the absence of a single, earthly spiritual government, the evangelical theologians argued from this invisible, abstract communion, according to moral consequences and property usage (defined as worship, education, and charity), not ownership.

Still, the religious justification for church property may seem to reinforce the impression that the early Protestants anticipated or began the European rebellion that transformed the church from the continent's richest and most pervasive government to an institution of spiritual care, a religious institution in the modern sense. It cannot be said, however, that the early Protestant movement began a chain reaction of secularization leading invariably to the modernity of either liberal or social republics.[28] The terms of debate in Germany throughout that first generation were deeply colored by traditional religious norms and preachers' agendas. The norms and the agendas were defined and maintained by a stubbornly privileged institution called the church.

---

[27] Benedict Anderson, *Imagined Communities* (London: Verso, 1983, 1991), p. 6 and passim.

[28] Neither has secularism displaced religion in political life today. Talal Asad, "Religion, Nation-State, Secularism," *Nation and Religion: Perspectives on Europe and Asia*, edited by Peter van der Veer and Hartmut Lehmann (Princeton University Press, 1999), pp. 178–196, here 192.

APPENDIX ONE

THE THEOLOGICAL RECOMMENDATION OF 1540

ON CHURCH PROPERTY

Saxony: Justus Jonas, Johannes Bugenhagen Pomeranian, Caspar Creuzinger, Philip Melanchthon.
Magdeburg and Duke Heinrich of Saxony: Nikolaus Amsdorf, Nikolaus Scheubell.
Hesse: Antonius Corvinus, Johannes Reimaus, Balthasar Reid.
Strasbourg: Martin Bucer.
Nassau: Erasmus Sarcerius. I, doctor Pomeranus, by my own hand sign for him, as he asked me by letter.
Bremen: Johannes Timan.

On Church Property

First, it is certain that every government is responsible in its territory to abolish improper divine worship and establish proper worship, to institute parishes and schools, and to provide for the sustenance of needy people. And that the government is responsible for this service and work of God is clear in many of our writings and irrefutably demonstrated. Thus, Isaiah says, "and the kings will be your nurturers and the queens, nurses,"[1] that is, princes and city[2] should feed the churches and support them. Indeed, the commonwealth also becomes God's maidservant, and so should it be in its highest office and work, that it serve the praise of God and support and protect the church, for on account of this work God established government and civil society, that in it God's name, doctrine, and church should shine. And where such is not the case, as among the pagans, there the government does not function in good order, and even if they are at the same time wise, clever people, like Alexander the Great and his associates were, it's still only a Cyclops gang,[3] which is godless

---

[1] Is. 49.23.
[2] *Stett*, "city," is feminine, as is its Latin equivalent, *civitas*. The text takes feminine *regine*, "queens," as a metaphor for cities.
[3] Erasmus' *Adagia* explains the Cyclops as an image of an ungoverned life. Erasmus, *Opera omnia*, 10 vols. (Louvain: Vander, 1703–6, reprinted London: Gregg Press,

and ordained for eternal damnation. And it is, in summary, certain that the legal basis remains sure, namely that the temporal government is responsible to institute correctly parishes and schools and to abolish idolatry.

Secondly, where now the government abolishes incorrect divine worship, there is no doubt that the parish property remains to the churches, since if there were no parish property there, the government would be responsible to establish new properties to that end and impose something [i.e. a tax] on all parishioners, as their ancestors have done, and as it stands written [in Paul's letter] to the Galatians,[4] the hearer is responsible to pay the teacher. And so the church has dominion of the same properties. But the temporal government is protector over the properties, and should sustain them and institute the sustenance of the personnel from them: this all is out in the open.

Third, just as an incompetent preacher or pastor is removed, so that the office can be given to a competent one, so it follows, the property should go to the competent and not the previous one, according to the rule, "the benefice is given on account of the office," and this is expressed openly in many places in laws. Thus Christ says, "the worker is worthy of his pay."[5] And is it not true now that some allege that if a prebend is lent to a person, one may not remove him for his entire life, as though like a knight he were enfeofed— for his entire life? These church benefices are offices, certain people boast. They sit in ownership; one cannot remove them!

Fourthly, about parish and school property it is easy to understand that such property would be justly held as said [namely, that it remains with the parish]. Now we want to say more about foundation and cloister property.

When the governments abolish incorrect divine worship, the property remains to the correct churches, as Augustine writes: that properties of the Donatist churches are justly transferred to the correct churches, and the temporal government is protector of them and

---

1962), 2:153A, 385F, 1132D. The last passage refers us to book 10 of Aristotle's *Nicomachean Ethics*, where (x.9, 1180a, lines 24–34) the philosopher notes that in contrast with the Spartan state, in most states people live like the Cyclops (κυκλωπικῶς), each living as one pleases. Erasmus explains the Cyclops-life as "ubi nullis publicis legibus vivitur, sed quisque suo arbitratu res gerit." It's like living in the mountains according to wim with no sight of civil life, religionless.

⁴ Gal 6.6.
⁵ Luke 10.7.

has to appoint them just like other public goods.[6] On that account the princes and estates did this rightly, that they in their territories in foundations and cloisters abolished incorrect divine worship and took the properties under their administration. For there can be no doubt that they are responsible for both, to abolish incorrect divine worship, as the first and second commandments teach, and to take up the administration of the properties as patrons and protectors of common property, and especially of church properties. Thus no one should have governing power besides the temporal government. For since such goods, like cities and villages, require one obligation and higher jurisdiction, it is fitting that not church personnel but rather the temporal government take up the same.

Fifthly, on that account the government is obliged not to alienate the same [church] property but rather to preserve it faithfully and from it, first of all, to attend to the office of preacher and schools according to need; secondly help should be given to poor people from it. And be there greater goods, it is reasonable that one give help to poor youth, noble and not noble, in the land, for study. Again, to provide support to ailing church ministers and those that have dutifully fulfilled their office.[7] Again, that one should receive a provision.[8] That one might help the poor in times of inflation, etc. If something is left over, the government as patrons may enjoy the same, since they must protect and manage such property, [and] also endure tremendous expenses on account of religion, as long as they first supply the parishes, schools, studies, poor, as said. But certain ones take to themselves not only the foundation and cloister property, but also injure the parishes and hospitals, which is much to be contested and is a theft that God would severely penalize. For that reason we admonish them that they would use and manage this property as said. It would also be reasonable that managers be chosen, to render account of the churches at any time, that is certain people chosen from the territory, that one can ascertain that such is maintained as church property and primarily stipulated for that end.

---

[6] C 23 q. vii.3, CICan 1:951–52, quoting Augustine's Ep.50.

[7] "those that have dutifully fulfilled their office," *emeriti*. The idea is to pension retired clergy.

[8] This apparently refers to clerical retirees. Or this is an abbreviated reference to pensions given to those who leave cloisters to return to secular life, which was also practiced.

Sixthly, because the cathedral foundations in great cities want to be their own lordships, as at Strasbourg, Augsburg, Constance, Bremen, Magdeburg, etc., or allege that the cities have no supremacy over them, as at Frankfurt, Esslingen, Hamburg, Braunschweig, etc., from these foundations, all of them equally, it is fundamentally true that there were and should be parish churches and schools at the place, and how then can it be thought, that at the same places there rather be no parish property because in certain cities the hospitals were converted into collegiate foundations for un-Christian papal use, as at Strasbourg, Memmingen, etc.?[9] Again, almost all foundations grew out of incorporated parishes.[10] There cannot be any doubt about this. The parishes, schools, and poor in cities should foremost be supplied from such properties, and after, from the oversupply, help should be given to the churches of the countryside and the poor nobility.

Therefore, that a settlement may be reached,[11] if such a city claims such great need, certain church property should be delivered to it, as much as they need to appoint their churches, schools, and hospitals, and then stipulate which foundations should be authorized to the nobility who need help and which should be handed over to the cities. For it is not possible for the cities to pay for their churches in the long term and openly arrange that they should be completely robbed of their foundations and fiefs, as all the city-emissaries suffi-ciently know to report. But if they cannot demand such through nego-tiation, so is it equally true that they do rightly to banish the idola-trous pastors and persecutors of correct doctrine from their midst,

---

[9] The cities of Strasbourg (1533 and 1536, by the bishop of Strasbourg), Constance (1536, by the cathedral chapter), Frankfurt (1533, by the archbishop of Mainz), Esslingen (1536), and Hamburg (1529, by the cathedral chapter of Hamburg), and the Duke of Braunschweig (1533) were all defendents in suits before the *Reichskam-mergericht*. The city of Constance, as administrator of a church made evangelical, appealed in 1537 the verdict of another court, the decision of which the *Reichs-kammergericht* upheld. Dolezalek, "Die juristische Argumentation," pp. 33–36.

[10] The allegation of this rather dense clause is that collegiate churches in cities accumulated parishes through "incorporation," the process stipulated by church law when a fraternal church body gains control of a parish church and the tithes asso-ciated with it. Moreover, cathedral foundations have title to most or all the churches in many towns, also encroaching on things originally intended for parish ministry. The origin justifies returning the property to the use of parish ministry, which causes conflict with collegiate foundations and cathedral chapters.

[11] That is, a settlement between the princes and the cities at the Schmalkald diet of 1540.

and thus is it possible for them to gather in the church properties to the extent that necessity demands, as they at Hamburg and Minden took away certain goods from the [cathedral] foundations for the necessary provisioning of their pastors.

But because someone will want to counter that the emperor alone is patron, and the emperor should arrange such properties for their proper use, to that there is a quick answer: because the emperor protects and maintains incompetent people in the control of these goods, so may the churches, upon his order or command, in this matter rely on us.[12] An example. The emperor Decius demanded from [St.] Lawrence the church treasure.[13] Then as now one had to recognize the emperor's supremacy, but Lawrence wanted to give him nothing. Likewise, Ambrose did not want, upon the emperor's command, to abandon the church to the Goths and said, although one truly acknowledges that everything belongs to the emperor, yet the church is the Lord Christ's.[14] Thus there remains to the true church its right to retain its property that it has in possession, and to confiscate it at the place where it was especially instituted for the support of the ministers, since the parish property should follow the right pastor, and one must remove the incompetent, as indicated above.

And the cunning of the poisonous snake in the Chamber Court is not to be tolerated, which does not want to understand church property as a matter of religion, yet this article is an article of doctrine,[15] that the papists, pastors, and monks sit on church properties as thieves and robbers, and the church property as parish property should follow the correct office and be not free fiefs that one should give to such an awful, godless lot, to waste uselessly and without

---

[12] The point here seems to be that, since the emperor expects the estates to protect religion, so must the estates protect religion from the emperor when he himself fails in the obligation. Or in other words, defense of religion does not imply treason.

[13] Cf. *Legenda aurea* 117, *The Golden Legend*, trans. William Granger Ryan, 2 vols. (Princeton University Press, 1993), 2:65–6. In Lawrence's legend, Decius' demand is based on a misunderstanding, having heard Lawrence refer to the "treasures" of the church, which he used as a metaphor for the poor. This reading suggests that Lawrence used the metaphor to protect church property.

[14] Ambrosius, *Sermo contra Auxentium* 35, PL16:1061A, *Decretum Gratiani*, C. 23, q. 8, c. 21, CICan 1:960. *Bucers Deutsche Schriften* 9/1:88 n. 17.

[15] "Leer artickell," probably meaning an "article of faith," an evident, preferably self-evident, premise of theological argument.

discipline, as Peter already prophesied,[16] that the church prelates will wantonly feast upon alms: they themselves know that their own canon laws don't hold this matter as a secular issue.

This our report on church property we wish to bid our most gracious, gracious lords to accept kindly from us. For this our report on church property we bid our most gracious [lords], and we have no doubt at all, that this opinion is truly founded upon God's word and the ancient canons and imperial laws, if one wants to understand them very appropriately, without sophistry, in their natural, correct meaning. On that account also one's conscience may be variously instructed and confirmed from this report. Would that God lend this grace to all Christian rulers that they generously help, maintain, and promote church offices and studies.

Edition

There has been much confusion over this text. According to Deetjen it was first published in the eighteenth century by Christian Sattler under the date 1535 and the title *Gutachten an die Fursten und Stände des Schmalkaldischen Bundes*.[17] Sattler's exemplar still exists in the Baden-Württembergisches Staatsarchiv in Stuttgart among materials, including inventory lists, from Duke Ulrich's confiscations in that year, under the title *Gutachten ausslaendischer Theologen ueber die Kirchenguetter, c. 1535*.[18] The Stuttgart copy was once bound in a codex, for which reason it bears folio numbers 211(v)–217(v). Yet the flyleaf/cover shows that it was originally written and folded as a single item, likely as a copy prepared for the duke or his counselors. Deetjen assigned it to 1537 and identified it with a letter by Melanchthon in the *Corpus Reformatorum*.[19] But the letter to which he referred is actually a different text, the 1537 advice of Wittenberg theologians to the Schmalkald League discussed in chapter 5, above.

A supplement to Melanchthon's letters in the *Corpus Reformatorum*

---

[16] 2 Peter 2.3.
[17] Deetjen, *Studien zur Württembergischen Kirchenordnungen*, p. 317 n. 172. C.W. Sattler, *Geschichte des Herzogtums Württemberg unter der Regierung der Herzogen*, 3 Bde. (Ulm 1769–71) 3:151f., Beilage Nr. 4.
[18] Stuttgart, Staatsarchiv, A63 Bueschel 4a.
[19] CR 3:288.

includes the text under the date 24 February 1537.[20] There, it is edited from a Vienese copy, which is an apograph and has Melanchthon's name subscribed at the end, "Philippus Melanthon von Kirchengütern. 49.," thus appearing to assign the document to 1549.[21] But the address to "unsre gnädigste und gnädige Herren" must refer, the editor tells us, to the electoral prince and the Landgrave of Hesse, and that suggests it was written before and not after the Schmalkald War, since both princes were in imperial custody after the war and, as a consequence of their defeat, the electorate passed from Johann Friedrich and the Ernestine succession to duke Georg and the Albertine succession. The *Corpus Reformatorum* compares the Vienna copy with an edition of a Kassel copy edited by Georg Neudecker in his *Urkunden aus der Reformationszeit*, and it claims that from the names subscribed at the end of the text, it should be dated to the Schmalkald convention of 1537. But this conclusion is based on a misreading of Neudecker. The *Corpus Reformatorum* alleges that Neudecker found the document included in a letter of Georg von Carlowitz to Landgrave Philip dated "Dresden Freytags Purificationis Mariä [i.e. 2 February] 1537," then the editor speculates that Carlowitz could not have sent this letter, concluding that it must rather have been written at Schmalkalden, not Dresden. The conclusion is based on a mistake. The *Corpus Reformatorum* confuses the *Gutachten* with the letter of von Carlowitz to the Landgrave of 2 February 1537, which is in fact a separate, previous item in Neudecker's volume.[22]

The correct date, 9 March 1540, was given by Heinrich Ernst Bindseil in his edition of previously unedited letters and texts by Melanchthon, and defended by Heinz Scheible, but the 1537 date still sometimes appears in the work of modern scholars.[23] The *Gutachten* was since edited by Cornelius Augustijn and Marijn de Kroon and included in their edition of Bucer's German works. They relied on the manuscripts represented by Neudecker, Bindseil, and the *Corpus*

---

[20] CR 4:1040–46 nr. 1532.
[21] Biblioteca Palatina, Theol. no. 908 fol 276f.
[22] Neudecker, *Urkunden*, pp. 298–310 nr. 99.
[23] Philip Melanchthon, *Epistolae, iudicia, consilia, testimonia aliorumque ad eum epistolae quae in Corpore Reformatorum desiderantur*, ed. Heinrich Ernest Bindseil (New York: Georg Olms, 1975), pp. 142–46. Heinz Scheible, *Melanchthons Briefwechsel* 10, T1–T3 vols. (Stuttgart: Fromann-Holzboog, 1977+) 3:2391 nr. 2391. Mencke, *Visitationen*, p. 61 and note 331, and Sieglerschmidt, *Territorialstaat*, pp. 143 and 284, repeat the 1537 date.

Reformatorum. It is the best edition produced thus far, although it does not include the Stuttgart manuscript. There is no edition representing all known manuscripts, nor has anyone given a complete account of the dating errors still in circulation.

The thirteen signatories represent the territories of Electoral Saxony, Hesse, Albertine Saxony (with the city of Magdeburg), and Nassau, and the cities of Strasbourg, Bremen, and as mentioned, Magdeburg.[24] Along with the well-known theologians of Wittemberg (Melanchthon, Jonas, Bugenhagen, Cruciger the Elder), Magdeburg (Amsdorf), and Strasbourg (Bucer), we find less known representatives of Ducal Saxony, Hesse, Nassau, and Bremen. Scheubel (representing Ducal Saxony) was the first Protestant theologian of the University of Leipzig. Antonius Corvinus, a pastor in Hesse, was placed by Philip of Hesse on all the religious colloquies of 1539–1541. Johannes Kymaeus was also a preacher in Hesse and advisor to Philip. Balthasar Raidt was pastor in Hersfeld in Hesse. Erasmus Sarcerius was a pastor in Nassau. Johann Timann was pastor in Bremen.

The known manuscripts are, with the sigla used in the edition that follows:

S = Stuttgart, Baden-Württembergisches Staatsarchiv, A63 Büschel 4a (according to old folio numbers in upper right corners, 211v–217v). Edited by Christian Friedrich Sattler, *Geschichte des Herzogthums Württemberg unter der Regierung der Herzogen* 13 vols., (Ulm: A.L. Stettin, 1769–1788), 3:151–54. Sattler slightly modernized word order and some spelling. I follow the manuscript.

K = a manuscript of the Regierungsarchiv in Kassel and edited by Christian Gotthold Neudecker, *Urkunden aus der Reformationszeit*, (Kassel: J.C. Krieger, 1836), pp. 310–15 nr. 100. In 1871, the Regierungsarchiv was moved to Marburg, but it is unclear what happened to Neudecker's exemplar. I searched Hessisches Staatsarchiv Marburg, Bestand 3, nr. 538 and 540, which includes materials pertaining to the Schmalkald diet of 1540, and Bestand 22a 3 Nr. 5, Bestand 22a 8 Nr. 24–26, Bestand 22a 2 Nr. 45–47, Bestand 22a 11, all potential places for a mislaid document, to no avail. Neudecker's exemplar may no longer be extant.

---

[24] *Bucers Deutsche Schriften* 9/1:89–90.

W = Österreichische Nationalbibliothek, Cod. 11551, b. 276a–82b, included in the very good edition by Cornelius Augustijn and Marijn de Kroon in *Martin Bucers Deutsche Schriften*.

G = Gießen, Universitätsbibliothek, Handschriftenbestand Nr. 651 f. 54–60. Edition: Philip Melanchthon, *Epistolae, iudicia, consilia, testimonia aliorumque ad eum epistolae quae in Corpore Reformatorum desiderantur*, ed. Heinrich Ernest Bindseil (Halle: G. Schwetschke, 1826; rep. New York: Georg Olms, 1975), pp. 142–46.

Cornelius Augustijn and Marijn de Kroon were aware only of Neudecker (for K), W, and G.[25] CR used Neudecker (for K) and W. Bindseil used G. Augustijn and De Kroon's edition is more careful than both Neudecker and Bindseil. I rely on their readings for W and G. I rely on Neudecker for K.

The edition below presents S with variations noted from the previous editions, and I try to note only those differences that, beyond regional orthography and dialect, may suggest the relation of manuscripts, since I was curious to see what the manuscript tradition might suggest about its circulation and use. Sentence and paragraph divisions vary as well. I note when different words occur, seldom note spelling differences or slightly variant case-endings. I follow the punctuation of S but not slavishly.

There appear to have been two or more stages of copying. If we exclude the most incidental variants and analyze the remainder, we may conclude the following. W is the most independent, improving the text by adding words or phrases, omitting an obscure term or writing in slight shorthand, or omitting or changing entire phrases. In some instances S departs from W, K, and G, suggesting its partial independence. In other cases K and W share a common reading and common omissions. K and G occasionally agree against the other witnesses, or G and W against the other witnesses. The closest family relationships therefore appear to be between W, K, and G, with at least one median stage of transmission to account for the independent affinities of G with W and G with K. S has an initial half-page flyleaf (f. 212, apparently an external cover) with these notes in four different contemporary hands, two of which may

---

[25] *Martin Bucers Deutsche Schriften*, vol. 9/1, ed. C. Augustijn, M. De Kroon (Gütersloh: Gütersloher Verlagshaus, 1995), 79–90.

correspond to the hand of the text. Hand 1 of S wrote a square
gothic title, whose serifs are similar to the text hand's serifs, and it
says: *von den Kurchengüeter*. Hand two, which appears to be the text
hand, says above the title and running through some of its serifs:
ausslendisch ewangelisch theologos bedencken. Hand three provides three
notes placed below the title. One says: *idem cum praecedente*. Another:
sine dato. The third: *153*, perhaps being an incomplete date. In the
upper right hand corner is another cancelled mark in this hand: 17b
(under it appears the modern folio number 212). In the lower left
hand area is hand four: *Archiv praelatis?* (illegible) L.A. 53. This last
hand matches that of 211v, an archivist's hand on a flyleaf who
gives the document a title and repeats the inventory number. The
format of S, sent as a parcel and placed in the Duke of Württemberg's
archive, further suggests that in spite of its relatively independent
orthography, it was a copy made probably at Schmalkalden from
the original and sent home (but K appears to represent the most
influential text). The edition below follows S, including punctuation
(the old folio numbers are included in footnotes), noting variant
readings from G, W, and K. I compare readings of K as they are
represented by CR 4:1040–46 and by Augustijn and De Kroon
and rely on the latter for readings of G and W, as I mentioned
above (their edition reproduces G and notes variants from W and
Neudecker/K). A plausible stemma would be (although it is possible that median versions exist between G and K/W):

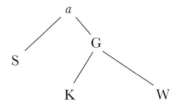

¹Von den Kůrchengůeter
²Sachsen.³
Justus Jonas d
Johannes Bugenhagen Bomer d
Caspar Croinzinger d   5
Philipus Melanchton

Magdeburg, Herzog Hanrich zu Sachsen.
Nicolaus Amsdorff
Nicholaus Scheubell   10

Hessen.
Antonius Corvinus
Johannes Rymauss
Balthassar Raydus   15

Strasburg.
Martinus Bucerus

Nassau.   20
Erasmus Sarcerius. Ego doctor pomeranus mea manu pro eo sub-
scribo ita ipse me per literas rogauit.⁴

Bremen.
Johannes Amsterdamus⁵   25

⁶Von den Kirchen Gueter⁷.
Erstlichen ist⁸ nicht zweifeln⁹ ein¹⁰ jede oberkeit ist schuldig in irren
gebieten unrechte gotz dienst abzuthun und rechte anzurichten, die

---

¹ S f. 212r.
² S f. 213r.
³ K omits the city/state names from the list. W omits the entire list.
⁴ Ego doctor . . . rogauit] S places this note after the list of subscriptions. G and K place this note with Sarcerius.
⁵ Johannes Timan
⁶ S f. 214r
⁷ Gothic hand matching the title on the flyleaf. W Philippus Melanthon von kurchen Guettern.
⁸ W *add* mir
⁹ CR Zweifel. G Zweinelh. W *add* das
¹⁰ CR eine

30 pfarren und schulen zubestellen und den personnen notturfftige underhaltung zuuerschaffen[11]. Und das die oberkeit dissen dienst und dises[12]
werck Got[13] schuldig seie ist in vilen unsern schrifften clar unnd
unwidersprechlich erwisen. So spricht Esaias[14], Et[15] reges erunt nutri-
tores vestri[16] et regine[17] nutrices, dass ist fursten unnd stett sollen die
35 kurchen erneren, unnd underhallten. Ja[18] also werden die polacie[19]
auch gottes[20] dienerin[21] unnd seind[22] in irem furnemsten ampt und
werck so sie zu Gottes lob dienen, unnd die kurch[23] underhallten
unnd schuzen, dann[24] umb dises wercks willen hatt Gott Regiment
unnd policitam societatem geordnet das darin leuchten sollen[25] sein
40 nam[26] ler[27] unnd kurche[28]. Unnd wo solchs nit ist, alls by den haiden,
da[29] gend[30] die regiment nicht in rechter ordnung, und wans[31] gleich
weise geschicke leut sind, Alls Alexander und seine gesellen gewesen[32], so ists doch nur ein hauff Cyclopum[33], der one Got[34] ist, unnd
zu ewiger verdamnis verordnet[35]. Und ist in somma[36] nicht zweifeln[37],
45 der gestzte grund pleibt vest, nemlich das die weltliche oberkeitt

[11] B zu schaffen
[12] *om* W
[13] *om* W
[14] Isaiah 49.23.
[15] *om* W
[16] W tui
[17] W regentes
[18] W Da
[19] CR, K Politiae. G policie. W Policeyen
[20] *om* W
[21] W dienern
[22] CR sind
[23] G, W Kirchen
[24] G, W denn
[25] W soll. G solle
[26] CR Nahme. G, W nham
[27] G, W leher
[28] CR Kirchen
[29] G, W do
[30] CR gehen
[31] G, W wens
[32] W gesellen gewesen] Haufe und Gesellen gewest sein. CR gewest seyn.
[33] W *om.* Erasmus, *Opera omnia*, 10 vols. (Louvain: Vander, 1703–6, reprinted London: Gregg Press, 1962), 2:153A, 385F, 1132D. See also Aristotle, *Nicomachean Ethics*, (x.9, 1180a, lines 24–34).
[34] W Geist
[35] unnd zu ewiger verdamnis verordnet] W zum ewigen feuer verdampt
[36] K, G, W Summa
[37] K Zweuel

schuldig[38] ist die pfarren[39] und schulen recht zu bestellen und abgot-
tery abzuthun.

[40]Zum anndern wo nun die oberkeit in pfarren die unrechten
gottes diennst abthut ist nicht zweifeln die pfargueter pleibenn der
kurchen, dann so keine pfargueter da werren[41], werre die Oberkeit   50
schuldig nuwe[42] gueter datzu zuverrordnen, unnd allen pfarleuten
etwas ufzuligen wie ire voreltern gethan haben[43], unnd wie[44] geschriben
stet[45] ad Galatas[46] der zuhorer ist schuldig dem lerrer zu lonen. Unnd
hatt also die kurch dominium derselbigen gueter. Aber die weltlich
oberkeitt ist schutzher daruber, unnd soll sie erhallten und den per-   55
sonnen ir unnderhaltung davon verordnen, dises alles ist offennlich[47].

Zum dritten so ain undichtiger[48] prediger oder pfarher entsezt wird
dass[49] das ampt ainem tuchtigen bevolhen, so volgt der solld dem
dichtigten[50] unnd nicht dem vorigen, lautt der Regell beneficium
datur propter officium[51], unnd ist dises offenlich an vilen orten inn[52]   60
rechten usgetruckt. So[53] spricht Cristus[54] dignus est operarius mercede[55],
und reymtt[56] sich nicht hieher[57] dass etlich furgeben, so ainem ain prebend gelihen[58] moge man[59] denselbigen nicht entsetzen[60] sein lebenlang[61], gleich alls ob[62] ime ain ritter lehen[63] sein lebenlang vershriben.

---

[38] schuldig . . . schulen] W die pfarrern unnd schulen schuldig ist

[39] K Pfarrer

[40] S f. 214v

[41] W *add* so

[42] G, W neue. K newe

[43] *om* W

[44] *om* W

[45] *om* W

[46] Galatians 6.6.

[47] dises . . . offennlich] *om* W

[48] G, W, K untuchtiger

[49] G, W *add* und

[50] G, W, K tuchtigen

[51] *Liber Sextus*, I.iii.15, CICan 2:943. *Martin Bucers Deutsche Schriften*, 9/1:85 n. 5.

[52] G im

[53] W Do

[54] Luke 10.7.

[55] W *add* sua

[56] W ruemb.

[57] W daher

[58] W *om*. W *add* wird

[59] moge man] W *om*

[60] W zuentsezen

[61] sein lebenlang] W *om*

[62] gleich alls ob] W gleichsamb wer. K gleich als sei. G gleich als so

[63] CR Lohn. ime ain ritter lehen sein lebenlang vershriben] W im sein lebn lang
ein [*del* . . .] reicher lohn verschriben

65 Dise kurchen lehen[64] sind Ampter, etliche rumen. Sie sizen in der possession man konne sie nicht entsetzen[65].

[66]Zum vierdten, von pfar[67] unnd schulguetern ists[68] leicht zuversten[69], das solche billich also gehallten wurd wie gesagt ist. Nun wollen wir weiter von stifft unnd closter gueter sagenn. So die oberkeiten[70] die
70 unrechten Gottes diennst darin[71] abgethann pleibenn die gueter der rechten kurchen wie Augustinus schreibet, das der donatisten kurchen gueter billich der rechtenn kurchen zugewandt werden[72] und ist die weltlich oberkeit schutzen[73] daruber hatt dieselbigen zubestellen wie andere publicabona. Darumb die fursten und stende[74] dises theils
75 recht gethan[75], dass sie in iren gebieten in stifften[76] und clostern die[77] unrechten gottes diennst abgethan, unnd die[78] gueter in ire verwaltung genomen. Dann[79] ganz kein zweifell daran, das sie beides schuldig sind, die unrechten gottes dienst abzuthun, wie das erst und ander gebot leren[80], und die verwaltung der guoter anzunemen alls patroni
80 und schutzhern gemeiner[81] gueter, unnd in sonderheit der kurchen guoter. So soll auch niemandt haben imperia, dan die weltlich oberkeit. Dann[82] dweill[83] solche gueter alls stett unnd dorffer eins zwangs, und der hohen[84] jurisdiction[85] bedorffen, geburt sich derselbigen[86] nicht

---

[64] W lohn
[65] G *add* etc.
[66] S f. 215r
[67] W pfarhen
[68] W, G ist
[69] W zuusteen. G zuuorstehenn (according to Augustijn and De Kroon: probably misreading zuuerstehenn)
[70] W oberkait
[71] K, W *om*
[72] K, G worden
[73] K, W, G schutzherr
[74] und stende] *om* W
[75] G (CR) *add* haben
[76] in stiften] *om* W
[77] K den.
[78] *om* W
[79] K, G Denn. W Denn es ist
[80] Augustijn and De Kroon refer us to the *Großer Katechismus* on the first two commandments, *Die Bekenntnisschriften der Evangelisch-lutherischen Kirche* 8th ed. (Göttingen 1979), pp. 560–80. *Bucers Deutsche Schriften* 9/1:85 n. 9.
[81] W der gemainen
[82] CR, G Darum
[83] G weil
[84] der hohen] W derhalben
[85] K, W, G Iurisdictio
[86] G dasselbige. K daselbige. W dieselben.

den[87] kurchen personnen sonder die weltlichen oberkeit anzunemen.

Zum funfften, daby ist aber[88] die oberkeit schuldig dieselbige gueter   85
nicht den kurchen zuempfremden sondern[89] sie trewlich zuerhalten[90]
unnd davon erßlichs das predigampt unnd schulen nach notturfft
bestellen, zum andern soll davon hilff gescheen den armen leuten.
Unnd so es grosser guoter seind ist[91] billich dass man davon der
armen jugend, edlen unnd unedlen[92] in landen[93] haff[94] thut[95], zum   90
studio[96].

Item[97] den kurchen dienern so schwach werden[98] unnd emeriti
seindt unnderhaltung zuverschaffen. Item das man[99] einen vorrath
erhalte[100]. Davon man in teuerungen[101] den armen helffen moge[102]
etc[103]. Ist um[104] etwas uberig, so mogen auch die oberkeit[105] als patroni   95
dasselbig[106] mitgeniessen, dweill sie solche gueter schutzen unnd ordnen muossen, tragen auch grossen uncosten der religion halben[107],
souern das[108] sie zuuor[109] die pfarren[110], schulen, studia[111] armen[112]
wie gesagt ist[113] versorgen[114].

---

87 den] G *korr* der
88 daby ist aber] W nichts desto weniger ist
89 S f. 215v
90 W erhalten
91 CR, W *add* es
92 armen jugend, edlten unnd unedlen] W den armen Edlen und Unedlen
93 in landen] *om* W
94 CR Hůlfe, G Hulf
95 W thuen
96 W studirn
97 Item den . . . zuverschaffen. Item . . . moge etc.] W *trans*
98 K, G worden
99 W *add* davon
100 W behalt
101 CR Theurungen
102 K könne. W kune
103 K, W *om*
104 K auch. G, W nu. CR nun.
105 G oberckeitenn. W *add* selbst
106 W desselben. G dasselbige
107 tragen . . . halben] W *om*
108 CR (K) *om*
109 si zuuor] W *om*
110 W pfarnkirchen und
111 W *add* und die
112 G *add* etc.
113 wie gesagt ist] *om* CR (K). W *add* zuuor
114 K besorgen. W verordtnen und besorgen

100   Etliche aber nemen nicht allein die stifft[115] und closter gueter[116] zu sich, sonder bestumpeln auch die pfarren unnd hospitalen, welches seer zubeclagen unnd ain[117] raub ist, den[118] Got ernstlich straffen wurdt. Darumb wir sie vermanen das sie dise[119] gueter wie gesagt ist[120] prauchen[121] und ordnen wollen. Ess were auch billich das
105   oeconomi gewechlet wurden, die der kurchen[122] das ist etlich gewechleten[123] von der lanndschafft[124] zu jeder zeit rechnung[125] thettenn das[126] man erkennen kondt, das sollichs[127] fur kurchengueter gehallten unnd furnemlich dahin verordnet[128] wurden.

       Zum sechstenn Dweill[129] aber die thumbstifft inn grossen stetten
110   aigne[130] herschafft[131] sein wollen, alls zu Strasburg, Augspurg, Costanz[132], Bremen, Magdeburg[133] etc.[134] oder wenden fur, die statt[135] haben[136] kein hochait uber sie, alls zu Frannckfurt, Esslingen, Hamburg, Brunschweige etc[137] von disen stifften[138] allen zugleich ist dises im grund die[139] warheit das es deren[140] ort pfarkurchen[141] unnd schulen gewese[142], unnd sein
115   sollten[143], wie sollichs darus auch[144] zuversten[145], das an denselbigen[146]

---

[115] K Stifter
[116] W om
[117] W om
[118] W welchen
[119] W solche
[120] W om
[121] W recht anlegen
[122] die der kurchen] om W
[123] G geweltenn
[124] die . . . lanndschafft] W das ist etliche Ehrbare von der Landschaft, die
[125] W rechenschaft. S f. 216r
[126] W damit
[127] G, W solche
[128] G verordenet. W verordnen
[129] W weil
[130] W eine
[131] K Herrschaften
[132] om W
[133] W Maideburckh
[134] W, CR (K) om
[135] G Stete
[136] wenden . . . haben] W wen von, die Stete halten. CR wenn von den Statthaltern.
[137] om K.
[138] W schrifften. G Stieften. K Stiftern
[139] G der
[140] W dieser
[141] deren ort pfarkurchen] K denen ortpfarrkirchen
[142] W gewest sein.
[143] sein sollten] K gewesen seyn sollen
[144] om W. darus auch] G trans
[145] Augustijn and De Kroon read: zuuorstehen
[146] W derselben

orten sonnst[147] keine pfarguoter[148] seindt, wie man dann weisst[149] das in etlichen stetten die hospitall in herrnstifft zu uncristlichen bopstlichen braacht verwandellt seindt alls[150] zu Strasburg, Memingen[151] etc[152]. Item es seind vast[153] alle stifft von den incorporierten pfarhen gestigen. Darumb ist nicht zweifell[154]. Ess sollen die pfarren[155], schulen   120
unnd armen in stetten furnemlich von solchen guetern versorget werden, darnach von der ubermas soldt[156] den kurchen uff dem land unnd dem armen adell[157] hilf gescheen. Darumb[158] so ain vergleichung[159] furgenomen wurde, fordert solcher statt[160] hohe notturfft, das inen etliche[161] kurchenguoter[162] zugestellt werden[163] sovill sie[164]   125
zu rechter unnd noturfftiger bestellung irer kurchen, schulen unnd hospitalen bedorffen[165], unnd wurde alls[166] dann zureden sein, welche[167] stifft dem adell unnd[168] der auch hilff bedarff zulassen und welche[169] den stetten ubergebenn sollten[170] werden[171]. Dann es ist den stettenn[172] nicht moglich ire kurchen in[173] die lennge zuerzallten[174], unnd leut[175]   130
uffzuziehen, so sie irer stifften[176] unnd lehen gannz[177] beraupt sein

---

[147] G *add* zu
[148] W Pfarrkurchen guetter sonst
[149] W was
[150] K also
[151] W *om*
[152] K, W *om*
[153] W sonst
[154] G, W zweiuelh
[155] W pfarherrn
[156] G solte. W soll
[157] W *add* zu
[158] G Derhalbenn
[159] K vergleichnus
[160] G Stete. K Stette
[161] S f. 216v
[162] K Kirchen zuvor
[163] W wurden
[164] W *om*
[165] W beturfften
[166] CR also
[167] W welches
[168] K, W, G als
[169] W *add* man
[170] W sollt
[171] W, K (CR) *om*
[172] ubergebenn . . . stettenn] K denen
[173] *om* W
[174] K, W, G zu erhalten
[175] K laut
[176] G, W Stieften. K Stiftern
[177] W, K gar

sollten[178] wie solchs aller stett botschafftenn gnugsam wissen zuberichten. Können sie aber solchs durch hanndlung nicht erlangen so ist gleich woll[179] die warheit, das sie recht thun, so sie die[180] abgottischen
135 pfaffen unnd verfolger rechter[181] leer von sich verjagen, unnd so es inen moglich die kurchenn gueter souill zu irer bestellung von notten zu sich[182] bringen. Wie die[183] zu Hamburg unnd Minden[184] etliche guoter den stifften entzogen zu notturfftiger bestellung irer[185] pfarren[186].

Das man aber dagegen sprechen will, es sye der kaiser allein
140 patronus, derselbig soll solliche gueter ordnen, zu[187] irem rechten prauch, daruff ist ain kurtze Anntwurt, dweill der kaiser undichtige[188] personnen[189] in disen guetern schuzet[190] unnd erhellt[191] so dorffen die kurchen uff sein verdernung[192] oder beuelch hierin uns warten.
[193]Exemplum. Der kaiser Decius[194] fordert von Laurentio der[195] kurchen
145 schatz. Nun hatt man[196] gleich wie jezund[197] des kaisers hoheit anziehen mogen, aber Lorentius wollt im nichts gebenn[198]. Also Ambrosius wollt uffs[199] kaisers gebott den götten[200] nicht die kurch einreumen[201] unnd sprach, ob man wol sagt alles sye des kaisers[202] so sy doch die kürch des herrn Cristi[203]. Also pleibet der warren kurchen ire gerechtig-

---

[178] sein sollten] werden W
[179] gleich woll] W ists gleich
[180] die warheit . . . die] W *om*
[181] K reinen
[182] *add* zu G
[183] W *om*
[184] *add* den Pfaffen W
[185] W der
[186] Wie die zu Hamburg . . . Pfarren] K, G *om*
[187] K in
[188] unnd nichtige *add* W
[189] W person
[190] W schuzt
[191] W helt
[192] G Verordenung. W verordtnen. CR Verordnung.
[193] S f. 217r
[194] W Donius. CR (K) Valerianus
[195] CR (K) den
[196] W *add* hier
[197] G itzo
[198] Cf. *Legenda Aurea* nr. 117 trans. W.G. Ryan, 2:63–74.
[199] CR *add* des
[200] K Gothen. W gotzen. G Gotten
[201] W *add* und ihm nichts geben
[202] ob man . . . kaisers] *om* K
[203] Ambrosius, Sermo contra Auxentium 35, PL16:1061A, *Decretum Gratiani*, C XXIII, q. 8, c. 21, CICan 1:960. *Bucers Deutsche Schriften* 9/1:88 n. 17.

keit ire gueter, so sie inhatt, zubehallten auch an denen orten 150
entzunemen²⁰⁴ dahin sie zu underhalltung²⁰⁵ der ministerien²⁰⁶ furnemlich gestifftet, wie das pfargut dem rechten pfarher volgen soll unnd
muss so man den²⁰⁷ untichtigen entsetzet, wie daroben²⁰⁸ anngetzaigt²⁰⁹.

Unnd ist den güfftigen²¹⁰ schlangen im camergericht, ire lisst²¹¹ nicht
zuzulassen²¹², welche die²¹³ sache von kurchenguotern nicht fur religion- 155
sachen versten wollenn²¹⁴, dann auch diser artikell ain leer artickell²¹⁵
ist, das die papistenn²¹⁶, pfaffen unnd munche, in den kurchenguotern
sitzen, alls²¹⁷ dieb unnd raober²¹⁸, unnd das kurchengueter wie pfargueter dem rechten ampt²¹⁹ volgen sollen, unnd seind nicht freie
lehenn, die man annem²²⁰ solche miessigen²²¹ Gottlosen hauffen gebenn 160
soll²²², unnuzlich²²³ unnd in unzucht zuverschwenden²²⁴, wie sonnst²²⁵
petruss geweissaget²²⁶, das die kurchen prelaten²²⁷ die elemosinen²²⁸
mutwilliglich verschlemen²²⁹ werden²³⁰, so wissen sie selbs das ir aig-
ine canones dise sach nicht fur ein weltliche sach halltenn²³¹.

---

²⁰⁴ inhatt . . . entzunemen] K denen Orten einzunehmen. entzunemen] W einzu-
reumen. G einzunehmen
²⁰⁵ W erhaltung
²⁰⁶ W ministros
²⁰⁷ rechten . . . man] W *om.* den] W droben
²⁰⁸ G oben. *om* W
²⁰⁹ G *add* ist
²¹⁰ G, W gifftigenn
²¹¹ W gift
²¹² W, K zu lassen
²¹³ W, K diese
²¹⁴ Augustijn and De Kroon point out that this is the position promoted by the
Reichskammergericht since the early 1530's. *Bucers Deutsche Schriften* 9/1:88 n. 18.
²¹⁵ ain leer artikell] W, K gar ein Clarer artickhel
²¹⁶ G papistischen
²¹⁷ W *add* die
²¹⁸ Jn 10.1
²¹⁹ das . . . ampt] *om* W
²²⁰ G eim. W in
²²¹ *om* W
²²² unnd seind nicht . . . hauffen gebenn soll] *om* CR (K)
²²³ W unuz
²²⁴ G zuvorschwenden. K zu uerschwendende.
²²⁵ G, W S[anktus]
²²⁶ W *add* hat
²²⁷ kurchen prelaten] K Prelaten
²²⁸ W allmoßen. S f. 217v
²²⁹ G vorschlemenn
²³⁰ Augustijn and De Kroon refer us to Luther's gloss on 2 Peter 2.13, WA
Deutsche Bibel 7:321. See also 2 Peter 2.3.
²³¹ Augustijn and De Kroon refer us to *Decretum Gratiani* C. 12, qq. 1, 2, especially
q. 2, c. 5, 6, 21. CICan 1:688, 693–94.

165   Disen unnsern bericht von kurchen guetern bitten wir wollen unnser gnedigiste unnd[232] gnedige herrn von unns gnediglich annemen. Dann wir gannz nicht zweifeln dise meynung seie warhafftiglich[233] gegrunndet in Gottes wort unnd den alten canonibus unnd kaiser-lichen gesetzen, so man sie in irem naturlichen rechten verstand[234],
170 one sophistery, verstenn will gannz gemess. Darumb auch meniglich aus disem bericht sein gewissen unnderrichten unnd troen[235] mag. Got[236] wolle allen cristenlichen regenten dise gnad verleihen das sie die kurchenn ampter[237] unnd studia stattlich helffen[238] erhallten unnd
175 furdernn[239].

---

[232] *om* W
[233] G wahrhafftiglichenn. CR wahrhaftig.
[234] *om* W
[235] G, W, K trosten
[236] W *add* der Allmechtig
[237] kurchenn ampter] W kurch
[238] W *om*
[239] W *add* Amen.

THE TITLE PAGE OF MARTIN LUTHER'S
*A TERRIBLE HISTORY AND THE JUDGEMENT OF
GOD ON THOMAS MÜNTZER*

THE TITLE PAGE OF MARTIN LUTHER'S
A TERRIBLE HISTORY AND THE JUDGEMENT OF GOD ON THOMAS MÜNTZER, IN WHICH GOD CLEARLY PUNISHES AND CONDEMNS THE SAME[1]

Luther wrote and published this pamphlet at the end of the Peasants' War, after Thomas Müntzer was taken captive at the battle of Frankenhausen on 15 May and before Münzter's execution twelve days later. Müntzer had been handed over to Count Ernst of Mansfeld, was imprisoned in the tower of the Heldrungen castle, tortured, and condemned. He was finally executed outside the city of Mühlhausen, the center of his activity before the battles were joined earlier that month. In *A Terrible History* Luther encouraged the princes and nobles of Saxony and Thuringia to suppress the revolt, as he did a few weeks before in his incendiary tract, *Against the Thieving and Murderous Hordes of Peasants*.[2] *A Terrible History* includes three Müntzer letters that give evidence of Müntzer's contribution to the revolt. Both tracts, *A Terrible History* and *Against the Thieving and Murderous Hordes*, give the exaggerated impression that Luther was responsible for revealing the danger of revolution in grandiloquent, religious terms, and that he raised the princely assault against it. This impression was more important in the war's aftermath than the point more commonly pondered, namely Luther's change of mind between *An Admonition to Peace*, written in April (it laments the exploitation of peasants and argues for princely concessions and an avoidance of hostility) and *Against the Thieving and Murderous Hordes*, completed in early May (it demands violent suppression).[3] Catholic opponents, for example the

---

[1] WA 18:362–74.

[2] *Against the Thieving and Murderous Hordes* (WA 18:344–61, *Selected Writings of Martin Luther*, ed. by Theodore G. Tappert, 4 vols. [Minneapolis: Fortress, 1967], 3:345–55) was written as a third part to the more merciful *Admonition to Peace* (WA 18:279–333b, *Selected Writings*, 3:303–43), which although written in April, was first published in early May. See WA 18:344. Also Brecht, *Martin Luther*, 2:172–94 and the literature noted there.

[3] Brecht, *Martin Luther*, 2:174–185. In the time between writing the two treatises,

theologian Johann Cochläus, and friends, such as the chancellor of the count of Mansfeld, Johann Rühl, commented on Luther's shift from peaceful admonition to violent antipathy. In letters of 21 and 26 May, Rühl complained to Luther that the reformer caused scandal among his own supporters.[4] Rühl reported the rumor that, with the death of Luther's protector Friedrich the Elector of Saxony (he died after a long illness on 5 May), the reformer meant to evade the imperial ban by endearing himself to the Catholic Duke Georg of Saxony. To rebut this allegation, Luther continued to defend the suppression of rebellion by force. After a private reply to Rühl, he published a public response in July and dedicated it to the chancellor, under the title, *An Open Letter on the Harsh Book Against the Peasants*.[5] In it, he justified the use of violence as appropriate to the temporal realm and accused his detractors of confusing the earthly and heavenly spheres. Few today believe that Luther's initial position in the revolt flatly contradicts his later advocacy of use of force. But even if he had changed his mind, there can be no doubt that his advocacy of force in May 1525 was consistent with a theological rationale justifying temporal power.

Lucas Cranach the Elder's workshop probably made the woodblock border to the first edition of the title page to *A Terrible History*.[6] The title page is divided into two registers that juxtapose two stories. The larger, lower register depicts the famous judgment of Paris, which was believed to precipitate the Trojan war. The scene had occupied Cranach before, and as Edgar Bierende has argued, it had

---

Luther traveled from the county of Mansfeld back to Wittenberg. During sermons en route, he admonished peasants to take Christ's passive suffering as their model, which his audience loudly protested. Their protest impressed on him the extent of sympathy for the revolt and the danger posed to Saxony.

[4] Cochlaeus believed Luther first incited the peasants, then the princes. See WA 18:376–77. See also Brecht, *Martin Luther*, 2:185–184.

[5] WA 18:375–401; *Selected Writings*, 3:357–85.

[6] This same border was used for the titlepage of Johannes Bugenhagen's *Von dem ehelichen stande der Bischoffe und Diaken, an herrn Wolffgang Keyssenbusch, der Rechte Doctor und Preceptor zu Lichtemberg Sant Anthonius ordens* (Wittemberg, 1525). Hans-Günter Leder, Norbert Buske, *Reform und Ordnung aus dem Wort. Johannes Bugenhagen und die Reformation im Herzogtum Pommern* (Berlin: Evangelische Verlagsanstalt, 1985), plate 3 (after p. 32). Georg Geisenhof, *Biblioteca Bugenhagiana* (Nieuwkoop: De Graaf, 1963), pp. 196–7 nr. 158. For Cranach and Wittenberg, Joseph Leo Koerner, *The Reformation of the Image* (University of Chicago Press, 2004), 76–8. The subsequent editions I've seen use embellished, floriated and/or colonnaded borders, namely, the editions by Michael Blum of Leipzig, Wolfgang Köpfel of Strasbourg, Paul Kohl of Regensburg, and Friedrich Peypus of Nürnberg. *Flugschriften des frühen 16. Jahrhunderts*, Fiche 198 nr. 568, Fiche 664 nr. 1750 and 1751, Fiche 1839 nr. 4703, Fiche 1945 nr. 4957.

special importance at the Saxon courts (Georg Spalatin, among others, had alleged Trojan origins of the Saxons and Thuringians).[7] The Trojan prince, his horse hitched to a post in the background, sleeps indifferently, oblivious to the three goddesses before him, naked except for their necklaces. Hermes bears the golden apple of Eris, or Discord, and prods the sluggish youth, trying to rouse him. Cupid hovers above with his bow at the ready.

The smaller upper register depicts a scene from the biblical story of Samson rending the lion (Judges 14), a scene portrayed elsewhere by Cranach.[8] Samson, in a slightly unusual pose (he typically straddles the beast), grabs the lion by gaping jaws, about to rip it apart.

The sleeping Paris alludes to Luther's text. Luther explains that Müntzer's prophecies are inspired by the devil. Then he repeats the summons to the princes made a little earlier in *Against the Thieving and Murderous Hordes*. The princes, he says, should immediately end the revolt by force. He scolds rulers for their slumber, as if to await a special revelation from God:

> For the sheer fear of God, dear brothers, why are you sleeping? . . . How long have I told you how it must be? God cannot reveal himself any longer. You must stand! If you don't, the sacrifice of a contrite heart is useless. You will come to grief again, that I tell you; would you not rather suffer on God's account? So must you torment the devil. Therefore gird yourselves, do not despair, be not negligent; fawn over the twisted fanatics no longer, the godless; begin and fight the Lord's fight, it is high time . . . At Fulda during Easter week, four collegiate churches were destroyed, the peasants at Klegen in the Hegau and Black Forest have risen up, three times a hundred thousand strong, and the longer the uprising, the greater the army. . . ."[9]

Princes must rouse themselves against the Peasants, as they, in fact, at the time of writing had already done.

Cranach's images suggest that German princes confronted the dilemmas of Greek and Hebrew heroes. Prince Paris, in deciding between the goddesses Hera, Athena, and Aphrodite, was choosing

---

[7] Edgar Bierende, *Lucas Cranach der Älterer und der deutsche Humanismus. Tafelmalerei im Kontext von Rhetorik, Chroniken und Fürstenspiegeln* (Munich: Deutscher Kunstverlag, 2002), pp. 195–212.

[8] E.g., in a drawing of 1509 or 1510, and later in the woodcut title page of Luther's sermons on baptism, published in 1535. *Lucas Cranach der Älterer, 1472–1553. Die gesamte graphische Werk, mit Exempeln aus dem graphischen Werk Lucas Cranach d. J. und der Cranachwerkstatt*, introduction by Johannes Jahn (Herrsching: Manfred Pawlak, 1972), pp. 19, 440.

[9] WA 18:367–8.

between princely desires—dominion (Hera), war-power (Athena), and
salacious love (Helen), according to the common allegory.[10] Choosing
love frivolously, Paris gave rise to the disaster of the Trojan War
and the destruction of his father's kingdom.

The story of Samson's rending of the lion poses a striking contrast
to this bucolic scene, both for Samson's sudden, bare-handed slaugh-
ter of the lion in the vineyards of Timnah and for his use of its
strange carcass, infested with bees and honey (Judges 14–17). He
consumed its ritually unclean honey and made the carcass the object
of a riddle, which through several turns of events marks the beginning of his skirmishes with the Philistines, until captured by his enemy
and displayed in chains, bound to two pillars at their banquet, he
tore the columns from their pedestals, collapsing the building on his
enemies and himself.

That was a godly prince. In Luther's early writings, Samson appears
as an example of a prophet and a divinely appointed ruler who had
the care of the Israelites and whose aggression was privileged, inspired,
and aided by the Holy Spirit.[11] It is the responsibility of the temporal office to answer revolt by spilling blood, as did Samuel, David,
and Sampson, Luther explained to the chancellor of Mansfeld.[12]
Cranach's juxtaposition of the two stories suggests Luther's own jux-
tapostion of *An Admonition to Peace* and *Against the Thieving and Murderous
Hordes*, when he added the latter as a third part to the former in
early May 1525. *An Admonition to Peace* presented the case for love.
Against the Thieving and Murderous Hordes simply promoted the military
solution, the necessity of violent, peremptory action by princes.

---

[10] Lucian of Samosata, as "The Judgement of the Goddesses," *Lucian*, trans. A.M.
Harmon, 8 vols. (New York: G.P. Putnam, 1921), 3:384–409. For its presence in
German literature, *Lexikon der antiken Gestalten in den deutschen Texten des Mittelalters*, ed.
Manfred Kern, Alfred Ebenbauer (Berlin: Walter de Gruyter, 2003), pp. 466–475,
and for its importance in the context of the belief in the Trojan origins of the
Saxons and Thuringians, Bierende, *Lucas Cranach*, pp. 195–212.

[11] A sermon preached on the Feast of St. Stephen, 26 December 1523, WA
14:321a–322a. *Praelectiones in prophetas minores*, on Amos 2 (1524), WA 13:111. The
story of his choice of a Philistine wife against the wishes of his parents appears as
evidence that in cases in which a clandestine vow of marriage could nullify a subsequent marriage, adult children should consult their parents, and parents should
indulge them. *Ein Sermon von dem ehelichen Stand* (1519), WA 2:169. A sermon preached
in 1523, WA 11:40–41. Samson is also taken as an allegory of Christ. *Praelectio in
librum Iudicum* (1516), WA 4:579–80.

[12] *Ein Sendbrief von dem harten Büchlein wider die Bauern* (1525), WA 18:400.

BIBLIOGRAPHY

Unpublished Sources

Braunschweig, Stadtarchiv
  B III 5:5

Marburg, Hessisches Staatsarchiv
  Bestand 3, Nr. 538, 540
  Bestand 22a 2 Nr. 45–47
  Bestand 22a 3 Nr. 5, 24–26
  Bestand 22a 11

Stuttgart, Baden-Württembergisches Staatsarchiv Stuttgart,
  A63 Büschel 4a
  A64 Nr. 1 Teil 1

Ulm, Stadtarchiv
  A1214

Published Sources

Acta Reformationis Catholicae Ecclesiam Germaniae Concernentia. 6 vols. Regensburg: Friedrich Pustet, 1959–74.
Akten der deutschen Reichsreligionsgespräche im 16. Jahrhundert. 2 vols.+ Göttingen: Vandenhoeck und Ruprecht, 2000–2+.
Akten zur Geschichte des Bauernkriegs in Mitteldeutschland. Edited by Otto Merx, Günther Franz. 2 vols. Aalen: Scientia Verlag, 1964.
Ambrose. *De officiis.* Edited and translated by Ivor J. Davidson. 2 vols. Oxford: Oxford University Press, 2001.
Anonymous. *Verbrantte unnd abgebrochne Schlosser unnd Cloester, so durch die Bawerschafft yhn Wuertzburger und Bamberger Stifften beschehen.* No place: no publisher, 1525. *Flugschriften des frühen 16. Jahrhunderts,* Fiche 287 nr. 828.
Anonymous. *Was Bebstliche heyligkeyt auß Teütscher nation järlicher Annata, und eyn yeder Bistum und Ebbtey, besondern taxirt.* No place: no publisher, 1523. *Flugschriften des frühen 16. Jahrhunderts,* Fiche 6 nr. 16.
Atlas zur Kirchengeschicht. Edited by Hubert Jedin, Kenneth Scott Latourette, and J. Martin. 2nd edition. Freiburg: Herder, 1986.
Bernard of Clairvaux. *Opera.* 9 vols. Edited by Jean Leclercq et al. Louvain: Brepols, 1957–1998.
Brenz, Johannes. *Werke.* Edited by Martin Brecht, Gerhard Schäfer. 3 vols. Tübingen: J.C.B. Mohr, 1970.
Briefwechsel der Brüder Ambrosius und Thomas Blaurer, 1509–1548. Edited by Traugott Schiess. 3 vols. Freiburg im Briesgau: F.E. Fehsenfeld, 1908–1912.
Bucer, Martin. *Common Places of Martin Bucer.* Translated by D.F. Wright. Appleford: Sutton Courtenay Press, 1972.
——. *Martin Bucers Deutsche Schriften.* Volume 9/1. Edited by C. Augustijn and M. De Kroon. Gütersloh: Gütersloher Verlagshaus, 1995.

——. *Martini Buceri Opera Latina*. 15 vols. Leiden: E.J. Brill, 1955–88.
Concilium Tridentinum. 13 vols. Freiburg im Briesgau: Herder, 1901–38.
Corpus Iuris Canonici. 2 vols. Edited by Emil Friedburg. Graz: Akademische Druck-
und Verlagsanstalt, 1955.
Corpus Iuris Civilis. 3 vols. Edited by P. Krueger. Berlin: Weidmann, 1954.
Corpus Reformatorum. 88 vols. Edited by C.G. Bretschneider et al. Halle: Schwetschke,
1835–1906.
Corpus Scriptorum Ecclesiasticorum Latinorum. 92 vols.+ Vienna: Hoelder-Pichler-Tempsksy,
Österreichische Akademie der Wissenschaften, 1866+.
Covarrubias y Leyva, Diego de. *Opera omnia*. 2 vols. Colonia Allobrogum: Samuel
de Tournes, 1679.
Das kaiserliche Buch des Markgrafen Albrecht Achilles. Edited by Julius von Minutoli.
Berlin: F. Schneider, 1850.
Decretum Gratiani emendatum et notationibus una cum glossis. Rome: In aedibus populi
Romani, 1584.
*Der Barfußer zcu Magdeburg grund yhres Ordens Nyderlegung desselbtigen ym wortte Gottes.
Erstlich eyn sendebryff, wy sulchs den von Hamburg durch die von Magdeburg zu geschryben.*
Magdeburg: Heinrich Oettinger, 1526. *Flugschriften des frühen 16. Jahrhunderts*, Fiche
433–434 nr. 1174.
*Der bock dryt frey auff disen plan/ Hatt wider Ehren nye gethan/ Wie sehr sie yn gescholten
han/ Was aber Luther für ein man/ Und wilch ein spyl ere gfangen an/ Und nun den man-
tel wenden kan/ Nach dem der wind thut einher gan/ Findstu in disem Büchlin stan.* No
place: no publisher, 1525. *Flugschriften des frühen 16. Jahrhunderts*, nr. 3375.
Der Briefwechsel des Justus Jonas. Edited by Gustav Kawerau, 2 vols. Hildesheim:
Georg Olms, 1964 reprint of the Halle, 1884–5 edition.
Desiderius Erasmus. *Opera omnia*. 10 vols. Louvain: Vander, 1703–6, reprinted
London: Gregg Press, 1962.
Ferber, Nikolaus. *Assertiones trecentae ac vigintisex fratris*. Cologne 1526. *Flugschriften des
frühen 16. Jahrhunderts*, Fiche 37, nr. 103.
Flugschriften aus den ersten Jahren der Reformation. Edited by Otto Clemen. 4 vols.
Nieuwkoop: B. De Graaf, 1967.
Marsilius of Padua: The Defender of Peace. 2 vols. Translated and edited with a study
by Alan Gewirth. New York: Columbia University Press, 1951, 1956.
Gleason, Elisabeth. Editor. *Reform Thought in Sixteenth-Century Italy*. Chico: Scholars
Press, 1981.
Glossen zum Sachsenspiegel-Landrecht. Buch'sche Glosse. Edited by Frank-Michael Kaufmann.
3 vols. Hannover: Hahnsche Buchhandlung, 2002.
Gratian. The Treatise on Laws (Decretum dd. 1–20.). Translated by Augustine Thompson.
Washington: Catholic University of America Press, 1993.
Gregory of Tours. *The History of the Franks*. Translated by Lewis Thorpe. London:
Penguin, 1974.
Johann Friedrich I, Philipp von Hessen Landgraf. *Responsio, quam in causa religionis
dedimus ad instructionen, quae allata est Smalcaldiam*. Wittenberg: Georg Rhau, 1540.
Flugschriften des späteren 16. Jahrhunderts. Fiche 1007 nr. 1766.
Legation Lorenzo Campeggios 1530–1531 und Nuntiatur Girolamo Aleandros 1531. Edited
by Gerhard Müller. Part 1, supplementary volume 1 of *Nuntiaturberichte aus Deutschland,
1533–1559, nebst ergänzenden Aktenstücken*. Tübingen: Max Neimeyer, 1963.
Lenz, M. *Briefwechsel Landgraf Philipp's des Grossmüthigen von Hessen mit Bucer*. 3 vols.
Leipzig: S. Hirzel, 1880–91.
Luther, Martin. *Sämmtliche Schriften*. Edited by Johann Georg Walch. 23 volumes.
St. Louis: Concordia, 1901.
D. Martin Luthers Werke, kritische Gesamtausgabe. 4 parts, 127 vols. Weimar: H. Böhlau,
1883–.
Melanchthons Briefwechsel. Volumes 1–11, T1–T6. Edited by Heinz Scheible. Stuttgart:
Fromann-Holzboog, 1977+.
Melanchthon, Philip. *Epistolae, iudicia, consilia, testimonia aliorumque ad eum epsitolae quae*

in Corpore Reformatorum desiderantur. Edited by Heinrich Ernst Bindseil. Halle, 1874, and reprinted Hildesheim: Georg Olms, 1975.

Melanchthon, Philip. *Opera quae supersunt omnia.* 28 vols. Volumes 1–28 of *Corpus Reformatorum.* Edited by C.G. Bretschneider. Halle: Schwetschke, 1835–60.

Nicholas of Cusa. *The Catholic Concordance.* Edited and translated by Paul E. Sigmund. Cambridge University Press, 1991.

Nützliche Sammlung verschiedener meistens ungedruckter Schrifften, Berichte, Urkunden, Briefe, Bedencken. Edited by Christian Gottlieb Buder. Frankfurt and Leipzig: Christian Heinrich Cuno, 1735.

Oldendorp, Ioannes. *De copia verborum et rerum in iure civili.* Cologne: Ioannes Gymnicus, 1542.

Olin, John C. *Catholic Reform from Cardinal Ximenes to the Council of Trent, 1495–1563.* New York: Fordham, 1990.

Osiander der Ältere, Andreas. *Gesamtausgabe.* Edited by Gerhard Müller et al., 8 vols.+ Gütersloh: Gerd Mohn, 1975+.

Patrologia Cursus Completus Series Latina. 221 vols., 5 supplementary vols. Paris: Garnier Frères, 1879–1974.

Pirkheimer, Caritas. *Die Denkwürdigkeiten der Äbtissin Caritas Pirkheimer.* Edited by Frumentius Renner. St. Ottilien: Erzabtei St. Ottilien, 1982.

Quellen zur Geschichte des Bauernkriegs aus Rotenburg an der Tauber. Edited by Franz Ludwig Baumann. Stuttgart: Literarischer Verein, 1878.

Reformation Kaiser Siegmunds. Edited by Heinrich Koller. Stuttgart: Anton Hiersemann, 1964.

Sachsenspiegel Landrecht. Edited by Karl August Eckhardt. Göttingen: Musterschmidt, 1955.

The German Peasants' War: A History in Documents. Edited by Tom Scott, Bob Scribner. New Jersey: Humanities Press, 1991.

Urkundenbuch der alten sächsischen Franziskanerprovinzen. 2 volumes. Edited by Leonhard Lemmens. Düsseldorf: L. Schwann, 1913.

Urkunden und Akten der Reformationsprozesse. Edited by Ekkehart Fabian, part 1: *Allgemeines 1530–1534.* Tübingen: Osiandersche Buchhandlung, 1961.

Urkundenbuch zur Reformationsgeschichte des Herzogthums Preußen. Edited by Paul Tschackert. 3 vols. Osnabrück: Otto Zeller, 1965 reprint of the edition of 1890.

Urkundliche Quellen zur hessischen Reformationsgeschichte. Edited by Günther Franz. 3 vols. Marburg: N.G. Elwerts, 1954–55.

Volz, Hans. *Drei Schriften gegen Luthers Schmalkaldische Artikel von Cochläus, Witzel und Hoffmeister (1538 und 1539).* Münster: Aschendorf, 1932.

Warhafftige neuewe zeitung. Von den Krieg zwischen keyserlicher Maiestat, dem hauss von Burgundi, Stifft Utricht, und hertzog Karol von Gellern etc. Wie das ergangen und gehandelt worden bis auff natiuitatis Marie, des achten tags September An. etc. xxviii. Constance: Johann Haselbergk, 1528.

Ioannis Wycliffe Tractatus de Civili Dominio Liber Primus. London, Truebner, 1885. Edited by R.L. Poole. Corrected by John Kilcullen (1999). http://www.humanities.mq.edu.au/Ockham/wlatcor.html.

Literature

Abb, Gustav and Gottfried Wentz. *Das Bistum Brandenburg.* Section 1, vol. 1 of *Germania sacra.* Berlin: Walter De Gruyter, 1929.

Abray, Lorna Jane. *The People's Reformation: Magistrates, Clergy, and Commons in Strasbourg, 1500–1598.* Ithaca: Cornell University Press, 1985.

Asmus, Helmut, et al. *Geschichte der Stadt Magdeburg.* 2nd edition. Berlin: Akademie-Verlag, 1977.

Auge, Olivier. *Stiftsbiographien. Die Kleriker des Stuttgarter Heilig-Kreuz-Stifts (1250–1552).* Leinfelder-Echterdingen: Weinbrenner, 2002.

Barge, Hermann. *Andreas Bodenstein von Karlstadt.* 2 vols. Leipzig: Friedrich Brandstetter, 1905.

Barnes, Robin Bruce. *Prophecy and Gnosis: Apocalypticism in the Wake of the Lutheran Reformation.* Palo Alto: Stanford University Press, 1988.

Barron, William Stanon. "The Controversy between Martin Bucer and Bartholomew Latomus." Ph.D. Dissertation, The Catholic University of America, 1966.

Beales, Derek. *Prosperity and Plunder: European Catholic Monasteries in the Age of Revolution, 1650–1815.* Cambridge: Cambridge University Press, 2003.

Becker, Hans-Jürgen. *Die Appellation vom Papst an ein allgemeines Konzil.* Cologne: Böhlau, 1988.

Behr, Hans-Joachim. *Franz von Waldeck. Fürstbischof von Münster und Osnabrück, Administrator zu Minden (1491–1553). Sein Leben in seiner Zeit.* 2 vols. Münster: Achendorf, 1996, 1998.

Berger, Adolf. *An Encyclopaedic Dictionary of Roman Law.* Philadelphia: American Philosophical Society, 1991.

Bildersturm. Wahnsinn oder Gottes Wille? Edited by Cécile Dupeux, Peter Jezler, Jean Wirth. Munich: Wilhelm Fink, 2000.

Biographisches-Bibliographisches Kirchenlexikon. 14 vols. Edited by Friedrich-Wilhelm Bautz, Traugott Bautz. Hamm, Herzberg, and Nordhausen: Traugott Bautz, 1990–2003.

Blaschke, Karlheinz. "The Reformation and the Rise of the Territorial State." Translated by Thomas A. Brady. Pages 61–75 of *Luther and the Modern State in Germany.* Edited by James D. Tracy. Kirksville, Missouri: Sixteenth Century Journal Publishers, 1986.

Blickle, Peter. *Communal Reformation: The Quest for Salvation in Sixteenth-Century Germany.* Translated by Thomas Dunlap. Atlantic Highlands: Humanities Press, 1992.

———. *Die Reformation im Reich.* Stuttgart: Ulmer, 1982.

Blickle, Peter. *The Revolution of 1525.* Translated by Thomas A. Brady and H.C. Erik Midelfort. Baltimore: Johns Hopkins University Press, 1981.

Borgolte, Michael. *Die mittelalterliche Kirche.* Munich: Oldenbourg, 1992.

Bornkamm, Heinrich. *Luther im Spiegel der deutschen Geistesgeschichte.* 2nd edition. Göttingen: Vandenhoeck und Ruprecht, 1970.

Brady, Thomas A. "In Search of the Godly City: The Domestication of Religion in the German Urban Reformation." Pages 14–31, *The German People and the Reformation.* Edited by Ronald Po-Chia Hsia. Ithaca: Cornell, 1987.

———. *Protestant Politics: Jacob Sturm (1489–1553) and the German Reformation.* Atlantic Highlands: Humanities Press, 1995.

———. "Reformation als Rechtsbruch: Nationalisierung und Territorialisierung der Religionen als Rechtsbruch." Pages 141–152, *Die Säkularisation im Prozess der Säkularisierung Europas.* Edited by Peter Blickle, Rudolf Schlögl. Epfendorf: Bibliotheca Academica, 2005.

———. "Rites of Autonomy, Rites of Dependence: South German Civic Culture in the Age of Renaissance and Reformation." Pages 9–23, *Religion and Culture in the Renaissance and Reformation.* Edited by Steven Ozment. Kirksville: Sixteenth Century Journal Publishers, 1989.

———. "The Holy Roman Empire's Bishops on the Eve of the Reformation." Pages 20–47. *Continuity and Change: The Harvest of Late Medieval and Reformation History.* Edited by Robert J. Bast, Andrew C. Gow. Leiden: E.J. Brill, 2000.

———. Editor. *Die deutsche Reformation zwischen Spätmittelalter und Früher Neuzeit.* Munich: Oldenbourg, 2001.

Brandis, Wolfgang. "Quellen zur Reformationsgeschichte der Lüneburger Frauen-klöster." Pages 357–398, *Studien und Texte zur literarischen und materiellen Kultur der Frauenklöster im späten Mittelalter.* Edited by Falk Eisermann, Eva Scholtheuber, Volker Honemann. Leiden: E.J. Brill, 2004.

Bräuer, Siegfried, "Der Briefwechsel zwischen Andreas Bodenstein von Karlstadt und Thomas Müntzer," Pages 187–209 of *Querdenker der Reformation.*

Brecht, Martin, and Hermann Ehmer. *Südwestdeutsche Reformationsgeschichte*. Stuttgart: Calwer, 1984.

Breul-Kunkel, Wolfgang. *Herrschaftskrise und Reformation: die Reichsabteien Fulda und Hersfeld, 1500–1525*. Gütersloh: Gütersloher Verlagshaus, 2000.

Brockmann, Thomas. *Die Konzilsfrage in den Flug- und Streitschriften des deutschen Sprachraumes 1518–1563*. Gottingen: Vandenhoeck und Ruprecht, 1998.

Brosius, Dieter. "Die lüneburgischen Klöster in der Reformation." Pages 95–111 of *Reformation vor 450 Jahren. Eine Lüneburgische Gedenkschrift*. Edited by G. Körner. Lüneburg: Museumsverein für das Fürstentum Lüneburg, 1980.

Buck, Hermann. *Die Anfänge der Konstanzer Reformationsprozesse: Österreich, Eidgenossenschaft und Schmalkaldischer Bund 1510/22–1531*. Tübingen: Osiandersche Buchhandlung, 1964.

Bünz, Enno. "'Die Kirche im Dorf lassen . . .' Formen der Kommunikation im spätmittelalterlichen Niederkirchenwesen." Pages 77–167 of *Kommunikation in der ländlichen Gesellschaft vom Mittelalter bis zur Moderne*. Edited by Werner Rösener. Göttingen: Vandenhoeck und Ruprecht, 2000.

Burke, Edmund. *Reflections on the Revolution in France*. New York: Anchor, 1973.

Cahill, Richard Andrew. *Philipp of Hesse and the Reformation*. Mainz: Philipp von Zabern, 2001.

Cameron, Euan. *The European Reformation*. Oxford: Clarendon, 1991.

Christin, Olivier. *Une Révolution symbolique*. Paris: Éditions de Minuit, 1991.

Cohn, Henry J. "Church Property in the German Protestant Principalities." Pages 159–62 of *Politics and Society in Reformation Europe. Essays for Sir Geoffrey Elton on his Sixty-Fifth Birthday*. Edited by E.I. Kouri, T. Scott. London: Macmillan, 1986.

Coing, Helmut. *Europäisches Privatrecht*. 2 vols. München: Beck, 1985, 1989.

Deetjen, Werner-Ulrich. *Studien zur Württembergischen Kirchenordnung Herzog Ulrichs 1534–1550*. Stuttgart: Calwer Verlag, 1981.

Delumeau, Jean, and Thierry Wanegffelen. *Naissance et affirmation de la Réforme*. Paris: Presses universitaires de France, 1997.

Deppermann, Klaus. *Protestantische Profile von Luther bis Francke*. Göttingen: Vandenhoeck und Ruprecht, 1992.

Deutsches Städtebuch. Handbuch städtischer Geschichte. Edited by Erich Keyser. 5+ volumes and numerous parts. Stuttgart: W. Kohlhammer, 1939+.

Dick, Betinna. *Die Entwicklung des Kameralprozesses nach den Ordnungen von 1495 bis 1555*. Cologne: Böhlau, 1981.

Dickens, A.G. *The English Reformation*. 2nd edition. University Park: Pennsylvania State University Press, 1989.

Dictionnaire de theologie catholique. Edited by A. Vacant, E. Maninot. 16 vols. Paris: Letouzey et Ané, 1908–72.

Die Bischöfe des Heiligen Römischen Reiches, 1448 bis 1648. Ein biographisches Lexikon. Edited by Erwin Gatz. Berlin: Duncker und Humboldt, 1996.

Die Schmalkaldischen Bundesabschiede, 1530–1532. Edited by Ekkehart Fabian. Tübingen: Osiandersche Buchhandlung, 1958.

Die Territorien des Reichs im Zeitalter der Reformation und Konfessionalisierung. Land und Konfession 1500–1650. 7 vols. Edited by Anton Schindling, Walter Ziegler. Münster: Aschendorf, 1991–6.

Diestelkamp, Bernhard. *Recht und Gericht im Heiligen Römischen Reich*. Frankfurt am Main: Vittorio Klostermann, 1999.

Dipple, Geoffrey. *Antifraternalism and Anticlericalism in the German Reformation*. Aldershot: Scolar Press, 1996.

Dixon, C. Scott. *The Reformation and Rural Society: the Parishes of Brandenburg-Ansbach-Kulmbach, 1528–1603*. Cambridge: Cambridge University Press, 1996.

Dolezalek, Gero. "Die juristische Argumentation der Assessoren am Reichskammergericht zu den Reformationsprozessen 1532–1538." In *Das Reichskammergericht in der deutschen Geschichte. Stand der Forschung, Forschungsperspektiven*. Edited by Bernhard Diestelkamp. Cologne: Böhlau Verlag, 1990.

Dommasch, Gerd. *Die Religionsprozesse der rekusierenden und die Erneuerung des Schmalkaldischen Bundes, 1534–1536.* Tübingen: Osiandersche Buchhandlung, 1961.

Duchhardt, Heinz. "Das Reichskammergericht." Pages 1–13 of *Oberste Gerichtsbarkeit und zentrale Gewalt.* Edited by Bernhard Diestelkamp. Cologne: Böhlau, 1996.

Duggan, Lawrence G. *Bishop and Chapter. The Governance of the Bishopric of Speyer to 1552.* New Brunswick: Rutgers, 1978.

Ehmer, Hermann. "Ende und Verwandlung: Südwestdeutsche Stiftskirchen in der Reformation." Pages 211–237 of *Die Stiftskirche in Südwestdeutschland.* Edited by Sönke Lorenz, Olivier Auge. Leinfelden-Echterdingen: Weinbrenner, 2003.

Eire, Carlos. *War Against the Idols.* Cambridge University Press, 1986.

Endres, Rudolf. *Adelige Lebensformen in Franken zur Zeit des Bauernkrieges.* Vol. 35 of *Neujahrsblätter der Gesellschaft für fränkische Geschichte.* Würzburg: Ferdinand Schöningh, 1974.

Estes, James Martin. *Christian Magistrate and State Church: the Reforming Career of Johannes Brenz.* Toronto: University of Toronto Press, 1982.

——. *Peace, Order and the Glory of God: Secular Authority and the Church in the Thought of Luther and Melanchthon 1518–1559.* Leiden: E.J. Brill, 2005.

——. "The Role of the Godly Magsitrates in the Church: Melanchthon as Luther's Interpreter and Collaborator." *Church History* 67(1998):463–483.

Felmberg, Bernhard. *Die Ablaßtheologie Kardinal Cajetans 1469–1534.* Leiden: E.J. Brill, 1998.

Fischer, Roman. "Das Barfüßerkloster im Mittelalter." Pages 9–109, *Von Barfüßerkirche zur Paulskirche. Beiträge zur Frankfurter Stadt- und Kirchengeschichte.* Edited by Roman Fischer. Frankfurt: Waldemar Karmer, 2000.

Fouquet, Gerhard. *Das Speyerer Domkapitel im späten Mittelalter (ca. 1350–1540). Adlige Freundschaft, fürstliche Patronage und päpstliche Klientel.* 2 vols. Mainz: Gesellschaft für Mittelrheinische Kirchengeschichte, 1987.

Fourneret, P. "Biens ecclésiastiques." 2/1:843–78 of *Dictionnaire de theologie catholique.*

Franz, Günther. *Der Deutsche Bauernkrieg.* 8th edition. Bad Homburg: Hermann Gentner, 1969.

Froehlich, Karlfried. "Saint Peter, Papal Primacy, and the Exegetical Tradition, 1150–1300." Pages 3–44, *The Religious Roles of the Papacy: Ideas and Realities, 1150–1300.* Edited by C. Ryan. Toronto: Pontifical Institute of Mediaeval Studies, 1989.

Fuchs, Ralf-Peter. "The Supreme Court of the Holy Roman Empire: the State of Research and Outlook." *The Sixteenth Century Journal* 34(2003):9–27.

Fuchs, Thomas. *Konfession und Gespräch. Typologie und Funktion der Religionsgespräche in der Reformationszeit.* Cologne: Böhlau, 1995.

Fuhrmann, Rosi. *Kirche und Dorf: religiöse Bedürfnisse und kirchliche Stiftung auf dem Lande vor der Reformation.* Stuttgart: G. Fischer, 1995.

Gabel, Helmut and Winfried Schulze. "Folgen und Wirkungen." Pages 322–349, *Der deutsche Bauernkrieg.* Edited by Horst Buszello, Peter Blickle, and Rudolf Endres. Paderborn: Ferdinand Schöningh, 1984.

Gäumann, Andreas. *Reich Christi und Obrigkeit. Eine Studie zum reformatorischen Denken und Handeln Martin Bucers.* Bern: Peter Lang, 2001.

Gebhardt, Bruno. *Handbuch der deutschen Geschichte.* 4 volumes. Edited by Herbert Grundmann. 8th revised edition, 2nd improved impression. Stuttgart: Union Verlag, 1958.

Glaube und Macht. Sachsen im Europa der Reformationszeit. Edited by Harald Marx, Cecilie Hollberg. 2 vols. Dresden: Michel Sandstein, 2004.

Gleason, Elisabeth. *Gasparo Contarini. Venice, Rome, and Reform.* Berkeley: University of California Press, 1993.

——. "On the Nature of Italian Evangelism: Scholarship, 1953–1978." *Sixteenth Century Journal* 9(1978):3–25.

Geisenhof, Georg. *Bibliotheca Corviniana. Eine bibliographische Studie.* Nieuwkoop: De Graaf, 1964 reprint of the 1900 edition.

Guggisberg, Hans R. *Basel in the Sixteenth Century*. St. Louis: Center for Reformation Research, 1982.

Günter, Wolfgang. *Martin Luthers Vorstellung von der Reichsverfassung*. Münster: Aschendorff, 1976.

Guttenberg, Erich Freiherr von. *Das Bistum Bamberg*. Section 2, vol. 1 of *Germania Sacra*. Berlin: Walter De Gruyter, 1937.

Hahn, Alois. "Religion, Säkularisierung und Kultur." Pages 17–31 of *Säkularisierung, Dechristianisierung, Rechristianisierung im neuzeitlichen Europa*. Edited by Hartmut Lehmann. Göttingen: Vandenhoeck und Ruprecht, 1997.

Hamm, Bernd. *The Reformation of Faith in the Context of Late Medieval Theology and Piety*. Edited by Robert J. Bast. Leiden: E.J. Brill, 2004.

Hammann, Gottfried. *Martin Bucer, 1491–1551: Zwischen Volkskirche und Bekenntnisgemein-schaft*. Translated by Gerhard P. Wolf. Stuttgart: Franz Steiner, 1989.

Handbook of European History. 2 volumes. Edited by Thomas A. Brady, Heiko A. Oberman, James D. Tracy. Leiden: E.J. Brill, 1995.

Hans, Wilhelm. *Gutachten und Streitschriften über das ius reformandi des Rates vor und während der Einführung der offiziellen Kirchenreform in Augsburg (1534–1537)*. Augsburg 1901.

Hastings, Adrian. *The Construction of Nationhood. Ethnicity, Religion and Nationalism*. Cambridge: Cambridge University Press, 1997.

Haug-Moritz, Gabriele. *Der Schmalkaldische Bund, 1530–1541/4*. Leinfelden-Echterdingen: DRW-Verlag, 2002.

——. "The Holy Roman Empire, the Schmalkald League, and the Idea of Confessional State-Building." *Identities: Four Dialogues*. Philadelphia: American Philosophical Society, forthcoming.

Heckel, Johannes. *Cura Religionis. Ius in Sacra. Ius circa Sacra*. Darmstadt: Wissenschaftliche Buchgesellschaft, 1962.

Heckel, Martin. "Das Problem der 'Säkularisation' in der Reformation." Pages 31–56 of *Zur Säkularisation geistlicher Institutionen im 16. und im 18./19. Jahrhundert*. Edited by Irene Crusius. Göttingen: Vandenhoeck und Ruprecht, 1996.

——. "Die Reformationsprozesse im Spannungsfeld des Reichskirchensystems." Pages 9–40 of *Die politische Funktion des Reichskammergerichts*. Cologne: Böhlau, 1993.

——. *Staat und Kirche nach den Lehren der evangelischen Juristen Deutschlands in der ersten Hälfte des 17. Jahrhunderts*. Munich: Claudius Verlag, 1968.

Henze, Barbara. *Aus Liebe zur Kirche Reform: Die Bemühungen Georg Witzels (1501–1573) um die Kircheneinheit*. Münster: Aschendorff, 1995.

Hermann, R. "Verzeichniß der in den Sachsen-Ernestinischen, Schwarzburgischen und Reußischen Landen, sowie den K. Preuß. Kreisen Schleufingen und Schmalkalden bis zur Reformation vorhanden gewesenen Stifter, Klöster und Ordenshäuser." *Zeitschrift für thüringische Geschichte und Alterthumskunde* 8(1871):1–176.

Hermelink, H. "Zwei Aktenstücke über Behandlung der Kirchengüter in Württemberg zur Reformationszeit." *Blätter für württembergische Kirchengeschichte*, n.s. 7 (1903): 172–185.

Hersche, Peter. "Adel gegen Bürgertum? Zur Frage der Refeudalisierung der Reichs-kirche." Pages 195–208 of *Weihbischöfe und Stifte. Beiträge zu reichskirchlichen Funktionsträgern der Frühe Neuzeit*. Edited by Friedhelm Jürgensmeier. Frankfurt: J. Knecht, 1995.

Hinschius, Paul. *System des katholischen Kirchenrechts mit besonderer Rücksicht auf Deutschland*. 6 vols. Graz: Akademische Druck- und Verlagsanstalt, 1959 reprint of the 1883 edition.

Hinz, Ulrich. *Die Brüder vom Gemeinsamen Leben im Jahrhundert der Reformation. Das Münstersche Kolloquium*. Tübingen: J.C.B. Mohr, 1997.

Hirsch, Emanuel. *Geschichte der neuern evangelischen Theologie*. 5 vols. Gütersloh: C. Bertelsmann, 1949.

Hoffmann, Christian. *Ritterschaftlicher Adel im geistlichen Fürstentum. Die Familie von Bar und das Hochstift Osnabrück: Landständewesen, Kirche und Fürstenhof als Komponenten der adeligen Lebenswelt im Zeitalter der Reformation und Konfessionalisierung 1500–1651*. Osnabrück: Verein für Geschichte und Landeskunde von Osnabrück, 1996.

Holl, Karl. *Gesammelte Aufsätze zur Kirchengeschichte.* 6th edition. 2 vols. Tübingen: J.C.B. Mohr, 1932.

Hortleder, Friedrich. *Handlungen und Ausschreiben. Von den Ursachen des teutschen Kriegs.* Gotha: Wolfgang Endters, 1645.

Hsia, R. Po-Chia. *Society and Religion in Münster, 1535–1618.* New Haven: Yale, 1984.

Hülße, Friedrich. "Beiträge zur Geschichte der Buchdruckerkunst in Magdeburg." *Geschichts-Blätter für Stadt und Land Magdeburg* 15(1880):21–49, 164–198, 275–295, 331–374.

Hülße, Friedrich. "Die Einführung der Reformation in der Stadt Magdeburg." *Geschichtsblätter für Stadt und Land Magdeburg* 18(1883):209–369.

Hunt, Edwin S. and James M. Murray. *A History of Business in Medieval Europe, 1200–1550.* Cambridge: Cambridge University Press, 1999.

Hütteroth, Oskar and Hilmar Milbradt. *Die althessischen Pfarrer der Reformationszeit.* Marburg: N.G. Elwert, 1966.

Immenkötter, Herbert. "Die katholische Kirche in Augsburg in der ersten Hälfte des 16. Jahrhundert." Pages 9–32, *Die Augsburger Kirchenordnung von 1537 und ihr Umfeld.* Edited by Reinhard Schwarz. Gütersloh: Gerd Mohn, 1988.

Isenmann, Eberhard. *Die deutsche Stadt im Spätmittelalter.* Stuttgart: Ulmer, 1988.

Katholische Theologen der Reformationszeit. Edited by Irwin Iserloh, Heribert Smolinsky, Peter Walter. 6 volumes. Münster: Aschendorf, 1984–1988, 2004.

Kaufmann, Thomas. *Die Abendmahlstheologie der Straßburger Reformatoren bis 1528.* Tübingen: J.C.B. Mohr/Paul Siebeck, 1992.

———. *Das Ende der Reformation. Magdeburgs 'Herrgotts Kanzlei' (1548–1551/2).* Tübingen: J.C.B. Mohr/Paul Siebeck, 2003.

Keen, Ralph. *Divine and Human Authority in Reformation Thought. German Theologians and Political Order 1520–1555.* Nieuwkoop: De Graaf, 1997.

Kess, Alexandra H. "Johann Sleidan and the Protestant Vision of History." Ph.D. Dissertation, University of St. Andrews, 2004.

Klausmann, Theo. *Consuetudo Consuetudine Vincitur. Die Hausordnungen der Brüder vom gemeinsamen Leben im Bildungs- und Sozialisationsprogramm der Devotio moderna.* Bern: Peter Lang Publishing, 2003.

Köhler, no first name. "Actenstücke der hessischen Reformationsgeschichte," *Zeitschrift für historische Theologie* 37(1867):217–247.

Kohn, Wilhelm. *Das Domstift St. Paulus zu Münster.* Vol. 4 of *Das Bistum Münster,* n. s. 17/1 of *Germania Sacra.* Berlin and New York: Walter de Gruyter, 1987.

Kohnle, Armin. *Reichstag und Reformation.* Gütersloh: Gütersloher Verlagshaus, 2001.

Körber, Kurt. *Kirchengüterfrage und schmalkaldischer Bund.* Leipzig: Verein für Reformationsgeschichte, 1913.

Kramer, Lloyd. "Historical Narratives and the Meaning of Nationalism." *Journal of the History of Ideas* 58(1997):525–545.

Kreiker, Sebastian. *Armut, Schule, Obrigkeit. Armenversorgung und Schulwesen in den evangelischen Kirchenordnungen des 16. Jahrhunderts.* Bielefeld: Verlag für Regionalgeschichte, 1997.

Kuhaupt, Georg. *Veröffentlichte Kirchenpolitik. Kirche im publizistischen Streit zur Zeit der Religionsgespräche (1538–1541).* Göttingen: Vandenhoeck und Ruprecht, 1998.

Kühn, Helga-Maria. *Die Einziehung des geistlichen Gutes im Albertinischen Sachsen, 1539–1553.* Cologne: Böhlau, 1966.

Kuropka, Nicole. *Philipp Melanchthon. Wissenchaft und Gesellschaft.* Tübingen: J.C.B. Mohr/Paul Siebeck, 2002.

Langholm, Odd. *Economics in the Medieval Schools.* Leiden: E.J. Brill, 1992.

———. *The Legacy of Scholasticism in Economic Thought.* Cambridge: Cambridge University Press, 1998.

———. *The Merchant in the Confessional: Trade and Price in the Pre-Reformation Penitential Handbooks.* Leiden: E.J. Brill, 2003.

Lausten, Martin Schwarz. *A Church History of Denmark.* Translated by Frederick H. Cryer. Burlington: Ashgate, 2002.

Laux, Stephan. *Reformationsversuche in Kurköln (1542–1548). Fallstudien zu einer Strukturgeschichte landstädtischer Reformation (Neuss, Kempen, Andernach, Linz)*. Münster: Aschendorff, 2001.

Lawless, George. *Augustine of Hippo and His Monastic Rule*. New York: Oxford University Press, 1987.

Lehnert, Hans. *Kirchengut und Reformation. Eine kirchengeschichtliche Studie*. Erlangen: Palm und Enke, 1935.

Lexikon der antiken Gestalten in den deutschen Texten des Mittelalters. Edited by Manfred Kern, Alfred Ebenbauer. Berlin: Walter de Gruyter, 2003.

Logemann, Silke. "Grundzüge der Geschichte der Stadt Halberstadt vom 13. bis 16. Jahrhundert." Pages 81–138, *Bürger, Bettelmönche und Bischöfe in Halberstadt. Studien zur Geschichte der Stadt, der Mendikanten und des Bistums vom Mittelalter bis zur Frühen Neuzeit*. Edited by Dieter Berg. Werl: Dietrich-Coelde-Verlag, 1997.

Lohse, Bernhard. *Mönchthum und Reformation. Luthers Auseinandersetzung zum Mönchsideal des Mittelalters*. Göttingen: Vandenhoeck und Ruprecht, 1963.

Looß, Sigrid. "Andreas Bodensteins von Karlstadt Haltung zum 'Aufruhr.'" In *Querdenker der Reformation*.

Lorz, Jürgen. *Das reformatorische Wirken Dr. Wenzeslaus Lincks in Altenburg und Nürnberg (1523–1547)*. Nürnberg: Stadtarchiv Nürnberg, 1975.

Losher, Gerhard. *Königtum und Kirche zur Zeit Karls IV*. Munich: R. Oldenbourg Verlag, 1985.

Luther and the Modern State in Germany. Edited by James D. Tracy. Kirksville, Missouri: Sixteenth Century Journal Publishers, 1986.

Lutherprozess und Lutherbann. Vorgeschichte, Ergebnis, Nachwirkung. Edited by Remigius Bäumer. Münster: Aschendorff, 1972.

Luther zwischen den Kulturen. Edited by Hans Medick, Peer Schmidt. Göttingen: Vandenhoeck und Ruprecht, 2004.

Luttenberger, Albrecht Pius. *Glaubenseinheit und Reichsfriede. Konzeptionen und Wege konfessionsneutraler Reichspolitik 1530–1552. Kurpfalz, Jülich, Kurbrandenburg*. Göttingen: Vandenhoeck und Ruprecht, 1982.

May, Georg. *Die deutschen Bischöfe angesichts der Glaubensspaltung des 16. Jahrhunderts*. Vienna: Vediatrix, 1983.

Melanchthon und die Marburger Professoren: (1527–1627). Edited by Barbara Bauer. 2 vols. Marburg: Universitäts-Bibliothek, 2000.

Mencke, Klaus. *Die Visitationen am Reichskammergericht im 16. Jahrhunmdert*. Cologne: Böhlau, 1984.

Meyer, Andreas. "Der deutsche Pfründenmarkt im Spätmittelalter." *Quellen und Forschungen aus Italienischen Archiven und Bibliotheken* 71(1991):266–79.

Midelfort, H.C. Erik. *Mad Princes of Renaissance Germany*. Charlottesville: University Press of Virgina, 1994.

Mikat, Paul. "Bemerkungen zum Verhältnis von Kirchengut und Staatsgewalt am Vorabend der Reformation," *Zeitschrift für Rechtsgeschichte, Kanonistische Abteilung* 67(1981):264–309

Miller, David Bruce. "The Dissolution of the Religious Houses of Hesse During the Reformation." Ph.D. Dissertation, Yale University, 1971.

Millet, Olivier. *Correspondance de Wolfgang Capito (1478–1541). Analyse et index*. Strasbourg: Mission de la Recherche du Ministère des Universités, 1982.

Moeller, Bernd. "Kleriker als Bürger." 2:195–224 of *Festschrift für Hermann Heimpel*. 2 vols. Gottingen: Vandenhoeck und Ruprecht, 1972.

Nipperdey, Thomas. *Religion im Umbruch, 1870–1918*. Munich: C.H. Beck, 1988.

Noonan, John T. *The Scholastic Analysis of Usury*. Cambridge: Harvard University Press, 1957.

O'Callaghan, Joseph F. *A History of Medieval Spain*. Ithaca: Cornell, 1975.

Ocker, Christopher. *Biblical Poetics before Humanism and Reformation*. Cambridge: Cambridge University Press, 2002.

——. "The Fusion of Papal Ideology and Biblical Exegesis in the Fourteenth Century." Pages 131–51, *Biblical Hermeneutics in Historical Perspective*. Edited by Mark S. Burrows and Paul Rorem. Grand Rapids: Eerdmans, 1991.

——. "'Rechte Arme' und 'Bettler Orden.' Eine neue Sicht der Armut und die Delegitimierung der Bettelmönche." Pages 129–57, *Kulturelle Reformation: Sinnformationen im Umbruch, 1400–1600*. Edited by Bernhard Jussen, Craig Koslofsky. Göttingen: Vandenhoeck und Ruprecht, 1999.

——. "Religious Authority and the Economy of Privilege in Late Medieval Germany." Pages 97–118, *The Growth of Authority in the Medieval West*. Edited by M. Gossman et al. Groningen: Egbert Forsten, 1999.

——. "Religious Reform and Social Cohesion in Late Medieval Germany." Pages 69–94, *The Work of Heiko A. Oberman*. Edited by Thomas A. Brady, Katherine G. Brady, Susan Karant-Nunn, and James D. Tracy. Leiden: Brill, 2003.

Oldenburg, Manfred. *Die Trierer Kartause St. Alban von der Gründung (1330/31) bis zur Mitte des 15. Jahrhunderts*. Salzburg: Institut für Anglistik und Amerikanistik, 1995.

Oppenheimer, Franz. *Der Staat*. 3rd rev. ed. Berlin: Libertad Verlag, 1990 reprint from the 1929 edition.

Ortmann, Volkmar. *Reformation und Einheit der Kirche: Martin Bucers Einigungsbemühungen bei den Religionsgesprächen in Leipzig, Hagenau, Worms und Regensburg 1539–1540*. Mainz: von Zabern, 2001.

Pánik, Jaroslav. "Land Codes of the Bohemian Kingdom in Relation to Constitutional Changes in Central Europe on the Threshold of the Early Modern Age." *Historica* n.s. 9(2002):7–39.

Der Passauer Vertrag von 1552. Politische Entstehung, reichsrechtliche Bedeutung und konfessions-geschichtliche Bewertung. Edited by Winfried Becker. Neustadt a.d. Aisch: Degener, 2003.

Paulus, Nikolaus. *Geschichte des Ablaßes am Ausgange des Mittelalters*. Paderborn: Ferdinand Schöningh, 1923.

Prodi, Paolo. *The Papal Prince*. Translated by Susan Haskins. Cambridge: Cambridge University Press, 1987.

Querdenker der Reformation—Andreas Bodenstein von Karlstadt und seine frühe Wirkung. Edited by Ulrich Bubenheimer, Stefan Oehmig. Würzburg: Religion und Kultur, 2001.

Rabe, Horst. *Reichsbund und Interim. Die Verfassungs- und Religionspolitik Karls V. und der Reichstag von Augsburg 1547/1548*. Cologne: Böhlau, 1971.

Ranieri, Filippo. *Recht und Gesellschaft im Zeitalter der Rezeption*. 2 volumes. Cologne: Böhlau, 1985.

Rawlings, H.E. "The Secularisation of Castilian Episcopal Office under the Habsburgs, c. 1516–1700." *Journal of Ecclesiastical History* 38(1987):53–79.

Reagin, N.R. "Recent Work on German National Identity: Regional? Imperial? Gendered? Imaginary?" *Central European History* 37(2004):273–289.

Reinhard, Wolfgang. "Die Kirchenpolitischen Vorstellungen Kaiser Karls V., ihre Grundlagen und ihr Wandel." Pages 62–100 of *Confessio Augustana und Confutatio. Der Augsburger Reichstag 1530 und die Einheit der Kirche*. Edited by Erwin Iserloh. Münster: Achendorf, 1980.

Reuter, Timothy. "The 'Imperial Church System' of the Ottonian and Salian Rulers: a Reconsideration." *Journal of Ecclesiastical History* 33(1982):347–74.

Reuter, Timothy, and Gabriel Silagi, *Wortkonkordanz zum Decretum Gratiani*. 5 vols. Munich: Monumenta Germaniae Historica, 1990.

Reynolds, Susan. *Fiefs and Vassals: the Medieval Evidence Reinterpreted*. Oxford: Clarendon, 1994.

Rößner, Maria Barbara. *Konrad Braun (ca. 1495–1563): ein katholischer Jurist, Politiker, Kontroverstheologe und Kirchenreformer im konfessionellen Zeitalter*. Münster: Aschendorf, 1991.

Roth, F. "Zur Kirchengüterfrage in der Zeit von 1538 bis 1540." *Archiv für Reformationsgeschichte* 1(1903):299–336.

Roth, Paul. *Durchbruch und Festsetzung der Reformation in Basel*. Basel: Helbing und Lichtenhah, 1942.

Rublack, Hans-Christoph. *Gescheiterte Reformation*. Stuttgart: Klett-Cotta, 1978.
Russel, William R. *Luther's Theological Testament: the Schmalkald Articles*. Minneapolis: Fortress, 1994.
Ruthmann, Bernhard. *Die Religionsprozesse am Reichskammergericht (1555–1648)*. Köln: Böhlau, 1996.
The Scandinavian Reformation from Evangelical Movement to Institutionalisation of Reform. Edited by Ole Peter Grell. Cambridge: Cambridge Unversity Press, 1995.
Scheib, Otto. *Die Reformationsdiskussionen in der Hansestadt Hamburg, 1522–1528*. Münster: Aschendorff, 1975.
Schilling, Heinz. "Charles V and Religion. The Struggle for the Integrity and Unity of Christendom." Pages 285–363, *Charles V, 1500–1558, and His Time*. Edited by Hugo Soly, Wim Blockmans. Antwerp: Mercatorfonds, 1999.
———. *Religion, Political Culture, and the Emergence of Early Modern Society. Essays in German and Dutch History*. Translated by Stephen Burnett. Leiden: E.J. Brill, 1992.
Schilling, Johannes. *Gewesene Mönche. Lebensgeschichten in der Reformation*. Vorträge 26 of *Schriften des Historischen Kollegs*. Munich: Stiftung Historisches Kolleg, 1990.
———. *Klöster und Mönche in der hessischen Reformation*. Gütersloh: Gütersloher Verlags-Haus, 1997.
Schlenck, Wolfgang. *Die Reichsstadt Memmingen und die Reformation*. Memmingen: Memminger Geschichtsblätter, 1968.
Schmuck, Josef. *Die Prophetie 'Onus Ecclesiae' des Bischofs Berthold Pürstinger*. Vienna: Verband der Wissenschaflichen Gesellschaften Österreichs, 1973.
Schneider, Bernd Christian. *Ius Reformandi. Die Entwicklung eines Staatskirchenrechts von seinen Anfängen bis zum Ende des Alten Reiches*. Tübingen: J.C.B. Mohr, 2001.
Schnitzler, Norbert. *Ikonoklasmus-Bildersturm. Theologischer Bilderstreit und ikonoklastisches Handeln während des 15. und 16. Jahrhunderts*. Munich: Wilhelm Fink, 1996.
Schrader, Franz. *Reformation und katholische Klöster: Beiträge zur Reformation und zur Geschichte der klösterlichen Restbestände in den ehemaligen Bistümern Magdeburg und Halberstadt*. Leipzig: St. Benno-Verlag, 1973.
Schroeder, Gabriele. "Speculation, History, and Politics: Richard Rothe's Negative Ecclesiology as a Response to the Transformation of Nineteenth-Century German Society." Ph.D. Dissertation, Graduate Theological Union at Berkeley, 1997.
Schubert, Ernst. "Vom Gebot zur Landesordnung. Der Wandel fürstlicher Herrschaft vom 15. zum 16. Jahrhundert." Pages 19–61, *Die deutsche Reformation zwischen Spätmittelalter und Früher Neuzeit*. Edited by Thomas A. Brady. Munich: Oldenbourg, 2001.
Schuchard, Christiane. *Die päpstlichen Kollektoren im späten Mittelalter*. Tübingen: Max Niemeyer, 2000.
Schulz, Peter. *Die politische Einflussnahme auf die Entstehung der Reichskammergerichtsordnung 1548*. Cologne: Böhlau, 1980.
Schulze, Manfred. *Fürsten und Reformation*. Tübingen: J.C.B. Mohr, 1991.
Schwarz, Brigide. "Klerikerkarrieren und Pfründenmarkt im Spätmittelalter." *Quellen und Forschungen aus Italienischen Archiven und Bibliotheken* 71(1991):243–65.
Schwineköper, Berent. "Klosteraufhebungen als Folge von Reformation und Bauernkrieg im Habsburgischen Vorderösterreich." *Zeitschrift des Breisgau-Geschichtsvereins* 97(1978):61–78.
Scott, Tom. *Society and Economy in Germany, 1300–1600*. Houndmills: Palgrave, 2002.
———. "Town and Country in Germany, 1350–1600." Pages 203–228, *Town and Country in Europe, 1300–1800*. Edited by S.R. Epstein. Cambridge University Press, 2001.
Seebaß, Gottfried. "Martin Bucers Beitrag zu den Diskussionen über die Verwendung der Kirchengüter." Pages 167–183, *Martin Bucer und das Recht. Beiträge zum internationalem Symposium vom 1. bis 3. März 2001 in der Johannes a Lasco Bibliothek Emden*. Edited by Christoph Strohm. Geneva: Librairie Droz, 2002.
Seyboth, Reinhard. "Kaiser, König, Stände und Städte im Ringen um das Kammergericht, 1486–1495." In *Das Reichskammergericht in der deutschen Geschichte. Stand der*

Forschung, Forschungsperspektiven. Edited by Bernhard Diestelkamp. Cologne: Böhlau Verlag, 1990.

Sieglerschmidt, Jörn. *Territorialstaat und Kirchenregiment.* Cologne: Böhlau, 1987.

Sitzmann, Manfred. *Mönchtum und Reformation. Zur Geschichte monastischer Institutionen in protestantischen Territorien (Brandenburg-Ansbach/Kulmbach, Magdeburg).* Neustadt a.d. Aisch: Degener, 1999.

Sperber, Jonathan. *The European Revolutions, 1848–1851.* Cambridge: Cambridge University Press, 1994.

Spieß, Karl-Heinz. *Familie und Hochadel im deutschen Hochadel des Spätmittelalters.* Stuttgart: Steiner, 1993.

Sprenger, R.M. *Viglius van Aytta und seine Notizen über Beratungen am Reichskammergericht (1535–1537).* Nijmegen: Gerard Noodt Institut, 1988.

Stamm, Heinz Meinlof. *Luthers Stellung zum Ordensleben.* Wiesbaden: Franz Steiner, 1980.

Starenko, Peter. "In Luther's Wake: Duke John Friedrich II of Saxony, Angelic Prophecy, and the Gotha Rebellion of 1567." Ph.D. Dissertation, The University of California at Berkeley, 2002.

Störmann, Anton. *Die städtischen Gravamina gegen den Klerus am Ausgange des Mittelalters und in der Reformationszeit.* Münster im Westfallen: Aschendorf, 1916.

Stratenwirth, Heide. *Die Reformation in der Stadt Osnabrück.* Wiesbaden: Franz Steiner, 1971.

Stroup, John. *The Struggle for Identity in the Clerical Estate: Northwest German Protestant Opposition to Absolutist Policy in the Eighteenth Century.* Leiden: E.J. Brill, 1984.

Stupperich, Robert. "Bucer und die Kirchengüter." In *Martin Bucer and Sixteenth Century Europe. Actes du colloque de Strasbourg (28–31 août 1991).* Edited by Christian Krieger and Marc Lienhard, 2 vols. Leiden: E.J. Brill, 1993.

———. Editor. *Die Reformation im Ordensland Preussen 1523/24.* Ulm: Verlag Unser Weg, 1966.

Swanson. R.N. *Religion and Devotion in Europe, c. 1215–1515.* Cambridge: Cambridge University Press, 1995.

The Work of Heiko A. Oberman. Edited by Thomas A. Brady, Katherine G. Brady, Susan Karant-Nunn, James D. Tracy. Leiden: Brill, 2003.

Trüdinger, Karl. *Luthers Briefe und Gutachten an weltliche Obrigkeiten zur Durchführung der Reformation.* Münster: Aschendorff, 1975.

Wandel, Lee Palmer. *Voracious Idols and Violent Hands.* Cambridge University Press, 1995.

Wendel, François. *L'Eglise de Strasbourg: sa constitution et son organisation, 1532–1535.* Paris: Presses universitaires de France, 1942.

Wentz, Gottfried. *Das Bistum Havelberg.* Section 1, vol. 2 of *Germania sacra.* Berlin: Walter De Gruyter, 1933.

Wentz, Gottfried and Berent Schwineköper. *Domstift St. Moritz zu Magdeburg.* Section 1, vol. 1, part 1 of *Germania sacra.* Berlin: Walter De Gruyter, 1972.

Wesel-Roth, Ruth. *Thomas Erastus: Ein Beitrag zur Geschichte der reformierten Kirche und zur Lehre von der Staatssouveränität.* Lahr: Moritz Schauenburg, 1954.

Witte, John. *Law and Protestantism: The Legal Teachings of the Lutheran Reformation.* Cambridge: Cambridge University Press, 2002.

Wohlfeil, Rainer and Hans-Jürgen Goertz. *Gewissensfreiheit als Bedingung der Neuzeit: Fragen an die Speyerer Protestation von 1529.* Göttingen: Vandenhoeck & Ruprecht, 1980.

Woker, Franz Wilhelm. *Geschichte der Norddeutschen Franziskaner-Missionen der sächsischen Ordens-Provinz vom heiligen Kreuz. Ein Beitrag zur Kirchengeschichte Norddeutschlands nach der Reformation.* Freiburg im Breisgau: Herder, 1880.

Wolf, Armin. *Gesetzgebung in Europa, 1100–1500.* München: Beck, 1996.

Wolgast, Eike. *Die Wittenberger Theologie und die Politik der evangelischen Stände. Studien zu Luthers Gutachten in politischen Fragen.* Gütersloh: Gerd Mohn, 1977.

Wolgast, Eike. *Hochstift und Reformation*. Stuttgart: Franz Steiner 1995.

Wood, Diana. *Medieval Economic Thought*. Cambridge: Cambridge University Press, 2002.

Woodward, George W.O. *The Dissolution of the Monasteries*. New York: Walker, 1967.

Zeeden, Ernst Walter. *Konfessionsbildung. Studien zur Reformation, Gegenreformation und katholischen Reform*. Stuttgart: Klett-Cotta, 1985.

Ziegler, Walter. "Reformation und Klosterauflösung. Ein ordensgeschichtlicher Vergleich." Pages 585–614, *Reformbemühungen und Observanzbestrebungen im spätmittelalterlichen Ordenswesen*. Edited by Kaspar Elm. Berlin: Duncker und Humblot, 1989.

Zimmermann, Gunter. *Prediger der Freiheit. Andreas Osiander und der Nürnberger Rat 1522–1548*. Mannheim: Palatium, 1999.

Zmora, Hillay. *Monarchy, Aristocracy, and the State in Europe, 1300–1800*. New York: Routledge, 2001.

INDEX

STUDIES IN MEDIEVAL AND REFORMATION TRADITIONS

(Formerly Studies in Medieval and Reformation Thought)

Founded by Heiko A. Oberman†
Edited by Andrew Colin Gow

58. GRAHAM, M.F. *The Uses of Reform.* 'Godly Discipline' and Popular Behavior in Scotland and Beyond, 1560-1610. 1996
59. AUGUSTIJN, C. *Erasmus. Der Humanist als Theologe und Kirchenreformer.* 1996
60. McCOOG S J, T.M. *The Society of Jesus in Ireland, Scotland, and England 1541-1588.* 'Our Way of Proceeding?' 1996
61. FISCHER, N. und KOBELT-GROCH, M. (Hrsg.). *Außenseiter zwischen Mittelalter und Neuzeit.* Festschrift für Hans-Jürgen Goertz zum 60. Geburtstag. 1997
62. NIEDEN, M. *Organum Deitatis.* Die Christologie des Thomas de Vio Cajetan. 1997
63. BAST, R.J. *Honor Your Fathers.* Catechisms and the Emergence of a Patriarchal Ideology in Germany, 1400-1600. 1997
64. ROBBINS, K.C. *City on the Ocean Sea: La Rochelle, 1530-1650.* Urban Society, Religion, and Politics on the French Atlantic Frontier. 1997
65. BLICKLE, P. *From the Communal Reformation to the Revolution of the Common Man.* 1998
66. FELMBERG, B.A.R. *Die Ablaßtheorie Kardinal Cajetans (1469-1534).* 1998
67. CUNEO, P.F. *Art and Politics in Early Modern Germany.* Jörg Breu the Elder and the Fashioning of Political Identity, ca. 1475-1536. 1998
68. BRADY, Jr., Th.A. *Communities, Politics, and Reformation in Early Modern Europe.* 1998
69. McKEE, E.A. *The Writings of Katharina Schütz Zell.* 1. The Life and Thought of a Sixteenth-Century Reformer. 2. A Critical Edition. 1998
70. BOSTICK, C.V. *The Antichrist and the Lollards.* Apocalyticism in Late Medieval and Reformation England. 1998
71. BOYLE, M. O'ROURKE. *Senses of Touch.* Human Dignity and Deformity from Michelangelo to Calvin. 1998
72. TYLER, J.J. *Lord of the Sacred City.* The *Episcopus Exclusus* in Late Medieval and Early Modern Germany. 1999
74. WITT, R.G. *'In the Footsteps of the Ancients'.* The Origins of Humanism from Lovato to Bruni. 2000
77. TAYLOR, L.J. *Heresy and Orthodoxy in Sixteenth-Century Paris.* François le Picart and the Beginnings of the Catholic Reformation. 1999
78. BUCER, M. *Briefwechsel/Correspondance.* Band IV (Januar-September 1530). Herausgegeben und bearbeitet von R. Friedrich, B. Hamm und A. Puchta. 2000
79. MANETSCH, S.M. *Theodore Beza and the Quest for Peace in France, 1572-1598.* 2000
80. GODMAN, P. *The Saint as Censor.* Robert Bellarmine between Inquisition and Index. 2000
81. SCRIBNER, R.W. *Religion and Culture in Germany (1400-1800).* Ed. L. Roper. 2001
82. KOOI, C. *Liberty and Religion.* Church and State in Leiden's Reformation, 1572-1620. 2000
83. BUCER, M. *Opera Latina.* Vol. V. Defensio adversus axioma catholicum id est criminationem R.P. Roberti Episcopi Abrincensis (1534). Ed. W.I.P. Hazlett. 2000
84. BOER, W. DE. *The Conquest of the Soul.* Confession, Discipline, and Public Order in Counter-Reformation Milan. 2001
85. EHRSTINE, G. *Theater, culture, and community in Reformation Bern, 1523-1555.* 2001
86. CATTERALL, D. *Community Without Borders.* Scot Migrants and the Changing Face of Power in the Dutch Republic, c. 1600-1700. 2002

87. BOWD, S.D. *Reform Before the Reformation*. Vincenzo Querini and the Religious Renaissance in Italy. 2002

88. PELC, M. *Illustrium Imagines*. Das Porträtbuch der Renaissance. 2002

89. SAAK, E.L. *High Way to Heaven*. The Augustinian Platform between Reform and Reformation, 1292-1524. 2002

90. WITTNEBEN, E.L. *Bonagratia von Bergamo*, Franziskanerjurist und Wortführer seines Ordens im Streit mit Papst Johannes XXII. 2003

91. ZIKA, C. *Exorcising our Demons,* Magic, Witchcraft and Visual Culture in Early Modern Europe. 2002

92. MATTOX, M.L. *"Defender of the Most Holy Matriarchs"*, Martin Luther's Interpretation of the Women of Genesis in the *Enarrationes in Genesin*, 1535-45. 2003

93. LANGHOLM, O. *The Merchant in the Confessional,* Trade and Price in the Pre-Reformation Penitential Handbooks. 2003

94. BACKUS, I. *Historical Method and Confessional Identity in the Era of the Reformation (1378-1615).* 2003

95. FOGGIE, J.P. *Renaissance Religion in Urban Scotland.* The Dominican Order, 1450-1560. 2003

96. LÖWE, J.A. *Richard Smyth and the Language of Orthodoxy.* Re-imagining Tudor Catholic Polemicism. 2003

97. HERWAARDEN, J. VAN. *Between Saint James and Erasmus.* Studies in Late-Medieval Religious Life: Devotion and Pilgrimage in The Netherlands. 2003

98. PETRY, Y. *Gender, Kabbalah and the Reformation.* The Mystical Theology of Guillaume Postel (1510–1581). 2004

99. EISERMANN, F., SCHLOTHEUBER, E. und HONEMANN, V. *Studien und Texte zur literarischen und materiellen Kultur der Frauenklöster im späten Mittelalter.* Ergebnisse eines Arbeitsgesprächs in der Herzog August Bibliothek Wolfenbüttel, 24.-26. Febr. 1999. 2004

100. WITCOMBE, C.L.C.E. *Copyright in the Renaissance.* Prints and the *Privilegio* in Sixteenth-Century Venice and Rome. 2004

101. BUCER, M. *Briefwechsel/Correspondance.* Band V (September 1530-Mai 1531). Herausgegeben und bearbeitet von R. Friedrich, B. Hamm, A. Puchta und R. Liebenberg. 2004

102. MALONE, C.M. *Façade as Spectacle: Ritual and Ideology at Wells Cathedral.* 2004

103. KAUFHOLD, M. (ed.) *Politische Reflexion in der Welt des späten Mittelalters / Political Thought in the Age of Scholasticism.* Essays in Honour of Jürgen Miethke. 2004

104. BLICK, S. and TEKIPPE, R. (eds.). *Art and Architecture of Late Medieval Pilgrimage in Northern Europe and the British Isles.* 2004

105. PASCOE, L.B., S.J. *Church and Reform.* Bishops, Theologians, and Canon Lawyers in the Thought of Pierre d'Ailly (1351-1420). 2005

106. SCOTT, T. *Town, Country, and Regions in Reformation Germany.* 2005

107. GROSJEAN, A.N.L. and MURDOCH, S. (eds.). *Scottish Communities Abroad in the Early Modern Period.* 2005

108. POSSET, F. *Renaissance Monks.* Monastic Humanism in Six Biographical Sketches. 2005

109. IHALAINEN, P. *Protestant Nations Redefined.* Changing Perceptions of National Identity in the Rhetoric of the English, Dutch and Swedish Public Churches, 1685-1772. 2005

110. FURDELL, E. (ed.) *Textual Healing: Essays on Medieval and Early Modern Medicine.* 2005

111. ESTES, J.M. *Peace, Order and the Glory of God.* Secular Authority and the Church in the Thought of Luther and Melanchthon, 1518-1559. 2005

112. MÄKINEN, V. (ed.) *Lutheran Reformation and the Law.* 2006

113. STILLMAN, R.E. (ed.) *Spectacle and Public Performance in the Late Middle Ages and the Renaissance.* 2006

114. OCKER, C. *Church Robbers and Reformers in Germany, 1525-1547.* Confiscation and Religious Purpose in the Holy Roman Empire. 2006